CW00765026

RESTORATION THEATRE AND CRISIS

Restoration Theatre and Crisis

SUSAN J. OWEN

CLARENDON PRESS · OXFORD
1996

Oxford University Press, Great Clarendon Street, Oxford OX2 6DP
Oxford New York
Athens Auckland Bangkok Bogota Bombay
Buenos Aires Calcutta Cape Town Dar es Salaam
Delhi Florence Hong Kong Istanbul Karachi
Kuala Lumpur Madras Madrid Melbourne
Mexico City Nairobi Paris Singapore
Taipei Tokyo Toronto
and associated companies in
Berlin Ibadan

Oxford is a trade mark of Oxford University Press

Published in the United States by
Oxford University Press Inc., New York

British Library Cataloguing in Publication Data
Data available

Library of Congress Cataloging in Publication Data
Owen, Susan J.
Restoration theatre and crisis / Susan J. Owen.
Includes bibliographical references.
1. English drama—Restoration, 1600–1700—History and criticism.
2. Literature and history—Great Britain—History—17th century.
3. Theater and society—Great Britain—History—17th century.
4. Great Britain—History—Restoration, 1660–1688. 5. Theater—
Great Britain—History—17th century. 6. Dryden, John, 1631–1700—
Dramatic works. 7. Behn, Aphra, 1640–1689—Dramatic works.
I. Title.
PR698.H5094 1996 822'.409—dc20 96-28238
ISBN 0-19-818387-9

1 3 5 7 9 10 8 6 4 2

Typeset by Best-set Typesetter Ltd., Hong Kong
Printed in Great Britain by
Biddles Ltd, Guildford and King's Lynn

Preface

THIS project began nine years ago as a chronological survey of all the plays of the Popish Plot and Exclusion Crisis period in their historical context. I was fascinated by the shift in dramatic form and content which the crisis produced. It seemed to me that the only way to avoid either under-, over-, or otherwise mis-reading the politics of the drama was by a complete survey of all the extant plays both inside and outside the theatres; and by locating this survey in relation to other contemporary political writing such as polemical pamphlets and *Poems on Affairs of State*, and to primary and secondary historical material.[1] This book takes a chronological perspective in the early chapters, looking at the nature of the historical period and the dramatists' extraordinarily sensitive and 'engaged' response to political shifts from one theatrical season to another. The later chapters move beyond a chronological approach, extracting an outline of the dramatic languages of politics and partisanship, and looking at contradiction in the drama. By contradiction, as will become clear, I do not mean a jumble of conflicting meanings, but tensions which lie at the heart of royalist and Tory drama; and a contradiction between such drama and a vigorous oppositional or Whig drama whose existence and vitality have not been sufficiently noticed. The drama of the Lord Mayor's Shows, outside the theatres, is also more oppositional than has been appreciated.

In critical terms this project developed out of a desire to bridge the gap between different sorts of criticism. Firstly, there seemed to me to be a gulf between criticism which looked very closely at the plays, but which limited its perception of political relevance to personal parallels and precise topical references, and thematic and tropological approaches which had a wider notion of political meaning, but paid less close attention to the plays, often selecting dramatic examples according to a precon-

[1] For a chronological survey of the first three seasons of the Exclusion Crisis, 1678–81, see my Ph.D. thesis, University of Leeds, 1992.

ceived schema. Secondly, it seemed to me desirable to bridge the gulf between political and apolitical criticism of a play like Thomas Otway's *Venice Preserv'd*, the former being frequently limited to questions such as whether the Venetian Senate represents the Whig leadership, the Common Council of the City of London, or the Stuart court; the latter noticing the issue of rape in the play or the disorientation of the pitiable and distressed characters but not the political resonance which these things might have. I have surveyed these issues in my 'Interpreting the Politics of Restoration Drama' and I shall say more about them below. More recently, the critical debate has moved on: there has been a spate of articles on gender issues in the drama, and some recent books which do not exactly fit the 'parallelism versus tropes' framework. My own project should be seen as complementary to such recent studies as Michael Dobson's *The Making of the National Poet*, Richard Braverman's *Plots and Counterplots*, and Nancy Maguire's *Regicide and Restoration*. Gerald MacLean's book of essays *Culture and Society in the Stuart Restoration* appeared as I was completing this book, but I have been able to make some response to one particular essay in my final chapter. Two very useful books which appeared after this was finished are *Cultural Readings of Restoration and Eighteenth-Century English Theater*, edited by Douglas Canfield and Deborah Payne, and Jessica Munns's *Restoration Politics and Drama: The Plays of Thomas Otway 1675–1683*.

This project has generated five published articles which the reader might find of interest: '"Partial Tyrants" and "Freeborn People" in *Lucius Junius Brutus*'; 'Interpreting the Politics of Restoration Drama'; '"Suspect my loyalty when I lose my virtue": Sexual Politics and Party in Aphra Behn's Plays of the Exclusion Crisis'; '"He that should guard my virtue has betrayed it": The Dramatization of Rape in the Exclusion Crisis'; and 'The Politics of John Dryden's *The Spanish Fryar; or, The Double Discovery*'. A revised version of the piece on Behn is due to appear shortly in *Aphra Behn Studies*, edited by Janet Todd for Cambridge University Press. There is inevitably some reiteration, but I have not recapitulated all of the published arguments, for reasons of space, and because I hope that they will not be entirely unknown.

The writing and revision of this book were made possible by the generosity of the William Andrews Clark Memorial Library in Los Angeles and the UCLA Center for Seventeenth and Eighteenth Century Studies, who jointly awarded me a three-month post-doctoral fellowship in 1993, and of the Leverhulme Trust, who awarded me a one-year research fellowship in 1994–5. I am also indebted to the University of Leeds undergraduate exchange scheme and to the Fulbright Commission for the opportunity to study at UCLA in 1989–90. I was extremely fortunate, too, in my employers: LSU College, which allowed me to take up the post-doctoral fellowship when I had just started teaching there, and the University of Sheffield, which permitted me to take up the research fellowship when I had just been appointed there. I could not have written the book without the help I have received from the staff of the Brotherton Library and Brotherton Collection at the University of Leeds, the Hartley Library at the University of Southampton, the Bodleian Library in Oxford, and the William Andrews Clark and Huntington Libraries in Los Angeles.

I owe a debt of gratitude to Paul Hammond for his advice and encouragement over the last nine years. I am also grateful to former colleagues at the University of Leeds for support and stimulation; to present colleagues, Sally Shuttleworth and Erica Sheen, for their friendship and advice; to my Ph.D. thesis examiners, Martin Butler, Derek Hughes, and Nigel Smith, for their helpful suggestions; to Robert Hume and Jonathan Scott for their encouragement; and to Jonathan Sawday for reading the first chapter and telling me to start again. He bears no responsibility for the final version, which has been reworked again in response to other readers' remarks. My warmest thanks are due to Jason Freeman and the editorial staff at Oxford University Press. I also want to thank the Oxford University Press reader for helpful comments, and everyone else who has read the manuscript and offered constructive criticisms.

Finally, I want to thank Mike Macnair for his invaluable assistance and support, and my daughters, Jenny and Alice, for putting up with the pressures caused by my writing. This book is dedicated to the three of them, with love.

S.J.O.

University of Sheffield
February 1996

Contents

Note on Terminology and Conventions

Two questions of terminology are problematic. Firstly, the terms 'Whig' and 'Tory' acquired wide currency in 1681.[1] There are earlier examples of use of the terms: 'Tory-rory' is used of the rollicking, cavalier mentality, for example in Dryden's *The Kind Keeper*, published in 1678, though written earlier. 'Whig' is used to mean dissenting Scottish rebel in *Ravillac Redivivus* (72), published in the same year. Yet the meaning here is not quite the same as the later explicitly factional usage. L'Estrange and Marvell were polemicizing against one another in the late 1670s in terms very similar to the Tory–Whig debates of the 1680s, but it does not seem legitimate to call Marvell a Whig. What should we call the factions prior to 1681? 'Loyalist' would not do for 'pre-Tory', as Whigs described themselves as 'Loyal Protestants'.[2] Contemporaries used 'Court' and 'Country' where we would use 'government' and 'opposition', but with an additional negative value attached to 'Court' as a locus of corruption.[3] These terms have been used by some twentieth-century historians and critics. However, recent history and criticism has tended to shy away from them. In the Exclusion Crisis, the 'Country' opposition to the Danby administration broke up in 1679; courtiers such as Buckingham and Sedley became Whigs, while countrymen submitted Tory 'abhorrences' as well as Whiggish petitions. I have therefore used 'royalist' and 'opposition' in contexts where chronology is important or where 'Tory' and 'Whig' would be misleading.

The terms 'popery', 'popish', and 'papist' were often used by contemporary English Protestants where we would use 'Catholic'. 'Roman Catholic' is sometimes used, but 'Catholic' in contemporary political writing usually refers to the true Church: 'the *Catholick Church*, which is composed of several distinct *Churches*', as John Nalson puts it in *The Project of Peace* (74). The appropriation of the word by the Roman Church was a Counter-Reformation strategy, an assertive and contro-

---

[1] Willman, 'The Origins of "Whig" and "Tory" in English Political Language'.

[2] Despite royalist attempts to depict them as rebels, the opposition in the Exclusion Crisis saw themselves as loyal defenders of sovereignty against popish desires to subordinate it to a foreign power. See e.g. Hunt, *Great and Weighty Considerations*, 6; and Lawrence, *Two Great Questions Determined*, 8–10. See also Ashcraft, *Revolutionary Politics*, ch. 5.

[3] See Burnet's *History of My Own Time*, i. 498 and ii. 82 and n.

versial act of self-definition. I find myself having to use the terms 'popery' and 'popish' to describe Restoration concerns and fears, but this should not be taken as implying any intentional rudeness towards present-day Roman Catholics.

References for quotations from plays are given in the form '2. 2. 5', where the first number represents the Act, the second number the scene, and the third number the line. In seventeenth-century editions there are no line numbers, so the reference is in the form '2. 2. p. 5', where the final number represents the page. The form '2. p. 5' indicates that there are no scenes in Act 2. Bare-number references, e.g. '(75)', refer to page numbers, unless otherwise stated.

Italic and roman type have been reversed in quotations from Restoration texts, except in the case of Shadwell's *The Lancashire Witches*. The censor deleted sections of this play in performance, and Shadwell printed these in italic type, which has been retain in the present volume.

CHAPTER 1

Reading the Politics of
Restoration Drama

IN autumn 1678 the English political regime was struck by two unrelated, yet related, sets of events. Titus Oates's allegations of a Roman Catholic conspiracy to assassinate the king were brought into the public eye by the precautionary actions taken by the government, and reinforced by the murder of Sir Edmund Bury Godfrey, the magistrate to whom Oates had originally given his evidence. Montagu, the former ambassador to Paris, revealed secret dealings between the Danby administration and the French monarchy at a time when the ministry had been asking Parliament for money, ostensibly to prosecute war with France.

These developments were unrelated: Oates's allegations were a matter of private enterprise, while Montagu's leaks were a part of the political game between Louis XIV and Charles II over the level of the French financial subsidy to Charles. They were related, however, by a common thread: the issue of Protestantism versus popery (or Catholicism versus heresy), which had been at the centre of both European and English politics for more than a century. English political life had been in a chronic state of tension over this issue since the king's brother James, heir-presumptive to the throne, had in 1673 publicly admitted that he was a Roman Catholic. The revelations of autumn 1678 therefore made the Parliament which had been sitting, on and off, since 1661 unmanageable, and the ministry was left with no option but to dissolve it in hope of better results from elections.

England now entered a four-year roller-coaster of political crisis, commonly known to historians as the Exclusion Crisis. These years saw three elections in as many years, as the Crown was unable to reach agreement with three successive Parliaments in which the Commons both insisted on the exclusion of James from the succession and steadily radicalized their other demands. Renewed civil war was feared. 'Forty-One is come again' was the cry. The crisis ended with Charles ruling without Parliament, the charters of the City of London and other boroughs under attack, and oppositional leaders executed or in exile.

This period represents our own history in the making. Aspects of the political language of the Toryism of the Exclusion Crisis have not yet gone out of use in England: the idea of the unity of the upper and middle classes in an aristocracy of taste, as against the lower classes and radicals who attack 'true culture', for instance, or the use of ideas of sexual deviation as an image of political disorder. In the United States the Whig language of republican virtue and radical Protestantism is equally in use in political discourse. Stephen Greenblatt explains our fascination with the Renaissance and its drama in terms which apply just as much to the Restoration:

We sense too that we are situated at the close of the cultural moment initiated in the Renaissance and that the places in which our social and psychological world seems to be cracking apart are those structural joints visible when it was first constructed. In the midst of anxieties and contradictions attendant upon the threatened collapse of this phase of our civilization, we respond with passionate curiosity and poignancy to the anxieties and contradictions attendant upon its rise. To experience Renaissance culture is to feel what it was like to form our own identity, and we are at once more rooted and more estranged by the experience.[1]

This notion of rootedness and estrangement precisely conveys the doubleness of our response to the Restoration Crisis and its drama. For it is not just the Renaissance, but the whole of the century of crisis from 1588 to 1688, which is important in initiating our culture. In seventeenth-century England there were three revolutionary crises: the Civil War, the Exclusion Crisis, and the 'Glorious Revolution'. The Exclusion Crisis did not lead to a revolutionary outcome, but its effect on literature and culture was nevertheless profound.

During the Exclusion Crisis some fifty-four new plays, or new versions of old plays, were written. The large majority of these plays engage with the political crisis in fascinating and complex

---

[1] Greenblatt, *Renaissance Self-Fashioning*, 174-5.

ways. The theatre dramatists responded to the beginning of political polarization with amazing vigour and promptitude. Their relationship to late Stuart ideology is quite as complex and contradictory as that of their Jacobean and Caroline predecessors: they strain every nerve to offer a royalism which is nevertheless tormented and fractured; or offer a message of moderation which insists upon the need for royal temperance; or launch boldly into a rhetoric of outright Whiggery. Incredible as it may seem, the same dramatist may veer from tormented quietism, to rousing royalism, to a Whiggish focus on antipopery and hostility to the court, to scathing Tory satire. Even 'canonical' authors such as Dryden respond flexibly and with enormous vitality and ingenuity to political shifts.

The drama, in other words, was involved in the debates which engaged the political nation. It entered a new phase of profound political engagement, and the nature of this engagement shifted in an extraordinarily responsive way, as the crisis itself moved from one phase to the next. The theatrical season, beginning in the autumn and ending in early summer like the legal and parliamentary year, seems also to have corresponded to the seasons or phases of the political crisis. At the same time as drama became political, politics seemed theatrical. From the outbreak of the Popish Plot scare in the autumn of 1678 onwards, the dramatists denounced the plot as a piece of theatre and suggested that there was more truth and less artifice in the theatre than outside it in the 'theatre of news': 'The Devil take this cursed plotting age,' wrote Aphra Behn, ''T has ruined all our plots upon the stage.'[2] Modern historians have written about the crisis as a kind of drama, sometimes as a dark farce, sometimes in Aristotelian tragedy terms of the fatal hubris of the opposition leader Shaftesbury, or, taking a longer view, of James Stuart.

The sensitivity of the drama to its times is reflected in the fact that the crisis had a profound effect on dramatic form. In the 1660s the king had promoted the royalist heroic play in rhyming couplets, a form characterized by baroque bombast. However, in the late 1670s this gave way to political tragedy in blank verse. Dryden makes the transition in *All For Love* (1678).

---

[2] Prologue to *The Feign'd Curtizans*.

There was also a spate of politically motivated adaptations of Shakespeare which foregrounded the message against rebellion, beginning with Crowne's *The Misery of Civil-War* (an adaptation of part of 2 *Henry VI* and of 3 *Henry VI*). Prior to the Exclusion Crisis, adaptations of Shakespeare, for example *Macbeth* and *The Tempest*, had stressed grandeur and spectacle. In the crisis there was a deepening of developments in the sexual politics of the drama, which had already begun with the appearance of women on stage for the first time in the early Restoration period. 'Love interest' had an increased prominence and was added to Shakespeare plays by Restoration adapters, as with Edgar and Cordelia in Tate's *Lear*. Young love and the violated woman were used in a histrionic way as tropes of the natural against unnatural political arrangements. In the heroic play, heroes had fallen into two types, parodied in Buckingham's *The Rehearsal* as the 'effeminate' Prince Prettyman and the 'huffing' Drawcansir. Now, politically quietist heroes were increasingly 'feminized' as the huffing character became a villain or a Whig. Toryism emphasized quietism;[3] and quietism is incompatible with the 'huffing' heroism of heroic drama, and needs the hero who, as Dryden says of his Antony, 'Weeps much; fights little; but is wond'rous kind.'[4] These developments prefigured the sentimental and affective tragedy of the eighteenth century.

In response to the crisis the dramatists used old themes in new ways: in tragedy the long-standing association of political and sexual excess took new forms, as lust, rape, and sexual perversion were associated with rebellion and republicanism by Tories and with tyranny and popery by Whig playwrights. Comedy was also adapted for the purposes of political critique: cuckolding is an ancient theme, and satire of puritans dates back to the sixteenth century. Both traditions were employed in the satire of

[3] Cf. Dryden's *Religio Laici* (1682): 'But Common quiet is Mankind's concern' (*Works*, ii. 122, line 450); also Barbeau, 'Free Will and the Passions in Dryden and Pope', 2–8. Quietism is both political and religious. In Nalson's *Project of Peace* (1678), an early document of quietism, dissenters are attacked because they disrupt the God-given unity and peace of the nation. Ch. 14 makes a plea for quiet on the grounds of the difficulty of right knowledge and action, leading to the need to respect existing civic and religious authority, a central theme in Dryden's and Lee's *Oedipus*.

[4] Prologue to *All For Love*, in *Works*, xiii. 20.

dissenting Whig citizens. Satire of interregnum radicals and rebel upstarts also became a staple of comedy: this had begun in the 1660s in plays such as Howard's *The Committee* and Tatham's *The Rump*. The regime was founded in fear of lower-class radicalism, and was persistently afraid that it might revive, blowing up small plots out of all proportion and episodically staging major crackdowns on dissent.[5] Comic satire of lower-class radicals both represents this fear and defuses it through laughter, drawing on the regime's political roots to solidify its immediate support.

This book is about the plays of the Exclusion Crisis and, more broadly, about the relationship of Restoration theatre and political crisis. In the first part of the book I shall consider initially the drama's engagement with its times from a precisely detailed, chronological perspective; then drama's relationship to political ideology in a wider sense. Chapter 2 sets the scene by examining the nature and significance of the revolutionary 'moment' which modern historians have labelled the Exclusion Crisis. The drama was intensely engaged with its times and the best understanding of the drama is achieved by the best understanding of those times. First, I give a narrative of events, because they are unfamiliar to many literary scholars. I have brought together from different sources a picture which is as inclusive as I can make it. Of course there is no such thing as an impartial narrative of events; but I think it is possible to try to avoid 'partial' history in the sense of an account of events which excludes factors which are inconvenient for a particular theory. I then consider various rival narratives which both historians and literary critics have used to explain the bigger picture, the larger movements of history of which the crisis was a part, concluding with an explanation of which narrative informs my own interpretation of the drama. I think this is the honest course for the literary historian. The fact that true impartiality is impossible should not mean that we take our account of history from whatever text we please, as some New Historicists do. Nor do I think it is proper to reject all 'narratives': we are bound to make sense of history by telling ourselves some kind of story, and literary scholars' rejection of 'grand narratives' of history is often an

---

[5] Hutton, *The Restoration*, pt. 4, and *Charles the Second*, chs. 10–15, *passim*.

excuse either for failing to try to get to grips with history or for refusing to make our own particular story clear.

In Chapter 3 I shall show the extraordinary flexibility with which the dramatists responded to the 'local' historical debates and shifts outlined in Chapter 2. I take the example of Crowne because I have considered the same phenomenon in other dramatists elsewhere. Why should Exclusion Crisis drama engage with the politics of its times so intensely that a single dramatist can shift from vehement Toryism to moderation or outright Whiggery and back again within the space of a few years? I shall suggest a variety of possible motivations: a desire to entertain, the popular nature of dramatic culture, the poverty and dependence of dramatists, and the fact that 'enthusiasm' was marginalized in 1660, so that the ability to switch attitudes and allegiances seemed proper.

Chapters 4–6 move beyond a chronological perspective to draw out an account of the dramatic language of politics. What exactly were the themes and tropes of Toryism and Whiggery? Chapter 4 deals with themes of social order and disorder, religion and class, Chapter 5 with sex and gender issues. The account of the dramatic language of politics in these Chapters has been carefully drawn out from a nuanced and complete reading of all the plays of the Exclusion Crisis. It is the fruit of that labour, but it is also a tool, to illuminate the discussion of Tory, Whig, and City drama in subsequent chapters. Some surprises are revealed: for example, through a careful reading of the language of Toryism it becomes clear that there was often a contradiction for Behn between Toryism and feminism, rather than a simple compatibility, as is often assumed. The existence of a vigorous and specific Whig dramatic language is a useful counter to assumptions about the hegemony of royalism in the Restoration: it is often assumed either that there was no Whig drama, or that it differed very little from Tory drama. This misunderstanding is due to a misreading of the themes and tropes of Whiggery, which are often conservative, but yet quite distinct from Toryism. The Whig rhetoric is one of 'Loyal Protestantism'. Chapter 6 looks at dramatists' attempts to intervene politically by deliberately reversing themes and tropes from other plays. Nowhere is the strenuous and ideological effort of the drama of this time more apparent than in this extraordinary attempt to rearrange and refocus meaning, to wrest it away from the enemy.

Chapters 7–10 explore the contradictory nature of drama, of politics, and of the relationship between the two. Before I describe their content, I want to explain what this means. By contradiction I mean something more precise than simply a clash or jumble of conflicting meanings. The Exclusion Crisis exposes and sharpens contradictions which already exist in society and in the theatre, and generates what may be called a drama of contradiction.

A Society of Contradiction

Royalist ideology portrayed the king's return as God's answer to the heartfelt prayer of a nation suffering under a band of greedy ruffians. Yet in reality many, including Dryden, had accommodated to Cromwell's regime; so many, in fact, that the vengeance which some old cavaliers wanted would have been impractical. The regime thus displeased its royalist supporters as well as the Presbyterians and dissenters whom it marginalized. Not only was Charles unable or unwilling to redress the balance completely against those who had profited in the interregnum; he also supported toleration for dissenters, as a way of introducing greater freedoms for Roman Catholics. Praise of his mercy to his enemies in royalist writing is often a backhanded way of criticizing him for being 'soft' on the opponents of his royalist supporters: the indulgent David of Dryden's *Absalom and Achitophel* is the epitome and culmination of this tradition.

The Restoration of 1660 offered triumphalist values around which to unify the nation; but these were more a literary fiction than a reality. Jonathan Sawday has argued that the triumphalism of 1660 had a forced element:

If, in the spring of 1660, there was widespread fear that the return of the monarch would precipitate reprisals, a settling of scores from the revolutionary period, then the production of [loyal] addresses, or the large-scale organization required to stage the elaborate civic festivities said to have taken place might be understood as demonstrations of a new-found loyalty motivated as much by a fear of the consequences of not indulging in such extravaganzas, as by a genuine conversion to the ideals of monarchism as opposed to republicanism. A fact which might alert us to this possibility, operating at a purely textual level, is the curiously homogeneous quality to the nature of the descriptions of the festivities said to have been mounted in urban centres throughout the country . . . Charles arrived at Dover on 25 May 1660, by which time the government had indulged in a virtual orgy of expenditure in which the symbolic forms representative of republicanism were replaced with the symbolic forms representative not just of monarchism, but of monarchism as it had existed at the moment of its dissolution in 1649.[6]

Moreover, the restoration of royal authority soon came up against a crisis of authority. Marvell's book-length pamphlet *An Account of the Growth of Popery and Arbitrary Government in England* (1677) merely crystallized concerns which had been simmering since the 1660s about Charles's dishonesty, crypto-Catholicism, and refusal to take a strong line against French Catholic expansionism. It is clear in Marvell's text that Charles's secret dealings with France were widely suspected, even if his subjects did not actually know the exact terms of the Secret Treaty of Dover (1672) in which he had promised to convert England to Catholicism using French troops if necessary, in exchange for money to rule without dependence on Parliament. Marvell is only the most famous of a large number of writers of satirical poems and prose. In John Ayloffe's *Britannia and Raleigh* (1674–5), Raleigh defends the 'long-scorn'd Parliament' as 'The basis of his throne and government' and Britannia replies, 'too long in vain I've tri'd | The Stuart from the tyrant to divide'. She concludes with the promise to England, 'No pois'nous tyrant on thy ground shall live.' The same author's 'Marvell's Ghost' (1678) concludes with the warning that England will:

> to those resentments come
> That drove the Tarquins out of Rome,
> Or such as did in fury turn
> Th' Assyrian's palace to his urn.[7]

The Assyrian here is Sardanapalus, described by the Whig writer

---

[6] Sawday, 'Re-writing a Revolution', 174, 175.
[7] *Poems on Affairs of State*, i. 234, 236, 286.

Shadwell as 'so excessively effeminate and luxurious that his captains conspired to kill him'.[8]

The same perceived royal 'effeminacy' and 'luxury' constituted another major site of contradiction for Stuart authority. The reintroduction of the court brought back the 'luxury' of conspicuous consumption that had angered many in the early Stuart period. 'Effeminacy' in the Restoration sense of enslavement to women and sexual desire was seen as one of Charles's major faults, the other side of the coin from his failure to be 'man' enough to square up to Louis XIV militarily. Marvell, in *Last Instructions to a Painter*, shows Charles awakened in bed by a symbolic female form representing his grieving kingdom. His response is not sympathy or shame but a fumbling amorousness. Yet it was not only parliamentarians like Marvell who mistrusted royal behaviour. Pepys and his friends frequently discussed such matters as the king's 'horrid effeminacy' and 'the viciousness of the Court' and the 'contempt the King brings himself into thereby'.[9]

Royal effeminacy was not just a moral problem, but also a political one. In *The Earl of Rochester's Verses For Which He Was Banished* effeminacy is associated with political irresponsibility, both in Charles and in his brother and heir, James:

> His sceptre and his prick are of a length,
> And she may sway the one who plays with t'other
> And make him little wiser than his brother.

It is also associated with impotence: Nell Gwyn has a 'painful' and 'laborious' effort to induce a royal erection. A similar point is made by Thomas Povey to Pepys: the king prefers fondling to 'doing the other thing'.[10] This associates him with the fumblers and gropers who are comic butts in the drama. The point is not simply a sexual one: the overtones are political. Charles is seen as being as impotent against French Catholic expansionism on the one hand, and warmongering parliamentarians and radical dissenters on the other, as he is in bed. Rochester offers an ironic context for the designation of Charles as the 'merry Monarch'

---

[8] From the note to his *Tenth Satire of Juvenal*, cited in *Poems on Affairs of State*, i. 286.

[9] *The Diary of Samuel Pepys*, vii. 323–4, viii. 288. See Hammond, 'The King's Two Bodies'.

[10] *Diary*, iv. 136–7.

which, divorced of its original sarcastic and critical connotations, has survived into our own time: Charles is 'A merry
Monarch, scandalous and poor'. Charles, the poet ironically
observes, is not such a fool as to strive, like the French king, to
defend and extend his kingdom: his only ambition is to conquer
'the best cunts in Christendom'. Moreover, his obsession with
sex is contrary to religion and law:

> Whate'er religion and the laws say on't,
> He'll break through all to come at any cunt.

Here Rochester, the *enfant terrible* of the Restoration court
whose witty posturings the easygoing Charles usually tolerated,
seems almost close to the political opposition who lump together criticism of Charles's supine foreign policy with attacks
on his widely hated French Catholic mistresses, thought to be
a bad political influence. The banishment from court which
inspired the verse was at the instigation of just such a French
Catholic mistress, the Duchess of Portsmouth. It is not simply
that Charles is lewd, but that he is endangering the Protestant
succession and the laws of the land by subordinating the interests of the Protestant nation to dalliance with the French Catholic enemy. Stuart ideology was patriarchal. Filmer's *Patriarcha*,
written in defence of Charles I, was published in 1680 as a
political intervention against the king's opponents. It defended
royal authority by analogy with that of the father: the king is the
father of the nation. While this may have worked well for
Charles I, who, whatever his failings as a ruler, was thought of
as a loyal husband and devoted father, it seemed disastrously
inapposite to Charles II, whose mistresses were the target of
hostility which ranged from courtly squibs to apprentice riots;
who scattered his seed irresponsibly throughout the land, in
Dryden's famous image from *Absalom and Achitophel*, failing
to produce a legitimate heir but strewing the kingdom with
troublesome bastards at least one of whom, Monmouth, posed
a threat to political stability.

Criticism of royal misbehaviour and political opposition to
the Stuart regime crossed political and class lines. Both the court
and the old cavaliers who had supported the Crown in the Civil
War and interregnum became politically divided. The Duke of
Buckingham, who was both a cavalier and a courtier, was an

opposition leader; Prince Rupert, who had commanded armies for Charles I, associated himself to some extent with the Whigs, and left the Council chamber rather than sign the warrant for the arrest of the Whig leader, Shaftesbury, in July 1681. The so-called Cavalier Parliament was by no means sycophantic to Charles, and blocked his proposals for religious toleration. In the 1670s such tenuous consensus as existed was placed under enormous strain, finally breaking down. The Exclusion Crisis exacerbated the divisions among courtiers and old cavaliers, and saw a larger division in the 'political nation' which was both horizontal and vertical. On the one hand, the Tory assertion that the royal cause had the support of 'the better sort' had some basis in reality: the Whigs really did draw more support from the merchant citizen class and the lower classes in the city than the Tories did. On the other hand, if the Whigs enjoyed support among the nobility, the Tories could also mobilize support from below: the court, the country gentry, the lawyers, the citizens were all divided.[11]

The Exclusion Crisis exposed and exacerbated the contradictions of Restoration society: between the notion of triumphant consensus and the reality of division; and between Stuart patriarchal ideology and the perceived reality of royal (mis-)behaviour and (mis-)government.

A Theatre of Contradiction

In the theatre, a similar contradiction was apparent between the assertion and the failure of royal authority. The Restoration of the theatres together with the king was to be a symbol of the rejection of the 'puritan' regime of the interregnum. Charles saw the drama as a political instrument: from the first, he was actively engaged in discussing with the dramatists what they should write,[12] and with the theatre management what should

---

[11] See the discussion of politics and class in Ch. 4.

[12] Braverman, *Plots and Counterplots*, 36–7, notes Charles II's invitation to Orrery to write a play in the style of the French tragedy, the result being the first heroic play, *The Generall*. Charles's letter to Orrery (quoted 37) reads as though the king was a theatrical producer rather than just a monarch with a general interest in the drama. Winn, *John Dryden and his World*, 394–5, shows Charles actively involved in persuading Dryden what to write in 1683–4.

and should not be staged.[13] The assertion of royal control took the form of censorship, and strict limits on theatrical outlets: only two theatres were licensed.

At first sight, it appears that censorship was a powerful limiting factor on dramatic expression, especially during the Exclusion Crisis. Plays banned included Lee's *The Massacre of Paris* and *Lucius Junius Brutus*, Tate's *Richard the Second*, and Crowne's *Henry the Sixth*. Dryden's and Lee's *The Duke of Guise* and Crowne's *City Politiques* were banned in summer 1682. Banks had *Cyrus the Great* banned in 1681, *The Innocent Usurper* in 1683, and *The Island Queens* in 1684. However, it is interesting to note that most of these plays were initially licensed without any problem. *The Massacre of Paris* was banned at the request of the French ambassador.[14] *Lucius Junius Brutus*, *Richard the Second*, and *Henry the Sixth* were banned after a few days' performance, following complaints to the Lord Chamberlain from powerful courtiers in the audience.[15] Shadwell's *The Lancashire Witches*, initially licensed with few alterations, was cut after similar complaints, as he notes in his preface to the reader. The two Tory plays *The Duke of Guise* and *City Politiques* were simply held up for a few months, almost certainly to avoid making a political provocation at a sensitive time when the government was trying to engineer a Tory victory in the City of London. The plays were put on in the autumn after the elections were past.[16]

Moreover, while censorship may have worked to some extent to limit criticisms of the authorities in performance, it did not stop publication. Even during the Exclusion Crisis play texts appeared in print uncensored. It made no difference if the play had been banned from performance. Control of printed material was never very effective, and was virtually non-existent between the expiration of the Printing Act in 1679 and 1681 when, following the Oxford Parliament, steps were finally taken to

---

[13] For example, he probably persuaded the theatre management to keep *The Maid's Tragedy* (with its depiction of royal lust, corruption, and heroic regicide) off the stage during the Exclusion Crisis: Hume, '*The Maid's Tragedy* and Censorship in the Restoration Theatre'.

[14] Dryden, *The Vindication*, 41.

[15] Loftis, introduction to *Lucius Junius Brutus*, 12; Tate, epistle dedicatory to *Richard the Second*, sig. A2ᵛ; Crowne, dedication to *The English Frier*, sig. A3ᵛ.

[16] See Chs. 2 and 3 below.

control the press.[17] Even so, play publication was unaffected. Shadwell published *The Lancashire Witches* in 1682 at the height of the Tory reaction period with the passages that the Master of the Revels had insisted be cut out in performance given extra prominence by being printed in italics.

A similarly contradictory picture emerges in relation to government control of the theatre. It used to be assumed that the theatre was a theatre of courtiers, which would strongly suggest that Charles's government achieved in reality the cultural hegemony which was proclaimed in royalist literature and propaganda. This view is now discredited: all classes to some extent attended the theatre.[18] However, it is fairly clear that though the audience was socially mixed, it was less so than in the Jacobean and Caroline periods: there were only two theatres, and the price of the cheapest ticket at one shilling was nearly five times that of a cheap meal at a cookhouse at twopence-halfpenny.[19] The plays themselves provide some evidence that dramatists thought of their audience as predominantly people of property; it is hard, otherwise, to explain the savage satire of citizens in many plays and the worsening of the plebeians in Shakespeare adaptations. In contrast in the drama produced outside the playhouses, the Lord Mayor's Shows and the Bartholomew Fair play *The Coronation of Queen Elizabeth*, the crowd might be gently mocked, but was not demonized. Dryden claims in *The Vindication of The Duke of Guise* that his detractors are wrong to accuse him of inciting the rabble, because the rabble did not go to plays:

But what *Rabble* was it to provoke? Are the *Audience* of a *Play-house* (which are generally persons of Honour, Noblemen and Ladies, or at worst, as one of your Authors calls his Gallants, *Men of Wit and Pleasure about the Town*) are these the *Rabble* of Mr. *Hunt*? I have

---

[17] Crist, 'Government Control of the Press after the Expiration of the Printing Act in 1679'.

[18] Avery, 'The Restoration Audience'; Danchin, *Prologues and Epilogues of the Restoration*, vol. ii, pt. 1, pp. xxiii–xxiv; Hume, *Development*, 23–8; Love, 'Who were the Restoration Audience?'; Scouten and Hume, '"Restoration Comedy" and its Audiences'; Holland, *The Ornament of Action*, 11 ff.; Roberts, *The Ladies*, 49–94 and *passim*.

[19] For the price of the cheapest theatre tickets, Sampson, 'Some Bibliographical Evidence concerning Restoration Attitudes towards Drama', 101; for that of a meal in a cookhouse, Earle, *The Making of the English Middle Class*, 55–6.

seen a *Rabble* at Sir *Edmundbury Godfreys* Night, and have heard of such a name, at *true Protestant Meeting-houses*; but a *Rabble* is not to be provoked, where it never comes. (14)

We must make due allowance for the polemical and slippery nature of this text, but it could hardly function even as polemic if it was patently absurd. Overall, it seems that, as Jocelyn Powell says, 'though it was not the mere plaything of the Court, the theatre was not for the people either'.[20] Moreover, as J. L. Styan argues, 'the playwrights, like the actors, aimed their wit at the highest social level of the house, indeed, at the better-paying part of the audience'.[21] The playwrights seem to be writing to an audience which at least aspired to identify itself, in class terms, with the aristocracy, or as part of an aristocracy of taste.

Similarly, it seems likely that the audience, though politically mixed, was probably predominantly Tory, reversing Whig predominance in the electorate during the crisis. Most plays, and more sharply most prologues and epilogues, were Tory. It was traditional in Restoration prologues and epilogues to tease the audience, usually for immorality and witlessness. The dramatists are able to exploit this tradition for the purposes of political propaganda. The prologues and epilogues were intended to involve and catch the attention of the audience, not to alienate them. If the majority of the audience were sympathetic to the opposition, these royalist prologues and epilogues would not work, would simply create hostility and drive away custom. One can only imagine them having worked by appealing to the majority and forcing an embarrassed minority into uneasy laughter.[22] Further evidence that the theatres were seen as Tory territory can be found in politically motivated disturbances in them in early 1680. These suggest that Whiggish perpetrators felt that they were on hostile ground, since they attacked the

---

[20] Powell, *Restoration Theatre Production*, 12–13.

[21] Styan, *Restoration Comedy in Performance*, 7. However, elsewhere Styan's argument seems to overstate the homogeneity of the audience.

[22] However, royalism did not guarantee success. Dryden's *Troilus and Cressida* and Crowne's *The Ambitious Statesman* failed in the 1678–9 season, and in the 1679–80 season Otway's *Caius Marius* succeeded not because of the message against 'faction', but because of the comic acting of Underhill as the bloodthirsty Sulpitius and Nokes as the nurse: see epilogue and *Works of Thomas Otway*, ed. Ghosh, i. 45.

theatre itself: 'calling all the women whores and all the men rogues', and 'flinging Links at the Actors', while Tory disturbances were aimed at individual Whigs in the audience.[23]

Yet there was room for contradiction. The dramatists address a politically divided audience, and they seek to persuade, not just to celebrate a monolithic absolutism. Moreover, it was possible for a play to succeed even when the court strongly disapproved of it. Settle's Whiggish *The Female Prelate* was popular and had a good run,[24] despite the fact that on the third night, when the author received the receipts, 'the Duchesse of Portsmouth to disoblige Mr Settle the Poet carryed all the Court with her to the Dukes house to see Macbeth'.[25] Settle describes this as an extraordinary circumstance, saying in his epistle dedicatory that he writes in accordance with his conscience, regardless of the affront he might give to 'so numerous a Party that are so powerful a Support of the Stage' (sig. A3ᵛ–A4ʳ). However, such rhetorical self-pity is a common strategy. Royalists do it constantly. Anti-popery was popular on stage in general,[26] despite the fact that during the Exclusion Crisis it became a Whig theme.[27] Even a Whig play could succeed. Shadwell's *The Lancashire Witches* has a strongly Whiggish dedication to Shaftesbury which says that many of 'the best sort of men' supported the play, which lived in spite of the Tories, who hired 'mercenary Fellows' to hiss it.[28] Moreover, it was unlikely that the nature of the audience remained constant. The king and

---

[23] Van Lennep *et al.* (eds.), *The London Stage*, 284.

[24] Lord Falkland's prologue to Otway's *The Souldier's Fortune* teases the audience for deserting the Dorset Garden theatre to see the female Pope at Drury Lane.

[25] *Newdigate Newsletters*, 3 June 1680, cited in Van Lennep *et al.* (eds.), *The London Stage*, 287.

[26] For example, Ravenscroft's epilogue to Whitaker's ultra-royalist *The Conspiracy* says the audience might have been better pleased if plotting papists had been depicted; Crowne sneers at papists in *Henry the Sixth* and in sundry prologues and epilogues, and makes murderous priests in association with tyranny in the state, central in his *Thyestes*, a play aimed at reviving the fortunes of the ailing King's Company. Dryden panders to anti-popery in *The Spanish Fryar*, a play he described as offered 'to the people' (preface to *De Arte Graphica*, in *Works*, xx. 76).

[27] For a challenge to the notion that anti-popery was apolitical or as much Tory as Whig, see the discussion of religion in Ch. 4.

[28] Of course we cannot take this on trust; but Shadwell's enemy Dryden mentions the play's success in *The Vindication*, though he attributes it to 'the favour of a Party' (5), i.e. the Whigs.

his immediate circle attended far fewer performances after the Popish Plot scare raised the spectre of possible assassination,[29] which must have opened up at least a small critical space. As we shall see in Chapter 3, the tone of prologues and epilogues changes dramatically in autumn 1680, sneers at Whig 'faction' giving way to politically neutral sexual taunts and complaints about poets' hardships. This is undoubtedly because the over-whelmingly Whig-dominated Second Exclusion Parliament was sitting. This gives an interesting context for the complaints from Tories in the audience which resulted in the banning of *Lucius Junius Brutus*, *Henry the Sixth*, and *Richard the Second*, also in autumn 1680. The Tories' actions seem more like political re-taliation or a response to political insecurity than the confident assertion of a position of strength.

A Drama of Contradiction

Perhaps the drama prior to the Exclusion Crisis might present a more unified picture? Not so. The libertine comedy which comes to most people's minds when they think of Restoration drama embodies a moral contradiction which is the subject of endless debate. Are sex comedies like Wycherley's *The Country Wife* and Etherege's *The Man of Mode* indulgent or satirical in their treatment of libertinism? The texts contain both possibilities. Such plays would have shocked some and titillated or amused others. More significant for the purposes of this book is the clash between sex comedies which could be taken as offering an indulgent portrayal of cavalier (in both senses) sexual mores, and the excoriating anatomization of Hobbesian libertinism in a play like Shadwell's *The Libertine*. However, as Robert Hume has pointed out, 'A less selective treatment of 1670s plays dem-onstrates that the sex comedies of Wycherley and Etherege were actually atypical and that the vogue for such plays was quite brief'.[30] In its own time, the heroic drama of the early Restora-tion period was more significant.

If the creation of the Restoration theatre was an act of state, more than anything else like the creation of the BBC, the new

---

[29] Milhous and Hume, 'Dating Play Premières', 382.
[30] Hume, 'Texts within Contexts', 77.

dramatic genre of the heroic play in rhyming couplets also came about through royal instigation.[31] As Nancy Maguire says, 'for the first time, those in power promoted a consciously contrived campaign to build a new monarchy and a new culture'.[32] Drawing on the earlier genre of the court masque, 'the rhymed heroic play functioned for Charles II as the court masque proper functioned for his father' (10). The politics of the heroic drama is the subject of debate;[33] but it seems clear that the model of submerged contradiction, which the Exclusion Crisis was to blast open, applies just as much to the drama as to the society and the theatre of which it was a part. Some critics have argued that contradiction between the ideal and a human reality is the subject of the heroic play. Derek Hughes in *Dryden's Heroic Plays* (152) argues that 'the disparity between heroic art and mortal life' is the mainspring of Dryden's dramas. Nancy Maguire has argued that the heroic play perpetuates in a somewhat more subtle form the 'unrelenting sense of division' (6) and the tensions between idealism and pragmatism (11) which characterize royalist tragi-comedy.

However, the greatest contradiction relates to the disparity between the perceived reality of 'effeminacy and luxury', corruption and division, and the heroic ideal depicted, which Richard Bevis sums up thus:

'Heroic drama' was to be a kind of grand opera without music, a splendid artifice in which monarchs, nobles and generals of astonishing virtue or evil endured momentous conflicts of love and honour while nations quaked and audiences admired the magnificence of the thought, language, scenes and costumes. Drawing its sentiments from chivalric romance and the etiquette of the most refined courts, it was to lift serious English drama from the muck of blood and revenge into which it had fallen up to a level befitting a nation whose theatrical establishment had recently sojourned in the capitals of Europe. The themes of honour and martial valour would brace the soul, while that

---

[31] See n. 12 above.

[32] Maguire, *Regicide and Restoration*, 7.

[33] For discussion of the politics of the heroic play, see Brown, *English Dramatic Form*, 25; Staves, *Players' Scepters*, Ch. 1; Stocker, 'Political Allusion in *The Rehearsal*', 16; Altieri, *The Theatre of Praise*, ch. 1; Canfield, 'The Significance of the Restoration Rhymed Heroic Play'; Barbeau, *The Intellectual Design of Dryden's Heroic Plays*; Evans, '"Private Greatness": The Feminine Ideal in Dryden's Early Heroic Drama'; Maguire, *Regicide and Restoration, passim*.

of love would soften the heart and the characters would provide patterns for imitation, ideals in the platonic sense.

Heroic drama may be considered baroque in the sense in which Walter Benjamin defined baroque drama in *The Origins of the German Tragic Drama*: characterized by an 'agonizing violence of . . . style' (49) and a 'desire for new pathos' (55), bearing the imprint of absolutism (48) and 'possessed of an unremitting artistic will' (55). For Benjamin, baroque drama is 'a literature which sought, in a sense, to reduce both its contemporaries and posterity to silence' (56). The same might be said of the heroic drama of the early Restoration period.[34]

The (unrealizable) high-flown aims of heroic drama are debunked in Buckingham's irreverent parody in *The Rehearsal*, but perhaps more tellingly in Lee's *The Princess of Cleve*, in which, as Robert Hume says, 'the apparently peculiar double plot is a brilliantly designed satiric debunking of both the libertine ethos of Carolean sex comedy and the heroic and précieuse conventions of contemporary tragedy'.[35] The characters in the heroic 'high-plot' are as tainted by all-pervasive court corruption as those in the sex comedy plot. The Princess hankers after the predatory libertine Nemours. The Prince is a whining fool and potential cuckold who dies a victim's death from unrequited love of his wife. This supposedly transcendent love is immediately debunked by the woman he has died for:

> Nor can I think his passion wou'd have lasted,
> But that he found I cou'd have none for him.
> 'Tis Obstacle, Ascent, and Lets and Bars,
> That whet the Appetite of Love and Glory.

> (5. 3. 169–72)

---

[34] Other features heroic drama shares with the baroque drama defined by Benjamin are a modified classicism which is imperfectly understood (50), violent actions and visual appeal which make it eminently theatrical despite modern notions that it is unsuited to performance (51), and the fact that it is considered insincere, or validated only in the kind of reading which posits 'either the positive worth or the futility of all value judgements' (52). However, there cannot be a simple equation between Restoration tragedy and German baroque drama. Differences between the two include a voracious linguistic innovation in the German drama which is more similar to English Renaissance drama. Moreover, Benjamin's description of the political absolutism under which the drama was produced is *too* absolute for English Restoration politics and society.

[35] Hume, 'The Satiric Design of Nat. Lee's *The Princess of Cleve*', 118.

High-flights are continually being deflated or exposed as futile posturing. The atmosphere is one of all-pervasive obscenity. It is stressed that, whatever their affectations, all men and women are the same. Nothing is pure, every feeling or action is alloyed, tainted, qualified, or undermined by the sneering of others. Words lose their value, and discourse seems merely contingent, as Nemours manipulates one language after another, including 'the Heroick Vein' (4. 1. 260). The lack of moral coherence, and of clear standards from the political centre of the nation, coupled with the lack of any alternative worthy of respect, is an indictment of the leaders of society whose ill-regulated desires reflect a society badly ruled.

In the divided society of the 1660s, in which Stuart ideology has to be reconstructed and reinstated after the rupture of the interregnum, the royalist heroic play represents an attempt to paper over ideological cracks. It is an attempt which, in its very artifice, reveals the constructed nature of late Stuart ideology. The definition of ideology is disputed among philosophers and critics.[36] I am using the term in the same sense as Jonathan Dollimore: 'ideology typically legitimates the social order by representing it as a spurious unity, metaphysically ordained and thereby forestalls knowledge of the contradictions which in fact constitute that order (such knowledge being a pre-condition for the recognition that change is possible)'.[37] From this point of view, the fact that the royalist ideology of the heroic drama appears as a construct obviously represents a crisis for its legitimizing function. Moreover, plays which agitate so hard on behalf of the dominant ideology expose the fragile nature of that ideology precisely in the fact that such agitation is necessary.[38]

[36] The discussion is reviewed by Eagleton, *Ideology: An Introduction*.

[37] Dollimore, *Radical Tragedy*, 14.

[38] Szanto, *Theater and Propaganda* identifies three kinds of dramatic propaganda: agitation, integration, and dialectical. A Whiggish anti-Catholic play such as Settle's *The Female Prelate* corresponds to his definition of the theatre of agitation propaganda, aimed at 'raising its audiences' consciousnesses to a point where social and political problems took on shape and immediacy' (73). However, so does an ultra-royalist play such as Whitaker's *The Conspiracy*. Whitaker revives the defunct form of the heroic play during the Exclusion Crisis to do the ideological work of royalism. It is a sign of the profundity of the regime's crisis that *The Conspiracy*, although celebrating the dominant order, cannot function as 'integration propaganda' as Szanto defines it (74): it cannot suggest that all is well. It must *agitate* on behalf of the dominant ideology.

In the Exclusion Crisis internal contradiction within royalist drama is dramatically sharpened, as is the division between it and a vigorous oppositional drama. That is the subject of the latter part of this book. Chapter 7 looks at Tory plays and the contradictions of royalism in crisis. These are greater than often supposed by critics who stress the resilience and cogency of Stuart royalism. Chapter 8 looks at the vitality of Whig plays in opposition, and Chapter 9 at Thomas Jordan's Lord Mayor's Shows, a vigorous drama outside the theatres which is opposed to Tory drama in the theatres in important respects. Critics have argued that there aren't any Whig plays, but there clearly are. The differences from Tory plays are significant, but have been missed because the Whig rhetoric of 'Loyal Protestantism' is misread or misunderstood. Recent criticism has also argued that the Lord Mayor's Shows are simply mouthpieces of authority, but a careful reading of the dramatic language of politics shows this is the reverse of the truth; the shows stand opposed to Tory drama in their emphasis on patriotism, trade, Protestantism, and class questions, notably defence of merchants and the City and an inclusive social vision which emphasizes the whole commonwealth.

Contradiction in the drama is thus to be understood in a precise way, not as a muddle of qualifications and uncertainties which obscure the existence of any partisanship or real political differences in the drama at all. Tory drama is fraught with contradiction which will be explored at length in Chapter 7, but which may be summed up here in the paradox: the vociferous assertion of a quietist message. There is also a contradiction between Tory drama and drama inside and outside the theatres which carries an oppositional or Whig message. The contradictions within Whiggism are less acute than those of Toryism, perhaps because it is easier to be in opposition than to defend the status quo; perhaps because the dominant ideology in crisis is inevitably less vigorous than an emergent ideology. The process of dramatization tends to bring out contradictions in the dominant ideology;[39] or, to paraphrase Dryden, to widen and not to heal the breaches in the nation.[40] The drama of the crisis thus reveals the fragility and the constructed nature of post-

---

[39] As Robert Markley has argued: *Two Edg'd Weapons*, 27–9.
[40] Cf. dedication to *Troilus and Cressida*, in *Works*, xiii. 221.

interregnum Stuart ideology and the disparity between this ideology and people's experience of political reality.

How should we Read the Politics of the Drama?

What makes the drama interesting is precisely its engagement with its peculiar times, and therefore its topicality and partisanship. This engagement is an engagement of the playwrights in the life of their society. Accordingly, though the author as God has left the scene in 'post-modern' thought, s/he must re-enter as a force in history: as Robert Hume argues, 'trying to discover what the author attempted to say (and why) is not the same as claiming that the author's intent determines the meaning of a text'.[41] The first step in reading the drama is to decide not to 'write out' the political impulses and commitment of the dramatists. The playwright lives within the discourse of the times, but she or he also *lives* within it and changes it. There is a very famous passage of Marx which is peculiarly appropriate to discussion of the political ideology and literature of the Exclusion Crisis:

Men make their own history, but they do not make it just as they please: they do not make it under circumstances chosen by themselves, but under given circumstances directly encountered and inherited from the past. The tradition of all the generations of the dead weighs like a nightmare on the brain of the living. And just when they seem involved in revolutionizing themselves and things, in creating something that has never before existed, it is precisely in such periods of revolutionary crisis that they anxiously conjure up the spirits of the past to their service and borrow names, battle cries and costumes from them in order to act out the new scene of world history in this time-honoured disguise and this borrowed language.[42]

People 'make their own history, but they do not make it just as they please'. This sentence expresses in a very clear way the fact that we can, in reading the drama, have regard both to authorial political aims and impulses, and to constraints on the expression of these, as well as unexpected and undesired results. These texts were closely and ferociously engaged with their times. Of course

---

[41] Hume, 'Texts within Contexts', 87.
[42] Marx, *The Eighteenth Brumaire of Louis Bonaparte*, 9–10.

they are written within the dominant discourse of their times, which they in turn employ and embody; but the playwrights also, successfully or unsuccessfully, wrench these discourses to their purpose. In the process they participate in 'creating something that has never before existed', in this case the political language of the Whig and Tory parties. Unexpected and undesired results may arise as internal contradictions within the text, as in the Tory dramas discussed in Chapter 7; or it may occur in a conflict between the author's aims and the play's reception. In the various prologues and epilogues to *Venice Preserv'd* Otway, the author, and Dryden on his behalf, assert strongly Tory intentions; yet the play was revived in the eighteenth century as a revolutionary fable, with the rebel Pierre as hero. Ravenscroft's *The London Cuckolds* satirizes citizens who have some Whiggish characteristics, in the manner of Tory comedy; yet the play was revived well into the eighteenth century at the behest of the citizens, with whom it was a firm favourite.[43] These (historical) contradictions have meaning and interest *as* contradictions: they do not necessarily mean that all political meaning and commitment is indeterminate.

We make our own history, but not just as we please. How we think and act is both determined by the past and undetermined by it. This contradiction is at the centre of Hegel's and Marx's idea of real historical contradiction. In this conception change is the underlying reality; stability, the tendency of things to go on as they are, is merely a phase of change. 'The present' is a name we give to the immediate past and the immediate future; in reality past and future are interpenetrated: the past determines, but does not determine, the future; the past, and therefore the present, is pregnant with alternative possible futures. To understand historical causation is to grasp these alternative possibilities, which exist in the past as contradictions, ways in which the apparent dominant characteristic negates or contradicts itself. Just as change is universal, so is contradiction. It only becomes apparent that this is the case, however, when a historical crisis

[43] For this reason, some critics have stressed the importance of audience applications as well as authorial aims in constituting political meaning: Roper, 'Drawing Parallels and Making Applications in Restoration Literature'; Wallace, 'Otway's *Caius Marius* and the Exclusion Crisis'; Hume, 'The Politics of Opera in Late Seventeenth-Century London', forthcoming. I am grateful to Robert Hume for sight of this piece.

causes an apparently solid and stable order suddenly to melt into fluidity and uncertainty, ending either by being reinstated or by being replaced by a different order.[44] This concept of contradiction can be of great value to us in grasping the historicity of political drama. Firstly, by recognizing the contradictions within a dramatist's treatment of a subject, and which side of the contradiction, if any, is dominant,[45] we can avoid both, on the one hand, the writing out of all meaning and intention, and, on the other, a forced reading which eliminates discordant notes. Secondly, by grasping the contradictions of the period both in the society and in its drama we can avoid both readings which over-emphasize stability and continuity, failing to recognize the existence of new elements, and readings which are teleological, under-reading the persistence of the old order and over-reading the elements of the new.

To elaborate on the first of these points, it is important not to understate or overstate partisanship in the drama. Grasping contradiction is distinct from positing a free play of meaning. Obviously all literary criticism must interrogate to some extent, must be aware of subtexts and interpretive plurality. However, an excessive focus upon interrogation can lead to the 'writing out' of partisanship and to missing political significance. This means missing the way in which drama engages with the burning issues of its time. It seems to me little different from the depoliticizing attempts of the New Criticism with its focus on rich ambiguity. Writing out partisanship has led to misreadings of Restoration drama. Necessary political distinctions are obscured, and it is wrongly asserted, for example, that Lee's Whiggish plays scarcely differ from the Tory plays on which he collaborated with Dryden.[46]

The deconstruction of political statement is not an enabling

[44] For a full account of dialectic and contradiction, see Bhaskar, *Reclaiming Reality* and *Dialectic* .

[45] Cf. *Brecht on Theatre*, 261, citing Mao Zedong 'On Contradiction'. Mao's account is rather mechanical, and the specific argument cited by Brecht is a spectacular piece of political mystification. Yet the notion of contradiction is enormously empowering for Brecht, and is an exciting feature of his reading, for example, of *Coriolanus*.

[46] See e.g. Brown, 'The Dryden–Lee Collaboration: *Oedipus* and *The Duke of Guise*' and 'Nathaniel Lee's Political Dramas 1679–1683'. I argue against this approach in my '"Partial Tyrants" and "Freeborn People" in Lee's *Lucius Junius Brutus*', and in Ch. 8 below.

tool of analysis. It renders meaning labyrinthine, and may obscure the subtle or strategic deployment of political themes and
tropes. For example, the Whig Settle produces a play in which
meaningful contradiction is, as it were, concealed within an
apparent labyrinth. It could easily be argued that there is in
Fatal Love (1680) a rendering provisional of all solutions. Rhetorical flights are consistently deflated and even the most poign-
ant moments of realization are qualified. The difficulties of
loving rightly are compounded by the problem of thinking
clearly and behaving suitably. The hero Philander's paralysis
reveals the complexity of the questions of marriage and remar-
riage, fidelity, gratitude, and human happiness in love. Believing
his first love dead, he has made new vows in all good faith. This
insoluble conflict leads him to reproach the Gods in outbursts
against creation. His *cri de cœur*, 'Guide me, ye Gods, in this
unhappy Labyrinth' (1. 2. p. 10), is echoed by the villain,
Pyrgus: 'In what a Labyrinth am I lost?' (5. p. 41). This image of
a labyrinth seems suggestive. However, the play is not value-
free. In the first place, there is a stringent and Whiggish critique
of royal lust, intemperance, and tyranny. Secondly, the contradictions in the plot are tentatively resolved in favour of a Protestant ethos of respect for—and within—marriage. As in other
Whig plays, married love is prized not merely as a matter of
sentiment, but as a social alternative to both tyranny and pam-
pered lust. It is hard to see how this could have been taken
as apolitical at this crisis point in the reign of Charles II.
Philander's abandonment of his unrealistic hankering after a
lost ideal love and attempt to make the best of a new marriage
seems opposite to the somewhat absurd posturings of the pro-
tagonists of the royalist heroic plays, and offers a model for
behaviour in difficult times.

The opposite danger is of not interrogating the text enough,
of not noticing contradictions and points of fracture at which
attempts to dramatize a political ideology become hollow and
unconvincing, so that tensions within the conservative ideology
of personal patriarchal monarchy are missed. This 'flattening
out' of contradiction is apparent in some of the readings of
Venice Preserv'd which I discuss in Chapter 7. For example,
Harry M. Solomon in 'The Rhetoric of Redressing Grievances'
(294) has little patience with the darkness of tone and 'rich

ambiguities' noticed in the play by others. Solomon's extraordinary subtitle is 'Court Propaganda as the Hermeneutical Key to *Venice Preserv'd*'. The idea that we can decode, unlock, or solve the mystery of the text by reference to court propaganda seems dubious in terms of literary critical method, and simplistic in political terms. More influential has been Douglas Canfield's 'Royalism's Last Dramatic Stand', according to which only three tragedies show disillusionment with Stuart aristocratic ideals: Lee's *Lucius Junius Brutus*, and Otway's *The History and Fall of Caius Marius* and *Venice Preserv'd*. However, 'in every other political tragedy from 1679–89 the royalist code of loyalty to a rightful monarch, however weak or indulgent, wrong or unfortunate, is strenuously maintained'.[47] This sweeping statement is without foundation, as I shall hope to show in this book. This implies no disrespect to Canfield, whose own piece is, after all, a stringent critique of Susan Staves and Laura Brown. It is simply to explain and justify my own method of reading. As Robert Hume argues in 'Texts within Contexts',

Few of us would recommend ignoring predecessors or eschewing the courtesies of scholarly discourse. But *deference* seems the wrong attitude. If we accept our predecessors' conclusions, what can we change? If we do not ask new questions then we consign ourselves to crumbs and bickering . . . even the most historicist of scholars needs to adopt a rigorously skeptical attitude toward the facts, questions, logic and conclusions of even the most respected predecessor. (90–1)

Precisely. To engage critically with other critics' work is a compliment, a sign that one regards that work as serious.

In fact, as we shall see, many plays are pessimistic in tone. Canfield makes much of the fact that most of the plays he considers soundly condemn rebellion. However, as I shall show in the ensuing chapters, many plays in this period are critical of misrule in high places, and have the force of opposition without advocating rebellion. Moreover, even when loyal playwrights are straining every nerve to justify the ways of the Stuart monarchy to men, the negative resonance of loyalty to vitiated kingship is apparent. As we shall see, recurring themes are bad fatherhood and the sovereign's unruly passions which jeopardize the state, inability or failure to reward loyal service, and

[47] Canfield, 'Royalism's Last Dramatic Stand', 238.

general political impotence or incompetence. Canfield's analysis writes out not only the political implications of suffering, but the suffering itself. An example is his optimistic reading of the ending of Crowne's *The Ambitious Statesman*. That the conflicts in the play are resolved in the direction of absolute loyalty is not in question; but the statement that the hero, Vendosme, dies 'At peace with his King and his Prince' (240) glosses over the negative reverberations of the king's inability to protect his loyal subject and the Dauphin's abuse of power to score over him, sexually, by stealing his bride. Royalism in the play coexists with an almost puritan disgust for court manners and mores in which the Dauphin is implicated. Canfield thinks 'Vendosme dies in full expectation of a happy afterlife with Louize' (241). Yet, as I shall argue more fully in Chapter 3, the play ends on a dark note as Vendosme speaks of reunion in the grave in terms which carry no suggestion of any joyous afterlife. Vaska Tumir states: 'I find unconvincing Douglas Canfield's claim that the destructive passions and deadly fates of the royalist characters in the drama of this decade do not signal a growing political pessimism about Stuart rule. In the theater, at least, seeing is believing, and what the audience observes fails to reassure and affirm.'[48] This accords with my own views.

For similar reasons I would take issue with Christopher Wheatley's reading of Otway in 'The Defense of the Status Quo and Otway's *The Atheist*'. Again, this is not in the least to devalue this critic's useful work, for example in reinstating the idea of arranged marriage as still potent in the drama.[49] Wheatley criticizes those who have perceived radical inconsistency, even chaos, in *The Atheist* (1683), and makes it clear that he is talking about more than just Otway's play:

I would like to argue that the romance in *The Atheist* makes perfect sense as an affirmation of tradition and existing social structures as ordering principles that create meaning in a world where certainty is impossible, and that restrain humanity's anarchic nature. Further, the failure of critics to consider this potential reading of the play is an example of how the Twentieth Century has marginalized conservative elements in Restoration drama. (14–15)

---

[48] Tumir, 'She-Tragedy and its Men', 427 n. 17.

[49] Wheatley, 'Romantic Love and Social Necessities: Reconsidering Justifications for Marriage in Restoration Comedy'. See also his pioneering study of Shadwell in *Without God or Reason*.

The cautionary point here is valuable: some critics have been too quick to marginalize conservative elements in the drama. Yet I would suggest that Wheatley's reading imposes excessive 'closure' on *The Atheist*. For example the fact that Courtine's breach with Sylvia is never healed affects the tone of the play's ending. Moreover, the theme of bad fatherhood resonates in a way which is problematic for Toryism. The play's father is a libertine, a fool, and an unnatural parent, but he also uses kingly language. The analogy between king and father is made and mocked in such paternal outbursts as, 'Why, Sirrah, you have lost all Grace; you have no Duty left; you are a Rebel' (1. 1. 72–4); and also by the spectacle of the father scrounging money from the son to gamble away or waste on wine and whores, whilst betraying the son to his enemies on the slightest provocation. It is the father who is changeable, mercenary, ungrateful, and disloyal. In Tory plays, as we shall see, these are qualities of the rebel son or subject. The father is a worse character than the eponymous atheist. It is notable in the context—the height of the Tory reaction—that the opportunity to make the atheist a Whig is largely missed.

To read the plays of this period, then, we need to recognize partisanship; but we also need to recognize that overtones and undertones may contradict explicit messages, and that the messages themselves may be contradictory.

The second way in which the idea of real historical contradiction may be useful to us is in viewing the politics of the drama of the period as a whole. To reach this point it is necessary to go beyond the traditional particularist approach to the politics of the plays of this period which reads the plays politically by attempting to discern topical allusions, coded references, and parallels, and to grapple with the weaknesses of thematic and tropological approaches.[50] What I have called the particularist approach has elsewhere been termed 'literalistic fantasy' and 'interpretations of the lock-picking type'.[51] This approach refuses to acknowledge the bigger picture of dramatic and political shifts; while thematic and tropological approaches, by failing to recognize historical contradiction, may overstate

---

[50] I have discussed this at length in my 'Interpreting the Politics of Restoration Drama'.

[51] Goldberg, *James I and the Politics of Literature*, 232; Hume, 'The Politics of Opera in Late Seventeenth-Century London'.

either conservatism and stability or radicalism and innovation in the drama.

The one Restoration text which every student knows is Dryden's *Absalom and Achitophel*. We can decode this satirical poem by discussing 'who's who'. This does not tell us all we need to know about Dryden's poem, but it has some value, and may be considered a necessary exercise. However, applying this method to Restoration political drama is very limiting. Political reference and engagement in the drama is much more subtle and profound. A few plays work by topical allusion and satire of individuals: Crowne's *City Politiques* (1683) is an example. Applied to other plays, especially of earlier seasons, the method can be misleading. On the one hand, the political significance of occasional and fleeting parallels and allusions might be over-stated, particularly since party politics was new in the Exclusion Crisis, and was seen as a problem: there is a danger in seeing political reference exclusively or mainly in terms of dramatists taking sides, or making the kind of political allusions which we might expect to find in a modern context of clearly defined political allegiances. On the other hand, the political significance of themes such as disharmony in the family may be missed; the powerful resonance in characters and situations which carry overtones of interregnum radicalism as well as Whiggery is missed by the cry of 'here is yet another portrait of the Earl of Shaftesbury'. There is some personation and caricature of Shaftesbury and other Whig leaders, but dramatic satire of the Whigs is far more diffuse and far-reaching than this.[52] Personations were certainly identified at the time,[53] and could be

[52] Scott, *Algernon Sidney and the Restoration Crisis*, ch. 1, argues that historians have been over-preoccupied by Shaftesbury and Exclusion, but this is controversial: cf. the reviews in *History*, 78 (1990), 114 and *Albion*, 24 (1992), 652. My reading of the plays may lend some support to Scott's view, since characters who can, like Achitophel, plausibly be read as Shaftesbury are not that common, and exclusion and banishment are no more prominent as themes of disorder than presumption by the lower classes, mob rule, and civil war.

[53] An example dating from before the outbreak of the crisis is Marvell, writing on Pope-burning night, 17 Nov. 1677: 'To day is acted the first time Sir Popular Wisdome or the Politician where my Lord Shaftesbury and all his gang are sufficiently personated' (*Poems and Letters*, ii. 356, cited by Novak, in *Works of John Dryden*, xiii. 463). A late one is the personations in *City Politiques*, reported in the *Newdigate Newsletters* for 20 Jan. 1682/3 (Wilson, 'Theatre Notes from the *Newdigate Newsletters*', 81).

dangerous for the dramatists,[54] but where a personal parallel was denied, this did not draw the sting of the satire, but if anything extended it: 'you are *all* rebellious villains'.[55]

Some criticism, therefore, has tended to move away from this method of reading the politics of the drama to one which approaches politics through the political resonance of themes and tropes.[56] This approach has great potential strengths: it can grasp the multifaceted nature of political engagement in the drama, avoid either writing out or overstating partisanship, and relate drama to social process by apprehending changes in the politics of the drama and their relationship to shifts in dramatic form and content. However, it also carries with it the danger of partial (in the sense of incomplete; and sometimes also of partisan) readings, which create a one-sided picture. Critics have produced in this way the conservative schema, illustrated above, which regards the plays almost entirely as 'royalism's last dramatic stand', in Canfield's phrase;[57] and a teleological schema which focuses almost entirely on aspects which foreshadow the coming revolution of 1688, as in the work of Susan Staves, Rose Zimbardo, and (in a more extreme form) Laura Brown.[58] I shall discuss these different methods of reading in the next chapter, in the context of the historical methods to which they correspond. However, I want to mention here some immediate critical problems.

Assumptions about the conservatism of Restoration drama have led to the marginalization of oppositional drama and to the

[54] For example, Crowne was cudgelled on 24 Jan. 1683 by supporters of the deceased Rochester, who was thought to have been personated in *City Politiques*: Van Lennep *et al.* (eds.), *The London Stage*, 318.

[55] A good example is the charge made against Dryden that the villain Guise in *The Duke of Guise* represented Charles II's illegitimate son, the Earl of Monmouth, who was associated with the Whig cause. Dryden's denial of the personal parallel in *The Vindication* only gives more wide-ranging relevance to the rebel qualities associated with Guise.

[56] The word 'trope' seems to be loosely and variously used by New Historicists. Douglas Canfield speaks of 'master tropes', by which he means important ways in which power relations are constituted through literary discourse: 'Dramatic Shifts: Writing an Ideological History of Late Stuart Drama'. To give a simple example of my own use of the term: the danger of rebellion is a Tory theme. The association of rebellion and rape for the purpose of arousing horror is a trope of Toryism.

[57] See also, for example, Matthew Wikander, 'The Spitted Infant', who adopts the phrase as a description of what the dramatists were about.

[58] Staves, *Players' Scepters*; Zimbardo, 'Toward Zero' and 'At Zero Point'; Brown, *English Dramatic Form*.

false idea that there is no Whig writing of any significance before
1688. There is no need to say more about this here, as it is the
subject of the latter part of the book. The problems of teleology
and anachronism include false assumptions which are frequently made about the rise of the sentimental and the development of a privileged private or domestic sphere. Those who do
not see the shift towards the sentimental in drama as a purely
aesthetic phenomenon tend to look back from an eighteenth-
century vantage-point and assume it must have to do with a shift
towards bourgeois notions. How should this be, in a period in
which it became increasingly necessary at the ideological level to
demonize the merchant citizens of London as an entire social
class? The rendering culturally visible and articulate of a bourgeoisie which could form a cultural alliance with its social
superiors needed the revolution of 1688. Whether or not the rise
of the sentimental in the eighteenth century can be traced to a
shift from feudal aristocratic to bourgeois values, in the Restoration the sentimental is associated with quietism. The impetus
for quietism comes from royalism and Toryism.

Similarly, the assumption that Restoration plays, like
eighteenth-century plays, privilege an apolitical private sphere
as a moral alternative or corrective to a sordid political sphere is
mistaken, partly because it fails to recognize the real political
engagement of this drama, and partly because the assumption is
anachronistic. It rests on notions of the separateness from and
superiority to politics of both the domestic and the literary
which could scarcely have been prevalent at a time when the
specialized sphere of party politics in the modern sense was only
just beginning to develop. Restoration drama retains a sense
that politics is inseparable from religion, ethics, and national
welfare. In Otway's *The Orphan*, as I shall discuss more fully in
Chapter 7, the exclusion of the sons from the public sphere
creates a kind of chaos in a domestic sphere which is experienced as utterly stifling. In *Venice Preserv'd*, Belvidera's assertion of her needs and rights as a wife is utterly unsuccessful:
she is marginalized into madness, while her husband prefers to
die heroically with his male friend, whom he regrets having
betrayed 'In fond compassion to a woman's tears' (4. 1. 16).
Likewise, the attempt to dramatize the virtues of retirement is

singularly ineffective.[59] Persuading the political nation to keep its nose out of politics requires a polemical battle. The conflict between love and honour which is a central theme in heroic drama modulates in the political tragedy of the Exclusion Crisis into a tormented sense that political conflict vitiates both the macrocosm of state and the microcosm of family; but the most we can say is that this prefigures the eighteenth-century focus on the domestic sphere.[60]

The idea of contradiction, then, is useful not only in avoiding under- or over-reading partisanship in the drama, but also in examining how drama is neither conservative, nor forward-looking, but a little of both. The problem with the conservative schema is that it overstates the extent to which there was any stability for the drama to assert. Not only was there disunity in the present, but the past also was a site of conflict: as we shall see in the next chapter, even before the Exclusion Crisis, political 'faction' led opponents to try to wrest the meaning and interpretation of recent history to their own purposes. The problem with teleology, on the other hand, is that it ignores the possibility of different futures. Neither the defeat of Whiggery in 1682–3, nor the revolution of 1688, was inevitable. Even more importantly, neither outcome was foreseeable in the Exclusion Crisis period. The drama is not monolithically conservative, but, in so far as it is forward-looking, it contains within it the seeds of a range of possible futures. It is my intention to uncover the complex intersection of the real polarities of Toryism and Whiggery with different kinds and degrees of conservatism and radicalism. The idea of real historical contradiction is useful in considering the extent to which the drama mediates the values of various possible pasts and futures.

One further point about the method of reading the politics of the drama also needs to be made. This concerns the perceived conflict between the desire of critics such as Canfield, Staves,

---

[59] See the discussion in Ch. 4.

[60] There is a difference of emphasis here between my analysis and that of Michael Dobson in his excellent discussion of Exclusion Crisis adaptations of Shakespeare in ch. 2 of *The Making of the National Poet*: 'With the public arena of political action in a state of confused and dangerous ferment, playwrights resorted increasingly to dramatizing a domestic sphere of private emotion now strenuously defined as its antithesis' (76).

Zimbardo, and Brown to look at wider dramatic and political shifts, and what might be described as the old historicist approach: a willingness to look at all the evidence, to proceed 'play by play'. Canfield castigates the play-by-play approach in his 'Dramatic Shifts: Writing an Ideological History of Late Stuart Drama', preferring a political history of the theatre which proceeds by the exploration of tropological shifts. However, the two need not be mutually exclusive. I think we can and must be willing to do both, and indeed that our ability to discern wider shifts depends on attention to detail. The problem with all schematic readings is that the discussion centres upon those plays or aspects of plays which most fit a preconceived idea about drama and society. The reading is thus circular: the theory informs the selection of plays (and parts of plays) and these, unsurprisingly, confirm the theory. Rather than applying particular abstract concepts such as royalism, aristocratic honour, and patriarchalism directly, I think it is important to start with the concrete (the drama in its period) and draw from it abstractions (the various themes and tropes which constitute the dramatic language of politics) which can then be recombined to give a comprehensible picture of the concrete, the drama. The concrete can now be perceived more fully as a totality which is a unity of opposites, which is in movement, and which has potential futures which are limited, but not fully foreordained. Because this method requires us to theorize, and to grasp the concrete as a totality, it is able to impose a pattern on the mass of detail, and escapes from the shortcomings of empiricism.[61] Because it requires us to start from and return to the concrete, the results are not self-validating but testable and falsifiable against readings of plays as a whole, and of a whole body of drama.

Attention to detail is not counterposed to considering broader political and dramatic shifts: the two things are complementary and one can explicate the other. The relationship between detail and the bigger picture in historical and critical methodology is the subject of Chapter 2. In Chapter 3 attention to literary detail—all the plays, prologues, and epilogues of the Exclusion Crisis—together with precise information about his-

---

[61] Useful critiques of empiricism may be found in Brown, *English Dramatic Form*, p. xiii, and Corman, 'What is Restoration Drama?', 63.

torical events produces a surprising picture of the intense relationship between drama and politics in this period of crisis. In the middle section of the book a detailed reading of all the plays has enabled the generalizations about the dramatic languages of Toryism and Whiggery which are important tools of literary analysis. Attention to detail is sometimes presented as a conservative method, and it has certainly been used by some conservative critics and historians to undermine radical 'grand narratives'. Yet it is only by reading all the plays that it is possible to discern, in relation to the argument of Chapter 7, that the ardent royalism of much drama, and the contradictions within the royalist perspective, are not local accidents, or confined to a couple of plays, but real, recurring, and significant phenomena. Similarly, it is precisely such attention to detail that has enabled me to discern the existence of the vigorous oppositional drama discussed in the final chapters as not merely occasional.

The need to read the plays as part of a totality which includes all the drama of the period in its political context necessarily limits the chronological range of this study. This book treats four years and fifty-four plays. These years and these plays have a particular advantage. Crisis illuminates and brings to the surface things which in more normal times are hidden from view. Change which had already been going on in a gradual and therefore almost invisible way becomes manifest and rapid. The Exclusion Crisis reveals in a striking way the political ideas, contradictions, strengths, and weaknesses both of the Stuart regime and of its opponents; and the contradictory place of the drama in the political life of Restoration society.

CHAPTER 2

The Politics of the Crisis

THE drama of the Exclusion Crisis was intensely engaged with its times and the best understanding of the drama is achieved through the best understanding of those times. I shall give in this chapter an account of the Exclusion Crisis and the events leading up to it to 'locate' my analysis of the drama. This account is not an impartial account, because there is no such thing, but it draws on a range of historical sources and aims to be inclusive, not conveniently excluding material which gets in the way of any particular theory. I then go on to consider the various theories or stories which literary critics as well as historians use to explain the larger historical movements of which the Exclusion Crisis was a part.

Everyone has such a story whether they like it or not. We have the choice either to discuss the various options explicitly and to express our own preference, or to plug in unconsciously to some kind of 'default narrative'. For example, simply to suppose, as many literary scholars do, that the Exclusion Crisis was not very important, was not a 'revolutionary moment', is to make certain assumptions about the shape of seventeenth-century history. Similar assumptions lie behind the notion that there was no real difference between Whigs and Tories. Both these notions—the unimportance of the crisis, the similarity of Whigs and Tories—are false in my view. To explain why, the nettle of history must be grasped. Why not leave it to the historians? Because literary scholars who want to locate their account of texts within a historical framework have certain responsibilities.

It is no longer fashionable to speak of text and context, for two reasons. The first is that the text is part of the context: the drama participates in history and in the creation of a language of politics. The second is that the context is not knowable outside the texts which tell us about it. Yet the fact that our knowledge of events can only be provisional and approximate should not mean that literary scholars should make no effort to understand history; nor, I believe, should we take our account of history arbitrarily from whatever text we want, ignoring the work of historians.[1] For this reason I think much excellent recent work is better described as historicist rather than New Historicist.[2] If the rejection of text–context becomes an excuse in some New Historicist work for not attempting to get the best possible picture of the history in which literary texts are embedded, the rejection of 'grand narratives' is a similar flaw within historicism. We all understand history by telling ourselves stories. People living through the Exclusion Crisis certainly saw their experience as part of the wider movement of history, making constant reference to a past which they interpreted through competing stories, as we shall see in a moment. I shall show in the second half of this chapter that literary critics just as much as historians locate the Exclusion Crisis within different versions of a grander narrative of seventeenth-century history. I shall discuss these various narratives in an explanatory way, but not an agnostic one: if impartiality is a myth, the bold course is to express clearly which narrative informs my own interpretation of the drama in subsequent chapters.

The Exclusion Crisis and what Led to It: A Narrative

Restoration politics was carried on under the shadow of the past, in the sense of the Civil War and interregnum; and in the shadow of European politics.[3] The politics of the 1670s were

[1] Hume makes a similar argument in 'Texts within Contexts'. He has some valuable observations on method, but I disagree with his view that literary scholars cannot take account of the 'large-scale "why" questions' in history (90) and that we are not properly concerned with broader historical perspectives: see below.

[2] See e.g. Butler, *Theatre and Crisis*; Dobson, *The Making of the National Poet*; Lindley, *The Trials of Frances Howard*; Hutson, *The Usurer's Daughter*; Hadfield, *Literature, Politics and National Identity*; Smith, *Literature and Revolution*.

[3] See the important arguments of Scott about the Europe-wide dimension of the 17th-cent. crises: *Algernon Sidney and the Restoration Crisis*, ch. 6 and *passim*. Information on the political situation is drawn mainly from: Scott; Jones, *Country and Court*; Kenyon, *The Popish Plot*; Haley, *Shaftesbury*; Hutton, *Charles the Second*; Henning, *History of Parliament*; Burnet, *History of My Own Time*; Luttrell, *A Brief Historical Relation of State Affairs*; Grey, *Debates in the House of Commons*.

especially overshadowed by recent events. It is an indication of the instability of the regime that a comparison between the 1670s and the 1640s had occurred to people even before the Exclusion Crisis. Milton's *True Religion, Heresy, Schism, Toleration: and What May Be Used Against the Growth of Popery* (1673) had already compared the 1670s to the 1630s. *A Letter From A Person of Quality to his Friend in the Country* (1675), attributed to Shaftesbury, introduces a parallel with the 1640s from an opposition perspective, through allusions to Laud and the canons of 1640. Marchamont Nedham retaliated in *A Pacquet of Advices and Animadversions Sent From London to the Men of Shaftesbury* (1676), a lengthy attack on Shaftesbury, who is seen as a Mephistophelian figure, entirely responsible for the nation's discontents, and aiming to revive the old faction of '41 for reasons of ambition. John Nalson's *The Countermine* (1677) and Samuel Rolle's *Loyalty and Peace; or, Two Seasonable Discourses* (1678) use a developed rhetoric of royalism, mobilizing the parallel of 1641, seeing the dissenters as a potential source of renewed civil war and asserting that there is not just an analogy between present and Civil War trouble-makers, but a literal continuity of personnel. In Marvell's *An Account of the Growth of Popery and Arbitrary Government in England* (1677) and L'Estrange's *An Account of the Growth of Knavery, Under the Pretended Fears of Arbitrary Government and Popery* (1678) accusations that ''41 is come again' are fairly flying. Marvell says that as early as 1673, when Parliament objected to James's Catholic marriage, the court party were claiming that 'the Nation was running again into *fourty One*', but it was they who 'indeed designed to have raised a Civil War' (56; cf. 63). L'Estrange's central thesis is clear from the latter part of his title: 'with a Parallel betwixt the Reformers of 1677, and those of 1641, in their Methods, and Designs'. The discontented 'knaves' of 1677 parallel the rebels of 1641, and the logical outcome of their 'knavery' will be renewed civil war. This was emphasized when the work was reprinted in 1678 with the title, *The Parallel; or, An Account of the Growth of Knavery, Under the Pretended Fears of Arbitrary Government and Popery*. The Civil War parallel was thus already present in the public mind well before the Exclusion Crisis.

1677–8 was the fourth year of the administration, whose leading figure was the Lord Treasurer, Thomas Osborne, Earl of Danby. This administration had come into being in the wake of a war in which England had fought on the side of Catholic France against the Protestant Dutch; the war had been popular enough until the need for supply had forced the Crown in 1673 to abandon its prerogative Declaration of Indulgence and accept a statutory Test excluding Roman Catholics from public office: this had flushed out both the previous Lord Treasurer, and the king's brother and heir apparent, as secret Roman Catholic converts. At this point a logical connection could be made between Catholics at court and the pro-French foreign policy of the Crown, and in the light of this connection the failure of the government to make peace with the Dutch and disband the army appeared highly suspicious. It is well known that large crowds attended 'Pope-burnings' during the Exclusion Crisis; perhaps less so that this was also the case in 1673.[4] In February 1674 ten bills were in progress in the Commons to reduce the power of the Crown over the judges, Parliament, taxation, and religion, and the Lords were considering proposals for the exclusion of James from the succession. Charles made peace with the Dutch and disbanded the army, but then prorogued Parliament. When he met it again, in April 1675, it was with a new policy of persecuting both dissent and popery and reaffirming the Restoration settlement, through a proposal that all MPs and office-holders should be required to take an oath not to attempt to alter the government of Church or state ('Danby's Test'). The latter was only lost because oppositionists fomented a jurisdictional clash between Lords and Commons which deadlocked all business. The administration, moreover, made determined efforts to increase its strength in the Commons through the use of places and other inducements.

However, the new religious policy was still overshadowed by the French threat. Parliament mistrusted Charles's preference for French fashions and mistresses as well as his foreign-policy intentions. The attempt to manage Parliament backfired in the form of a bill to eliminate Catholics and office-holders from Parliament (May 1675) and a Commons investigation into

---

[4] Miller, *Popery and Politics*, 182–8, Williams, 'Pope-Burning Processions'.

government pensions for members (October 1677). Even when, in spring 1677, the government offered to act against France, the Commons refused supply until they saw evidence, in the form of alliances concluded, of the king's commitment to act. Even the marriage between James's daughter Mary and William of Orange in October 1677 and the formation of an alliance with the Dutch in winter 1677–8 only led to an agreement in principle to give supply, coupled with the adoption by the Commons of extreme war aims.

By now the French government was bribing opposition MPs to make trouble, and rumours began to circulate that the forces which were being raised with the new tax revenues were for internal rather than external use. These rumours seemed to be corroborated by two circumstances. The first was that rather small numbers of troops were actually sent to Flanders and that they seemed to be inactive. The second was that in Scotland the administration of Lauderdale was from January 1678 using a 'Highland Host' to dragoon the principal areas of Protestant dissent in Scotland, plundering not only dissenters but gentry supporters of toleration of Protestant dissent. Scottish dissenting and covenanting opposition was to give the appellation 'Whig' to English politics. Though Charles got Lauderdale to withdraw the 'Highland Host' in March, preparatory to the meeting of Parliament, the Commons still called in May for the removal of certain ministers, and particularly of Lauderdale, and, as peace negotiations in Europe were now obviously under way, refused supply for the maintenance of the forces in June, giving only seven weeks' supply for the purpose of disbanding.

Politics were thus dominated by the Roman Catholic threat centred in France, which was also associated with trade issues: in March 1678 the Commons tacked a ban on French imports to a revenue bill. The corollary of the 'popish' threat was that issues of Protestant unity versus Anglican exclusivism were prominent, and a division opened up between those who prioritized one or the other. Moreover, public disorder and possible rebellion in Scotland also created division: it could be an issue of government strength, reviving gentry fears of the interregnum and dissent; or it could focus the need for Protestant unity; or, by the use of the 'Highland Host', it could focus fears of a move to arbitrary government through a standing army. Fears of a standing army were not entirely groundless: James had, in fact, advised his brother in April 1678 to abandon Parliaments and rule through the new army supposedly raised to fight France; and since the source of this information is the French ambassador, who was in close touch with oppositional elements in Parliament, it is probable that this was widely known.[5] A polarization developed between two views. The parliamentary opposition feared French popish expansionism, popish conspiracies at court, and the possibility of arbitrary government through a standing army. To these dangers they counterposed law, liberty, property, Parliament, and Protestant unity both with the Dutch and through some degree of toleration of Protestant dissent. From the point of view of government supporters, in contrast, what was at stake was factional opposition led by discontented ex-ministers, and a dissenting conspiracy to overthrow the Restoration Settlement.

The Exclusion Crisis itself fell, roughly, into four phases. The first phase was opened by the discovery of the murder of Sir Edmund Bury Godfrey (17 October 1678) immediately before the opening of Parliament (21 October); the disclosure of the Popish Plot allegations to Parliament, followed by the appearance of the treasonable correspondence of Coleman, James's confessor (late October to early November), and the disclosure by Montagu, the former ambassador to Paris, that Danby had engaged in secret negotiations with France (19 December). Political affairs were conducted in an atmosphere of hysteria driven by the plot revelations, which reached boiling-point in January 1679 when on 'Black Sunday' freak weather conditions brought darkness at eleven in the morning, the most acute of various astronomical and meteorological 'portents' which terrified the nation.[6] The result was the dissolution of the Cavalier Parliament (24 Jan 1678) and elections, in which there was a massive swing against the court. James was exiled on 3 March and Danby fell on 21 March. On 21 April Charles reconstructed the Privy Council to include leaders of the opposition in Parlia-

[5] The information and the source, though not this inference, are in Hutton, *Charles the Second*, 353 and 525 n. 71.

[6] See Ogg, *England in the Reign of Charles II*, ii. 557–61 and Kenyon, *The Popish Plot*, 172.

ment and on the 30th offered Parliament 'limitations' on the powers of a popish successor.

The actions of Charles, and of Danby and his supporters, indicate that they believed that what was going on was a court intrigue for power against Danby led by Shaftesbury, Buckingham, and others, exploiting the plot and being given French support because of Danby's anti-French policy.[7] If this had been the case, the reconstruction of the ministry, with a display of commitment to prosecute the plot and other concessions to anti-popery, could have been expected to resolve the problem. None the less, this period which coincides roughly with the 1678–9 theatrical season, was dominated by a crisis atmosphere, doubt, and uncertainty. In mid-December 1678 Secretary of State Coventry wrote to Ormonde, the Lord-Lieutenant of Ireland, 'we are all, I think, in a mist'.[8]

The second phase was opened by the refusal of supply by the new House of Commons on 14 May 1679 and their vote for Exclusion on the 21st. These events indicated that the system of parliamentary management of the 1670s had broken down and the 'grievances before supply' pattern of 1638–41 re-emerged. The period was, therefore, one of manœuvres for time by Charles, while he moved back to resting on and building up the support of the 'church' or 'cavalier' party on which Danby had based himself. Charles prorogued Parliament on 27 May, and dissolved it on 11 July to prevent a triumphal return by Monmouth after his victory over the Scottish Covenanters.[9] The court gave assistance to plot suspect Sir George Wakeman, who was acquitted on 18 July. These actions were regarded as provocative,[10] and elections in August–September produced a House of Commons of the same political character as the previous one. Charles in October prorogued Parliament before it could meet, exiled Monmouth, sent James to govern Scotland, and dismissed Shaftesbury from the Privy Council. In November–December the government began to remodel the appoint-

---

[7] The distribution of French money to opposition MPs was revealed in Coleman's letters, but largely ignored by Parliament, though court supporters tried to push an investigation on 6 Nov. 1678: Jones, *Country and Court*, 203.

[8] Hutton, *Charles the Second*, 364.

[9] Ibid. 376–7.

[10] Scott, *Algernon Sidney and the Restoration Crisis*, 56.

ments of sheriffs and Justices of the Peace to ensure Tory control. Meanwhile, the clergy began to preach the dangers of civil war and of a repetition of 1641. June and July 1680 saw acquittals in several Popish Plot trials. For some 'the authorities, and especially Lord Chief Justice Scroggs, were determined, come what may, to frustrate the people's desire for justice on the nation's enemies; for others present it was a serious blow at the authority of the Plot witnesses'.[11] The opposition had for years made political capital out of Charles's immorality. Now the government tried to regain the moral offensive. Buckingham was arrested for sodomy in 1679. Ford Grey was prosecuted for seducing his sister-in-law in 1680.[12] Government supporters persistently slandered the elderly Shaftesbury for lechery, a charge which modern critics have repeated uncritically, though there is no evidence that it was true.[13] Government supporters also tried to portray the opposition as rebels and rabble-rousers.[14]

However, the period from autumn 1679 to summer 1680 also saw an offensive by the opposition. When Monmouth returned illicitly to London in November, an action which Dryden was to satirize in *The Duke of Guise*, he was stripped of all his offices; but he remained popular. When he attended Dryden's parish church on 27 November, he was greeted by a spontaneous demonstration of support.[15] In the streets Monmouth tended to be cheered, James jeered at.[16] On 17 November the opposition organized a Pope-burning, said to have been attended by 200,000 people.[17] During the late autumn and winter they organized mass petitioning, calling for Parliament to be allowed to meet. Charles prohibited petitioning, but it continued regardless. The petitioning movement was a mass political movement[18] and thousands of signatures were collected. The government encouraged 'abhorrences' of the petitions, but these

[11] Haley, *Shaftesbury*, 578.
[12] Wilson, *A Rake and his Times*, 256. Price, *Cold Caleb*, 98 ff.
[13] Haley considers the allegation at length and finds it unsubstantiated and unlikely to be true: *Shaftesbury*, 211–15.
[14] In reality, both sides engaged in crowd politics during the Exclusion Crisis: Harris, *London Crowds*, chs. 6 and 7 and *passim*.
[15] Winn, *John Dryden and his World*, 325.
[16] Harris, *London Crowds*, 157–9.
[17] Haley, *Shaftesbury*, 557. See also Miller, *Popery and Politics*, 182 ff.
[18] Ashcraft, *Revolutionary Politics*, 171–6.

had less popular support than the petitions and mainly originated from official bodies such as loyal corporations.[19] The
Licensing Act had lapsed in spring 1679 and a pamphlet war
now raged.[20] The prologue to a lost play, *Fools Have Fortune;
or, Luck's All*, suggests that in these hard times, 'Poetts cann
fall aWriting those Romances | Which they call Protestant
Intilligences.'[21] Shadwell's epilogue to Maidwell's *The Loving
Enemies* complains, 'Those who once loved the Stage, are now
in years, | And leave good Poets for dull Pamphleteers' (74). In
summer 1680 Opposition leaders sent Monmouth on a successful speaking tour of the West Country. They also induced a
Middlesex Grand Jury to present James for trial as a recusant
and the king's mistress, the Duchess of Portsmouth, as a prostitute. The Crown squashed the prosecution, but it was a bold
move which showed opposition self-confidence. Opposition
tactics and government intransigence had opened up a bitter
polarization: 'the political nation was becoming divided into
irrevocably hostile factions'.[22]

The third phase began with the election of two radicals,
Henry Cornish and the republican Slingsby Bethel, as sheriffs of
London in July 1680. The court in response made its policy
more conciliatory, ordering the execution of anti-papist laws,
and giving assurances that Parliament would be allowed to
meet. Though the Whig sheriffs and Lord Mayor were snubbed,
a plan to apply the anti-dissent Corporation Act to London
livery companies was shelved, and a Tory propagandist ordered
not to write divisive tracts.[23] These developments, and the fact
that Parliament was allowed to meet, created a widespread
belief that Exclusion was inevitable, which extended even to
several Privy Councillors and the royal mistress, the Duchess
of Portsmouth. The French ambassador thought 'the King's
brother could only be saved by a miracle'.[24] The Crown's position was, in fact, stronger than it appeared, as the Treasury
Commission appointed in April 1679 had carried out a radical

[19] Jones, *Country and Court*, 210.
[20] Ashcraft, *Revolutionary Politics*, chs. 5 and 6 gives a detailed survey of this
propaganda battle.
[21] Milhous and Hume, 'The Prologue and Epilogue for *Fools Have Fortune*', 314.
[22] Jones, *Country and Court*, 211.
[23] Hutton, *Charles the Second*, 392.
[24] Haley, *Shaftesbury*, 588; see also Hutton, *Charles the Second*, 394.

cut-back of civil expenditure and the budget was more or less in balance, so that supply was not required. The seal was set on this by Charles's conclusion of a new subsidy agreement with Louis XIV in March 1681. There are three possible explanations of the conciliatory course of the government at this period. Firstly, it is possible that Charles did not know until March that he could do without supply; secondly, he may have been giving the Commons a last chance to co-operate; or, thirdly, he may have been giving the opposition enough rope with which to hang itself in the eyes of the middle ground. The phase of apparently impending victory of the opposition none the less continued up to the Oxford Parliament in March 1681, though Charles's refusal of a Commons demand for Exclusion (7 January), dissolution of Parliament (18 January) and purge of Exclusionist office-holders (January–February), and the summoning of the new Parliament to meet at Oxford, all pointed to a return of the court to a hard line.

The dissolution of the Oxford Parliament after a week's sitting (28 March) marked the beginning of the fourth phase, the Tory reaction, which was to continue into the reign of James. The court now went on the offensive, both ideologically and through the machinery of law. Besides the trial of the 'Protestant joiner' Stephen College for treason, and the attempt to try Shaftesbury, the purge of JPs continued, and the militia commands were also remodelled. Luttrell's *Brief Relation* from summer 1681 onwards is full of accounts of prosecutions and persecutions.[25] The court pursued a policy of ruining Whigs through a variety of civil suits.[26] For a contemporary comment on this development and on the Rye House Plot trials of 1683,

[25] For example, for action against dissenters, see Luttrell, *Brief Relation*, i. 148, 153, 165, 193, 213, 216, 229, 242, 245; for (sometimes dubious) legal proceedings against Whigs, i. 170, 195–6, 202, 222, 228, 229, 240–1, 244; action against Monmouth (for disturbing the peace), i. 222, and against Ford Grey (for abducting his sister-in-law) and Oates (for sodomy), i. 248; action against Parliament via its serjeant-at-arms: i. 182, 194, 211–12; action against the charters of Whig-dominated cities: i. 169, 181, 184, 193, 201–2, 207, 223–4, 227, 230, 236, 240, 242; moving trials outside London in cases where Whigs were plaintiffs: i. 183–7, 211–12; the suppression of newspapers, i. 231; the prohibition of the usual November 'Pope-burning' celebrations, and of bonfires generally, i. 237. This is a small selection of examples.

[26] Keeton, *Jeffreys*, 364–5; Landon, *Triumph of the Lawyers*, chs. 3–4. For government designs on Buckingham's estates, see Melton, 'A Rake Refinanced'.

which mirrored the Popish Plot trials of 1679–81, Jonathan Scott cites the Earl of Anglesey: 'The old civil war had now, as it were, transformed itself into a judicial war: men fought with one another in judicial battle—for what was right troubled neither grand nor petty juries.'[27]

The opposition responded by clinging to the City of London as a bulwark of defence (most strikingly when Shaftesbury was arrested for treason in July 1681 and acquitted by a Whig grand jury in November). The game was not over until the Tories had obtained control of the City. This took three steps. In June 1681 the court obtained the election of a Lord Mayor who, though not a Tory activist, was friendly to the court. In December 1681 the Tories obtained a majority on the Common Council of the City. Finally in June 1682 these developments gave legitimacy to the use of electoral fraud, backed by military force, to secure the election of Tory sheriffs.[28]

The victory of the Tories in the City opened the way for a more vigorous move to take revenge on the Whigs. Shaftesbury fled to Holland. A new persecution of dissenters began, and an unprecedented campaign of remodelling borough charters (often promoted by local Tories) was designed to give control to Crown nominees and Tory gentry. Whig notables who had not already fled were assailed with a series of dubious prosecutions and civil lawsuits. The final act in the drama of the crisis was the discovery of the Rye House Plot of 1683, an amalgam between two schemes to overthrow the regime promoted by different sections of the opposition.

Stories

To theorize from these events, and to make sense of the crisis, a historical narrative is needed. Broadly speaking, three sets of interpretations have been offered by historians: Whig, Marxist, and 'revisionist', or Tory. Literary critics, consciously or unconsciously, use similar stories. There are two points I want to emphasize. Firstly, the terms 'Whig', 'Marxist', and 'Tory' in this context characterize the views of history, not the people

---

[27] Scott, 'England's Troubles', 120, 130.
[28] Haley, *Shaftesbury*, 700–4.

advancing them. In particular, though the impulse for revisionist history has been rightist in recent years (indeed leading exponents of it have been proud to associate with today's Tory Party) it is certainly not necessary to be right-wing to have a Tory interpretation of seventeenth-century history. Secondly, there is no criticism intended in characterizing the views of historians and critics as partisan. On the contrary, I think this is helpful, and more likely to lead to clarification and ultimate convergence than muddying the waters by pretending no real differences exist. A good example is Douglas Canfield's clear counter-position, in his view of the tenacity of Stuart royalism in 'Royalism's Last Dramatic Stand', to the different views of Laura Brown and Susan Staves. In my opinion this is both more honest and more useful than the common tendency to cite everyone impartially and gloss over the existence of real differences of perspective.

Let us consider the three interpretations of Restoration history in more detail. In the classic 'Whig interpretation', the seventeenth-century Whigs' underlying principles were those of the future, but their methods those of the past. The crisis thus looked forward to 1688 and the development of parliamentary government though its immediate result was the establishment of an Anglican Tory despotism. Thus G. M. Trevelyan writes in his *England under the Stuarts* that in 1683,

The [Whig] party had fallen because its leaders had been ill-advised, selfish, and violent in the methods they chose; but not because they lacked faith in its principles of Parliamentary government and religious Toleration, or because those principles were unsuited, like those of the regicides who had suffered twenty years before, to the social conditions of the age and the temper of the English people. And therefore the new party did not perish on the scaffold with Sidney and Russell. (408)

From this perspective, the crisis was about the constitution, and also about religion, which was intimately associated with the constitution since 'Catholicism and despotism, in their natural alliance against all liberty of action and thought, were in these years regarded as the ideal polity, in Italy, in Austria, in Spain, in many of the German states, but most pre-eminently in France' (353). The opposition exploited Oates's Popish Plot allegations, but Oates's lies symbolized Charles's and James's real commitment to French Catholic despotism; thus in 1678 'The truths that would have saved the Whigs remained hid, but a liar came to their deliverance' (367). The weaknesses of this account are that it reduces religion to liberty or despotism; it cannot account for the strength of the Tory Party, which appears merely myopic; and it is manifestly teleological, seeing progress in terms of constitutional development leading up to nineteenth-century liberalism.

The Whig view of history is widely regarded as discredited; though it should be noted that at least one literary critic thinks it is still going strong, in a disguised form.[29] However, it has had a distinguished exponent in Susan Staves, whose *Players' Scepters* examines the drama alongside the law and moral philosophy in order to show how 'The idea of authority changed . . . in the early modern period' (p. xi). She looks at ideas of sovereignty in the state and in the family, at oaths and vows, and at ideas about the law of nature, in order to show how the idea of authority was questioned, modified, and secularized, examining how new meanings are generated in a period of political change. For Staves our qualified sympathy for those who suffer, rebel, and break their promises in a corrupt society points to the need for the new political order which was to be established post-1688. Like Trevelyan's, Staves's perspective is teleological. This need not in itself be an absolute weakness: one of the jobs of history is to explain how we got to where we are now, and this cannot be done without appearing somewhat teleological. However, there is a problem that seeing Whiggism as an ascendant philosophy, gradually coming into its own, can lead to reading back a post-1688 mentality into the drama of the Restoration; and to seeing the overthrow of James as historically inevitable, leading to an over-reading of those aspects of the drama which seem critical of the Stuart regime. Staves is honest about her 'Whig view of history', suggesting that it 'may be a useful corrective to the revisionist Tory views expressed in so much modern Restoration and eighteenth-century literary criticism' (p. xviii). In this she may be at least partly right.

The Marxist interpretation of seventeenth-century history built upon the Whig interpretation. Christopher Hill comments:

---

[29] Pittock, *Poetry and Jacobite Politics in Eighteenth-Century Britain and Ireland.*

'We shall be looking for those elements of the new which are emerging. This is sometimes criticized as a "Whig" approach . . . It seems to me on the contrary the only possible historical attitude: anything else involves the dangers of sentimental anti-quarianism.'[30] In the Marxist interpretation, the rise of capitalism is substituted for the rise of parliamentary democracy as the process at work. This requires the overthrow of the feudal absolutist state (Charles I), but also the maintenance of control over the lower classes, which 1640–60 had endangered. Thus Hill comments in his *Century of Revolution*: 'The Restoration of 1660 was a restoration of the united class whom Parliament represented, even more than of the King . . . The propertied classes could not forget the lesson they had learnt in 1646–60, just as kings did not forget the lesson of 1649. So political opposition was never pushed to extremes: if it was, it tended to disintegrate' (195, 204). This account has the advantage over the 'Whig interpretation' of offering an explanation of the existence of the Tory Party. It also locates the political language of class which is prominent in the drama. It has two difficulties. The first, which all critics of Hill's thesis have pointed to, is the identification of the country gentry, let alone the 'Parliamentary party' as a revolutionary bourgeoisie opposed to a feudal aristocracy.[31] The second is that Hill's account is if anything more teleological than the Whig interpretation, and therefore makes both the Exclusion Crisis and 1688–9 appear rather trivial: the decisive battles having been fought and won in 1638–60, the outcome of the battles of the 1680s is foreordained.

Amongst literary critics, Laura Brown is influenced by Hill's view, valuing those plays and aspects of plays which are seen as participating in a challenge to Stuart 'absolutism' which was both inevitable and right. The problems with her approach are threefold. Firstly, it is schematic, selecting only those plays or aspects of plays which fit the schema. For example, Crowne must be entirely omitted from the discussion because his plays

---

[30] Hill, *Reformation to Industrial Revolution*, 20.
[31] The objections to a social-change account of 17th-cent. history are collected, albeit in an incoherent way, in Clark's *Revolution and Rebellion*. For a sharp critique of Clark which reformulates the thesis of the rise of capitalism in terms less dependent on precise class analysis, see Wood, *Pristine Culture of Capitalism* and Mooers, *Making of Bourgeois Europe*.

do not fit the model. Secondly and paradoxically, Brown's approach misses the oppositional nature of drama which uses a rhetoric of Whiggery which is cautious rather than triumphant: the themes and tropes of Exclusion Crisis Whiggery are frequently conservative rather than revolutionary. Thirdly, there is an extreme teleology, even verging at times upon failure to realize that Toryism has a relationship to the *dominant* ideology in the Exclusion Crisis period, whereas Whiggism is an *opposition* philosophy. For example, discussing Otway's tragedy, Brown speaks of 'the new, democratic Toryism that was beginning to form in opposition to the consolidation of the aristocratic Whig oligarchy' (92). As a description of life under Walpole this might begin to apply; as a description of the political situation in the Exclusion Crisis, it goes beyond teleology to sheer anachronism. Brown draws directly on Hill's *Century of Revolution* here, though the condensation which might be allowable in Hill's historical survey seems less forgivable in the literary critic. Moreover, Hill does not collapse as many distinctions as Brown: he sees Otway's literary achievement under Charles II as *foreshadowing* the 'new popular Toryism' of the early eighteenth century (258).

What Staves calls 'revisionist Tory' interpretations predominate among both historians and literary critics. Among historians, revisionism often disavows the notion of a grand narrative of historical events, stressing short-term contingency, misunderstanding, and the personalities of individuals in the causation of great historical events. Yet there are revisionist narratives, and they tend to cluster in three strands. The first is that Charles II and his advisers (and even James II) had no intention of creating a French-style Catholic despotism, intended to rule constitutionally, and had a good legal case to support their actions. Conversely, oppositional politics are reinterpreted partly in terms of aristocratic faction centred in the court and the House of Lords, reflected through client groups and interlocked with fundamentally local factional struggles in the counties and towns; partly in terms of a real continuity of old Commonwealth-dissenting opposition.[32]

[32] A strong recent argument for Charles's limited objectives is made by Hutton, *Charles the Second*, and for James's, by Miller, *Popery and Politics* and *James II: A Study in Kingship*. The legal case was made earlier, most forcibly in Keeton's

The second strand is a criticism of Whig and Marxist teleology. It is claimed that if there was a dominant trend in seventeenth-century politics, it was the strengthening of the central state. In this context there was continuity across 1688, not rupture. 'Stuart absolutism' represents a modernizing tendency and 'country opposition' a conservative one which, on the face of it, was doomed to defeat. The fall of James II in 1688 was thus not inevitable but on the contrary unlikely, and was in substance the result of Dutch invasion. J. C. D. Clark goes further to argue that the 'country' opposition, to the extent that they really objected to strong government and sought religious freedom, actually lost: Hanoverian England was an aristocratic confessional absolutist regime with a standing army like those on the Continent, only differing in being an Anglican confessional absolutism.[33]

Support from a perhaps unexpected quarter is lent to this view by some recent studies of the Exclusion Crisis which have stressed the influence of radical ideas. Haley's *The First Earl of Shaftesbury* and Jones's *The First Whigs* stress the moderation of the Whig leadership in both social terms (defence of aristocracy and property) and political ones (monarchism and reluctance to resort to force until it was too late). However, Ashcraft's *Revolutionary Politics and Locke's Two Treatises of Government* stresses the connection between the ideas of Whigs of the Exclusion Crisis period and those of interregnum republicans and Levellers, giving Locke a much more radical cast than is traditional, and Scott's *Algernon Sidney and the Restoration Crisis* argues for a view of the crisis as recapitulating 1638–42, and for the presence in the House of Commons and the City in 1681 of a radical leadership with a Commonwealth background.[34] If these were the politics of

Jeffreys. The various work reinterpreting 'party' politics in terms of faction is discussed critically by Clark, *Revolution and Rebellion*, ch. 7; Clark uses it to demolish Whig and Marxist accounts, but then criticizes it in favour of his own account in terms of political theology.

[33] On the conservative character of opposition to Charles I, see Ashton, *The English Civil War*, Morrill, *The Revolt of the Provinces*; on the 'unlikeliness' of 1688, Western, *Monarchy and Revolution*, Jones, *The Revolution of 1688 in England*. Clark's argument is in *English Society 1688–1832* and *Revolution and Rebellion*.

[34] De Krey, 'London Radicals and Revolutionary Politics', argues for a strong radical movement in London. It seems to me that there are flaws in De Krey's

the Exclusion Crisis Whigs, they were unquestionably not victorious in 1688.

The third strand of the revisionist interpretation is insistence that the historian should 'take religion seriously' in the sense of interpreting religious belief as a historical factor in itself, not just an ideological cover for political concerns (in the Whig account) or class ones (in Marxist accounts). It would follow that the crisis was really, as it appeared to be, about religious issues, indeed theological ones.[35] Putting these strands together, the picture that emerges is one of an English society which was naturally stable and held together by bonds of hierarchy and deference articulated by Anglicanism: there was therefore a natural Anglican Tory majority. In 1640–60, and again in 1678–81, aristocratic faction and misguided fears of the king's intentions among part of the gentry betrayed this stability and temporarily let in chaos and the mob, but order was in the end restored. This account is in substance that offered by contemporary Tories like L'Estrange and Roger North.

The strength of revisionist interpretations lies in two aspects. First, it is true that both seventeenth-century Tories and a large part of the Whigs did believe in strong personal monarchy. Connected to this point, individual personalities and religious beliefs are important in history. This is particularly important in the case of the Stuart brothers: whether Charles was 'an agent of the Counter-Reformation advance', as Scott puts it,[36] or merely lied to everybody, his personal unreliability in the eyes of the political nation was, from the mid-1660s, an important factor in politics. Similarly, both brothers were seen as sexually and politically irresponsible, and their court as a centre of sexual immorality, luxury (in a pejorative sense), and financial waste.[37] Secondly, revisionist interpretations remind us of the strength both of the position of the Crown, and of the Tory Party; and thus that there might have been an alternative course of development to the one which actually occurred, and that there

methodology, e.g. the uncritical citation of the Tory propagandist L'Estrange, and the unconditional acceptance of the evidence of arrested extremists about their own power and influence.

[35] This view is most forcibly argued by Clark, *English Society 1688–1832*, chs. 4 and 5; *Revolution and Rebellion*, 101–111.

[36] Scott, 'England's Troubles', 116.

[37] Hutton, *Charles the Second*, 185–9 and *passim*.

was division of the political nation, not an irresistible Whig tide.

However, there are two issues which the revisionist approach cannot explain. Firstly, both the view of an underlying tendency towards the strong state, and that of a natural Tory majority, fail to explain why quite well-informed contemporaries thought in 1680–1 that the Whigs might win, and why in 1688 William III thought an invasion necessary to avert a republic[38] and James himself lost his nerve and ran away. Contemporary perception of a weak regime at risk of collapse should be taken seriously as an item of evidence—especially when it did collapse in 1688. The second problem is the electoral strength of Whiggism in 1679–81 and, indeed, the relative equilibrium between the parties, shifting now one way, now another, between 1689 and 1715. This is hard to make fit with the idea of a natural Tory majority in the political nation. As far as the lower classes without the franchise are concerned, Tim Harris has argued for a predominant Toryism, but Buchanan Sharp, using a different methodology, has produced the opposite result, and there is other evidence for Whig popularity.[39]

There is also a problem with the idea that the crisis was purely and simply about religion. To be sure, James fell because of his religious convictions, and religion was at the centre of the Popish Plot. However, the 'Anglican political theology' discussed by Clark in his *English Society 1688–1832* could have been tailor-made as an example of politics, and at that class politics, dressed up as religion in the crudest possible way. Moreover, in political discourse about religion in the Exclusion Crisis period theological issues play a rather minor part. Transubstantiation and auricular confession appear not as devilish heresies but as frauds whereby the popish clergy exploit the laity; dissent not as heresy but as lower-class presumption, sexual hypocrisy, and sedition. As is clear from Scott's work, concerns about the spread of popery are animated by the strength of French Catholic despotism in Europe, the apparent

---

[38] Baxter, *William III*. The point is not that the belief was correct but that it was held.

[39] Harris, *London Crowds*, and 'Was the Tory Reaction Popular?'; Sharp, 'Popular Political Opinion in England 1660–1685'; see also Haley, *Shaftesbury*, 552; Ashcraft, *Revolutionary Politics*, 171–80.

alliance between the French monarchy and Charles II, the influence of popery at court, and the king's failure to pursue the
Protestant foreign policy Parliament wanted. In other words,
they bring us back to politics.

Many literary critics accept the model of the Stuarts and their
Tory apologists as representing an order and tradition which the
Whigs, an extremist minority, sought in vain to disrupt. In this
narrative, the Tories are conservative, the Whigs radical. The
side-effects are that texts which are not radically 'disruptive' are
not seen as Whiggish when they really are; and that Toryism is
seen as producing good literature, whereas Whiggism is thought
to have nothing of cultural benefit to offer. This is an old view,[40]
but one which has gained a new lease of life due to the work of
J. Douglas Canfield. The view that Tory literature is the best is
so widespread as to be regarded as definitively proven. I argue
for a more positive reading of Whig plays in Chapter 8.
Amongst feminist critics, it is taken as gospel not only that
Aphra Behn *thought* Toryism fruitful and sustaining, but that
this was really true.[41] It is considered that work of Catherine
Gallagher has proved for all time that there is a symbiosis
between Toryism and feminism.[42] I have challenged such views
in my article ' "Suspect my loyalty when I lose my virtue":
Sexual Politics and Party in Aphra Behn's Plays of the Exclusion
Crisis', and will discuss this issue further when considering the
dramatic language of politics in Chapters 4–6.

Tory criticism is open to the same charge as Tory history: it
writes out the Whigs' perceived success and electoral strength
during the Exclusion Crisis, and fails to explain the events of
1688. Tory criticism is more misleading in that it has a more
simplistic paradigm. The underlying assumption of Tory conservatism and Whig radicalism will not fit in a period in which
the very nature of radicalism and conservatism are hard to
define. What is radical and what is conservative after a counter-

[40] See e.g. the editorial comments by Montague Summers in his editions of the
works of Behn, Otway, and Shadwell; Wilson, introduction to Crowne's *City
Politiques*, pp. x, xi; Kaufman, 'Civil Politics–Sexual Politics in John Crowne's *City
Politiques*', 72; Fujimura, 'Dryden's Changing Political Views', 93.

[41] For a judicious account which distinguishes between what Behn thought and
the realities of Restoration politics, see Todd, *Sign of Angellica*, ch. 1.

[42] See also Kinnaird, 'Mary Astell and the Conservative Contribution to English
Feminism'.

revolution, and in a period in which commitment to the people's liberties may be seen as a residual, rather than an emergent, component of contemporary ideology?[43] The Restoration of 1660 was a disruption of a situation to which a majority of the nation had adapted. Thus it was possible for Shadwell in *The Woman-Captain* to portray the degenerate, 'cavalier' younger generation as iconoclasts against the decency of their godly forefathers: the returned cavaliers become the radical disrupters and the old puritans represent conservatism.

Toryism was in a sense conservative, but also innovative. On the one hand it drew on early Stuart ideas of divine kingship. Its central text, Filmer's *Patriarcha*, published as an intervention in the Exclusion Crisis in 1680, was written in defence of Charles I.[44] On the other hand, Toryism developed new themes and tropes and developed old ideas with a new intensity. Toryism also had a new stridency and went against the spirit of compromise and 'oblivion' of 1660. This can be seen in Roger L'Estrange's *An Account of the Growth of Knavery*. L'Estrange's aim is to discredit the parliamentary opposition utterly, placing them beyond the pale. Members of Parliament are placed on the same footing as dissenting 'fanatics'. Initially, L'Estrange poses as the champion of Parliament against criticism (28–30, 37), but this is disingenuous: he slips from the faction of 1641, which he equates with the opposition of 1677, to puritans, to Presbyterians, to rebels, to what is essentially an attack on Parliament itself. There is a continual thrust in his argument towards a militant Toryism which involves marginalizing the centre. There is no room for negotiation or compromise. In particular, the view that the law is in the king leads to the doctrine of quietism, or non-resistance under any circumstances, which is the crux of his argument. To say that

[43] For the concepts of residual and emergent ideologies, see Williams, *Marxism and Literature*, 121–7, and Dollimore, *Radical Tragedy*, 7 ff. Of course it could be argued that the idea of the people's liberties was emergent in the period prior to 1688; but it is important not to underestimate the extent to which the Restoration of 1660 was experienced as a counter-revolution.

[44] Tuck, 'A New Date for Filmer's *Patriarcha*' argues for 1628 as a date of composition. Scott, *Algernon Sidney and the Restoration Crisis*, 208 n. 11 points out that a tract, *The Power of Kings . . . Learnedly Asserted by Sir Robert Filmer, Kt. With a Preface of a Friend: Giving an Account of the Author and his Works* (1680) describes *Patriarcha* as 'written about the year 1642'. Sommerville, introduction to *Patriarcha*, pp. xxxiii–iv, supports Tuck.

the people have any part in making laws is to make them partners in sovereignty and pave the way for deposing the king, as in 1641 (44–5, 64). There can be no lawful resistance to the king's officers (58–9). There can be no defence of the interests of the kingdom, separate from the king: 'Who are they, I pray, that he calls the *Kingdom*, but the *Rabble* still of 41; the Execrable *Instruments* of *That Rebellion*, and the *Hopes* of *Another?*' Tyranny or oppression cannot justify resistance: 'What would be the Fruit of such a *Resistance*, but the Turning of an Oppression on the *One* side, into a *Rebellion* on the other' (61). This attempt to reimpose early Stuart political philosophy in an extreme form, in the wake of the necessary compromises of 1660, seems aggressive. Similarly, in the Exclusion Crisis, and especially in the Tory reaction period, moves such as the repeated proroguing and dissolution of Parliament, attacks on the charters of cities, including London, persecution of Whigs, and ultimately the king's personal rule from spring 1681 seemed extremist and innovative rather than conservative and traditional.

Conversely, the Whigs were innovative, but also traditional. Whig arguments drew upon those of Civil War radicals;[45] though their radicalism was often covert, perhaps unconscious, denying any connection with a discredited past and loud in professions of loyalty to the restored monarch. Whig ideas had revolutionary implications, and in some sense foreshadowed 1688. Yet the Whigs were also able to figure as the custodians of tradition and the exponents of the views of the sane majority. Moreover, there was a sense in which it was not the Whigs who disrupted the status quo, but James who was perceived by contemporaries as 'rocking the boat' by acknowledging his Roman Catholicism in the early 1670s. The Whig Exclusion campaign did not disrupt a stable situation, as the situation was already destabilized.

The Whigs used a rhetoric of 'Loyal Protestantism' and country gentry values, and owed their success partly to their ability to appeal to conservative instincts in the face of what was perceived as royal and 'popish' innovation. Whigs saw themselves as upholders of tradition, perpetuating Protestantism against

---

[45] Ashcraft, *Revolutionary Politics*; Sensabaugh, 'That Grand Whig Milton'.

popery, English independence against France, and the liberties of property owners against arbitrary power. Though there were a minority of republicans such as Sidney, most Whigs were monarchists and traditionalists: they sought, and after 1688 got, a strong central government to pursue an aggressive foreign policy.[46] Thus, they were not really disingenuous in calling their philosophy 'Loyal Protestantism'.

As Tories were forced on to the defensive by Whig successes during the Exclusion Crisis, Tory ideology increasingly fell back upon élitism and the claim to represent the better sort, abandoning the middle ground to the Whigs and not even claiming to be the best defenders of Protestantism, or the good of the nation. Yet this is a problematic endeavour and fraught with doubt and contradiction, as we shall see in Chapter 7. Quietism, with its emphasis on passive obedience, makes dramatic heroism difficult. It is also a self-defeating philosophy, implicitly advocating the severance of the very social bonds on which it relies. It depends upon vaguely feudal notions of subordination, but without reciprocity, service to the king, but without reward, the subordination of the individual to the community, but the denial of any right to the individual to relate to the community at any normal human level, as privacy and retirement are privileged over politics.

Moreover, the disparity between the heroic ideal of Toryism and the reality of Charles II's lies and political irresponsibility and both royal brothers' libertinism was a real problem for supporters of their regime. Since I shall illustrate this fully in subsequent chapters, it will suffice to give two examples here. In 1672 Charles made a secret treaty with Louis XIV, promising to convert England to Catholicism using French troops if necessary. That Charles's secret dealings with Louis were widely suspected is clear from a reading of Marvell's *Account of the Growth of Popery and Arbitrary Government*.[47] There was nothing secret about the libertinism of both royal brothers, and this created a crisis of political credibility and legitimacy throughout the late Stuart period. Charles was thought of even

---

[46] Western, *Monarchy and Revolution*, 19 ff., 43 ff., and ch. 2, *passim*. Even the notorious Earl of Shaftesbury was no egalitarian: Haley, *Shaftesbury*, 312, 386, 396.

[47] See also Scott, 'England's Troubles', 117–18.

by friends and supporters as one who 'spends his time in imploying his lips and his prick about the Court, and hath no other imployment'.[48] James made a habit of seducing nobly born young women. As Bishop Burnet put it, he 'had always one private amour after another'.[49] During the Exclusion Crisis his seduction of Catherine Sedley was probably a factor in driving her father, Sir Charles Sedley, from support for the court to moderate Whiggery.[50] Sedley is said to have remarked in 1690 that he was 'even in civility with King James, who had made his daughter a countess, by helping (through his vote [for William] in the Covention parliament) to make the king's daughter a queen'.[51] A rhyme circulated in 1688:

> But Sedley has some colour for his Treason
> A daughter Ravished without any Reason.[52]

There was a sense, then, in which Toryism was a disabled and disabling political philosophy.

Which historical narrative informs my own arguments in the ensuing chapters? In Chapter 1, I outlined a method for reading plays which attempted to combine a grasp of totality and change with attention to specificity. The same is true of history. We need a history which pays sufficient attention to particularity, 'grounding' a reading of plays in an understanding of the precise nature of the times which produced them, but which will also look at the 'whole'. My discussion will, accordingly, range from an account of the way in which dramatists participate in local and particular political debates and shifts, to a consideration of the drama's role in the ongoing dynamics of Toryism and Whiggism.

The framework for the discussion is the assumption that change did happen, though it proceeded in a somewhat contradictory way, by fits and starts. So on the one hand, as historian

---

[48] Thomas Killigrew, cited in Pepys's *Diary*, vii. 400. Paul Hammond, in 'The King's Two Bodies', gives an account of the way in which Charles's immorality was seen as political irresponsibility from early in the Restoration, e.g. in political poetry and comments by Pepys.

[49] Burnet, *History of My Own Time*, i. 405.

[50] For the affair with Catherine, see Fraser, *Weaker Vessel*, 453. For Sedley's moderate Whiggery, see Pinto, *Sir Charles Sedley*, 168 ff., and Henning, *History of Parliament*, iii. 409–10.

[51] Cited in *DNB*. *DNB* is wrong in describing Sedley as a moderate Tory.

[52] Pinto, *Sedley*, 174.

Scott and literary critic Sawday have argued, there was a decisive counter-revolutionary shift in 1660.[53] On the other hand, as Hutton notes, Restoration political institutions covertly allowed a continuity with the 1650s which was denied at the level of ideology and propaganda.[54] Moreover, the regime of the 1650s was less stable than it might appear from some revisionist accounts: in 1688 James fell in spite of sound finances and a standing army. The ensuing period saw significant changes at the level of law and constitutional reform, foreign policy, political philosophy, party-political pluralism, and, as Lear puts it, 'Who loses and who wins; who's in, who's out' (5. 3. 15).[55] The period after 1688 saw a transformation of England's status in Europe, based upon the mobilization of the resources of the nation for an aggressive anti-French foreign policy, through the link between the Crown, the City, and the country gentry incarnated in the Bank of England and the rise of the London financial markets. As Rose Zimbardo puts it, the Restoration period and the period after the 'Glorious Revolution' are 'distinctly different from one another and therefore understandable, in the Foucaultian sense, as different "ages" '.[56]

Moreover, in spite of the difficulties with Hill's account, the case remains strong that the upheavals of seventeenth-century England produced something radically new: a capitalist polity. This view has recently been strongly argued by Ellen Meiksins Wood in *The Pristine Culture of Capitalism*. Robert Brenner in the postscript to his book *Merchants and Revolution* offers an explanation of seventeenth-century history in these terms which is of great assistance in understanding the Exclusion Crisis. Brenner's account has the double strength of acknowledging that a shift to a capitalist regime occurred, without assuming as Hill does that a bourgeois revolution was completed in the 1640s. His analysis can also help explain the continuing tension

---

[53] Scott, *Algernon Sidney and the English Republic*; Sawday, 'Re-writing a Revolution'.

[54] Hutton, *The Restoration*, ch. 2 and 155–6, 182, 288.

[55] For the complete reversal of foreign policy, see Jones, *Country and Court*, ch. 13. The legal changes included the Bill of Rights, Toleration Act, Treason Act of 1696, and Act of Settlement of 1700; see also Landon, *Triumph of the Lawyers* and Schwoerer, *Declaration of Rights*. On shifts in the structure and language of politics, see Kenyon, *Revolution Principles*; Hill, *Growth of Parliamentary Parties*; Horwitz, *Parliament, Policy and Politics*.

[56] Zimbardo, 'At Zero Point'. See also her *A Mirror to Nature*.

between court, Country, and City which is so important in the drama.

Brenner argues that feudalism consists essentially in the fact that the revenues of the upper classes are politically constituted. That is, they get their income from exactions from lower classes, particularly the peasantry, who actually possess their means of production, the land they work. These exactions are only possible because they are authorized by tradition and backed by force. In capitalism, in contrast, the upper classes own and control the means of production, and get their revenue by employing free labourers at a wage to produce for the market. What is protected by force (the state) is simply the upper classes' rights of ownership and the sanctity of contract. Looking at the matter in this perspective, Brenner argues that by the early seventeenth century the English landowning class as a whole had become a capitalist class: it owned its land and employed free labour, or let it to capitalist farmers who employed free labour. In the process, moreover, it had become committed to Protestantism, partly because it had benefited extensively from the dissolution of the monasteries, partly because of the assertion of state power over the Church. There remained, however, feudal elements in the polity. The Crown remained 'patrimonial': its revenues were politically constituted, and it disposed of offices which gave politically constituted revenue, so that it could create a feudal following around the court; and its motivations remained those of dynastic aggrandizement. The Church derived much of its revenue from politically constituted sources (tithe and other exactions, particularly those of the Church courts). In the City of London and the towns there was a 'feudal' merchant class which derived its revenue from monopolistically regulated trades; but there were also 'outsiders', lesser traders and artisans, and merchants outside the regulated company system.

The differing motivations of the Crown and the landowning class explain the repeated political conflicts of the century, which focused on the interrelated questions of foreign and religious policy. Protestantism in the seventeenth century appeared threatened by developments on a European scale; so that the two issues of religion and foreign policy were inextricably intertwined. In contrast to the landowning class, the monarchy had strong reasons, both of class solidarity with other monarchs against rebels, and of dynastic interest, for not pursuing an aggressively Protestant foreign policy, and for leaning on episcopacy at home. These conflicts of interest made it difficult for the Crown and the parliamentary classes to work together even though they sincerely wanted to, promoting conflicts over money and the rights of Parliament. Eventually the Crown was driven to try to rule without Parliament (1630s) and a section of the landowning class to respond by an alliance with the 'outsiders' in the City.

This alliance precipitated the Civil War, because 'Parliament could not hope to defend (let alone impose on the King) its program of 1640–1 without the power that could be supplied by the London mass movement; and . . . an alliance with the London mass movement had certain unavoidable results that could not but precipitate division' (689). In particular, it required standing for further religious reform, which alienated many MPs because of fears for social hierarchy which proved in the event to be justified: the struggle, and political debate, was radicalized, ending in the rise of radical sects.[57]

In the end the landowning class restored the patrimonial monarchy, albeit with some attempt to limit its powers, as a guarantee of its own class position; but the monarchy followed its class position in attempting to get financial independence from Parliament and allying with the dominant Catholic absolutist power, now France. In consequence, opposition leaders were driven in the Exclusion Crisis to re-create 'an alliance of forces very much like that of 1641 for a Protestant and politico-constitutional program analogous to that of 1641'. However, having been burned once in 1641–60, the majority of the parliamentary classes were unwilling to resort to a mobilization of the lower classes, and the king was able to regain control. The result was a new experiment with absolutism between 1682 and 1688. Meanwhile, however, Brenner argues that during the Restoration socio-economic forces worked heavily in favour of agricultural capitalism and unregulated foreign trade. Thus when William III rescued the parliamentary classes in 1688, this

[57] Cf. Hutton's analysis of the dynamic of events leading to the Restoration as in part driven by the rise of Quakerism as a subversive lower-class movement in the countryside: *The Restoration*, pts. 1 and 2, *passim*.

represented 'the victory of a program quite similar to that of 1641 and the establishment in power of an alliance of forces behind that program quite analogous to that of 1641' (714) and these developments and those of the 1690s 'cut short the tendency to absolutism' (715) and created an aggressively imperialist capitalist trading power.

This interpretation has the very great advantage over Hill's that it is not teleological. It does not see the fundamentals as being settled in 1640–60: 1660 was a genuine counter-revolution and part of a counter-revolutionary dynamic driven by the landowning class's fear of lower-class radicalism; and it opened the way for new experiments in absolutism and alliance with Catholic powers on the part of the Crown. Everything was, therefore, still to play for in 1660–88. It also explains one of the great questions of the politics of the century, why the Stuart kings repeatedly chose to pursue policies which put them at loggerheads with parliaments who sincerely wanted to work with them: their class position, shared with the Spanish and French kings. This, in turn, explains why Exclusion, though it failed in 1679–81, could be the possibility that eventually came true; and therefore 'Whig' and 'Tory', names from the Exclusion Crisis, could be the two great parties of capitalist England into the nineteenth century. Besides the constitutional reforms of 1688–1700, William III and the first two Georges shared a great advantage for the landowning class over the Stuarts: their own commitments abroad forced them to adopt a Protestant, anti-absolutist policy in European politics. In the Exclusion Crisis it explains the character of the crisis as a rerun of the Civil War on a smaller scale, and the prominence of certain survivors from the interregnum, as does Scott's more detailed and more purely political treatment.

This explanation informs the rest of this book. A perception of the development of capitalism in a partial way before 1688 and more fully afterwards is helpful in understanding the use of class themes by the parties, for which neither Whig nor Tory interpretations are helpful. It enables us to understand the dramatic language of politics through which Tory plays sharply associate dissent, citizens, and class presumption; why issues of court corruption, royal extravagance, and the lack of rewards for loyalty are problematic for Tories; and why, in several cases,

Tories stress class solidarity between monarchs of opposed nations. On the other side, we can begin to see why themes of national solidarity including all classes tend to be associated with Protestantism, patriotism, and liberty in a Whiggish counter-ideology. A fuller exploration of this dramatic language of politics is the subject of Chapters 4–6.

Change really happened in the drama as well as in society at large; just as the heroic drama of the 1660s developed in response to the counter-revolution but also the anxieties of 1660, so the political blank-verse tragedy which developed in response to the crisis of the late 1670s had its own peculiar character— and its own influence on subsequent generic shifts, particularly towards the sentimental. Yet the drama of the Exclusion Crisis is not the same as the 'bourgeois' sentimental drama of the next century. The nature of the changes which occurred, as explained above, helps us understand why Tory drama mobilizes old themes and tropes with a new stridency, but also seems to have a sense of quite extraordinary doom and desperation about it, as we shall see in Chapter 7. It enables us to say that the drama does contain elements of the new, without subscribing to a crude teleology (because change had already begun to come about in a partial way, so we are not merely concerned with elements which foreshadow future developments). It can help us understand why Whig drama has vitality, but also expresses itself in terms which do not seem radical, stressing the interests of trade and the Protestant nation, and the new ruling class. This is the subject of Chapter 8. These tendencies are even more pronounced in the City drama which forms the subject of the final chapter.

However, the first thing to show is how the dramatists responded to the 'small picture'. In the first part of this chapter I gave an account of debates and of shifts in the political balance of forces during the Exclusion Crisis and the years which led up to it. I shall now show that playwrights showed an extrordinary flexibility in responding to these 'local' shifts. This will not only transform our understanding of the drama of the Exclusion Crisis, but also say something about the role of drama in moments of revolutionary crisis.

CHAPTER 3

Dramatic and Political Shifts: The Example of John Crowne

DID the politics of the drama change in response to the seasons of the Exclusion Crisis described in the previous chapter, and if so to what extent? The answer is that the dramatists were extremely sensitive to political changes and flexible in responding to them. Perhaps this is partly because the big political shift in 1660 had already taught flexibility; perhaps it is also because, as I have argued elsewhere, 'a willingness to uproot the self as the balance of power in society shifted had become synonymous with loyal, socially responsible and civilized behaviour. "Zealots" were marginalized after 1660.'[1] This chapter will map the theatrical seasons against the seasons of the crisis, examining the dramatists' sensitivity to the shifting political mood through a consideration of prologues and epilogues, and of the work of a particular playwright. I have chosen John Crowne for two reasons: firstly, he is both interesting and neglected.[2] Secondly, I have already argued in published articles that Lee, Behn, and Dryden are intensely responsive to 'local' political shifts.[3] I have limited myself to one playwright here for reasons of space, but I want to emphasize that a similar case could be made for other dramatists.[4]

[1] Owen, ' "Partial Tyrants" and "Freeborn People" in *Lucius Junius Brutus*', 477.

[2] Nancy Maguire's 'Factionary Politics: John Crowne's *Henry VI*' appeared after this book was finished. She discusses Crowne's shifting politics between *The Misery of Civil-War* and *Henry VI*, but makes no reference to my own discussion of Crowne's dramatic and political shifts in 'Interpreting the Politics of Restoration Drama' in spring 1993 and in subsequent articles.

[3] Owen, ' "Partial Tyrants" and "Freeborn People" in *Lucius Junius Brutus*'; ' "Suspect my loyalty when I lose my virtue": Sexual Politics and Party in Aphra Behn's Plays of the Exclusion Crisis'; and 'The Politics of John Dryden's *The Spanish Fryar; or, The Double Discovery*'. See also my 'Interpreting the Politics of Restoration Drama'.

[4] For example, D'Urfey 'hedges his bets' in 1679–80 with *The Virtuous Wife*, a play in which political references are confined to an extraneous royalist remark in the epilogues, and a Whiggish song in the play itself which is unrelated to the

We shall see that the overall tone of prologues and epilogues in the theatres shifts in response to the political changes outlined in Chapter 2; and, perhaps more surprisingly, that the politics of Crowne's plays shifts in a similar way: in the dark days following the outbreak of the Popish Plot scare, Crowne in *The Ambitious Statesman* (probably premièred spring 1679) displays royalism, but also an overall pessimism and darkness of tone. As polarities deepen in 1679–80, *The Miseries of Civil-War* (probably premièred January 1680) offers a more vigorously royalist focus on the evils of rebellion and civil war. In the following season, however, Crowne reworks similar historical and Shakespearian material in *Henry the Sixth: The First Part* (probably premièred between January and March 1681) to focus on weak kingship and popery in high places: an apparent adaptation to Whiggism. This was the time of apparent Whig ascendancy and the sitting of the second Exclusion Parliament. *Thyestes*, probably premièred in spring or summer 1680, seems politically transitional between *The Misery of Civil-War* and *Henry the Sixth*. *City Politiques*, dating from the Tory reaction period of summer 1682, shifts back to offer a savage satire of the Whigs and the City. Of course this is not to say that all contradiction is absent. However, the dramatic shifts are significant and, I suggest, can be explained by the shifts in the political situation between 1678 and 1682.

1678–1679: Darkness and Difficulty

In the 1678–9 season the political situation adversely affected the two London theatres. The King's Company at Drury Lane was already in difficulties, and during this season Dryden, who had a contract with them, offered both *Oedipus* and *Troilus and Cressida* to the rival Duke's Company. As noted in Chapter 1, Aphra Behn complains in her prologue to *The Feign'd Curtizans*: 'The devil take this cursed plotting Age, | 'T has ruin'd all our Plots upon the Stage' (sig. A4ʳ). In her epilogue she adds, 'So hard the Times are, and so thin the Town, | Though

---

action. *The Injur'd Princess* is somewhat Whiggish, and may date from the 1680–1 season (see the Appendix). In the autumn of 1681 there is satire of Whig citizens and criticism of Shadwell in *Sir Barnaby Whigg*, then in 1682 the fervent Tory idealism of *The Royalist*.

but one Playhouse, that must too lie down' (p. 72). People are
no longer content to be spectators in a theatre when they can
fancy themselves involved in a real-life plot:

> Suspicions, New Elections, Jealousies,
> Fresh Informations, New discoveries,
> Do so employ the busie fearful Town,
> Our honest calling here is useless grown;
> Each fool turns Politician now, and wears
> A formal face, and talks of State-affairs.   (sig. A4^r)

The lines are coloured by the royalist view that people should be
'quiet' and refrain from presumptuous interest in the business of
the country's rulers. Behn seems to be suggesting that the Popish
Plot scare is dishonest, a sign that scepticism coexisted with anti-
papist hysteria from the earliest stages. The usual teasing of the
audience for immorality becomes a taunt at the hypocrisy of
those who 'piously pretend, these are not days, | For keeping
Mistresses and seeing Plays' (ibid.). Teasing the audience for
lack of wit, also common, becomes a complaint that the hysteria
of the Popish Plot leads to crude and philistine artistic judge-
ments: 'But Wit as if 'twere Jesuiticall, | Is an abomination to ye
all' (ibid.).

This mockery of the Popish Plot scare is repeated by others.
Dryden's prologue to Lee's *Caesar Borgia*, a play which attempts to exploit prevailing anti-papism, complains that the
citizens have deserted the playhouses for the superior attractions
of newsmongering, mocks their credulity, and suggests that the
plot scare is dishonest. In the epilogue to *Troilus and Cressida*,
Dryden mocks the plot through the irreverent character
Thersites.[5] However, Lee's epilogue to *Caesar Borgia* takes a
different tone from Dryden's prologue, attacking popery, not
the plot scare and alluding in sinister terms to the murder of Sir
Edmund Bury Godfrey, an interesting example of how dramatists attempted to 'manage' audience reaction to a play through
prologues and epilogues. This suggests that, though the Whig–
Tory division had not yet fully developed, political polarization
is already apparent. In his prologue to *The Ambitious Statesman*, Crowne makes the parallel between papists and dissenters
which was in the process of becoming a stock royalist motif:

[5] As Paul Hammond has demonstrated: *Dryden: Literary Life*, 93.

But now the Nation in a tempest rowles,
And Old St. *Peters*, justles with St. *Pauls*,
And whilst these two great Ladys fight and braule,
Pick pocket Conventicle Whore gets all.
Ungrateful Jade, from *Rome* it is most clear,
She had the stinking Fish she sels so dear.

(sig. B3ᵛ)

Thus both partisanship and a sense of strain are apparent in prologues and epilogues.

The political problems with which the dramatists are preoccupied include corruption at court and intemperance in high places; the dangers of superstition and credulity, of ambition and popular uprising; the problems of rebellion against tyrants and the dangers of rebellion against true kings. Though it would be premature to speak of Tory and Whig plays in this season, a difference is already apparent in how these issues are treated by different playwrights. Dryden and Crowne tend to stress the dangers of political rebels stirring up the 'rabble' and the importance of social order and stability, although they also explore the problem of immorality in high places. Political dissidence is seen as being motivated by personal ambition. The use of machiavellian methods to maintain order is given qualified sanction, especially in *Troilus and Cressida*. Mistrust of popular presumption and valuing of 'quietness' and civility are shared by Dryden, Crowne, and Behn.

Bancroft and Lee on the other hand show the threat of popular discontent emanating from bad government or popery, rather than political agitation. The traumatic and far-reaching effects of misgovernment are explored. There is sympathy for those whose concern for the people's grievances leads them to oppose the government. Lee's *The Massacre of Paris* was the first play of the period to be banned and he had difficulty in getting a licence for *Caesar Borgia*. However, royalist plays in particular convey a sense of difficulty about taking sides. The drama is characterized by a sense of crisis affecting individual, family, and state. We find both political partisanship and political anxiety. There is a pervasive sense of darkness and difficulty. Of the eight known new plays in the season, *The Feign'd Curtizans* is the only comedy. In the previous season, so far as is known, there were twenty-one new plays, of which nine could be classed as comedies.

Crowne's play in this season was *The Ambitious Statesman*, a play in which he strains after a partisanship which is difficult to dramatize successfully due to doubts about royal impotence and impropriety, and in which quietist heroism seems fraught with difficulty. Crowne attributed the play's lack of success directly to the political season in which it was produced:

We cannot think our soft Songs shou'd be heard, when Church-Musick grumbles with loud and unpleasant Discords, and the whole State seems out of Tune . . . This Play, which I think the most Vigorous, of all my foolish Labours, was born in a time so unhealthy to Poetry, that I dare not venture it abroad without as many Cloaths as I can give it to keep it warm. Let this excuse then serve to cover some of the nakednesses and deformities of it, that they are not so much mine as the Faults of the troublesome times. (sig. [A1^v–A2^r], B2^r)

The play itself exhibits a blend of royalism and pessimism which the nature of the period renders explicable. That Crowne strives for a royalist outlook is made explicit. He says in the epistle dedicatory that he has offered an '*Image* of that *Vertue*' loyalty, 'And truly at this time both *Image* and *Substance* seem to need *Protection*, when some are endeavouring to reduce again the *Substance* to an *Image*' (sig. B1^r). The memory of the Civil War is evoked, using the common image of a flood.[6] Crowne's mind seems to be equally divided between the danger posed by the political opposition and the fact that '*Fools* damn good Playes, and *Fortune* good Poets' (sig. B2^v). The prologue links the two themes: in the playhouse, 'Wit will find but Rods to switch her well' (B3^v). In the political sphere dissenters (associated with the opposition) profit from the Popish Plot scare. The association of the enemies of culture with the enemies of the state was a standard royalist topos. It is continued in the play, as we learn that the ambitious statesman of the title regards his son, the loyal favourite, as 'A studious, moral Fool' (1. p. 4).

---

[6] In the interregnum period see e.g. Marvell's 'Upon Appleton House' and Denham's 'Cooper's Hill'. In the Restoration period see e.g. Dryden's *Astraea Redux*. Ogilby's coronation pageant for Charles used the image of the Flood in association with satanic rebellion, in opposition to Eden and the Augustan golden age, which were associated with the Stuart Restoration.

As the title suggests, Crowne's image of loyalty has two aspects: the positive exemplum and the counter-example. The loyal favourite is Vendosme. Even when he is wrongly imprisoned and insulted by the Dauphin, who has stolen his beloved, Vendosme refuses to embrace 'The Heiress of all Hell, *Rebellion*' (4. p. 51). When his soldiers rise in insurrection to protest against his wrongs, he quells them with a burst of absolutist rhetoric: 'Princes are sacred, | What e're Religion (*sic*) Rebels may pretend, | Murderers of Kings are Worshippers of Devils' (5. p. 85). The ambitious statesman is Vendosme's father, the villainous Constable, who has all the qualities of the Renaissance machiavellian villain. He is clever and cunning, and derides fools: 'For as the Money's false that's mixt with Brass, | So he is a False Man, who is an Ass' (2. p. 25). He has a 'Philosophy' that nature is on his side (1. p. 5). He speaks of his 'Designs' in imagery of monstrosity (2. p. 19) and has an atheistic reliance on 'Fortune which always takes into her Favour | A hundred Villains for one honest Man' (1. p. 6). He revels in chaos and destruction:

> I ought not to get Children of a Woman,
> I ought to mix with nothing but a Chaos,
> And get Confusion to the Universe,
> And then the Children wou'd be like the Father.

> (4. p. 52)

Above all he is overweeningly ambitious; 'In short, Power is my pleasure' (1. p. 8).

Whig noblemen such as Shaftesbury were seen by royalists as ungrateful because disobedient, despite being forgiven in 1660 and granted high office. Similarly, the Constable is seen as guilty of ingratitude: 'Old Favours are Old Almanacks, ne'r lookt on' (2. p. 25). The Constable abuses rhetoric of 'revenge and freedom' (1. p. 5), spreads lies against the government (1. p. 7), and pretends religion:

> I'le seem religious to be damndly wicked,
> I'le act all villany by holy shews,
> And that for piety on fools impose,
> Set up all Faiths, that so there may be none,
> And make Religion throw Religion down.
> I will seem Loyal, the more Rogue to be,

> And ruine the King by his own authority:
> Pretending men from Tyranny to save,
> I will the foolish credulous World enslave.   (1. p. 8)

This speech is purely of topical application, relating to nothing which we see the Constable do in the play. The pretence of piety seems to allude to dissenters who supported the opposition. The fourth line seems to refer to the Declaration of Indulgence, supported by Shaftesbury, who was believed by some to be virtually an atheist.[7] The fifth line seems to refer to 'true Protestantism' as a cloak for anti-establishment policies. Seeming loyalty and ruining the king in his own name recall both the opposition of the 1670s and Civil War parliamentarians. The Constable sends dispatches to foment rebellion in the provinces. We also see him negotiating with his country's enemies, which reminds us of the fact that some members of the opposition in the 1670s took French bribes. Guise in *The Duke of Guise* similarly takes money from his country's enemies.

However, the Constable is not a personation of Shaftesbury. Shaftesbury was not accused of taking bribes. Moreover, unlike Shaftesbury (the dutiful father of a retarded son, and a fond grandfather), the Constable is the unnatural father of a good son. Crowne's technique is to associate topical allusions with a spectacle of monstrousness.

There are several features of this play which seem problematic from a royalist point of view. Some are attributable to inherent difficulties with the royalist paradigm, despite the author's best efforts. Thus in order to endure injustice Vendosme needs to be a stoic, but this tends to lead to pessimism, even bitterness. Loyalty is associated with quietism: Vendosme condemns warmongering in terms which may allude to opposition desire for a more active Protestant foreign policy (2. p. 26), and counters his father's desire to stir up trouble with a passivity which at times comes close to paralysis. His one action, to disarm the Dauphin after the latter has stabbed Louize, is regretted with his dying breath: 'I lifted up my Arm against the *Dauphin*, | It ought to have dy'd and rotted in the Air' (5. p. 86). The stoic hero is not charismatic. Loyalty as a transcendent value is difficult to

---

[7] Clarendon accused him of 'indifferency to religion': *The Continuation of the Life*, ii. 93, cited in Haley, *Shaftesbury*, 141. Haley says he 'favoured toleration for Dissent because he inclined to a rationalist, latitudinarian freedom of thought and because he retained a Puritan dislike for clerical authority' (ibid.).

dramatize convincingly: Vendosme's repudiation of his defence of Louize against the prince's murdering frenzy seems like a betrayal of his love. In moral terms the abject royalism of the ending seems a falling off from Vendosme's earlier priorities, as when he refuses to swear falsely that he and Louize are adulterous to protect the Dauphin from the revenge of his own angry troops: 'I will not be made to speak a Falshood | By any Sons of Earth, or Sons of Kings' (5. p. 79).

Moreover, Vendosme's *contemptus mundi*, expressed in bitter speeches which seem to castigate the universal folly and pretension of the author's own times, is oddly close to his father's. Vendosme sees 'a World of Vanity . . . Where massy substances of things sink down, | And nothing stay's but Colours, Sounds, and Shadows' (3. p. 32). Only the thought of heaven prevents him from seeing the world as 'The bloody Slaughter-house of some Ill Power', for 'Ev'ry thing here breeds misery to man' (5. p. 70). For the Constable,

> Who ever wou'd be vertuous, is a Fool;
> For he endeavours to plant Vertue here
> In a damn'd world, where it no more will grow
> Than Oranges in *Lap-land*.
>
> (5. p. 71)

The Dauphin is equally cynical: 'Nature now is us'd to barbrous deeds' (5. p. 80). Louize, speaking ironically, satirizes the hardened sensibilities of the age: 'A Woman dye for love! Oh! infamous! . . . Indeed 'tis never done, or if it be | 'Tis never own'd' (3. p. 42).

The resulting pervasive darkness of tone is not counteracted at the end. Although the Constable has taunted his son for being a 'Priest-ridden Slave' (5. p. 75), Vendosme appears to have little sense of Providence and retains his conviction that the world is better lost. Although he comforts Louize with talk of meeting in death, his own final words seem bleak:

> But in the Grave there's no Propriety,
> In Death's dark ruinous Empire all lye's waste . . .
> Then come cold Bride to my as cold Embrace,
> The Grave's our Bed, and Death our Bridal-Night,
> None will disturb, or envy our Delight.
>
> (5. 1. p. 86)

The first two lines are offered as reassurance to the Dauphin that there will be no loving communion after death. Vendosme accordingly receives the Dauphin's permission for a shared grave. In the context, the word 'Delight' seems to be used ironically. Douglas Canfield argues that 'Vendosme dies in full expectation of a happy afterlife with Louize.'[8] However, I can see little sense of transcendence.

There is also a bleakness, probably unintentional, about the spectacle of unhappiness in the family, emblematic of civil strife. The fact that royal authority is upheld in opposition to, not in parallel with, authority in the family has the effect of making royal authority seem less 'given', less part of an inevitable scheme of things, and more something which is vulnerable and requires an effort to maintain. More disturbingly, vitiated authority in the microcosm, not only in the Constable, but also in the Dauphin's 'Tyranny' (1. p. 10) over Louize, draws attention to the spectacle of misleadership in the macrocosm. In particular the Dauphin is attacked by both Vendosme and the king as a warmonger and a hothead. The king alludes disparagingly to his 'licentious followers' (2. 1. p. 27). His marriage to Louize, in defiance of a previous obligation, has brought trouble upon his country, but he does not care: 'My Country's welfare! why shou'd Princes marry | To make their Country happy?' (2. 1. p. 17).

There seems to be an allusion here to James, a military hero known for intemperance, intransigence, lust, and a politically problematic marriage. Crowne's Dauphin is an unsympathetic character. Towards the end he is almost machiavellian as he tricks the Constable: 'Princes no more shou'd keep their words with Villains | Than Priests with Hereticks' (5. p. 79). This profoundly emotive statement touches a raw nerve: the fear of the opposition was that a popish successor would not keep faith with his Protestant subjects, as religious loyalty would override all else, even the coronation oath.[9]

However, the Dauphin does at least act. The king is powerless to protect his loyal subject. His very integrity makes it impossible for him to understand why the Constable should make false

[8] Canfield, 'Royalism's Last Dramatic Stand', 241.
[9] Kenyon, The Popish Plot, 2–3, 38, 262–5. In reality Roman Catholic opinion was divided on the question.

accusations against his own son. When he does act, he is not only ineffectual, but disastrous: he confiscates the Constable's estates, so the villain has nothing more to lose; then, to be even-handed, he gives the Constable custody of the falsely accused Brisac, which plays into the villain's hands and furthers his plots. We cannot help but recall that Charles's refusal to act caused suspicion. He had been considered by royalists to be too merciful to parliamentarians ever since 1660, and others considered him too backward in rooting out popery.[10] The king's inability to act, like the prince's inability to behave, renders loyalty somewhat problematic.

The same might be said of the corruption which infests the centres of power. Crowne is scathingly critical of the court as the home both of scheming malcontents and of fickle yes-men, concerned only with appearances and hostile to wit. The Constable's sneering indictment rings disturbingly true in the play, and is embarrassingly topical: 'Oh! surfeited with fulsom Ease and Wealth, | Our Luscious hours are candied up for Women, | Whilst our Men lose their appetite to Glory' (3. p. 36). By the end, the best that can be said of loyalty is that it is the only alternative to chaos. Perhaps this is the reason for the play's lack of success. Whom can it have pleased? Hatred and mistrust of opposition are counterbalanced by an almost puritan disgust for the falsity of society in general and the court in particular.[11]

1679–1680: Polarization

In this season the focus of Tory drama shifted decisively to the

---

[10] Ibid. 119, 121.

[11] This may seem an odd adjective to apply to a royalist playwright, but Crowne grew up among dissenters in New England, where he attended Harvard University. The bitterness underlying his loyalty and apparent in his preface might owe something to the Restoration authorities' refusal to uphold his title to his father's lands in Nova Scotia, captured by the French. See Sengupta, 'Biographical Notes on John Crowne' and Neman, 'Setting the Record Straight on John Crowne'. In his preface, Crowne mentions enemies, possibly a reference to the fact that Rochester is said to have withdrawn his patronage: see the satire of 'Little starch'd Johnny Crowne', in A Session of the Poets (1676), in Poems on Affairs of State, i. 355. This poem may be by Rochester or by Rochester and Buckingham jointly. In either case it may partly account for Crowne's bitterness towards courtiers in the preface and the play itself.

danger of civil war arising from rebels inciting the rabble. Only in *London in Luster* and in *The Coronation of Queen Elizabeth*, both produced outside the theatres, are artisans regarded as rational and as an important part of the political nation. Settle's dedication of *The Female Prelate* to Shaftesbury portrays the Whig leader as a patriot, defending the liberties of property-owners, and opposed by 'a sort of People of neither Birth, Principles, nor Estates; a kind of indigent Bullies, who in all Companies run down Religion and Property, because they have neither Conscience nor Lands to lose; and therefore are for Change at any Rate, and desire Tumults onely to scramble for Bread' (sig. A2ᵛ). Settle's play, like Lee's *The Massacre of Paris*, shows mob violence unleashed not by opposition, but by papist savagery. The opposition, unlike their detractors, did not see the term 'Loyal Protestant' as a contradiction: Lee's Protestant hero, like Shaftesbury in Settle's dedication, is shown as loyal to the king, though for Lee and Settle loyalty means not being afraid to give the king good advice.

In the theatres those who see popery as the main danger are outnumbered by those who point to rebellion as the chief threat, though the stridency of Tory prologues and epilogues is perhaps a response to the popularity of Whiggery among the electorate. By summer 1680 the reality of the Popish Plot was openly questioned. Scepticism is evident in William Whitaker's prologue to *The Conspiracy* (March 1680). In *The Revenge*, probably performed in the spring, and in *The Souldier's Fortune* (June 1680) citizens who believe tales of popery are satirized.[12] Settle's *Female Prelate* was the only anti-papist play produced in the theatres in this season. The Protestant farce *The Coronation of Queen Elizabeth* was performed at Bartholomew and Southwark Fairs. 'Loyal Protestantism' is also seen outside the theatres in Jordan's Lord Mayor's Shows. Opinion in the theatres was more conservative. Politically inspired disturbances in the audience become frequent in this season and, as indicated in Chapter 1, when oppositionists were the instigators they seemed to feel themselves to be in hostile territory. The royalist intentions of the majority of dramatists are apparent in the prologues

---

[12] There is also a prologue by Dryden to an Oxford performance of Settle's *The Female Prelate*, in which the existence of the Popish Plot is questioned. Paul Hammond convincingly dates this summer 1680: *The Poems of John Dryden*, i.

and epilogues of this season. The tone varies: Otway's fervent prologue to *The History and Fall of Caius Marius* laments Charles's absence from the theatres and rapturously anticipates his return in miraculous terms similar to those employed in the Caroline court masque. His prologue to *The Orphan* praises James as the cure for the ills of the times in similar tones of quasi-religious triumphalism, though shot through with anxious, reiterated admonition: 'Receive him! Oh, receive him as his friends; | Embrace the blessings which he recommends' (p. 7). Very different in tone is Whitaker's wholesale satirical attack on the opposition in the prologue to *The Conspiracy*: 'Men of Business' are comprehensively indicted for presumption, irreverence, faction, disloyalty, petitioning, and scaremongering about a make-believe plot:

> Let *Politicians* too not be so *hot*
> To swear that a *Spring-tide's* a *Popish-Plot*.
> Do not too eagerly that scent persue,
> Least hunting an *Old Plot* you *make* a *New*.
>
> (sig. [A2]ʳ)

Criticism of the French king is condemned as disrespectful to majesty, Pope-burning is uncivilized, and at the very least people should 'Burn too the *Rump* and *Westminster Petition*'.[13]

Unlike Whitaker, most dramatists at least affect to situate themselves in the centre. Crowne's prologue to *The Misery of Civil-War*, Dryden's prologue to Tate's *The Loyal General*, and Settle's dedication to *The Female Prelate* all lay claim to moderation—but go on to castigate their political enemies in no uncertain terms. Equally disingenuous—or wisely cautious—is the denial of topicality in Ravenscroft's epilogue to *The Conspiracy*: 'the modest stage | Forbears to represent the present age' ([55]).

Strongly foregrounded in the prologues and epilogues in this season is the class-based association of political meddling and philistinism. Dryden tells Tate's audience that players might go out of business, 'Whil'st you turn Players on the Worlds great

---

[13] Sig. [A2]ʳ. The Tories were in fact to organize a rump burning, recalling those of 1660, at Whitsuntide 1680: Harris, *London Crowds*, 166. The demonstration was banned, presumably for reasons of public order. The boys of Westminster School burnt 'Jack Presbyter' in Nov. 1681: Miller, *Popery and Politics*, 186; Haley, *Shaftesbury*, 673.

Stage, | And Act your selves the Farce of your own Age'.[14] Philistinism and political agitation and true wit and order find similar association through metaphor in Maidwell's prologue to *The Loving Enemies*. The people defend their 'property' of 'folly' and 'knavery' and complain of the poet's 'arbitrary Government'. In 'each Town' petitioners 'swear all Satyr with bold truth shall down' (sig. [A4ʳ]). A similar theme recurs in the prologue and epilogue to *The Misery of Civil-War*, while Crowne's prologue to *Thyestes* calls the audience 'upstart Sectaries of wit' (sig. [A2]ʳ). Even the future Whig Shadwell associates newsmongering and lack of artistic taste in the prologue to *The Woman-Captain*, though he blames irresponsible and degenerate aristocratic youths as well as cits. The prologue to *Fools Have Fortune* says poet, players, and audience should unite against the common enemy, politics, instead of fighting each other while 'Plotters and pollitickes devour you all.'[15] He asks, 'Will you Witt Women, love and plasure Chuse | or pamphletts prating Foppes or lying Newes' (ibid.). Similarly, Crowne's epilogue to *The Misery of Civil-War* claims that vice is better than politics, gambling and sex preferable to 'damn'd senseless bloudy strifes' ([72]).

'Knavery' and 'folly' are common charges. Behn's pastoral epilogue to *The Young King* offers an example of other common tropes. The opposition to James is accused of 'Ambition', 'insolence', 'emulation', 'politick mischiefs', 'malice', 'sedition', 'Plots', 'outrages which Knaves and Fools procure', being improperly 'busie', and, reversing the charge against the Stuarts of 'arbitrary power', of 'Arbitrary Votes' ([64]). It is also common for the audience to be satirized for hypocrisy: Shadwell's prologue to *The Woman-Captain* and Behn's to *The Young King* satirize the audience for francophobia and Behn points out that

---

[14] Dryden refers in this prologue to rebels and to libels, supposedly for the public good, which stir up 'the Shrove-tide Crew to Fire and Blood', a reference to opposition activity inciting apprentice riots. It seems clear that Dryden is attacking the opposition, as well as newsmongering and general meddling. I disagree with Phillip Harth's reading this prologue in such a way as to confirm his view that Dryden was politically uncommitted prior to 1681 ('Dryden in 1678–1681'). Dryden had already offered a royalist treatment of rebellion and faction in *Oedipus* and *Troilus and Cressida*. See also my 'The Politics of John Dryden's *The Spanish Fryar*'.

[15] Milhous and Hume, 'The Prologue and Epilogue for *Fools Have Fortune*', 314.

this is hypocritical given their predilection for French wine and fashions. She also taunts them for religious concerns when they are really irreligious, a theme reiterated in Crowne's prologue to *The Misery of Civil-War*: ''Tis pleasant, Sirs, to see you fight and brawl | About Religion, but have none at all' (sig. [A2]ʳ).

In the epilogue to *The Misery of Civil-War* Crowne describes religious fanaticism as sickness and madness, recalls the horrors of the 1640s, and likens them to today's 'Religious Brawls' (72). At least the contenders in the Wars of the Roses fought for 'loyalty' and 'Royal Right' (ibid.). Contenders in the 1640s and 1680s have no such excuse:

> Yet those rich Ornaments were very far
> From gracing that foul Monster Civil-War.
> How ugly then is she when ridden blind,
> With Pope before, but Presbyter behind? (ibid.)

The plays continue the themes of the 1678–9 season, but the tone is more factional. Though contradictions and anxieties persist, there is a sense that the dramatists are working harder to clarify and make explicit connections such as that between filial piety and natural affection in the family, and political propriety. The dramatists make effective use of family themes to offer a message of quietism. Political faction by parents disrupts young love in *The Young King, Caius Marius, Thyestes*, and *The Conspiracy*. Powerful use is also made of women out of place, a theme associated with the lower orders being out of hand. The effect is royalist in the case of the Queen in *The Young King*, Myrrhoe and the Queen in *The Loyal General*, and the ambitious Flatra and the Queen Mother in *The Conspiracy*. In *The Female Prelate* the effect is to demonize popery; while in *The Woman-Captain* Mrs Gripe's cross-dressing seems to reflect the idea that degenerate times need desperate (Protestant) remedies, a theme which Shadwell was to develop in more Whiggish vein in *The Lancashire Witches*.

There is some recurrence in this season of the anxieties of royalist playwrights. The theme of lack of reward for loyal service is found in *The Orphan*, the *The Souldier's Fortune* and its epistle, and the epilogue to *Caius Marius*. The long-suffering and self-sacrificial heroism of Dryden's Troilus and Crowne's

Vendosme in the 1679–80 season has its counterpart in this season in Theocrin in *The Loyal General*, Philisthenes in *Thyestes*, and Castalio in *The Orphan*. The only aggressive, 'manly' hero is Saxony in Settle's Whiggish *The Female Prelate*. Sometimes unease about the court or about royal impotence or impropriety escapes the bounds of royalism and creates a tension, as in *The Loyal General* and *The Orphan*. However, elsewhere court corruption is merely a stock theme, as in the comic courtier Pimante in *The Young King*; or is contained and explained away, as in *The Conspiracy*. Overall, there is a hardening of polemical distinctions.

In this season of polarization, 1679–80, when ''41' was on everyone's lips, Crowne produced *The Misery of Civil-War*. This adaptation of Shakespeare's 2 *Henry VI*, Acts 4 and 5, and 3 *Henry VI*[16] is more persuasive as royalist drama than *The Ambitious Statesman*, but contains some residual anxieties. The play succeeds as royalist drama, but some uneasiness about royal promiscuity is apparent. Matthew Wikander has shown that Crowne uses 'scenic emblem' and particularly the image and spectacle of dead babies to render Shakespeare 'more politically conservative and more iconographically simplistic' (342). In particular, in 3. 2, Crowne adds an exemplary spectacle of the horrors of civil war. Soldiers are shown robbing and tormenting peasants and raping their daughters. The peasants have only themselves to blame, for they have railed seditiously in alehouses instead of living 'honestly and quietly' (3. 3. p. 36). The soldiers repeatedly sneer 'How do you like Rebellion?' Then 'The Scene is drawn, and there appears Houses and Towns burning, Men and Women hang'd upon Trees, the Children on the tops of Pikes' (ibid.). Wikander does not mention that these are royalist atrocities; it is the queen's forces who are creating in Yorkist lands 'An Orchard for the Devil'. However, this only serves to point up the universally corrupting effects of civil war and to recall the realities of the English Civil War.[17]

[16] Oddly, Crowne says in his prologue that 'The Divine Shakespear did not lay one Stone' of his 'poor Work' (sig. [A2]ʳ). This may be modesty; more likely it is to draw attention to his own politically motivated alterations.

[17] Stocker discusses Restoration awareness of royalist atrocities in the Civil War, e.g. the sacking of Brentford, though a loyal town: 'Political Allusion in *The Rehearsal*', 19. Staves points out that in *The Old Troop* (1664?, 1668) John Lacy, a royalist lieutenant in the war, shows undisciplined royalist soldiers plundering. Such

The popular menace is depicted in the Jack Cade scenes, which Crowne worsens to problematize rebellion. The first Cade scene in Shakespeare is 2 *Henry VI*, 4. 2, but Crowne's play opens with the spectacle of upstarts executing summary justice. The execution of Lord Say is brought forward and his learning adduced as an added reason for his death, enhancing the philistinism already depicted in the source and reinforcing the equation of ignorance and political activity in Crowne's prologue:

> Thou hast caus'd wicked Printing to be us'd,
> And contrary to the King, his Crown and Dignity,
> Hast built a Paper-Mill. It will be prov'd,
> That thou hast Servants talk of Nouns and Verbs
> And such vile Words no Christian er'e can here.

> (1. p. 3)

Cade's defence of the poor and illiterate is thus parodied and rendered dangerous nonsense. The fact that Say is unknown to us in Crowne's version turns a tragic incident into a satiric cameo. The rebels will attack historical records: 'Pluck down the Tower, and burn all the Records, | Why shou'd we keep | Mouldy Records of what our Grandsiers did?' (7). This philistine iconoclasm is probably intended to recall the 1640s from a royalist perspective. Crowne's Cade is also like a 1640s radical in the way in which he attacks the legal system (6) and the Church (7).[18]

To further worsen the mob, the self-justification of Shakespeare's 4. 2 is omitted. Crowne also leaves out the satirical asides with which Shakespeare's butcher and weaver debunk Cade's pomposity, so that his rebels are more united in ambition. Crowne inserts an obviously topical warning that the rebels will spare neither the lords who have been their particular friends nor the rich citizens who have sought to lead them in 'Plotting, and Caballing' (5). As in the 1640s, disloyalty in the

realism is rare, and it is a sign of Crowne's political morale and dramatic energy in this play that he is able to turn it to good account.

[18] While Cade attacks the law, the heroic Young Clifford attacks the venality and political presumption of lawyers in a way which alludes to the opposition in the 1640s and 1679 (1. p. 13). Crowne seems to relish jibes at lawyers and priests. For further instances of anti-clericalism in the play, see 1. 2. p. 13; 4. 4. p. 55, 5. 3. p. 61.

upper and middle strata of society will unleash forces which will
threaten the instigators themselves. Thus Crowne has Clifford
explain to Warwick:

> by the same law,
> Thou tramplest on thy King, a sawcy Groom
> May set his dirty foot upon thy jaws,
> And tell thee they were made both of one Clay.
>
> (1. p. 13)

In the same vein he adds a curse by the dying old Clifford on the
Yorkists: 'Rebels you thrive, and may Rebellion thrive | That
Rogues may cut your throats as you do ours' (4. p. 45). Crowne
also has the rabble fall out among themselves (1. p. 6), showing
that rebellion breeds internecine strife.

Crowne's rebels are less volatile and hence more terrible than
Shakespeare's, muttering doubtfully after Clifford's persuasions
to loyalty in 1. 1, rather than shifting their allegiance with every
alternating speech. Crowne omits Cade's stifled remorse in
Shakespeare's 4. 7. Where Shakespeare's Cade is pitiable in
death, weakened by starvation, but determined to fight on until
he is finished by the sword (2 *Henry VI*, 4. 10), Crowne's is
killed off-stage to avoid any misplaced sympathy. He is killed
not, as in Shakespeare, by a country gentleman, hostile to the
court, but by that ubiquitous nobleman young Clifford. This
enhances Clifford's heroism, but also there is a suggestion of the
upper-class values that prevail in *Oedipus* and other royalist
plays. The king's true friends are courtly aristocrats. The country gentry cannot be relied on.

Crowne eliminates extraneous nobles to focus interest on
Clifford, who becomes a royalist hero who 'fought not for
rewards' (1. p. 9). Crowne co-opts for him an image which
Shakespeare has Warwick use to refer to his standard (2 *Henry
VI*, 5. 1): he is a mountain on which Henry may stand as a
strongly rooted cedar (1. p. 14). He is also made into a mouthpiece for moralizing speeches against rebellion (e.g. 1. p 10). If
Clifford is somewhat rash and intemperate on occasion, this
only serves to point up the integrity of Henry.

To Henry is given the key moralizing speech in the play.
In Crowne's Act 4, based on Shakespeare's 3 *Henry VI*, 2. 5,
Henry witnesses the grief of a son who has killed his father

and a father who has killed his son, a depiction in microcosm of unnatural division in the national family. In Henry's response, Crowne minimizes the self-pity in Shakespeare, stresses the thankless burdens of kingship, and draws the lessons of the spectacle:

> Oh you, who when you suffer by your Kings,
> Think to mend all by War, and by Rebellion!
> See here, your sad mistakes! how dreadfully
> You scourge your selves! learn here the greatest Tyrant
> Is to be chose before the least Rebellion.
> And Oh you Kings, who let your people rule,
> Till they have run themselves into confusion,
> See here your gentleness is greatest Tyranny!

(4. p. 44)

In this speech, dissatisfaction with the monarch is acknowledged but confidently made irrelevant. The latter part reminds us of the prologue, where the kingdom is described as the contrary wife of a gentle husband who ought to beat her. Charles has been indulgent for too long and is being invited to 'put his foot down'.

Crowne's improvement of Henry's character goes beyond giving him the authority to draw a moral, serving two other functions: firstly, to dignify royalty, making rebellion and civil war seem more horrific, and, secondly, to show how interfering with the succession will backfire upon future generations. Shakespeare's Henry is a weak and vacillating figure whose downfall is due in part to his inadequacy as a ruler. Crowne omits Henry's admission of ineptitude (2 Henry VI, 4. 10. 47–8) and also the rather undignified parley with Cade. He has Henry agree to meet York not from fear of antagonizing him, but so 'He shall not say that I refus'd to hear, | Or to redress any just grievances' (1. p. 10). Crowne's Henry is given two excellent motives for failing strenuously to resist the Yorkists. Firstly he cares for his people:

> But I confess I do fear Civil War;
> Not for my own, but for my people's sake,
> I am afraid to shed the blood of *English* men,
> But you indeed are bold in cruelty.
> By which (oh Heaven!) judge whose is the Child,

His who desires to have it cut in pieces,
Or mine, who strive in tenderness to save it.

(2. pp. 23–4)

Secondly, Henry gradually comes to realize:

I find my Title's weak,
And to defend it were to fight with Justice.
Besides, there lyes already on my head
The Blood of *Richard*, murder'd by my Grand-father.

(2. p. 25)

Where Shakespeare's Henry vacillates between yielding the
throne and hoping for revenge through Margaret, Crowne's
Henry, once convinced of the Yorkists' right to restore the true
line interrupted by the deposing of Richard II, swears to defend
them even against his wife, if necessary (2. pp. 26–7). He is only
persuaded to resume the throne by Warwick's threatening to kill
his son (5. p. 59). Crowne has the ghost of Richard II appear to
Henry in the Tower in Act 5 to warn of the horrors which ensue
from tampering with the succession. A singing spirit then comforts Henry with the knowledge that he is being punished not
for any crimes of his own, but for his grandfather's sacrilege in
interfering with the divinely ordained line of hereditary kingship. Anyone else whose 'bold Ambition' makes him 'presump-
tuously pretend a Right, | Because he stands upon the peoples
heads' (5. p. 68) will be similarly blasted. This may be a reference to Monmouth. Henry is not weak but saintly in his acceptance of heaven's decree.

Edward's accession is thus transformed from a usurpation to
a restoration, and Crowne improves him accordingly. Where
Shakespeare's Edward withholds Lady Grey's lands initially in
the hope of making her his mistress, even though her husband
fought on the Yorkist side, Crowne's marries her even though
her husband was 'a most vehement *Lancastrian*' (4. p. 50).
Crowne's Edward is continually in conflict with his brother
Richard's 'bloody cruelty, | Lean envy, and insatiable Ambition'
(2. p. 22). The contrast between them is earlier and more fully
developed than in Shakespeare. Where Shakespeare's Edward
leads his brothers in stabbing the Prince of Wales (3 *Henry VI*,
3. 5), Crowne's merely strikes the prince and is annoyed when

Richard and George kill him. Crowne's Edward forbids his brothers to insult Henry's queen and is furious at Richard's murder of Henry. Crowne ends the play with two long speeches by Edward, addressed more or less directly to the audience, in which he recapitulates the horrors of civil war and expresses the hope that the present generation 'Will prove exceeding honest Loyal Subjects, | For by their Fathers Ruine they have learnt Wit' (5. p. 71).

With a possible allusion to his own monarch, Crowne both foregrounds and palliates Edward's lust. He creates the character of Edward's mistress, Lady Elianor Butler, and adds a scene, 3. 3, in which his followers almost rebel because he has spent the night before an important battle in dalliance with her. However, appearances are deceptive: Edward has in fact mustered his troops, and he goes on to moralize at length upon their presumption in censuring his frailties, especially given the freedom with which he pardons theirs. They are also hypocrites because they would all do the same, given the chance. Anxiety about royal promiscuity is acknowledged and contained. Crowne works hard to absolve the king's immorality from censure and dissociate it from political untrustworthiness.

Crowne also makes Warwick's desertion of Edward result from sexual rivalry over Lady Grey. However, the conflict has a different resonance from the rivalry between prince and subject in *The Ambitious Statesman*. Warwick, the vainglorious and ambitious 'kingmaker', is not sympathetic, and it is liberating for Edward to realize that he does not need to rely on men like this. Nevertheless, there is some residual uneasiness about Edward's marriage. Politically it is a blunder. He offends the French king, whose hand he has been soliciting. The English nation will probably be hostile. Like the Dauphin in *The Ambitious Statesman*, Edward cries, 'What? is the people free, and not the King? | Not free where every Slave is free, his bed?' (4. p. 51). However, there is a mitigating irony here: what Englishmen will object to is his marrying an English commoner who already has children. Given contemporaries' objections to a barren foreigner as queen, the objections to Edward's marriage seem comical. The implication is that all such objections in all ages are presumptuous and ridiculous.

However, more seriously, Edward's marriage leads him to abandon Lady Elianor, who dresses as a boy and induces him to slay her in a fight. At the moment when he renounces his vows to Lady Elianor, Edward is associated with popery:

ED.   I, when I please
Can have a dispensation from his Holiness.
LADY EL.   What then his Holiness will be your pardon?
A very excellent office for a Pope!
To be the Universal Bawd of Christendom!

(1. p. 55)

This might just be gratuitous anti-papism, but the association of popery and royal promiscuity cannot but touch a raw nerve. Horrified by his killing of Lady Elianor, Edward vows henceforth to change his ways and live in marital constancy. It is as if Crowne cannot ultimately sustain the effort of vindicating a lustful king and is forced to impose moral improvement on him even if the process reflects on his own monarch.

Or is it? Might not the association of popery and selfish caprice, repented of as rule brings a new sense of responsibility, suggest James rather than Charles and be intended to *allay* anxiety? Just as heaven has restored the true line, so the new king has providentially become worthy of his office. The play is a comprehensive indictment of rebellion against royal right and the succession. There are some anxieties about royal impropriety which seem contradictory, but in the end even these are subsumed into the triumphant royalist schema.

1680–1681: High Tide of the Opposition

The mood of belief that the opposition might win in autumn 1680 to early 1681 also appears in the theatres in the 1680–1 season. The tone of prologues and epilogues is markedly different from the previous season. I have discussed the prologues and epilogues of this season at length in my 'The Politics of John Dryden's *The Spanish Fryar*'. What follows is therefore a brief summary. No longer is the focus on criticism of the opposition and of the presumption and witlessness of those who do not leave politics to His Majesty. Tory themes are sharply expressed only in Behn's prologue and epilogue to *The Second Part of The Rover*, which sneer at the 'Almighty Rabble' and associated images of dissent and presumption, insist on quiet, and offer some criticism of other playwrights who have 'flatter'd all the Mutineers'ith' Nation' with 'Giants, fat Cardinals, Pope Joans and Fryers' ([86]). This stands out sharply as atypical, emphasizing the absence elsewhere in this season of themes common in 1679–80 and 1681–3. The hardships of poets seems to be the predominant theme. There is less sneering at the Popish Plot and a mild kind of anti-popery is common. Misogyny and sexy teasing are often substituted for political invective; for example, in the prologue to *Richard the Second* the male speaker says that men and women have changed places: 'Their property of Falsehood we invade, I Whilst they usurp our Mid-night Scouring Trade' ([A4]ʳ).

It is perhaps unsurprising that the fervent praise of James which Otway contributed in the previous season should be lacking in this,[19] but it is quite remarkable that anti-populist virulence, sneering at the Popish Plot scare and demonizing opposition which characterized royalist prologues and epilogues in the previous season should be so much in abeyance in this one. In the autumn and winter the fact that Parliament was sitting must have been an important factor: this undoubtedly affected the composition of the audience. Yet moderation and restraint persist after the dissolution of Parliament in January.

In the plays Whiggery and moderation predominate: a startling about-turn. Lee was inspired to follow *The Massacre of Paris* with *Theodosius*, a play which is critical of royal irresponsibility, and with the banned Whiggish play *Lucius Junius Brutus*. Dryden offered in *The Spanish Fryar* a combination of popular, though not inflammatory, anti-popery and cautious, moderate royalism. Tate allowed disquiet about royal impropriety to rupture the fabric of royalism and got into trouble: *Richard the Second* was banned in December, and when the

---

[19] There is a 'Prologue to His R. Highness the D. of York at Edinburgh by the late E. of Roscommon': Danchin, *Prologues and Epilogues*, vol. ii, pt. 1, pp. 303–4. This sycophantically praises James's royal virtue, military heroism, and loyalty, and contrasts strikingly with prologues spoken in London and even Oxford at this time.

King's Company tried to stage it under the title of *The Sicilian Usurper*, their theatre was closed as a punishment.[20] Shadwell and Banks contributed plays which emphasized Protestant values. Shadwell also got into trouble, being forced to cut out substantial portions of *The Lancashire Witches*. There was an extraordinary preponderance in this season of plays which stressed Protestantism or moderation. There is little or no evidence of the strident Toryism of the following year.

Crowne's response seems equally remarkable. His *Henry the Sixth: The First Part, With the Murder of Humphrey Duke of Gloucester* is a striking example of the shift I have described. Before discussing this play, however, I want to consider the transitional *Thyestes*. I think this play was probably first performed in spring or summer 1680 (see Appendix). The play deals with two royal brothers, one of whom is in exile. It turns on a problem with the succession, as Atreus has usurped Thyestes' right to rule. Unnatural political arrangements are mirrored in the family: as in Otway's *Caius Marius*, the family is torn apart by internecine strife, and as in Otway's *The Orphan* one brother has committed rape and incest on the other's wife. Also as in *The Orphan* there is an atmosphere of suspicion and mistrust, of darkness and dissimulation, and universal disruption is invoked to express private anguish: Thyestes at the grisly banquet at which he unknowingly eats his children and drinks their blood cries, 'Old *Chaos* is return'd' (5. 5. p. 49). In *The Ambitious Statesman* Crowne had a father rack his son on stage. Here the younger generation is literally devoured. Further thematic similarity may be found in Crowne's introduction of star-crossed young lovers, Antigone, daughter of Atreus, and Philisthenes, son of Thyestes.

The Misery of Civil-War contained a few jibes at priests. This play depicts a tyrant (Atreus) in league with wicked priests. The priests conspire with Atreus to murder the young hero, which gives Philisthenes the opportunity for several bitterly anticlerical tirades towards the end of Act 4. The topical resonance here makes it hard to dismiss the atrocities as pagan savagery, and Crowne does not wish us to do so. He says in his epilogue:

---

[20] Hume, *Development*, 345, challenges the view (in Van Lennep *et al.* (eds.), *London Stage*, 293) that there were two performances before the ban.

We shewed you in the Priests to day, a true
And perfect Picture of old *Rome* and new;
One Face serves both; Pagan and Popish Priests
Are but two names for the same bloody Beasts.   (p. 56)

Equally problematic from the royalist point of view is the fact
that the tragedy is precipitated by royal lust: Thyestes' seduction
of Atreus' wife has not only resulted in his own exile and
estrangement between Atreus and the Queen, but also seems to
have driven Atreus demented. At the beginning of the play the
ghost of Tantalus, grandfather of the royal brothers, announces
that incest and murder run in the family.

The horrors which occur at the palace are the occasion for
aspersions against the court by the Captain who arrests
Philisthenes in Act 2, by the virtuous philosopher, Penteus, and
by Thyestes himself. Both Penteus and Thyestes are careful to
distinguish 'the wickedness of Courts' (3. 3. p. 34) from the
king. Act 1 concludes with a moralizing speech by Penteus on
the burdens of power and merits of passive obscurity, a recurring royalist theme. However, this is unconvincing after the
spectacle of Atreus' entirely blameworthy cruelty. The ideology
of the king as victim is hollow indeed when all the horrors in the
play result from Atreus' plots. Thyestes implausibly lumps together foreign wars, political factions, assassination plots, and
other kingly worries with 'Intemperance' which may afflict the
king, as though the latter were also an outside agency. Royal
intemperance is 'A lingring Poyson that consumes our time, |
Our Nights in drunkenness, our Days in sleep' (3. 3. p. 33).
Moreover, the 'good' royal brother, Thyestes, who was sympathetic in his desire to heal the rifts in family and state, descends
to Atreus' level in the banquet scene.

Crowne also makes use of the theme of right behaviour
without reward, and, as with Vendosme in *The Ambitious
Statesman*, faith without hope. We cringe as the repentant
Thyestes, returning from exile, prays to the wood gods,
'My only Friends of all the Heavenly Powers' (3. 3. p. 34),
for the hellish fury, Megaera, announced his predetermined
doom at the beginning of the play. The point is laboured as
Thyestes asks, 'For who will Virtue follow, and obey, | If when
she is their Guide, men lose their way' (ibid.). It is usual for

loyal dramatists to agonize over whether virtue is its own reward in unjust times, but Crowne seems to be emphasizing that virtue is futile and the virtuous doomed and damned. This is reinforced by the play's ending. As in *The Ambitious Statesman*, the hero who trusts the king is dead, but whereas the Dauphin in that play is chastened, Atreus is unrepentant. The play ends with his psychotic maunderings about how men are worse than beasts and vagabonds whipped by the gods. Mankind deserves to be oppressed and he will rear his sons to tyrannize over future generations. This takes the world-weariness of the hero of *The Ambitious Statesman* into another dimension. From the thought that only the hope of heaven makes virtuous effort in an unjust world endurable, we have come to the position that mankind is only fit for tyranny. This seems dangerously close to parody of the royalist justification of kingly power by reference to ordinary men's unworthiness. It seems as if Crowne is parodying his own previous preoccupations, or redressing the balance, counteracting *The Misery of Civil-War* with a play which concentrates primarily on royal and popish excess.

An anti-Whig note might be struck in the tyrant's concluding rant. When he calls mankind a 'mutinous Impostour' (5. 5. p. 56) and asks 'Can baseborn Bastards lawful Soveraigns be?' (p. 55) we think of Monmouth. However, the allusion is purely gratuitous. The depiction of corruption, tyranny, and priestly falsity at the centres of power is extremely emotive. This was the first play to be put on by the King's Company after a six- or seven-month interlude. Crowne's task was to revive the fortunes of the ailing company. He undertakes it with a play full of titillating horrors, but he must also have felt that his depiction of wicked tyrants and evil priests would not be taken amiss.

In *Henry the Sixth*, like Tate in *Richard the Second*, Crowne allows disquiet about royal impropriety to gain ascendancy over royalism and gets into trouble. As he was to explain in 1690: 'my aversions to some things I saw acted [at court] by great men, carried me against my Interest, to expose Popery and Popish Courts in a Tragedy of mine, call'd *The Murder of Humphry, Duke of Gloucester*, which pleas'd the best men in England, but displeas'd the worst; for e're it liv'd long, it was stifled by command'.[21] In the prologue and epilogue Crowne departs from his habit of coupling satire of Rome and of dissent. The absence of any reference to the latter is significant. The play is dedicated to Sir Charles 'Sidley' (i.e. Sedley), now a moderate Whig.[22] The epistle dedicatory makes it clear that the focus of Crowne's hostility has shifted from rebellion, of which there is no mention, to popery: 'this Play is no indifferent Satyre upon the most pompous fortunate and potent Folly, that ever reigned over the minds of men, called Popery' (sig. A3ʳ).[23] The bulk of the dedication is taken up with a description of his attempts to develop and foreground the anti-Catholicism of his source, by emphasizing that the murder of Duke Humphrey was the work of papists, by deploying the rhetoric of papist atrocity, and by satirizing popish credulity and miracle-mongering in added exchanges between the murderers: 'To expose these Follies to the People is the business of this Play' (A4ʳ).

It is clear that Crowne's extraordinary volte-face is motivated at least in part by his own long-suffering in the royal cause. The familiar spectre of lack of reward for loyalty rears its head, and Crowne's patience has worn thin. His opening metaphor describes the attempt to succeed with poetry as building castles in the air, 'but I never heard of one inch of firm Land be gained'(A3ʳ). This is not an arbitrarily chosen image: it relates to the grievance concerning the loss to the French Crown of his American property, which Crowne attributes to 'the advice of some ill great Men, who sacrifice both private and publick Interest to their own' (A4ʳ–A4ᵛ). There is a bitter reference to English inability to counter France: 'And if that fortunate Kingdom strove for it, you may imagine they got it' (ibid.). Here and elsewhere Crowne seems to go beyond criticism of courtiers and to verge on political criticism of his monarch. We may even say that he verges on Whiggery. He says, 'I have so deeply felt, what the loss of Property is, that I cannot but honour the Defenders of it' (A4ʳ). Whigs claimed to be defenders of property against

---

[21] Crowne, dedication to *The English Frier*, sig. A3ᵛ.

[22] See the discussion in Ch. 2.

[23] I have used the first edition in the Brotherton Collection at Leeds University. Page references in the Huntington Library edition and on Wing microfilm are slightly different. The division between Acts 4 and 5 is not given. I assume a break on p. 52 after the murderers go out: they then return, having sworn a religious oath to do the Cardinal's will and proceed to murder Gloucester.

royal arbitrariness. Sedley's wit, which has long delighted the nation, is now directed to 'the Defence of what is very dear to it, Truth, Liberty, and Property' (A4^r). Crowne adds that he and Sedley share the goal of exposing popery.

The play's ending might suggest that the play conforms to royalist expectation, for Buckingham tells the king, 'The Rascal People all joyn with the Traytors, | Threatning to spoil the City, and your Court' (5. 2. p. 68). The queen warns, 'yield not, Sir, to Rebels' (p. [69]). However, the play confounds expectation. First, let us look at the context of the queen's words, cited above, in speeches added by Crowne at the end of the play. The king says:

> Pray let as little Blood be shed as possible.
> . . . I will promise e'm
> To mend my Government, for I confess,
> *England* may yet Curse my unfortunate Reign.

The Queen replies:

> Come, Sir, take Spirit in you; Men like Buildings
> Fall to the Ground, if never Fire burn in e'm
> To harden e'm; King's a Royal Building,
> That shou'd have no soft Clay in it at all.
> Adversity has always reign'd upon you,
> And made you soft; but yield not, Sir, to Rebels.
> Royalty like great Beauty, must be chaste,
> Rogues will have all, if once they get a taste.   (ibid.)

The monarch is morally improved by Crowne, but nothing like as much as in *The Misery of Civil-War*: these speeches show his weakness.[24] Henry's final admission is extraordinary and must have had topical resonance in the theatre. The queen's penultimate line, with the pun on 'chaste', seems to be a gratuitous topical allusion, to the present monarchy's discredit.

---

[24] Wikander (340–1) makes much of the point that, as Gloucester is led off by the plotters, Crowne replaces Shakespeare's image of Henry as a mother cow bereft of her calf with the image of a mother whose infant is carried off on a soldier's spear (4. p. 45). It is true that slaughtered children functioned to demonize rebellion in *The Misery of Civil-War*, but here there is a problematic resonance which Wikander fails to notice: the substitution of woman with panting breasts for mother cow still leaves Henry embarrassingly passive and unable to protect his loyal subject. This point may acquire more force in the context of my discussion below of the treatment of women.

If the king's weaknesses are not palliated as much, conversely the mob is not demonized in this play as it was in the previous one. Henry's concern for the people here is mirrored by the hero Gloucester's. Gloucester resembles Lee's Brutus: he is concerned about the people's welfare, but not populist. In Act 3 he comforts his publicly humiliated wife by saying commoners cannot help jeering any more than wild beasts can help their wildness, a statement which combines a perception of the need for good government with tolerance and insight (by the standards of the period). Crowne repeatedly stresses Gloucester's popularity with the common people, as against the plotters (Cardinal, queen, Suffolk, York), who show contempt for the needs of the commonwealth. Similarly, Crowne stresses Gloucester's respect for the law and the plotters' disregard for it, adding in Act 2 demands by Henry and Gloucester that the conspirators bring proof of their allegations against Gloucester. The overtones here are parliamentarian, not Tory.

The commoners have good instincts: York is only able to raise the people at the end because they are already angry at the murder of the virtuous Gloucester. The Commons' demand for Suffolk's death or banishment is not presented as presumptuous. Where the king's safety is in question, they must act to prevent his death just as they would wake him even though he had told them not to if they saw a serpent in his bosom. As Salisbury tells Henry, 'out of Loyalty they drive [Suffolk] from you' (5. 1. p. 59). It is interesting that Crowne leaves in this material from Shakespeare, because applied to the situation in 1680–1 the paradigm is Whiggish. Crowne even alters Shakespeare to stress that the people give advice from loyalty: Shakespeare's Henry is grateful for 'their tender loving care' (2 *Henry VI*, 3. 2. 280), Crowne's 'for their Loyal care' (5. 1. p. 59).

Crowne condenses several scenes in Shakespeare to a report that a patriotic pirate chief has killed the fleeing Suffolk in a loyal act of popular revenge for the king's injuries: '[he] said the Duke had murder'd good Duke *Humphry*, | Begger'd the King, lost *France*, and ruined *England*' (5. 2. p. 66). He also 'said the Duke had injur'd the King's Bed' (ibid.). Crowne makes explicit a hint in Shakespeare of an actual affair (rather than just attraction) between Suffolk and the queen. The people's knowledge and resentment of royal adultery shows the great cannot hide their sins. The political resonance is quite opposite to that in Tory prologues and epilogues where the people's 'busy' interest in the affairs of the great is seen as dangerous. The people's anxieties about royal behaviour mirror those of virtuous statesmen. In the opening scene, Gloucester, as in Shakespeare, praises the victories won against France by his brother Henry V, and criticizes the sacrificing of England's gains in France to please a woman. The reference is to the king's French marriage, the arrangements for which will involve giving back conquered land. Warwick weeps to think of the lands he has won with his wounds being given away. Gloucester notes that the king 'might have Married one of His fair Subjects, | And had more Beauty at a cheaper rate' (1. p. 3). Concessions to France, royal 'effeminacy', foreign marriage against the nation's interest: there is enough here to make Tories wince.

Crowne emphasizes the heroism of 'the good and wise Duke *Humphry*, | Whose Vertues are so many Guardian Angels | Both to the King and Kingdom' (3. p. 28), by various alterations which emphasize his dignity and loyalty. For example, Crowne omits the unseemly *sotto voce* arrangement of a duel between Gloucester and the Cardinal (Shakespeare's 2 *Henry VI*, 2. 1). Loyal speeches are added at 2. 1. p. 14, 3. 2. p. 30, 3. 3. p. 36, and 4. pp. 43–5. Gloucester stands against the demonic spectacle of corruption and popery rampant at court. He is a 'manly man', having some of the positive qualities of dynamism and hostility to court 'effeminacy' which confused us in the Constable, a virile, quasi-Protestant patriot, similar to the Admiral in Lee's *The Massacre of Paris* and Saxony in Settle's *The Female Prelate*: both Whig plays.

For Gloucester, the king is 'Begirt by Wolves, and none to be his guard' (4. p. 45). One of these is Suffolk, whose character is worsened by additions which emphasize his plots against and cuckolding of the king. Those who plot against the throne are in league with popery, court faction and popery being two sides of the same corrupt coin. Thus the Cardinal is the biggest wolf of all. He is given a ranting soliloquy (2. 1. p. 17) in which, like Edmund in *Lear*, he broods on his bastardy, envy, and ambition and vows to have Gloucester's blood. In 2. 2 he has machiavellian asides, one about how he and Henry should change places, another about how a miracle which is being cried up probably is not true: 'I who wait at the Altar, | Know well what tricks are plaid behind the Altar' (p. 22). The queen is also given an aside on how friars 'cheat the silly people: | They are all a pack o' Rogues' (p. 23). The credulous king, like the people, is inclined to believe the miracle, but Gloucester disproves it rationally. There is then an exchange, aside, between the Cardinal and the friars about using rogues and fools to cozen the foolish multitude: 'Fools are those that we must hope to stand by' (p. 26). In this play Crowne shares Marvell's mockery of belief in miracles and transubstantiation, and mistrust of idolatrous worship of images; as well as his depiction of priests as deceiving the people by using Latin, keeping knowledge to themselves, and engaging in 'Phanaticall Rites' which resemble 'the pranks and ceremonies of Juglers and Conjurers' (*An Account*, 6). To Gloucester's patriotic vigilance against France is added exposure of popish malpractice. Anachronistically, but with powerful ideological effect, the mantle of Whiggish 'Loyal Protestant' heroism falls upon Crowne's hero.

It is in Acts 4 and 5 that Crowne alters Shakespeare most significantly. His purpose is to bring out the evils of popery in high places. If the moralized spectacle in *The Misery of Civil-War* is soldiers on the rampage shouting 'How do you like rebellion?', here it is the spectacle of the loyal subject foully murdered by papists, not in France, or Italy, but at the English court. As a prelude to the murder Crowne gives the Cardinal several speeches of hypocrisy and blatant speciousness: the murder will be a damnable crime, but he has power to damn those who refuse to do it. Using what he calls the priest's weapon, 'A kind of two-edge Knives, call'd Subtilties' (4. p. 48), he argues that the crime is 'A most religious, meritorious deed' (p. 47). He offers sophistical arguments as to why false reports to the people that Gloucester committed suicide from shame and a broken heart will not be lies, but 'Most sacred truths' (p. 48).[25] He argues for a double standard of morality, telling the nobles they can live by a more self-serving code than the people and still get into heaven by the back stairs:

> My Lords, the Church has several kind of Garments,
> Course home-spun Clothes for Fools, fine Robes for Wits.
>
> (p. 49)

---

[25] This seems to be a satirical reference to the notion that Godfrey had committed suicide (see e.g. Kenyon, *Popish Plot*, 302–3).

Here the Cardinal resembles the royalists in Lee's Whig play *Lucius Junius Brutus*, whose contempt for the common people is negatively depicted.

Suffolk is complicit in the murder, relishing the deed in antici-pation, though it is the Cardinal who will provide 'soft Church Tools' to do the job (p. 50). The Cardinal has promised these men reward in heaven for 'stopping of a Heretick's Windpipe' (p. 51). The third murderer has quasi-Protestant doubts: 'How do I know Duke *Humphry* is a Heretick? . . . How if the Cardinal | Shou'd be mistaken?' (p. 52). He tells his companions how the Church has cheated him in the past. The Cardinal advises, 'Believe your Priests, and not your Consciences, | For Priests are to direct your Consciences; | Your Consciences are silly, false, corrupt' (5. 1. p. 53). The third murderer asks, 'Suppose a Priest, an't please you, | Mistake, and I shou'd sin by his command, | Will he be damn'd for me? and shall I escape?' (ibid.). The Cardinal answers this home question by threatening to burn the doubter as a heretic and repeating that the Church is infallible by its own decree. The gruesome scene which then follows is as horrific as anything in *The Female Prelate*. Like the murder of Gandia in Lee's *Caesar Borgia*, the murder of Gloucester is carried out in the same fashion as that of Sir Edmund Bury Godfrey, as contemporaries understood it: Crowne repeatedly stresses that strangling is the method used. The murderers place the body in a chair. Gloucester's final speech, 5. 1. p. 55, is a moving display of loyalty and forgiveness of his enemies. Crowne's paradigm here, exemplary loyalty poignantly counterposed to popery and plots, is the same as that in *The Massacre of Paris* and *The Female Prelate*. After the king regrets giving Gloucester up to his 'too cruel Enemies' (p. 56), 'The Scene is drawn, and the Duke of *Glocester* is shewn dead in a Chair' (p. 57). In Shakespeare the body is brought in on a bed. The point could hardly be clearer: the spectacle of Gloucester's martyrdom, mirroring Godfrey's, shows what happens if weak kingship allows popery to gain power at court.[26]

---

[26] Matthew Wikander notes this anti-popery, but sees it as secondary and perhaps accidentally over-emphasized ('The Spitted Infant', 342, 348, 349). This misses the significance both of the dedication and of the way in which themes and tropes work together in the play in one overall direction.

In addition to quasi-Protestant heroism, Crowne also gives Gloucester the manly vigour and hostility to effeminacy of Whig heroes. This fits with the masculinism of the dedication, in which Crowne, like Settle in the dedication of *The Female Prelate*, eschews the usual 'courtly' style[27] in favour of a bluff and manly Protestant style. After likening the sufferings of unappreciated dramatists to the beleaguered but true Protestant religion, he says that too many plays are written to please women: 'For what vigour soever is necessary to please Ladies elsewhere, Impotence best delights e'm upon the Stage' (A3ᵛ). To emphasize Gloucester's manliness, Crowne makes the women worse, an influence for evil at Henry's court, just as many thought they were at Charles II's. Crowne makes his ambitious Elianor competitive with the queen, whom she regards as an unsuitably elevated inferior. Gloucester rebukes her, 'Talk not of ruling Kingdoms, rule your self' (1. p. 6), and adds that he abhors the king's marriage

> not for Womanish causes,
> Because my Wive's inferior goes before her;
> But because *France*, *England's* inferior,
> Will by this Match ascend above her Conqueror:
> We give two Provinces to buy a Wife,
> Who brings with her but a shameful Peace.   (ibid.)

Patriotism, anti-popery, and masculine dignity are associated. Presumption is represented not by citizen interference in politics, but by papists, plotters, and unruly women. In 2. 1 Gloucester rebukes the Queen for butting in to a discussion of affairs of state: 'Madam, the King is old enough himself | To speak his Mind; these are no Womens matters' (p. 13). Crowne also adds interference by the Queen and reproaches by the King in 2. 2 (p. 21). When Elianor is arrested Crowne's Gloucester responds to the Queen's taunts, 'Madam, I will not answer for a Woman' (2. 2. p. 26). That we are meant to regard this manliness positively is suggested by the fact that Crowne has the scene conclude with the Queen gloating nastily over her fallen rival and drooling adulterously over Suffolk. Both the gloating and the lovemaking continue in Act 3.

[27] Cf. the negative reference to 'Courtly Stile' in Bancroft's Whig play *The Tragedy of Sertorius*, 1. 6. p. 9.

Crowne develops the association of unnatural ambition and female monstrosity by additions in 1. 3 and 2. 2 which stress Elianor's active role in conjuring the Devil, and associate conjuration and popery. In 2. 2 Elianor is more brazen on arrest than in Shakespeare. When she is finally banished for conjuring the Devil, Gloucester says, 'Did I not timely warn thee of Ambition; | And say, one day 'twould do some dismal deed?' (3. 2. p. 29). Both the queen and the Cardinal taunt and exult over him. Crowne's use of female monstrosity to demonize popery and plotting is similar to Settle's in *The Female Prelate*. The women's self-interest also reinforces the isolated virtue of Gloucester, who alone thinks of the nation's good.

John Wallace includes this play among those which contain politically significant banishments, leading to an anti-Exclusion moral.[28] However, the banishments of Elianor and Suffolk are entirely just and merited even in Shakespeare, and Crowne's worsening of these characters removes any doubt. Nor does Crowne's ending seem to offer an anti-Exclusion message. The emphasis on the monarchy's weakness in the final speeches is coupled with a stressing of papist culpability through increasing the Cardinal's demented guilt: first we see the Cardinal troubled in his conscience, but using specious arguments to quell the urge to confess his sins. Then the ghost of Gloucester appears and the Cardinal is thrown into a torment of fear, promising to 'do cruel Pennance all my life' (5. 2. p. 64) if the ghost will leave him alone. The first murderer comments, 'Is his Infallibility come to that? A Pox of his Doctrines, | He has damn'd himself and me too' (p. 63). Later he repeats, 'Oh! gallant, brave Infallibility!', and the second murderer tells the King, 'He's fallen into a fit of Infallible Madness' (ibid.).

The queen blames her own ambition for Suffolk's death, and asks heaven's forgiveness. She utters a curse upon England which is actually a comprehensive indictment of Crowne's own times, like Vendosme's in *The Ambitious Statesman*. It is here that we might expect to find anti-Whiggery:

> May'st thou ne're breed brave Man, or if thou dost,
> Oh! let him be thy Ruine, or thou his.
> May all thy Witty men be sadly Vitious,

Let sloth devour their Fortunes, Fools their Fame,
Lewdness their Souls, their Bodies Foul Disease.
May thy Wise Men be Factious, and head Fools,
If they be honest let e'm lose their Heads.
Let thy Brave Men against thy self be bravest,
Be Men at foreign, Devils at Civil War.
Let all thy Pious Sons with Zeal run mad,
And make Religion thy Reproach and Curse.
May'st thou have all Religions to confound thee,
And none to save thee.

(5. 2. p. 67)

There does seem to be satire of Whigs and dissenters here. There is also a rather obvious satire of Crowne's *bête noire* Rochester. If dissent is alluded to, so is popery. The supineness of the Church of England seems to be the subject of the last line: a Whiggish theme in Shadwell's *The Lancashire Witches*. Criticism of Whigs is not only rather token, but offset by satire of court corruption. It is the latter which is Crowne's focus in the play as a whole. Lust and corruption at court in *The Ambitious Statesman* were secondary to the demonization of rebellion in the Constable; but here York's rebellion is marginal, and Suffolk's is associated with popery, not Whiggery. The hero is not a tormented quietist, like Vendosme, but a virile, quasi-Protestant patriot. The spectacle of weak monarchy surrounded by a court where lust, ambition, and popery are rampant is highly provocative, and it is as unsurprising that the play offended the authorities as it is extraordinary and striking that Crowne should have given his 'aversions' such free rein.

1681–1683: Reaction and the City

The prologues and epilogues of the phase of the Tory reaction are comparatively uniform in tone and content. A couple of examples will serve to illustrate the new, shriller Toryism in the theatres. D'Urfey's *The Royalist* (January 1682) seems to epitomize royalism's new ascendancy. It manages to convey at the same time both the inevitable triumph of royalism, and a sense that the royalists are beleaguered and worthy of pity and admiration; that royalism is defensive of a threatened order, but also going on the offensive. The prologue associates better times for the theatre with the Tory victory, and affects to believe that the Whigs were previously in the theatrical ascendant: 'How! the House full! and at a *Royal Play*!' There is the familiar association of the Whigs and critics who rail against Monarch Wit. Satirical targets include '*Factious Juries* and *Associations*' and 'Petitions', as well as those who, like the author's Sir Barnaby Whigg in the play of that name, have changed sides, and those who are royalists for reasons of 'Art' rather than 'Nature', unlike the hero of the present play. This hero, Sir Charles Kinglove, speaks the prologue. He is 'a Lover of Monarchy and Prerogative' (actors' names). In him we find the associated qualities of royalism, good-hearted simplicity, civility, honour, stoicism in the face of adversity, friendship, and good living. Like Dryden's Antony as described in the prologue to *All For Love*, and like the merciful Charles of royalist ideology, he is 'wondrous kind'. The speaker facetiously suggests himself for City office: he would be a better Common-Councilman than the present 'Factious Furies'. The City is a necessary target, remaining a Whig stronghold despite the election of Tory Sir John Moore as Lord Mayor. Wondrous kindness is not the prevailing note as the speaker concludes by condemning the 1660 Act of Oblivion, suggesting that the City Whigs are the radicals of 1660 not by analogy but in the flesh, and foreseeing 'justice' in the City:

> Hang up all those for an Example show,
> That have deserved it Twenty years ago.　(42–3)

The epilogue is spoken by the comic actor Cave Underhill, who played the part of one of Sir Charles's tenants who 'afterwards made Evidences against him' (actors' names). He thus resembles not only interregnum turncoats, but Popish Plot witness Stephen Dugdale. The speaker humorously protests that he is 'Tory Cave' (l. 6). There is the familiar idea that those who oppose James do so for (financial) 'Int'rest' (l. 10); whereas the speaker 'rores in Coffee-house, and wasts his Wealth, | Toping the Gentlemen in *Scotland's* Health [i.e. that of James and his entourage]' (7–8). As in the prologue to Behn's *The False Count*, there is a sarcastic appeal to the theatre's 'Friend's i' th' City' (l. 15). The speaker will change his honest Tory ways, and learn to lie and swear falsely, in exchange for citizen applause. This would make him a good candidate for Sheriff.[29]

The preface form lends itself to a more uncompromising tone than would an epistle dedicatory. In his preface D'Urfey affects to believe that the times are so disrupted by fanaticism that his published play can hardly be expected to succeed, yet he simultaneously boasts of its theatrical success. Foreshadowing Dryden's epilogue to *The Duke of Guise*, there is an attack not only on Whigs, but upon waverers. As in the prologue, it is asserted that those who 'side with *Rebellion* and *Faction*' do so 'for the sake of *Interest*' (sig. A1r). Most of the preface is devoted to satire of Whigs and fanatics, with all the familiar tropes of Toryism in virulent form. Whigs are equated with papists, likened to radical commonwealthsmen of the interregnum, and tarred with the brush of republicanism. They are mischief-making rabble-rousers, base-born artisans. They hypocritically fight for religion, though they are irreligious, and for property, though they are thieving tradesmen. They are hostile to art and wit. The idea of sexual monstrosity is invoked in the comparison of Titus Oates to a shrewish woman (sig. A2v). Oates is also likened to a snapping dog, perhaps reversing Whig satire of L'Estrange as dog Towser, barking for his royal masters. The tone throughout is scathing and abusive.

The virulence of the Tory reaction may also be illustrated by Dryden's prologue and epilogue to *The Duke of Guise*, spoken in November 1682 and both printed as broadsides. The attack on Whigs in the prologue also embraces both Parliament and the City. The familiar accusation that the Whigs want 1641 to come again is made in a gloating way which envisages their downfall. They are ironically addressed:

> Go on; and bite, ev'n though the Hook lies bare;
> Twice in one Age expell the lawfull Heir:
> Once more decide Religion by the Sword;
> And purchase for us a new Tyrant Lord.
> Pray for your King; but yet your Purses spare;
> Make him not two-Pence richer by your Prayer.
> To show you love him much, chastise him more:
> And make him very Great, and very Poor.

---

[29] For the political controversy surrounding the sheriffs' elections, see Haley, *Shaftesbury*, 409, 582, 657, 693, 697–703; also the discussion in Ch. 2.

> Push him to Wars, but still no Pence advance;
> Let him lose *England* to recover *France*.
> Cry Freedom up with Popular noisy Votes:
> And get enough to cut each others Throats,
> Lop all the Rights that fence your Monarch's Throne;
> For fear of too much Pow'r, pray leave him none.
> A noise was made of Arbitrary Sway;
> But in Revenge, you Whiggs, have found a way,
> An Arbitrary Duty now to pay.
> Let his own Servants turn, to save their stake;
> Glean from his plenty, and his wants forsake.
> But let some *Judas* near his Person stay,
> To swallow the last Sop, and then betray.
> Make *London* independent of the Crown:
> A Realm apart; the Kingdom of the Town.
> Let *Ignoramus* Juries find no Traitors:
> And *Ignoramus* Poets scribble Satyres,
> And, that your meaning none may fail to scan,
> Doe, what in Coffee-houses you began;
> Pull down the Master, and Set up the Man.

In the epilogue, which Winn describes as 'the most vindictive of all Dryden's partisan writings'[30] Dryden excoriates not only Whigs but Trimmers, following the example of L'Estrange, who attacked Trimmers in *The Observator* in November 1682:

> Now since the Weight hangs all on one side, Brother,
> You *Trimmers* shou'd, to poize it, hang on t'other.
> Damn'd Neuters, in their middle way of steering,
> Are neither Fish, nor Flesh, nor good Red-Herring:
> Not Whiggs, nor Tories they; nor this, nor that;
> Not Birds, nor Beasts; but just a Kind of Bat:
> A Twilight Animal; true to neither Cause,
> With Tory Wings, but Whiggish Teeth and Claws.

This strident piece shows the shrillness of someone who has had a bad scare. The effort of persecution of Whigs and dissent in this period, discussed earlier, belies the inevitability of Tory victory which is claimed in prologues and epilogues. The naturalness of the victory is an ideological construct, involving an effort of will.

---

[30] Winn, *John Dryden and his World*, 371.

The fate of Crowne's *City Politiques* illustrates the narrowness and initial uncertainty of Tory victory. The play was licensed on 15 June 1682, but the licence was withdrawn on 16 June and not granted again until 18 December. The play finally had its première on 19 January 1683.[31] The same problem affected *The Duke of Guise*, banned in July 1682 and not performed until late November. It was necessary to the court to avoid additional provocations around the time of the rigged sheriffs' elections, themselves enough of a provocation. What is also suggested by these events is how quickly (even to the point of being a little premature) and strenuously Crowne had adapted to the Tory reaction in his play. ˊ

City Politiques is a work of great ideological ingenuity, in which the need to resort to vote-rigging backed by force is covered over, as the Whigs are most effectively rendered ridiculous through satire. The play really does contain the personations of notable Whigs which critics have been so excessively fond of discerning in other plays, though Crowne denies this in his preface to the reader for reasons of tact or tactics (4). Dr Sanchy represents Titus Oates, as Crowne admits in his preface, and the Catholic Bricklayer represents Stephen College, the so-called Protestant joiner executed in 1681. Other supposed personations may be generic, rather than specific. The Podesta is probably, as Wilson argues, a composite of City Whigs, of which Slingsby Bethel is the chief component.[32] The old lawyer, Bartoline, is said by Crowne in his preface to represent 'the general corruption of lawyers' (ibid.), but has been plausibly identified with Sir John Maynard.[33] The bad poet, Craffy, may also represent supposedly dull Whig poets in general, although Wilson argues quite plausibly for a possible iden-

[31] As a reference in the *Newdigate Newsletters* makes clear: Wilson, 'Theatre Notes from the *Newdigate Newsletters*', 81.

[32] Wilson, in introduction to *City Politiques*, pp. xv–xvi. In addition to the points about puritanism and parsimony referred to by Wilson, a particular focus on Bethel and/or Cornish is suggested by the choice of *podestà*, a judicial officer in Italian cities and therefore more directly comparable to the sheriffs than the mayor; also by the Podesta's being refused a knighthood, 2. 1. 1–3: for Charles's refusal to knight Bethel and Cornish, see Hutton, *Charles the Second*, 392. Arthur F. White's argument that the Podesta may represent Shaftesbury, though 'only in a general way' (*John Crowne: His Life and Dramatic Works*, 130), seems untenable

[33] McMullin, 'Serjeant Maynard's Teeth'.

tification with Samuel Pordage.[34] One or more of the rakes was identified by contemporaries with Rochester.[35]

Crowne's prologue and epilogue are virulently Tory pieces, similar in ideological content to many others in this period. In the prologue, Tory ascendancy is portrayed as the abatement of 'frenzy' and the rise of 'wit'. Whigs are accused of treason, being worse than Oliver Cromwell, friendship with the Devil, drunkenness, lechery, rebellion, and having too much money to spend. The familiar parallel between papists and dissenters is invoked. City Whigs are attacked both for packing juries and for choosing dull poets. The epilogue spoken by Leigh, who played the lawyer, associates Tories and good poets as poor but honest, while the lawyers are time-servers who will change sides if paid enough. We are informed that 'Wit is a Tory'.

The play's topicality is transparent, despite Crowne's setting the action in Naples. This is a means of ostensibly denying topical allusion, whilst covertly drawing attention to it. It may also have a more subtle motive, suggesting that the City of London Whigs aspire to the power and autonomy of an Italian city-state. Topical references are copious. Craffy is shown to write the Whig responses to Dryden's *Absalom and Achitophel* and *The Medal*. The characters refer to each other as Whigs (e.g. 1. 2. 243; 2. 1. 297), and Tories (e.g. 1. 1. 188, 2. 1. 124–5, 148). There are repeated allusions to the conflict over the sheriffs' election, presumably added between first composition and performance. The tone is royalist: the 'foolish headstrong city' is 'factious' because it elects the candidate of its choice. The Governor says, 'I thought his Excellency the Viceroy had given you intimation another person would be more pleasing to him, and in this juncture more fitting for office' (1. 2. 6–8). It is interesting that the Bricklayer's assertion that tricks were used to hinder the election is not denied: Crowne is not concerned to assert that the people's choice is Tory rather than Whig, but to

---

[34] Wilson, in introduction to *City Politiques*, p. xvii.

[35] Kaufman, in 'Civil Politics–Sexual Politics', argues for an identification of Florio with Rochester. Rochester disguised himself, for example, as a tradesman or a quack (Winn, *John Dryden and his World*, 590), and this resembles Artall's masquerade. There may, then, be a double satire of Rochester here. As noted above, Crowne was cudgelled on 24 Jan. 1683 by supporters of the deceased Rochester, thought to have been satirized in the play (Van Lennep *et al.* (eds.), *London Stage*, 318).

deny them a choice. The Bricklayer's claim that 'we have a charter for the free election of our magistrate and what we have done our charter will justify' (1. 2. 29–30), though it may seem reasonable to the modern reader familiar with the rule of law, seems in context to set an ideological framework for the impending attack upon the City of London's Charter. Action against the Whigs is justified because they threaten the social hierarchy, as is shown by the fact that a bricklayer presumes to tell the Governor the law.

Tory pamphlets and prologues commonly refer to Whigs as fools and knaves, and *City Politiques* is an anatomy of Whiggish folly and knavery. Crowne speaks in his preface of the importance of 'good manners' (6), and the Whigs are satirized for their bad manners, especially in the person of Craffy. In 1. 2 the Governor's mercy and good manners are contrasted to the Whigs' uncouth insistence on the letter of the law. The Podesta wants to regulate people's pleasures and 'have all persons eat and drink according to the law' (1. 2. 59). Whig philistinism is also satirized in Craffy's bad poetry and in the Podesta's perception of him as a great wit. This misperception is coupled with mistrust of poetic endeavour: 'Well, the Lord bless thee and deliver thee from poetry, say I' (4. 1. 188). Sanchy's ignorance and pretence of learning reinforce the idea that 'Wit is a Tory'. Philistinism is associated with the general frenzy and impropriety to which Crowne draws attention in his preface and prologue: Craffy is not only a bad poet, but also a drunkard and supposedly mad; Sanchy is 'a little cracked' (5. 3. 69–70).

Credulity is also satirized: 'What an excellent thing and how useful in the world is credulity' (3. 327–8), exclaims Rosaura, as the lovers get rid of the Podesta with false news of a French invasion. We also learn that the quality is useful to the fop who wants credit from tradesmen, the politician who misleads the rabble, and the 'swearer' (3. 333). The credulous citizens are much given to seeing plots where none exist (3. 493, 522; 4. 1. 272). In more sinister vein, they construct sham plots, as when Craffy is ordered by his father to 'affront the clergy and make 'em suspected for plotters' (1. 1. 302–3). The Oates figure, Dr Sanchy, is confident that he can impose on the credulity of the multitude in making ridiculous accusations against the Viceroy:

'The Viceroy is a pure canary bird; I'll have him turned out of his place. I'll prove he is a Mahometan; he was circumcised at Bar-bar-badoes' (5. 2. 151–3). The Popish Plot accusations are rendered ridiculous by association. The Whigs do not perceive real plots: Craffy's true statement that Rosaura and Florio are cuckolding his father in the bedroom is seen as a 'sham plot' (4. 3. 50). The Popish Plot scare is clearly shown as a fraud. The real plot is the 'true Protestant' one. The Whigs, though legalistic, pervert justice.

Pride is a prevalent quality. The Podesta in particular is much given to remarks such as 'I'm never mistaken' (2. 1. 393). His thwarted pride is partly responsible for his political opposition, as we see when he is passed over for favour by the Viceroy: 'Not knight me? When he knew I was a proud man, a very proud man, opposed him out o' pride, and a knighthood might ha' bought me. He shall repent it' (2. 1. 1–3). Pride is thus coupled with ambition. It is also associated with presumption, as when the Podesta lays claim to 'reasons of state' (3. 227), and with money-mindedness: he will receive Bartoline's wife into his house gladly when offered a piece of plate and jewellery, though he demurred before. He is depicted as excessively wealthy, with the resentment often shown by poor Tories— and poets—towards rich merchants and citizens, and he also makes free with civic funds. Similarly, Bartoline only cares about money and self-interest. In a parody of the Exclusion issue, he is asked to draw up articles against the Viceroy. He refuses, but pockets the fee. Appeals to his patriotism utterly fail, but he agrees to advise the City privately for £1,000, whilst also consenting to advise the Viceroy privately for cash. This changeability and fundamental self-interest is also apparent when the Bricklayer is arrested and tells the Governor, 'Procure me a pension, I'll come over to your party' (1. 2. 112–13). Like D'Urfey's Sir Barnaby Whigg, the Podesta is tricked with spurious promises of advancement, on condition he sacrifices his allegiance and his comrades. He replies: 'Ay, and my father too, if he were alive; he should hang 'em all' (5. 3. 11–12). Moreover, like the rebels and conspirators in other Tory plays, Crowne's Whigs are constantly fighting among themselves.

Irreligion and anti-clericalism are satirized in Craffy:

... for the locking of a man to a woman in marriage, or in a pew at church, are only a couple of church tricks to get money, one for the priest and t'other for the sexton; that's all. (1. 1. 265–8)

I don't know whether I have a soul or no. (1. 1. 320)

... you know we use to jeer the church, sir. (2. 1. 80)

I hope shortly to leave never a priest in Christendom. (2. 1. 86)

To his mother-in-law, with whom he wants to commit incest, he says, 'Thou art only tacked to my father's side by a priest' (3. 454–5). Dr Sanchy is similarly atheistical: 'Hang conscience! I do it out o' matter o'honour and matter of revenge. The priests are rascals and slight me, and I'll slight their prayers' (2. 1. 260). Prayer 'is but a thing of form to please the people' (2. 1. 289).

There is also satire of puritanism: the Whigs are 'dull lewd saints' (1. 1. 24), godly and humourless. Puritanism is the velvet glove on the iron fist of an assault on Church and state which could culminate in interregnum-style sequestration: 'You have a worse design on religion, to make her a bawd to carry on some lewd project' (1. 1. 103); 'You would babble and scribble us out of our estates' (1. 1. 127; cf. 4. 1. 402–3). The claim to be true or loyal Protestants is derided in the preface (7) and the play:

> There is in every true Protestant breast
> A Heraclitus Ridens, his contest,
> A knave in earnest and a saint in jest.
> The saint looks up to heaven, the knave that while
> Your pocket picks, and at the cheat does smile.

> (1. 1. 152–3; cf. 1. 1. 309–11, 323–4)

The Naples setting permits an association with popery and Roman Catholic forms of worship also, which fits with the coupling of papists and dissenters in the prologue (e.g. 1. 1. 228–30, 309–11; 4. 1. 396). Thus the City Whigs are associated with both dissent and popery, as well as with 'Hobbism' and 'atheism' (cf. 4. 1. 295).

Francophobia is satirized in the Podesta's fear of Florio's tale of a French invasion. Like fear of plots, Francophobia is false, hysterical and silly, and deliberate and self-serving: as the Podesta remarks, 'I can put the city in arms upon pretense of a

French invasion, but when they see no invasion, and the fright is over, how shall I keep up that army?' (2. 1. 94–5). Also touched upon in the Podesta's reference to his army is the tendency towards arbitrary power, which emanates not from the Viceroy, but from the Podesta and his city cronies. This reverses parliamentary concerns about Charles's 'arbitrary government' and failure to disband the army in the late 1670s. A 'Tory association pledge' written by Florio makes the accusation that 'a certain sort of people, consisting of Hobbists, atheists, fanatics, and republicans, have for several years past pursued a pernicious plot to root out the true religion, subvert our laws and liberties, and set up arbitrary power' (4. 1. 295). They design to bring the rabble to power through '*ignoramus* garrisons' (306), a reference to the City juries which had freed Whigs, including Shaftesbury, on a verdict of 'ignoramus'. Artall uses similar language more facetiously when he says, 'I venture boldly into the dominion of these arbitrary rogues, who have a strange, absolute authority over their own consciences in lying and swearing' (4. 3. 113–16).

This primary message of the play against the folly and knavery of political and social presumption is summed up by the Governor at the end:

The Viceroy and all of us will put an end to his absolute negative voice, his great power of degrading lords and dukes into rogues and rascals, if they will not purchase of him the confirmation of their titles by capping to him—nay, of deposing kings if they slight his counsels. We will also dissolve all his privy council. And so, gentlemen, henceforward be wise, leave off the new trade you have taken up of managing state affairs, and betake yourselves to the callings you were bred to and understand. Be honest; meddle not with other men's matters, especially with government; 'tis none of your right. (5. 3. 385–95)

The role of libertinism in the play is more complex, and may represent a contradiction in its Tory message. The primary function of the libertines is, of course, to represent the Whig cits as cuckolds who cannot govern their own households, let alone the state. Yet the clear positive value placed upon rakishness in Behn's and D'Urfey's analogous anti-cit comedies *The City Heiress* and *Sir Barnaby Whigg* is lacking. Libertinism is satirized in the foolish Craffy. It is less clear what Crowne's attitude to it is in Artall, and in Florio, self-styled 'king of libertines' (3. 353–4). The Whigs are satirized for their unsusceptibility to women: when Rosaura swoons, Dr Sanchy says, 'Carry her away, don't let us be troubled with women' (4. 1. 283). Later the Bricklayer tells her, 'woman; don't make more fiddle-faddle than needs, and hinder us from business of consequence' (5. 2. 24). This should suggest that the rakes' susceptibility is to be viewed indulgently. Cuckolding the Whig seems a worthy Tory aim, and libertinism is expressed in Tory metaphors. At one point Florio's use of metaphor even associates him with Charles II, the restored monarch in 1660:

FL. Then we may securely hoist sail for the haven of love. All the mud that barred it up we have conveyed away, and I will come ashore on these white cliffs, and plant my heart there forever.
ROS. Do so, and I'll promise thee the happiness and wealth I gain by the residence of my prince shall not make me ungratefully factious. Be true to me. and I'll be most loyal to thee. (5.2. 199–205)

However, this kind of language is mocked and subverted by Florio's use of similar metaphors to reproach Craffy for wanting to do what he himself aims to: seduce Rosaura:

FL. I'll fortify her.
CR. With godly counsels! Putting forces into her head will never fortify her tail. What signifies fortifying the capital city when the remote provinces rebel?
FL. I shall bring down the prince of the country, your father, sir, upon you, who if he cannot quell the rebellion shall deal with you. (1. 1. 288–94)

Florio's specious deployment of the language of Tory patriarchalism masks his purpose to undermine the family. The language itself is tainted or trivialized in the process.

Moreover, Florio conquers Rosaura in a metaphor of tyranny and political irresponsibility:

Then will I be a second Nero; I have put all my city in a flame.
And now, with harp in hand I will survey
My burning Rome, and whilst it burns I'll play.

(4. 1. 426–9)

This seems thoroughly to compromise his Tory rhetoric of libertinism. Paradoxically, Florio is morally better in his pious pretence than in his real persona. Furthermore, it seems odd from a Tory point of view that Florio makes the same mocking use of Tory language, above, as he does of Whig language here: 'He is not to be regarded who has a right to govern, but he who can best serve the ends of government. I can better serve the ends of your lady than you can, so I lay claim to your lady (5. 3. 179–82). He tells the Podesta Rosaura 'is a true Whig and has revolted from you because you did not pay her nightly pension well' (5. 3. 172–3). Florio here 'outwhigs' the Whigs, outdoing the Podesta in the specious use of language as a cover for self-interest and the denial of sacred bonds. In this context, he is no better than they are, and possibly worse.

Artall is in some sense the play's debunking centre. He is also 'a debauch that follows the Court' (dramatis personae). When Florio, feigning Whiggery, calls Artall an atheist (1. 1. 143), he is probably right. Artall, pretending to be Florio, calls himself an atheist (2. 1. 473, 501, 503). Like Florio, Artall is politically irresponsible, and not just at the level of metaphor. When the Whig lawyer whom Artall has cuckolded threatens to ruin him, Artall exclaims, 'in a little time will I have forty swords at your throat, French swords. I'll let in the enemy, and cut the throats of such rogues as you . . . Better be ruled by the swords of gallant men than the mercenary tongues of such rascals as you are' (5. 1. 100–5). This seems like a parody of Tory concern to validate class distinction against patriotism. It is a mirror image of Whig Francophobia. Kaufman points out that Florio and Artall, 'Although they embody audacious wit and perform the necessary political ritual of "horning the cit," . . . are nonetheless ambiguous and finally inadequate characters who represent for Crowne a sense of debasement.'[36]

Moreover, the triumphant success of the cuckolding raises moral problems. Such success is not as universal in comedies as might be supposed. Behn avoids it in *The Round-heads*. I do not only mean that the rakes and the heroine are morally compromised by it in seventeenth-century terms, but also that the supposed villains, the Podesta and Bartoline, are thereby transformed into sympathetic victims. Similarly, the idea that libertinism might be palliated in the rakes but derided in Craffy is

---

[36] Kaufman, 'Civil Politics–Sexual Politics', 77.

problematic, not only because the rakes are not distinguished from Craffy by personal or moral superiority, but also because Craffy is a victim, duped and left out in the cold. He is quite pitiable in the extremity of his passion, prepared if necessary to defy his father and be turned out. Staves notes that Craffy also has the role of exposing the folly and hypocrisy of his father and the Whigs, so that 'we do not entirely despise him'.[37] Conversely, there is a moment when Craffy is not critical of his father, when he becomes (momentarily) positively sympathetic: 'Nay, prithee father, don't take on thus; thou'lt make me cry too' (4. 3. 148).

These aspects do pose some contradiction for the play's Toryism. Wilson's suggestion that the rakes represent aristocratic Whig leaders does not seem tenable. Leaving aside the similarity of their role to that of rakish heroes in Behn and D'Urfey, the rakes are masquerading as Whigs, and make it clear from the start that this is a distasteful necessity in the cause of amorous intrigue. Florio is a 'Tory in masquerade' (5. 3. 145). The statement in the dramatis personae that Artall 'follows the Court' means he is of the opposite political persuasion to that of the Whigs; thus the Podesta says at the end, 'So the Whigs are all to go to pot, and the Court to win the game' (5. 3. 61). As we shall see in Chapter 5, libertinism was consistently associated with the court and with royalism, and attacks on it such as Shadwell's *The Libertine* (1675) were seen as having the force of political opposition. It seems unlikely, then, that the libertine characters suggested primarily to contemporaries another aspect of Whiggery, or a composite of leading Whigs. We are told that 'there were mighty clappings among the people of both partyes in Expressing either their satisfaction or displeasure'.[38] So the Tories did not clap all the time, nor did the Whigs continually boo. Perhaps the satire of court rakes was pleasing to the Whigs and gall to the Tories.

City Politiques succeeds in demonizing the Whigs wholeheartedly, without offering a positive image of the court, which is to 'win the game' now that the Whigs have gone to pot.

* * *

---

[37] Staves, *Players' Scepters*, 239.
[38] Wilson, 'Theatre Notes from the *Newdigate Newsletters*', 81.

In his epilogue to *City Politiques* Crowne alludes to himself as a 'swingeing Tory'. However, in his preface, he claims for himself a past of virulent Tory partisanship, and a calmer present. Crowne's persona in the preface is custodian of reason and moderation against faction and frenzy, and in between papists and Whigs. What is interesting about the preface is not the superficially obvious Tory partisanship, but precisely the difference in tone from the play and its prologue and epilogue.[39] If a text in which Crowne asserts his consistent Toryism is itself somewhat inconsistent in political tone with the play it prefaces, it seems surprising that modern critics have taken the assertion at face value. It is important to recognize Crowne's adept and subtle shifts in political tone and perspective.[40] As I pointed out at the beginning of this chapter, this characteristic is shared by other dramatists.

Crowne's plays, like the tone of other plays and of prologues and epilogues, shift from season to season with the shifts in the immediate political situation. This does not mean that Crowne was simply opportunistic. Underlying these shifts in emphasis seems to be a consistent nexus of attitudes and opinions: anti-dissent, anti-papist, anti-court, anti-rebel, anti-lawyer. His plays emphasize different aspects of this nexus at different political times. Even so, the shifts are striking. Crowne's poverty and dependence must have been a factor. The playwrights of this period certainly aspired to be more than mere 'hired pens',[41] but

---

[39] Crowne's preface is probably less partisan than Wilson's introduction to the modern edition, in which all mention of Whig successes is omitted, and the description of Shaftesbury (p. xvi) is taken from a Tory pamphlet.

[40] Neman, in 'Setting the Record Straight on John Crowne', takes account of Crowne's changing political perspective, but errs in conflating *The Misery of Civil-War*, *Thyestes*, and *Henry VI: The First Part* as royalist dramas of equal fervour, and in regarding the introduction of anti-Catholicism as a miscalculation (16–17). Her statement that in *City Politiques* Crowne 'did not have the political foresight to discern the emerging parliamentary power and thus realize the dangers in offending important Whigs' ignores the Tory reaction of 1682–7.

[41] The accusation of being a hired pen was commonplace. Like the charge of lechery, it was a slur with which to taint enemies. L'Estrange accuses Marvell of it (*An Account of the Growth of Knavery*, 6), Marvell accuses Nedham of it (*An Account of the Growth of Popery and Arbitrary Government*, 121). In *The Vindication* Dryden accuses Shadwell and Settle of being pensioners of the Whigs (45) and denies that he is a 'Mercenary Scribler' (20), a response to allegations that his views are prompted by his government pension. In this context I think Chernaik's certainty in *The Poet's Time* that Marvell was Shaftesbury's hired pen is misplaced (cf.

they also wanted to succeed in a period in which patronage was normal and had by no means been replaced by the market. They dedicated their work to patrons or potential patrons, and complained of the want of patronage and the failure of the age to place a proper valuation on poets. Moreover, the period was one in which 'enthusiasm' was condemned and satirized, while moderation and willingness to accommodate one's ideas to the powers-that-be were positively valued.

We might speculate that the drama was more likely to be intensely topical because it was still perceived as essentially popular rather than 'high' culture.[42] We can say, cynically, that catering to shifting opinion is good box office, or, positively, that the drama as popular culture has its finger on the pulse of popular feeling. Whatever the reason: need of patronage, desire to be in tune with the times, or simple pragmatism, the intense topicality of the drama is not in doubt.

In the next two chapters I want to 'stand back' from this topicality and take a different perspective, drawing out from the plays an account of the dramatic language of partisanship which has so often been misread. Chapter 6 re-enters the historical arena, showing how dramatists bandy this dramatic language of politics to and fro in an attempt at political intervention.

Wallace, *Destiny his Choice*, but contrast the more cautious view of Legouis in *Andrew Marvell: Poet, Puritan, Patriot*).

[42] Sampson, 'Some Bibliographical Evidence concerning Restoration Attitudes towards Drama'; Peters, *Congreve, the Drama and the Printed Word*.

CHAPTER 4

The Dramatic Language of Politics

THROUGHOUT the Exclusion Crisis period we can identify a common dramatic language of politics in the work of dramatists of differing political persuasions and perspectives. Within the framework of this common dramatic language of politics, there are distinctly royalist and opposition ways of treating common themes, and specifically royalist and opposition themes and tropes. This is true even at the early stage of the crisis when few dramatists take sides. As the crisis develops, the distinct political language of Whig and Tory plays can be clearly identified. Of course this does not mean that all plays are either Whig or Tory, or that contradiction is absent.[1] However, discovering and defining the themes and tropes of Toryism and Whiggery is necessary in order to see where they are absent, break down, or are used in a way which seems contradictory. We need to break the pieces apart in order to put them back together again and see the complexity of the whole.

I shall attempt to offer a careful account of the dramatic language of politics, which attempts to distinguish between Whig and Tory versions of common themes and to reveal the distinct tropes of Whiggism and Toryism. I shall divide my account into three sections: social order and disorder, religion, and class. First I want to make some basic and very important points about how to read the language of politics.

Reading the Language of Politics

The language of political partisanship has to be read carefully. At first it may appear as if everybody appears to be saying the

---

[1] Moreover, political reference may be gratuitous, as in D'Urfey's *The Virtuous Wife* where there is a Whig song in the text (included in *Choice Ayres and Songs* under the title 'The Loyal Protestant': Van Ennep *et al.* (eds.), *London Stage*, 281), sung by a nonentity and ignored by the characters, and an equally casual Tory jibe in the epilogue.

same thing. The rhetorics of Toryism and Whiggery have much in common, and this can be misleading.[2] However, this does not mean that they are not distinct. Both sides had a plausible claim to represent tradition: Tories could claim continuity with the rudely interrupted reign of the sainted martyr Charles I, and Whigs could profess to stand for traditional parliamentary, Protestant, and legal liberties. Both sides claimed to stand for the defence of property; but the threat to property was seen by Whigs as popery and by Tories as puritan-inspired interregnum-style sequestration. Both sides raised the undesirable spectre of renewed civil war, though they disagreed on the source of the danger: Tories accused Whigs of fomenting rebellion; Whigs asserted that foreign and popish influence in high places and the intransigence of the king's 'bad advisers' was the problem.

Everyone professed to agree on loyalty to the existing sovereign. However, loyalty meant different things for Tories and Whigs. Loyalty to the king and the hereditary succession becomes an absolute value in Tory plays, associated with quietism. It takes no account of the monarch's faults (which are palliated anyway), and it must be loyalty without thought of self, or hope of reward. As Kinglove, hero of D'Urfey's *The Royalist*, a play set in the interregnum, puts it: 'true Loyalty expects no reward' (53). He gives everything he has to the exiled king because:

> A Loyal Subject thinks himself repaid
> By purchasing his Country peace and Honour.
>
> (5. 1. p. 53)

This can be a problem for Toryism, since the old cavaliers had complained bitterly throughout the 1660s that the king had pardoned rebels and ignored their own claims to favour and redress: Marvell is able to exploit this in his *Account*.[3] William Whitaker tackles this directly in *The Conspiracy*, a fervently royalist drama which, as I noted in Chapter 1, revives the

---

[2] See e.g. Brown, 'The Dryden–Lee Collaboration' and 'Nathaniel Lee's Political Drama' for the view that Whig and Tory plays scarcely differ; and my critique in ' "Partial Tyrants" and "Freeborn People" ' in *Lucius Junius Brutus* and 'Interpreting the Politics of Restoration Drama'.

[3] 'These Conspirators are such as have not one drop of *Cavalier Blood*, or no *Bowels* at least of a *Cavalier* in them; but have starved them, to Revel and Surfet upon their Calamities, making their Persons, and the very Cause, by pretending to it themselves, almost Ridiculous' (Marvell, *An Account*, 15).

defunct form of the royalist heroic play in rhyming couplets. A character called Ipsir complains:

> none prosper well of late,
> But the meer Rogues, the Weather-cocks of State:
> The Wealth which in Rebellious times they gain'd,
> Has favour in succeeding Courts obtain'd:
> The Royalist in vain to Court does go;
> The Rogue that made him needy, keeps him so.
>
> (4. pp. 41–2)

He is rebuked by the saintly Kuperli, who is 'all Soul, his Soul all loyalty' (5. p. 44):

> we blame the Emperour
> Sometimes for things that are not in his pow'r . . .
> We never can with all our care avoid,
> But some rich Villains will be still imploid.
>
> (4. p. 42)[4]

Moreover, the complaint is voiced in the play in a context which renders it untrue and ridiculous; and in any case the whole question is overshadowed by the primary problem posed by rebels and traitors. At the end of the play, loyal service is rewarded, but loyalty would have been its own reward if necessary: 'the virtuous and the Loyal mind | Within it self its own reward does find' (5. p. '54' [52]).

In Whig plays the construction of loyalty is different. Where Whitaker sees loyalty as unswerving obedience to the king, for Whigs it means not being afraid to advise the king for his own and the country's good. In his epistle dedicatory to *The Female Prelate* Settle says his patron, the Whig leader Shaftesbury, is truly loyal because he scorns the 'flattering and mercenary service' of those who merely reflect the king's wishes rather than advising him as he needs to be advised, 'for without derogation to the Divinity of a Crown, Kings are sometimes but Men' (sig. A1ᵛ). Settle also co-opts the language of virtue for its own sake, rather than for selfish or ambitious motives; 'If Loyalty were ever truely generous, 'tis in your Lordship; for with the Philosophers description of Vertue, 'tis alone its own Reward.' Shaftesbury's pursuit of his political principles had led to loss of

---

4 Cf. the conversation between Ipsir and Kuperli in Act 2, p. 18.

office and to expenditure which was almost to bankrupt his estate. Like the villainous Constable in Crowne's *The Ambitious Statesman*, Shaftesbury risked confiscation of his estates.[5] For Crowne willingness to risk all is dangerous fanaticism; for Settle it is patriotic self-sacrifice.[6]

In Dryden's and Lee's *The Duke of Guise* Whig claims to be the best loyalists because they were not afraid to advise the king for his own good are depicted as a deliberately disingenuous 'show of Loyalty' (4. 1. 41). The rebels' aim to 'preserve the King, his Pow'r and Person' is 'A pretty Blind to make the Shoot secure' (1. 1. p. 2). Guise continually professes to be a 'Dutious Loyal Subject' (4. 3. p. 47), while plotting treason.[7] Whigs responded angrily to this. Thomas Hunt's *A Defence of the Charter and Municipal Rights of the City of London and the Rights of Other Municipal Cities and Towns of England* attacks *The Duke of Guise* as the epitome of pernicious and deluded Toryism: 'Their Loyalty is Slavery, their Religion the Princes pleasure' (11). Whig loyalty involves defending 'our antient Government, our pretious liberties, our Religion it self . . . We do not show our Loyalty, but discover an ignominious baseness, if we yeeld up our rights at the perswasion of a Courtier, who tells us it is for the Kings Service: when he is thereby promoting his own advantages and projects' (44–5). As for Settle, so for critics of *The Duke of Guise*, Whig loyalty involves self-sacrifice. This is brought out in '*Sol* in Opposition to *Saturn*; or, A Short Return to a Late Tragedy Call'd *The Duke of Guise*' which offers praise of Monmouth, considered to have been maligned in the play:

> Wert thou ambitious, thou hadst yet been high,
> But this thy fall doth prove thy Loyalty.[8]

[5] Haley, *Shaftesbury*, 578, 725–7. See also the discussion of the persecution of the Whigs in Ch. 3.

[6] Price notes, 'In their propaganda the Country party made much of the fact that they were honest men willing to risk their fortunes to ensure that parliament was not composed of courtiers drawing pensions from the King' (*Cold Caleb*, 43).

[7] Cf. Grillon to Alphonso (5. 1. p. 57) and *The Vindication*, 8.

[8] The reference to Monmouth's fall refers to his arrest in autumn 1682 after his progress in Cheshire. Hunt says that loyalty to Monmouth and loyalty to the king are the same thing: 'the People honor him and love him, and every where publiquely and lowdly shew it. But this they do, for that the best People of England have no other way left to shew their Loyalty to the King, and love to their Religion and Government, in long intervals of Parliament than by prosecuting his Son, for the

Grasping the fact that both Whigs and Tories had a genuine rhetoric of loyalty and that they conceived of the idea differently is really essential in reading the dramatic language of politics, especially the Whig language of 'Loyal Protestantism', which is often misread or not perceived for what it is.

Equally confusing at first is the fact that both sides pose as custodians of moderation. This presents two problems for the modern reader. Firstly, a rhetorical deployment of a moderation topos often disguises partisanship. Partly, this is because it was necessary to pose as moderate since party political partisanship was not yet socially accepted or normal. Partly, it represents an appeal by both sides to the middle ground while trying to capture this middle ground for themselves and exclude their opponents. This means we have to try to distinguish between the polemical use of tropes of moderation and genuinely moderate views. Examples of the deployment of a rhetoric of moderation for effect are numerous. The first prologue to D'Urfey's Tory play *Sir Barnaby Whigg* (autumn 1681) offers Tory factionalism in the guise of loyalty, virtue, calm impartiality, and true wit:

> When shall we see an Audience in the Pit,
> Not sway'd by Factions, that will silent sit,
> And friends to th'Poet, calmly judge his Wit?   (sig. A4ʳ)

The poet will go on to satirize the Whigs. The poet affects to criticize the factiousness of his audience, but he also assumes that they will be Tories. The use of the second-person pronoun is revealing as he says the Whigs 'grieve ye, | With names of Masquerader and Tantivy'.[9] His own play's affiliations are clear; he will know 'By Hisses th'Whiggs, and by their Claps the Tories'. Thus the poet glories in partisanship and the word 'Tory' is openly and proudly used. A later, virulently Tory prologue, spoken before the king, discards the pose of artistic

sake of the King and his own merit, with all the demonstrations of the highest esteem' (*A Defence of the Charter*, 28).

⁹ 'Tantivy' was a nickname arising from a caricature of 1680–1 depicting High-Churchmen mounted upon the Church of England and 'riding tantivy' to Rome behind the Duke of York. 'Masquerader' carries implications of false pretences: Whigs see the Tories as quasi-papists masquerading as Protestants. It also suggests a predilection for acting and show. Perhaps this Whig term of abuse associates the Tories with the theatre just as the poet's claims for his audience do.

impartiality. In the epistle dedicatory, D'Urfey complains of the hard fate of poets in a factious age, and assumes the mantle of moral superiority, moderation, and true wit; then he goes on to make factional attacks on the Whig dramatist Shadwell.[10]

Similarly, the anonymous author of the Whig play *Rome's Follies* offers a swingeing Whiggish attack on popery and dedicates his published text to Shaftesbury; but he affects in his prologue to be 'neither Papist, Whigg nor Tory'. Many critics have misread the rhetoric of Whiggery or 'Loyal Protestantism' as non-partisan because it is often couched in moderate terms. This can clearly be seen in the case of Marvell's *Account of the Growth of Popery and Arbitrary Government*. Marvell achieves his effect by alternating between sarcasm and emotive rhetoric, and full and factual documentation of governmental and parliamentary proceedings, which gives an impression of impartiality and moderation at the same time as it exposes the contradiction between government theory and practice. He includes direct quotations from opposing points of view, without editorial comment, for the same reason.[11] Marvell's rhetorical strategy is to present arguments deeply offensive to royalists as though they were simply reasonable common sense: 'And as none will deny, that to alter our *Monarchy* into a *Commonwealth* were *Treason*, so by the same Fundamental Rule, the Crime is no lesse to make that *Monarchy Absolute*' (14). Posing as moderate is coupled with an avowedly loyal stance: the insistence on a group of conspirators who mislead the king is a device for criticizing

---

[10] Tory or proto-Tory pamphlets engage in similar ploys. For example, Nalson is a self-styled moderate, placing himself between the extremes of popery and dissent, but dissenters are his target and likening dissenters to papists is not so much a statement of moderation, as a tactic to discredit the dissenters. See e.g. *The Project of Peace*.

[11] This rhetorical sophistication leads to puzzlement about Marvell's politics. Wallace, *Destiny his Choice*, Legouis, *Andrew Marvell*, and Klause, *The Unfortunate Fall* all argue for a moderate, or 'trimming', stance; but Condren sees moderation, balance, and modesty as 'important rhetorical credentials' which were 'vital precisely because of the shrill extremity of his message' ('Andrew Marvell as Polemicist', in Condren and Cousins (eds.), *The Political Identity of Andrew Marvell*). For the strategic deployment of the modesty topos in Marvell, see also Patterson, *Marvell and the Civic Crown*, 183, 214. Those who have argued that moderation is a rhetorical strategy are, in my view, correct; but labelling Marvell's message extremist misses the point about the extent to which it was the Stuart monarchy, not the parliamentary opposition, who were seen as violating English Protestant tradition: hence the electoral and parliamentary success of the Whigs.

the king by implication, in the tradition of criticizing the king's 'bad advisors', rather than the monarch himself. Marvell makes similarly strategic use of praise, for example of the Protestant foreign policy Charles sought with 'great sincerity' and achieved 'according to that felicity which hath allways attended him, when excluding the corrupt Politicks of others he hath followed the dictates of his own Royal wisdom' (18). Elsewhere, Marvell slips into criticism of Charles, for example for paying more attention to French opinions than to his own Parliament (e.g. 120–21). James is praised with faint damns (40, 49), and the proceedings of Parliament presented in such a way as to make it clear that Marvell and his fellow MPs did not trust Charles an inch. The whole work ends on a note of praise and exculpation of Charles. It is asserted that the piece 'was written with no other intention than of meer Fidelity and Service to his *Majesty*' (156). This stance of Loyal Protestantism is encountered in the plays. It is clear that the oppositional nature of the text is in no way diminished and may be enhanced by it.

If rhetorical affectations of moderation pose one problem, a second arises in defining what 'real' moderation might be. What might constitute a genuine position of the centre in between extremes of partisanship? We cannot impose our own notions. For example, the 'Trimming' position of Halifax and others seems to modern readers to be a moderate position; yet in the Tory reaction period Trimmers were to be attacked as little better than, and in some ways worse than, Whigs.[12] John Humfrey seems moderate: the titles of his numerous works invariably contain words like 'peaceable', 'healing', 'pacification', 'modest', 'impartial', 'Union', 'middle-way', and 'moderate' itself. He seems sincere in urging the union of all Protestants and wider toleration: he was evidently a man of conscience, since he was a monarchist in the Civil War and a Nonconformist after the Restoration, and he was respected throughout a long life (1621–1719) for integrity. However, contemporaries would never have considered a dissenter a moderate. After 1660 dis-

---

[12] Halifax, *Character of a Trimmer*; Dryden, epilogue to *The Duke of Guise*; L'Estrange in *The Observator* (Nov. 1682). There was some basis for this: Halifax was described by Burnet as a leader of the 'Country Party' in the 1670s, and his scheme for Limitations was rejected by Shaftesbury as 'too like a republic'. See Haley, *Shaftesbury*, 517, 530–1, and Scott, *Algernon Sidney and the Restoration Crisis*, 23.

senters were extremists and outsiders by definition. Yet nobody agreed on who was really a moderate. When one writer styles himself moderate, another will indignantly rebut the claim; thus, Bishop William Lloyd speaks of his own 'known moderation', but is referred to by Marvell as an apologist for popery.[13]

Conceptions of moderation could shift, sometimes within the work of a single writer, as in the case of Dryden. In the dedication to Danby of *All For Love* (1678) he insists on the importance of moderation, and appears to deny absolutism. His tone is judicious rather than shrill. However, like royalist pamphleteers, he sees moderation as being located not in some compromise between the king and Parliament, or the government and its critics, but in the government itself, the Church of England, and 'A King, who is just and moderate in his Nature' (5–6).[14] Dryden goes on to make the association of rebels and the Devil and the parallel between present-day malcontents and the rebels of 1641, both common in royalist polemic during the 1670s, as we saw in Chapter 2. In fact Dryden's apparent statement of moderation is an explicit and uncompromising royalist and quietist statement, similar to the views of L'Estrange quoted in the same chapter: 'Every Remonstrance of private Men, has the seed of Treason in it' (7).

However, in the 1678–9 season, as the Popish Plot scare opened up a period of hysteria and uncertainty, Dryden offered a different sort of moderation in *Troilus and Cressida* (early 1679). The subtitle is *Truth Found Too Late*, which suggests the need to avoid precipitate action based on hasty assumptions. Dryden was to dedicate his published text to Sunderland, who is said to have 'put a stop to our ruine, when we were just rowling downward to the precipice' because 'his principles were full of moderation, and all his Councils such as tended to heal and not to widen the breaches of the Nation' (p. 221). In the play moderation is celebrated in the form of control over rebellious passions. In the Greek camp control is enforced by means closer

---

[13] Lloyd, *Considerations Touching the True Way to Suppress Popery*, sig. A2ᵛ. *Considerations* is universally attributed to Lloyd, but the preface states that it is 'by two several hands' (A2ʳ), the second author contributing 'chiefly from p. 80 till the Conclusion' (A3ᵛ); Marvell, *An Account*, 67.

[14] Cf. Shelton's *Discourse of Superstition*, a defence of 'The Moderation of our Church' (sig. A3ᵛ), which attacks dissenters and discredits them by paralleling them with papists (a recurring theme of Tory propaganda in the Exclusion Crisis).

to the *realpolitik* for which Sunderland was really famous[15] than the more elevated virtues for which he is praised by Dryden. The Trojan princes are capable of self-control: Troilus is tempted to put his love before his country, but is persuaded by the noble Hector to subordinate love to duty in a scene which Dryden adds to Shakespeare, 3.2. Thus it is clear that in this play he has a 'moderate' view of order flowing from virtuous rule as well as from the suppression of faction.[16]

In the autumn of 1680, at the height of the Whig ascendancy, Dryden offered yet another message of moderation and reconciliation in *The Spanish Fryar*. I have demonstrated this at length and responded to other critics' views of the play in my 'The Politics of John Dryden's *The Spanish Fryar*'. The political vision in the play is inclusive and criticism is even-handed. As in Tory plays, ambitious statesmen like Bertran represent a threat, but Bertran is not all bad and his faults are partly courtly as well as partly parliamentarian. Moreover, the royalist hothead Raymond also poses a threat and raises a 'vile blaspheming Rout' (5. 1. p. 69). No one is right or wrong all of the time. The usurper's offspring Leonora can learn and change. Torrismond's marriage to her brings about unity and forgiveness. Accusations of plotting prove unfounded and silly. Attempts to force the pace of history through precipitate action prove misguided: patience brings the reward of a providential solution, as the restoration without bloodshed of the old king Sancho recalls the values of 1660.[17]

Thus a clear political perspective, adapted to changing circumstances, lies behind an apparently pervasive value placed upon moderation.

[15] In addition to Kenyon, *Robert Spencer, Earl of Sunderland*, see Jones, *Country and Court*, 20; Haley, *Shaftesbury*, 350; Hutton, *Charles the Second*, 367.

[16] The force of this political message of moderation has been missed by readings in terms of parallels and personation such as those of McFadden, *Dryden the Public Writer*, 213, Novak, in *Works of John Dryden*, xiii. 551, and Moore, 'For King and Country', 100; but equally, in my view, by Winn, who rejects this approach, only to fall into under-reading the play's political message as fleeting: *John Dryden and his World*, 317.

[17] My perspective differs from that of Phillip Harth, who argues that Dryden was politically uncommitted prior to the publication of *Absalom and Achitophel* in autumn 1681: 'Dryden in 1678–1681'. For an extended engagement with Harth's analysis, see my 'The Politics of John Dryden's *The Spanish Fryar*'.

Social Order and Disorder

Reading the language of politics becomes further complicated by the fact that it is sometimes symmetrical, with both Whigs and Tories claiming to be the best champions of a certain virtue or value, and sometimes asymmetrical: particular ideological 'counters' may be more use to one faction or the other, though usually the other side will make at least a token effort to reverse whatever is said and reapply the accusations which are made. In relation to liberty and law both these things apply: both sides claim to be the best custodians of liberty and law; yet a focus on liberty and law as transcendent values is Whiggish. There is a further asymmetry in the fact that Whigs counterpose English liberty to French slavery: Whigs talk much more about the patriotism and the interests of trade than Tories. Tories satirize Whig concerns here, rather than reversing them. Conversely, Tories extol peace and quiet more than Whigs. However, the language of politics becomes symmetrical again in relation to sovereignty: both sides share a strong conception of sovereignty, though they deploy the notion in different ways. Both talk about the threats to sovereignty. Some of these are the same. For example, both factions make use of the idea of tyranny, though they see it as emanating from different sources: for Whigs, from popery or royal misrule; for Tories, from rebels and usurpers. Another threat to sovereignty is court corruption. Corruption at the centres of power is a powerful Whig theme, though Tories do make some use of it. Conversely, Tories make extremely powerful use of a nexus of negative values: faction, ingratitude, banishment, and exclusion. These are central Tory themes: Whigs try to respond to and reverse them, but not very much or very successfully. Tories raise the spectre of rebellion as the principle threat to sovereignty; Whigs try to reverse the application of rebel qualities, connecting them instead with papists. Toryism derives its greatest force from invoking the threat of civil war. The need to guard against this danger can be presented as overriding all other contradictions stemming either from foreign enemies or from corruption and misrule at home. This describes the shape of the argument in this section. I am isolating the themes and tropes under consideration for clarity, but of course in the plays they often run into one another, or are combined in complex ways.

Both Tories and Whigs claimed to stand for the liberty and law.[18] Indeed, in 1675 an opposition pamphleteer had begun to advance what were to be typical Whig arguments that '*English Law* and *Liberty*' were threatened by popery and 'Encroaching Prerogative'; that dissenting Protestants were '*Friends* to *Liberty*', whereas prelates were '*Creatures* to *Prerogative*'; and that the militia defended liberty, whereas a standing army defended prerogative.[19] Royalists, meanwhile, were arguing that 'Country, Prince, Laws, Liberty, and Religion' were threatened by dissenters,[20] and by, as Dryden puts it,

Malecontents amongst us, who surfeiting themselves on too much happiness, wou'd perswade the People that they might be happier by a change. 'Twas indeed the policy of their old Forefather [Satan], when himself was fallen from the Station of Glory, to seduce Mankind into the same Rebellion with him, by telling him he might yet be freer than he was: that is, more free than his Nature wou'd allow, or (if I may so say) than God cou'd make him. We have already all the Liberty which Free-born Subjects can enjoy; and all beyond it is but License.[21]

Thus in D'Urfey's Tory play *The Royalist*, the interregnum is depicted as a time when 'the ancient Laws are turn'd topsy-turvy' (3. 2. p. 26) and the Protector enforces his will through 40,000 armed men, a salutary reminder to those parliamentarians who have complained about violation of the law and failure to disband the army under Charles II. The royalists, also called Tories in the play, stand for the rule of law and are beset by rogues and false witnesses. In *The Duke of Guise* the rebels stand 'Against the King, his Government and Laws' (3. 1. p. 21). As Dryden puts it in *The Vindication*, 'I write for a *lawful establish'd Government* against *Anarchy, Innovation,* and *Sedition*' (p. 21). Conversely, in Whiggish plays like Settle's *The*

---

[18] For the dominance of law as a language of political discourse on both sides, see Nenner, *By Color of Law*, 48, 198.

[19] *A Letter From a Parliament Man to His friend, Concerning the Proceedings of the House of Commons*, 3. This is signed 'T.E.' (The Earl?) and usually attributed to Shaftesbury.

[20] Nalson, *The Countermine*, 316; cf. *The Common Interest*, sig. A4ʳ.

[21] Dryden, *Works*, xiii. 6. Cf. Rolle, *Loyalty and Peace*, 213–14.

Female Prelate, popery is the threat to law. Pope Joan is able to get away with murder because the cardinals obligingly judge the victim to have been a heretic, and a nobleman is excommunicated, dispossessed, and imprisoned 'Against all Honour, Conscience, Law, Religion' (2. 1. p. 21). In *The Coronation of Queen Elizabeth* papists violate the law, but the English common people, in law-abiding contrast to papist arbitrary violence, carry the would-be assassins of the Queen 'before a Justice of Peace to have 'um Examin'd' (2. 2. p. 11).

Thus we can see that both sides saw their opponents as the violators of the law. They also tended to see them as outside the law. For Whigs, cruelty to papists was justified because they had cast off humanity and lived outside the bounds of natural law. In Whig plays such as *The Coronation* and Shadwell's *The Lancashire Witches* doubts arising from the dubious legality of the Popish Plot trials and the refusal of the defendants to confess are assuaged by the notion that the Pope has given them leave to regard themselves as above the law and its processes—so they deserve what they get. Similarly, Tories argued that Whigs were beyond the law, as a reason for going beyond it themselves. In *The Duke of Guise* the king orders the murder of the rebel Guise in the name of 'Soveraign Justice' and rejects the notion that he ought to use the processes of the law:

> Yes, when th'Offender can be judg'd by Laws,
> But when his Greatness overturns the Scales,
> Then Kings are Justice in the last Appeal:
> And forc'd by strong Necessity may strike,
> In which indeed they assert the Publick Good,
> And, like sworn Surgeons, lop the gangren'd Limb:
> Unpleasant wholsom work.

> (5. 1. p. 59; cf. 5. 1. p. 64, 5. 1. p. 69)

The same point is made by the soldier Grillon, overriding his own doubts.

However, the matter is more complicated because a focus upon law and liberty as transcendent values is Whiggish in the Exclusion Crisis. This is basically because Whigs and Tories had a different understanding of *natural* law. For Tories kingly power rested upon natural law both in terms of divine right and in terms of being an extension of 'natural' patriarchal authority.[22] So all law is a concession by the monarch as God's agent and the king cannot be challenged by 'inferior' human law. Whigs, in contrast, argued that an individual right to protect life and liberty was fundamental according to natural law for three reasons: (1) the law of nature was given by God to man to protect the common good; (2) natural law requires the keeping of agreements and contracts; (3) the community and (secondarily) individuals have a right to preserve themselves against the unauthorized use of force. Thus the king is, in the last analysis, under rather than above the law; and resistance can be justified if he illegally breaks his contract with the people.[23] So, Whig heroes show a positive concern for both law and liberty.[24] Tories satirize Whig legalism and litigiousness.[25] Sarcastic references to the Popish Plot trials and to 'ignoramus' juries like those which freed Whigs, including Shaftesbury, are common in Tory plays, and in prologues and epilogues. Whig concern for the violated liberties of subjects is parodied in Tory plays in the spectacle of rebels misusing libertarian rhetoric to mislead the mob.[26]

Lying behind Whig preoccupation with defending English liberties and laws was the comparison with 'a *French* slavery', as Marvell puts it (*An Account*, 14). Anti-French feeling derived from political and religious concern about Louis XIV's expansionism and apparent concern to stamp out Dutch Calvinism, and from fears about the extent to which Charles was colluding with Louis.[27] Francophobia also had economic roots. In 1675

[22] Filmer's *Patriarcha* brought these two arguments together and emphasized their natural-law basis.

[23] See Ashcraft, *Revolutionary Politics*, 186–96. Marvell accuses the government of illegal breach of contract with the people: *An Account*, 31.

[24] e.g. Saxony in Settle's *The Female Prelate*, the Admiral in Lee's *The Massacre of Paris*, and Sertorius in Bancroft's *The Tragedy of Sertorius*.

[25] e.g. Crowne's *City Politiques*, *passim*, and Otway's *The Souldier's Fortune*, 2. 156–9.

[26] e.g. Dryden's and Lee's *Oedipus* and *The Duke of Guise*, Behn's *The Young King*, Crowne's *The Misery of Civil-War*, Tate's *Richard the Second* and *The Ingratitude of a Common-wealth*, Otway's *Caius Marius*, Southerne's *The Loyal Brother*.

[27] Throughout 1677 there were secret negotiations between Charles and Louis, the latter granting sums of money in exchange for the repeated prorogations which incapacitated Parliament. It was the revelation of these secret dealings which led to the fall of Danby in the following year.

weavers had rioted against French competition.[28] Complex
manœuvres for and against the French in Parliament in the
1670s had culminated in a vote for a ban on French imports.[29]
Marvell summarizes the feeling of Parliament: 'the debate of this
day is as great and weighty as ever was any in *England*[;] it
concerns our very being, and includes our Religion, Liberty and
Property; *The doore towards France must be shut and Garded,*
for so long as it is open our Treasure and Trade will creep out
and their Religion creep in at it . . . We must destroy the French
Trade' (129, 145). Charles's ministers feel obliged to reassure
Parliament that the king has the interests of trade at heart;[30] but
Marvell says Louis has met with no resistance in his concern to
further French trade, and that Britain has exhausted revenue
in the purchase of French exports such as wine, brandy, and
'manufactures' (39, 41, 53, 107).

A similar connection between war with France and the promotion of trade is apparent in Thomas Jordan's Lord Mayor's
Shows, especially *London's Glory* (1680). Such Whiggish
concerns are satirized in plays such as the anonymous *Mr.*
Turbulent, in which a character called Sneak credulously ab-
sorbs a tale of a project to build ships of stone: 'Because we may
not be beholden to Forreign Nations, and to promote the
Growth of our own Nation, all the Sales are made of Tinn, and
the Shrouds, Tackle and Cables of twisted Wires' (4. p. '57'
[49]). Sneak hopes the scheme will be promoted 'for the Good of
the Nation' (ibid.).

Francophobia is sometimes mocked by reference to wine. An
example is *The Revenge; or, A Match in Newgate*, an adaptation of Marston's *The Dutch Courtesan*, probably by Behn.[31] In

---

[28] Harris, *London Crowds*, 215–16.

[29] Jones, *Country and Court*, 194.

[30] Marvell cites Lord Keeper Bridgman's speech of Oct. 1670 (20 ff.). Cf. Rolle's
royalist response to parliamentary anxiety about trade in *Loyalty and Peace*, 215:
the king 'maketh it his business to promote the *Trade* and *Traffique* of his people'
and cannot help it 'if after all this Trading be but dead, as that is the great
complaint', any more than a diligent but poor man can help his family's poverty.

[31] This play was published anonymously. Attribution to Behn was made by
Narcissus Luttrell in a note on his copy, bought in July 1680. A later attribution to
Betterton is probably erroneous. See Van Lennep *et al.* (eds.), *The London Stage*,
287, Hughes and Scouten, *Ten English Farces*, 203–4, and Milhous and Hume,
'Attribution Problems', 29. I would add that the political slant of the play accords

2.3 Behn adds to Marston's satire of the canting puritanism of the vintner and his wife fear that heaven is displeased because they have disguised English Protestant wines with 'heathenish names' (p. 22). Fear of French influence and imports becomes mere boorishness and stupidity as Trickwell, disguised as a dissenting preacher, reminds Dashit of his sins:

but Brother, you must remember your sins too, and iniquities; you must consider you have been a Broacher of prophane Vessels, you have made us drunk with the juice of the Whore of *Babylon*: for whereas good Ale, Perry, Syder, and Metheglin, were the true Ancient *British* and *Trojan* Drinks, you have brought in Popery, meer Popery—*French* and *Spanish* Wines, to the subversion, staggering, and overthrowing of many a good Protestant Christian. (5. 4. p. 67)

Similar arguments appear in Behn's prologue to *The Young King*, where anti-papist Francophobia is mocked by reference to the audience's preference for 'dangerous' French wine; Dryden's prologue to *Caesar Borgia*, in which he mocks the patriotic forsaking of claret for bottled ale; and an 'Epilogue at the Theatre in Drury-Lane. 1680',[32] in which satire of the Popish Plot scare and of Whigs and dissenters follows an ironic claim that French wines have emasculated the English.

In general, patriotism is extolled in Whig texts and satirized in Tory ones. The Whigs made most of the running with patriotic arguments, since the Stuarts were very vulnerable to the charge of fraternizing with France. However, Tories could counter by extolling peace and quiet, and so condemning the anti-French Whigs as warmongers. This went hand in hand with celebrating political quietude and demonizing troublers of the peace. The paradigm in Tory plays such as Whitaker's *The Conspiracy* is that if only subjects would be quiet, all would be well. Dryden in *Oedipus*, *Troilus and Cressida*, *The Spanish Fryar*, and *The*

---

with Behn's Toryism, and the sympathy accorded to the prostitute character, which I discuss below, might be internal evidence to support the attribution to Behn, who, in previous plays such as *The Rover* and *The Feign'd Curtizans*, had expressed more sympathy for sexually compromised women than was customary.

[32] Printed in Danchin, *Prologues and Epilogues*, vol. ii, pt. 1, pp. 233–4. Appears in the 1704 collection of Buckingham's works with an attribution to Otway. This is rejected by Ghosh, in *Works of Thomas Otway*, i. 64, on stylistic grounds. I think that the piece lacks the emotional quality and self-consciousness of Otway's prologues and epilogues in this season.

Duke of Guise places a positive value on 'Peacefull order' (*Troilus and Cressida*, 5. 2. 323), on subjects being quiet and keeping out of the business of kings. Attempts to act precipitately always lead to disaster because God's purposes in human history cannot be fully known. The merits of quiet also appear in the form of the virtues of retirement, scorned by ambitious politician villains such as the Constable in Crowne's *The Ambitious Statesman* (1. pp. 7–8).[33] Dryden praises retirement and private virtue in his dedication of *Amboyna* (1673) to Clifford (sig. A4ʳ) and the Dedication of *Aureng-Zebe* (1676) to Mulgrave; while in *The Duke of Guise* praise is accorded to retirement and 'inward gallantry' (1. 3. p. 8), as against the ambition of the Guisards.

Given these divergences between Whig and Tory views, it may seem odd that both shared a strong belief in sovereignty, though their ideas about it differed. The royalist and Tory message is that the king's sovereignty must be respected above all else. A very clear example of such exaltation of sovereignty is Dryden's revision of Shakespeare's *Troilus and Cressida*. Dryden has a firm but not rose-tinted vision of sovereignty. He alters Shakespeare to draw out the theme that respect for royal rule must be enforced by authoritarian means if necessary. The Greek council of war is made the first scene, rather than the third, as in Shakespeare. This gives greater prominence to the speech on degree, and other changes give the speech political force. Dryden shortens the speech and concentrates on subordination to the Crown. Shakespeare's 'O, when degree is shak'd, | Which is the ladder of all high designs, | The enterprise is sick' (1. 3. 101–3) becomes 'Or when Supremacy of Kings is shaken, | What can succeed?' (1. 1. 38–9). For Dryden it is the rebel quality of 'wild Ambition'[34] rather than 'appetite' which 'Must make an universal prey of all' (47). The distraction—and humiliation—of Aeneas' interruption is omitted and the scene ends forcefully,

[33] In Feb. 1676 at the same time as the attempt to suppress the coffee-houses and moves against dissenters, the Secretary of State had conveyed a message to Shaftesbury 'that he had information that he was very busy here in town in matters that he ought not, and that His Majesty thought it were much better he were at home in the country'. Shaftesbury refused to go: Haley, *Shaftesbury*, 404. This may be the basis for Dryden's remark in *Absalom and Achitophel*: 'Why should he, with Wealth and Honour blest, | Refuse his Age the needful hours of Rest?' (165–6).

[34] Line 45. This phrase also occurs in *Absalom and Achitophel*, l. 198.

with Agamemnon asking Ulysses and Nestor to 'vindicate the Dignity of Kings' (1. 1. 108).

The tone of the play's ending is completely altered by replacing Pandarus' cynicism with a speech by Ulysses, celebrating royal authority:

> Hayl *Agamemnon*! truly Victor now!
> While secret envy, and while open pride,
> Among thy factious Nobles discord threw;
> While publique good was urg'd for private ends,
> And those thought Patriots, who disturb'd it most;
> Then, like the headstrong horses of the Sun,
> That light which shou'd have cheer'd the World, consum'd it:
> Now peacefull order has resum'd the reynes,
> Old time looks young, and Nature seems renew'd:
> Then, since from homebred Factions ruine springs,
> Let Subjects learn obedience to their Kings.
>
> (5. 2. 316–26)

The fourth and fifth lines of this speech seem to have a particular topical application. The last two lines express 'the Moral that directs the whole action of the Play to one center' (preface, 234). If subjects persist in causing trouble and in interfering in government business which they are no more fit to understand than Phaeton was to control the 'horses of the Sun', the king or his ministers will have to act forcefully. 'Peacefull order' can only be restored by decisive political leadership and necessary action to deal with the king's enemies. Thus Dryden's ideal of sovereignty here, as in *Absalom and Achitophel*, is bound up with the idea that the monarch must act strongly, must 'put his foot down'.

The royalist notion of sovereignty is associated with an emphasis on royal virtues and an exculpation of royal faults. In *The Conspiracy* monarchs have godlike qualities and every character who is loyal to the true king is morally superior to every rebel. Even in plays with flawed monarchs, the true king's virtues are magnified and his faults at least partially wished away. For example, in several plays 'Royal Mercy' (*Duke of Guise*, 1. 3. p. 9) is shown as a personal virtue and political fault in the king: it becomes 'dangerous Mercy' (2. 1. p. 12), and must be abjured in order to suppress the kingdom's enemies. The king in *The Duke of Guise* progresses to a reluctant appreciation of the need for a firmness which is alien to 'the Natural Sweetness of his Temper'

(2. 1. p. 12): 'I will no more by Mercy be betray'd' (5. 1. 60). A rather different example is Behn's *The Young King*, in which the true king, Orsames, is exiled as a baby, but possesses inherent royalty. This idea of discernible superiority in the displaced or disguised prince was a commonplace in the heroic plays of the 1660s and 1670s. Vallentio recognizes the unknown and shabbily dressed Orsames by a certain royal quality:

> Ye Gods instruct me where to bow my knee—
> But this alone must be the Deity.

> (5. 3. p. 56)

In 2.1 Urania, not knowing his identity, perceives, 'He looks above the common rate of men' (p. 14). Orsames' faults are palliated, and shown as due to his exile. He has never learned decorum and has a tendency towards high-handed behaviour such as grabbing women's breasts and condemning to death anyone who displeases him. However, he improves a bit when he is restored to power and treated with kindness. Behn's palliation of royal faults does not entirely work, and we are left with a pity for Orsames which borders on fascinated repulsion, but we can detect an implication that faults of temper in James and of decorum in both royal brothers are to be attributed not to nature, but to their respective exiles.

Another aspect of the royalist treatment of sovereignty is a recurring emphasis on the burdens of kingship. For example, in *The Conspiracy*, the royal couple are lulled to sleep in Act 2 with a song: 'See, see how full of troubles are | The Crowns which wakeful Monarchs wear' (2. p. 14). Then a chorus of shepherds and shepherdesses offer the platitudes of courtly pastoral: 'happy are we who attend on our Sheep', for 'More refin'd are our pleasures, the meaner we are, | When the greatest of Kings are most subject to care' (2. p. 14).[35] Quite often royal lovers are depicted as victims who must sacrifice the love that common people enjoy as of right, just because they are royal.[36] This neatly reverses opposition criticism of the Stuart brothers' promiscuity.

[35] Cf. the self-pitying emphasis on the cares of kings at 5. p. 48; also *Duke of Guise*, 5. 1. p. 60; *Young King*, 4. 3. p. 45 and 5. 4. p. 62.
[36] See e.g. *The Young King*, *Oedipus*, and *Troilus and Cressida*.

Sovereignty is also an important ideal in oppositional or Whig plays, a fact which has misled critics into thinking them conformist or apolitical. However, the concept of sovereignty is different. The king's sovereignty is like the sovereignty of all men of property. It gives him the right to hold on to his own, but not to tyrannize over his subjects. The greatest threat to sovereignty is popery. This can be seen in Settle's *The Female Prelate*. The noble hero, the Duke of Saxony, warns that when a monarch embraces Catholicism,

> *Romes* upstart Idol 'bove his Throne he rears,
> And servilely creates the God he fears,
> Down goes his Majesty, and down his Fame,
> Pope is the King, and Monarch but the name.

(1. 2. p. 19)

He repeatedly stresses that popery upsets the natural order of things and that 'Princes | Are less than Dogs, where base-born Priests controul' (2. 1. p. 20). Saxony responds to being excommunicated and dispossessed of his property by the Church in quasi-Protestant and monarchist terms: 'I am a Soveraign Prince; | And faults of Princes stand accountable | Only to Heaven; and that too not till death' (2. 1. p. 22). Upholding sovereignty is associated with defending property and is absolutely dependent upon attacking popery. It is those who are vigilant against papist atrocity who are the true defenders of the established order.

There are several threats to the ideal of sovereignty. The first is tyranny, a theme used by both Whigs and Tories. Whigs make powerful use of the idea of tyranny, and associate it with popery. Marvell had asserted: 'There has now for diverse Years, a design been carried on, to change the Lawfull Government of *England* into an Absolute Tyranny, and to convert the established Protestant Religion into down-right Popery: than both which, nothing can be more destructive or contrary to the Interest and Happinesse, to the Constitution and Being of the King and Kingdom' (3); and he went on to discuss in detail measures through which Parliament's authority and Protestant interests had been overridden and undermined. In Whig plays tyranny in association with popery may be seen, for example, in the corrupt regime of Pope Joan in *The Female Prelate* with its arbitrary judgements, expropriations, rapes, tortures, and murders. In Lee's *Caesar Borgia*, Borgia is Machiavel's 'Championprince, Italian Tyrant' (1. 1. 206). The heroine, Bellamira, dies cursing him as 'thou Tyrant, double damn'd' (5. 1. 121). Tyranny is portrayed not only as the concomitant of depraved lusts, as in Lee's *Nero*, but also as a political mentality which leads to the alienation of essential human capacities, which destroys the family, and which damages perpetrator as well as victim.

Elsewhere tyranny is associated with royal faults in a way which seems to relate to the perceived faults of the Stuart brothers: uncontrolled lust combined in Charles's case with political ineptitude, inappropriate withdrawal into private concerns, and inability to distinguish friend from foe; and in James's with arrogance, arbitrariness, and self-centredness. For example, in Settle's *Fatal Love* questions of excess and moderation seem to take on a generalized significance so that difficulties of right action in love have a bearing on the problem of right behaviour in rule. Misbehaviour in love is 'Tyrannick Cruelty' (1. 2. p. 11). Prince Artaban, the 'Jealous Tyrant' (1. 1. p. 3), is the embodiment of excess. He is arrogant, absolutist, intemperate, credulous of lies, and unable to recognize integrity. He broods vengefully over imagined grievances and precipitates the tragedy by withdrawing from the scene. He is absent when needed and then consistently fails to negotiate or compromise, rebuffs attempts at reconciliation, and is himself destroyed by his failure to be conciliating until it is too late. Artaban's ranting caricatures the huffing hero of royalist heroic drama. He presents us with an object lesson in the dangers of royal excess.

Tories associate tyranny with usurpers and rebels. As L'Estrange puts it '*Rebellion* and *Tyranny* were brought in by the *Remonstrants*, under the Profession of *Loyalty* and *Duty* to their Country'.[37] Usurpers and rebels in plays are tyrannical: Flatra in *The Conspiracy* claims, 'Our Will's our Law, and whensoere we please | We alter or abolish our decrees' (1. p. 8). In *The Spanish Fryar* Queen Leonora inherits some of the faults

---

[37] L'Estrange, *An Account of the Growth of Knavery*, 19. 'Remonstrants', used loosely here of interregnum parliamentarians, usually refers to the Dutch Arminian republicans or the Scottish extreme Calvinists of the 1650s. There may also be a reference to the Grand Remonstrance of 1641.

of her usurper father, who exercised an iron rule over his people: 'He rein'd 'em strongly and he spurr'd them hard' (3. 2. p. 39). On his death he bequeathed to the nation, 'A Council made of such as dare not speak, I And could not if they durst; whence honest men I Banish themselves for shame of being there' (4. 2. p. 53).

Tyranny is often associated with court corruption, an old theme used with topical significance. Criticism of the court often tends to be Whiggish, since the Tory faction had its roots in what was called the court faction in the 1670s. Marvell describes the court faction as 'Flatterers' (156) and enemies of the people: MPs should not be court pensioners (74–81) because the interests of 'the court of *England*' are opposed to those of 'the People of *England*' (132) whom MPs are supposed to represent. In Lee's Whig play *Lucius Junius Brutus*, Brutus begins by making attacks on court lewdness under the guise of madness, and goes on to make the lust of the tyrant Tarquins the occasion for their expulsion from Rome. *Fatal Love* opens with a spectacle of sexual harassment and abuse of power at court, which is a place of 'loose Desires, gay Dayes, and wanton Nights' (4. 1. p. 33). In *Fatal Love* there is a critique of present corruption from the perspective of a more godly past and an older Puritan generation: Panthea invokes her parents' morality against the prince who wants to rape her: 'O hold, Sir! I had a Virtuous Father' (4. 2. p. 37). This is a notable feature of Shadwell's plays. For example, in *The Woman-Captain* the aristocratic wastrel Sir Humphrey Scattergood is criticized by reference to his late father, who was religious, thrifty, moderate in his pleasures, generous to his loyal dependants and appreciative enough of wit to keep a Fool. He kept English servants and enjoyed plain English cooking. Sir Humphrey is an extravagant sensualist, keen to follow the latest French fashions. Before he sets about wasting his inheritance on eating, drinking, whoring, and entertaining, he turns off his father's faithful English servants, replacing them with 'French Rogues' who are only fit 'for Slavery, They are born and bred to it' (1. p. 19). Sir Humphrey's old-fashioned steward acts as the ignored voice of his master's conscience. The Fool, turned off for censuring the folly, witlessness, and Francophilia of the Age, associates his misfortune metaphorically with court intrigue: 'Some body I see has us'd wicked Court Policy to supplant me in my employment' (1. p. 2).[38]

Whereas in Whig texts court corruption is associated with misrule, in Tory ones it tends to be associated with rebel noblemen such as the Constable in Crowne's *The Ambitious Statesman* and Ismael in Southerne's *The Loyal Brother*. Southerne mobilizes anti-court feeling against disloyalty by making Ismael typify the court: 'The court has been my Sphear, | Where, with the musick of my tongue in counsel, | I've charmed opinion after me' (1. 1. 307). This reflects the fact that Tory texts see the main threat to sovereignty as emanating not from the throne, but from the 'faction' and 'ingratitude' of such figures as the Constable and Ismael. 'Faction', a word which occurs frequently in prologues and epilogues, conveys not just criticism of political opposition but hostility to any political activity or interference in the business of kings. Rebels are also guilty of the unnatural crime of ingratitude, since the patriarchal model suggests that subjects should be as grateful for the benefits of kingly government as children are to their parents. The faction and ingratitude of villains is often associated with the wrongful banishment or exclusion of loyal heroes.[39]

Thus in Otway's *The History and Fall of Caius Marius*, a politicized adaptation of *Romeo and Juliet* in a Roman setting, ingratitude is rife and exclusions repeated, leading to civil war. Specifically, Marius is ungrateful for Metellus' political assistance, Rome for Marius' years of loyal military service. Metellus excludes his daughter, Marius his son, Rome banishes Marius and then Cinna, just as Marius earlier banished Metellus, and the young lovers are forcibly parted not by family feud, but by political faction. The cumulative effect is to offer a powerful royalist message against ingratitude (the perceived fault of factious subjects), banishment (the unjust fate of the heir to the throne), and exclusion (the avowed goal of the political opposition).

In his dedication to *The Ingratitude of a Common-wealth*,

---

[38] Cf. Thomas Porter's *The French Conjurer*, in which satire of Francophilia is associated with criticism of the court, and there is also a plain-speaking servant.

[39] For a useful discussion, see Wallace, 'Otway's *Caius Marius* and the Exclusion Crisis'.

Tate says his adaptation of *Coriolanus* emphasizes the parallel with 'the busie Faction of our own time . . . those Troublers of the State that out of private Interest or Mallice, Seduce the Multitude to Ingratitude, against Persons that are not only plac't in Rightful Power above them; but also the Heroes and Defenders of their Country'. This clearly associates his hero with James, whose military heroism was much celebrated (and exaggerated) by royalists.[40] Tate's aim is clear: 'The Moral therefore of these Scenes being to Recommend Submission and Adherence to Establisht Lawful Power, which in a word, is *Loyalty*' (sig. A2[r–v]). Tate 'improves upon' Shakespeare, to sharpen the political lessons. He adds a speech by Menenius, welcoming Coriolanus back from war and criticizing 'base Repiners' who do not appreciate him (2. 1. p. 16). In 4. 1 he has Coriolanus speak of 'ingrateful Rome' (39) instead of Shakespeare's 'my canker'd country' (4. 5. 95). He gives Coriolanus two speeches denouncing the ingratitude of factious peacetime politicians who feed off the efforts of warrior heroes, then engage in rabble-rousing against them: a clear reference to Whig leaders like Shaftesbury and Buckingham. To mitigate the unfortunate contemporary resonance of a man betraying his country to a foreign enemy, Tate improves his hero, replacing the moment of human weakness in Shakespeare's 1. 9 where the weary Coriolanus forgets the name of his benefactor, with a speech showing his hero's justice, piety, and concern for his troops (1. 4. pp. 14–15). Tate reduces the powerful mutual fascination of the two enemies, Coriolanus and Aufidius, which in Shakespeare's play makes the hero interestingly complex but also politically suspect. He also plays down in his hero the uncompromising temperament for which James was famous, omitting Menenius' disloyal criticism that things 'might have been much better, if | He could have temporized' in the exchange with the tribunes (Shakespeare's 4. 6. 16–17). Tate's improvement of the James figure does not really work: nothing can assuage the uncomfortable resonance of a man in league with his country's enemies making a war on his own people, and there was enough apparent criticism of James in the play for it to be revived as an anti-Stuart one after

---

[40] Marvell is sarcastic about this in his discussion of the mismanagement of the recent Dutch War: *An Account*, 40.

1715 and 1745.[41] However, he strains every nerve to offer an exemplary spectacle of the dangers which can befall a nation which is ungrateful to its military heroes and natural leaders.

Whig dramatists do use the charges of faction, ingratitude, and wrongful banishment, though more as a counter to Tories than as weapons which fall readily to hand in the ideological struggle. In the dedication to *The Female Prelate* papists become the 'dangerous Faction'. The Whig pamphlet *A Just and Modest Vindication* strives to palliate the charge of wrongful banishment and turn the charge of ingratitude against the king:

> Or if it be true that all obligations of Honor, Justice and Conscience, are comprehended in a grateful return of such benefits as have been received, can His Majesty believe that he doth duly repay unto his Protestant Subjects, the kindness they shewed him, when they recalled him from a miserable helpless banishment, and with so much dutiful affection placed him in the Throne, enlarged his Revenue above what any of his Predecessors had enjoyed, and gave him vaster sums of Money in twenty years, than had been bestowed upon all the Ks. since William the first; should he after all this deliver them up to be ruin'd by his Brother?[42] (29)

In *The Coronation of Queen Elizabeth*, Elizabeth offers reward and speeches of gratitude to her loyal subjects (e.g. 3. 2. p. 21), and Charles II is criticized by implication for failure to reward loyal service, and for ingratitude.

Besides ingratitude and faction, the other main weapons in the Tories' ideological arsenal were the charges of rebellion and civil war. A comprehensive anatomization of rebellion's many-headed monstrosity may be found in *The Conspiracy*, a play in which 'All plot the Sultan's fall for different ends' (1. p. 10). The Sultan's mother and his sister Flatra are motivated by ambition. The former is a liar and hypocrite, and the latter has absolutist urges. The disgruntled Bectas, Kara, and Kulchaia lead armies of discontented janizaries and use misplaced rhetoric of courage. The Grand Vizier, 'a Traytor' (actors' names), is a weak man, led astray by love for Flatra. Oglar's lust for the Queen allows the rebels to manipulate him. The rebels attract a rag-bag of the

---

[41] McGugan, introduction to *The Ingratitude of a Common-wealth*, p. lxxv.

[42] Wing attributes this to Robert Ferguson, but Scott, surveying the possibilities, suggests that Sidney's was the chief among several hands at work: *Algernon Sidney and the Restoration Crisis*, 186 ff.

discontented and inspire misplaced loyalty, as in the character of Lentesia, who makes obeisance to Flatra in Act 4 and nobly elects to die with the Queen Mother in Act 5. More dangerously, the people are misled, as Ibrahim laments in a passage from which all pretence of non-topicality has disappeared: 'The City Rages in Rebellious Flame: | The Commons are incourag'd by the Peers' (3. p. 20). Because rebellion breeds rebellion, rebels fall out, as we see when the Vizier turns on Flatra and Bectas in turn falls out with the Vizier; and when Ibrahim's nobility in death moves some of the mob so that 'The People quarrel and are divided' (3. p. '28' [26]).

Rebellion has several characteristics and associations. Firstly, the rebels are motivated by ambition. This is a recurring theme.[43] They are also arrogant and presumptuous: the Vizier at the head of the mob in Act 3 announces with what must have seemed to royalists the arrogance of opposition noblemen in January 1680, 'We come not with petitions, but demands' (3. p. 25). Rebellion is associated with specious logic and with inversion of the truth. In Act 2 Whitaker inverts the Popish Plot witnesses' unconvincing assertion that the assassination plot against Charles was to be accompanied by an attempt by the queen and her physician to poison him. This had been discredited by Wakeman's acquittal the previous summer.[44] The rebels' assassination plots against the royal family are accompanied by a plot to poison the Young Queen, which is foiled by her physician, who orders 'That she no Cordial take, but from his hand' (2. p. 13). Inversion of the truth is seen when the Vizier calls Ibrahim a 'lustful Tyrant' (2. p. 16) or calls for justice and relief for those who groan beneath his 'lustful Scepter' (3. p. 27). It is of course they who are lustful, arbitrary, and unjust. Bectas misappropriates a standard royalist image of king and state as

---

[43] L'Estrange argued that Marvell was a 'Pragmatical *Mal-content*' (33) motivated by malice and envy of 'those that are uppermost' (*Account of the Growth of Knavery*, 6), one of those who impugn office-holders because they are ambitious for office themselves (26–7). Marius Senior in *Caius Marius* utters a machiavellian hymn to 'Ambition! oh Ambition!' (1. 428) and we are told in Act 3 that his 'Ambition' and 'Pride' have led to 'Civil Wars in Rome' (448, 450). We are warned that 'Ambition is a Lust that's never quencht, | Grows more inflam'd and madder by Enjoyment' (5. 479–80). Other examples of rebels who revel in their own (disastrous) ambition are the Constable in *The Ambitious Statesman* and Guise in *The Duke of Guise*.

[44] Kenyon, *The Popish Plot*, 60, 191–201.

head and members: 'As many as dare follow, I dare lead, | Find me a Body, and I'le find a head' (2. p. 16). The image is recuperated by Solyman in Act 5 and combined with the standard topos of rebellion as disease: 'The gangrin, Sir, through the chief limbs is spread; | And will, 'tis fear'd, e're morning reach the head' (5. p. 49).

Rebellion is associated both with religious hypocrisy and with irreligion, as I shall discuss more fully below. It is also monstrous. This is shown by the gruesome excess of the spectacle in Act 5:

Scene drawn, discovers a Room hung all with black; the Old Queen, Lentesia, Bectas, Kara, and Kulchaia seated, while several of the Royal Party are plac'd in Order, with Coffins before them, on which stand a dim Tapier, and Mutes standing ready as to strangle them; then Enter eight or ten Blackmoors, drest like Fiends, and dance an Antic; having done, they go out, and after fearful groans and horrid shriekings; some of them return with burnt Wine, which they fill, out in Sculls to the King's Friends, who as fast as they drink, dy: at which the Queen and all the rest seem pleas'd. (5. p. 51)

This use of multiple murder methods may mock the Popish Plot witnesses' allegations of various parallel murder plots. However, it may simply be intended to arouse pity and horror. In the same way, Tate piles up atrocities to increase pity and strengthen his message against ingratitude at the end of *The Ingratitude of a Common-wealth*: the villain Nigridius gloats that he has killed Menenius and tortured Coriolanus' little son and thrown the mangled body into Volumnia's arms, thus driving her demented. Coriolanus does not die until he has been subjected to Volumnia's ravings and the boy's pathetic dying speech, in addition to the wounding and threatened rape of his wife.

Both Whitaker and Tate depict rebels as plotters, countering the Popish Plot allegations upon which Whigs capitalized and which Tories wished to see discredited. Accusations and counter-accusations of plotting flew to and fro during the Exclusion Crisis. In *The Ingratitude of a Common-wealth* Coriolanus says the tribunes and people are in a 'plot' against nobility (3. p. 25). Brutus retorts, 'Call't not a Plot' (p. 26). In *The Royalist*, set in the interregnum, there are pronounced similarities between the rebel plotters and the Popish Plot witnesses. One of the most persuasive Plot witnesses was Stephen Dugdale, former steward to the Catholic Lord Aston, who turned on his master when arrested as a Catholic in December 1678.[45] In the play, the treacherous tenants Copyhold and Slouch give false evidence against Kinglove to 'the Protector's Plot-makers' (3. 2. p. 27). The reward of their opportunism is to be beaten in 3. 2 by soldiers of both sides in succession, as they try but fail to adjust their protestations of loyalty to the demands of the moment, and ultimately to be whipped, a fate which was to befall Titus Oates only later in 1685. There is also Captain Jonas, 'A Seditious Rascal that disturbs the People with News and Lyes, to Promote his own Interest', who may recall Popish Plot witness 'Captain' William Bedloe, described by Kenyon as an accomplished conman.[46]

Rebellion is also associated with madness. In *Mr. Turbulent* the physical presence of Bedlam looms over the action and we are told its location in Moorfields is appropriate: madmen belong with the low-class fools, cheats, and puritan hypocrites of the city (1. pp. 2–3). Madness is also associated with literary ignorance: Friendly's response to Cringe's bad verse is, 'why this Fool is madder than any in *Bedlam*' (1. p. 7). Sneak's profiteering projects make him fit for Bedlam (4. p. '58' [50]), and he finally ends up there. Political discontent is associated with both madness and disease: the French doctor says Turbulent suffers from:

de colorick mellancholly dat causes all de quarrels in de vorld, and makes de fiting, de Riots, de Routs, de peevishness, de angriness, de beating one another, de disputing, de Railings, de Revilings, de Treasons, and de Treasonable Speeches, de Turbulences, de Rebellions, and opposition of de Governours, and de Government, of de Kings and his Laws, and of all unquietness in de vorld.   (2. p. 21)

The madness which is in Turbulent is the associated political madness of 1641 and 1681. A search of his room reveals interregnum literature, including various visions and prophesies, and works by Muggleton, the Levellers, Quakers, Anabaptists, Ranters, and the Family of Love. Furnish's comment is, 'No

---

[45] Kenyon, *The Popish Plot*, 157.
[46] Ibid. 57.

wonder that he is mad when he studies these.' Now the 'Gall and Venom which he sucks from these Weeds . . . feeds the foolish Hopes, and idle Fancies of such Lunatick Brains' as would 'rail against the Times—meddle with Government' (4. p. '60' [52]). The suggested treatment for Turbulent is a sojourn in Bedlam, and this is where he ends up, able at last to speak treason without fear of punishment, and railing against the times in a frenzy of rage which is indistinguishable from true madness. Learning of his diagnosis and fate, his cabal's response is to welcome the overthrow of 'the Idol Reason' (4. p. '67' [59]).

Opposition or Whig texts offer a mirror image of some of these aspects of rebellion. Marvell's court 'conspirators' are motivated by the qualities royalists attributed to rebels, 'Malice and Ambition' (16), and, similarly, in *The Female Prelate* it is ambition that drives the monstrous figure of Pope Joan, who typifies the horrors of popery. Lee's *Caesar Borgia* offers the spectacle of popish ambition rampant in Rome. Atrocities are also used in Whig plays, to arouse horror against priests and papists. For example, *The Female Prelate* offers a monstrous spectacle which rivals anything in *The Conspiracy* or *The Ingratitude of a Common-wealth*. In Act 3 the persecuted hero, Saxony, is taken into a chamber where the scene-opening 'discovers variety of Hereticks in several Tortures' (p. 40); in Act 4 the imprisoned heretics set the prison on fire and the ghost of the old Duke of Saxony, murdered by Pope Joan in her youth, writes 'MURDER' on the wall in 'bloudy fire' (4. 3. p. 50); and in Act 5 'The Scene opens, and discovers a Stake and Faggots, with Priests with Lighted Torches to kindle the Fire, and the Rabble hurrying Saxony to the Fire' (5. 2. p. 70). Plotting becomes a popish characteristic in *Caesar Borgia* and *The Coronation of Queen Elizabeth*; while in *Lucius Junius Brutus* it is associated with royalism: the attempted royalist counter-revolution is 'the royal plot' (3. 2. 149). The royalist plotters are in league with treacherous priests, and most of Act 4 is devoted to royalist and quasi-papist atrocities, as conspirators and priests engage in bloodthirsty ranting, and burn, crucify and consume their victims.

In Whig plays madness may be associated with popery. For example, in *Caesar Borgia* popery and political ambition are ranged against love, and the effect on the central character is literal madness. Machiavel's plot to toughen Borgia by inducing him to love and then lose Bellamira misfires. The memory of the wronged Bellamira induces not Roman greatness, but lunacy:

> Name not a Woman, and I shall be well.
> Like a poor Lunatick that makes his moan,
> And for a time beguiles the lookers on;
> He reasons well; his eyes their wildness lose,
> And vows the keepers his wrong'd sense abuse:
> But if you hit the Cause that hurt his Brain,
> Then his teeth gnash, he foams, he shakes his Chain,
> His Eye-balls rowl, and he is mad again.

(5. 1. 261–7)

The effect of this vivid description, poignantly prophetic of Lee's own impending madness, is to show that popish ambition causes not only political problems but emotional trauma, and damages both the perpetrators and their victims to the extent of striking at the roots of their identity.

Finally, Tory dramatists frequently raise the spectre of 1641, draw parallels between the Whigs and interregnum radicals, and claim that the Whigs pose the threat of civil war in the present. Sometimes the interregnum period is referred to directly, as in *The Royalist*, which invokes a mythologized 'memory' of royalist heroism and republican villainy in the Civil War period.[47] Behn's *The Round-heads; or, The Good Old Cause* is also set in the interregnum. Published with a vehemently Tory epistle dedicatory, this piece attacks the Whigs through comparison with interregnum parliamentarians, offering a warning of what Whigs would be like in power through a reminder of the past. Behn sharpens the satire in her source play, John Tatham's *The Rump*, adding a hypocritical puritan 'elder', Ananias Gogle, and royalist heroes, Loveless and Freeman, who are referred to as Tories. She also adds Corporal Right, 'An Oliverian Commander, but honest, and a Cavalier | in his heart' This figure illustrates a groundswell of hidden, 'natural' royalism, as do Ladies Lambert and Desbro, who have an affinity for the sexy cavaliers.

---

[47] For a valuable discussion of the contradictory process of remembering (in constructed ways) and forgetting the Civil War, see Sawday, 'Re-writing a Revolution: History, Symbol, and Text in the Restoration'.

Sometimes the tyrannies of republicanism are depicted in a different context, such as Venice in Otway's *Venice Preserv'd*, or ancient Rome, as in Tate's *The Ingratitude of a Commonwealth* and Otway's *Caius Marius*. In *The Ingratitude* the excessive power of the tribunes in the Roman republic leads to disaster, and the parallel between Coriolanus and James reflects the concern that James, if excluded, might start a civil war.[48] In his prologue to *Caius Marius* Otway refers to Charles II as 'Caesar'. Charles was ill at this time, and his return to the theatre is anticipated as crucial to peace, prosperity, and poetry. The play dramatizes political ambition running amok to the destruction of the state in the absence of a Caesar. The play's opening words set the framework. Public order depends upon social hierarchy:

> When will the Tut'lar Gods of Rome awake,
> To fix the Order of our wayward State,
> That we may once more know each other; know
> Th'extent of Laws, Prerogatives and Dues;
> The Bounds of Rules and Magistracy; who
> Ought first to govern, and who must obey?

> (1. 1–6)

Such divinely ordained order is never established, for it is antithetical to the republican condition. The world of Otway's play is one of 'Horrour, Confusion, and inverted Order, | Vast Desolation, Slaughter, Death and Ruine' (2. 506–7). As in the 1640s, viewed through royalist eyes, the citizens are incited to rebellion by references to 'the hard Yoak of Lordly pow'r' (2. 434) and 'Tyrannick pow'r' (4. 460, 464). Marius Senior becomes a 'Plebeian Tyrant' (1. 129), a Cromwellian figure who uses his army to suppress the senate and condemns the innocent and guilty alike.

Tories derive enormous ideological strength from raising the spectre of civil war. In fact this increasingly tends to be their central theme, overdetermining any difficulties or contradictions

---

[48] Parliament discussed this possibility in the 1670s, and Halifax repeatedly warned of the danger: Kenyon, introduction to Halifax, *Works*, 13–14; Haley, *Shaftesbury*, 483, 602. Halifax's warning that James might start a civil war if provoked was not disloyal, being aimed not at James but at exclusionists. However, some Tories coupled loyalty to Charles with criticism of James: Danby and Bishop Compton argued in 1676 that James's intransigence was the cause of Charles's political difficulties (Miller, *James II: A Study in Kingship*, 80).

which may arise, for example, from the depiction of royal faults or the lack of reward for loyal heroes.

Religion

Modern critics often fail to perceive as Whiggish anti-Catholic plays which were seen as oppositional in their own time. This is partly because the plays dramatize 'old-fashioned' values: the defence of sovereignty against popery in Settle's *The Female Prelate*, for example, or the defence of the traditional values of the Protestant country gentry in Shadwell's *The Lancashire Witches*. Partly, it is because critics do not see anti-Catholicism as political in itself at this time;[49] or believe that anti-popery only became Whiggish in about 1681.[50]

It is important to understand that even before the Popish Plot scare of autumn 1678, there was already a political division around issues of anti-dissent and anti-popery. Of course, this does not mean that all religious writing is political: the debate about religion in the 1670s encompasses tithes, episcopacy, clerical absenteeism, pluralities, and the forms and ceremonies of the Church of England. However, the Exclusion Crisis was overshadowed by the political and religious conflicts of the past. The sixteenth-century religious wars in Europe are recalled in *The Duke of Guise* and the pamphlet controversy surrounding it. Beleaguered Elizabethan Protestantism is recalled in plays such as *The Coronation of Queen Elizabeth* and Banks's *The Unhappy Favourite*, as well as in pamphlets and Pope-burnings on the anniversary of Elizabeth's accession, 17 November. The same is true in the pamphlet literature of 1677–8. Printed in 1678 were several histories of the St Bartholomew's Day Massacre in France in 1572 (and its bloody aftermath), of the

---

[49] Staves calls *Caesar Borgia, The Massacre of Paris*, and *The Female Prelate* 'simply . . . anti-Catholic' because they contain 'none of the abstract political theorizing that characterizes a genuine Whig play': *Players' Scepters*, 79. Her point of comparison is the Whig rhetoric of the period after the 1688 revolution, expressed in plays like Rowe's *Tamerlane* and Addison's *Cato*.

[50] As Robert Hume puts it, 'In 1679 and 1680 anti-Catholic hysteria is happily exploited by both Whig and Tory partisans: only later are cracks at priests taken as whiggish sentiment': *Development*, 342; cf. Brown, 'Nathaniel Lee's Political Dramas', 45.

sufferings of Protestants in the reign of Mary, and of the Gun-powder Plot, and a reprint of the English translation of Davila's *The History of the Civil Wars of France.* Marvell's *An Account of the Growth of Popery and Arbitrary Government,* like other anti-papist pamphlets, makes reference to Catholic atrocities in the reigns of Mary, Elizabeth, James, and Charles I. Above all, debates about religious matters tend to recall Civil War polarities. In Marvell's *Account,* fear of popery is coupled with fear of Counter-Reformation Catholicism and the government's weakness towards it, and of government attacks on Parliament. Attacks on dissenters by Nalson, L'Estrange, and others are mingled with royalist polemic against fomenters of rebellion who will bring back the terrors of ''41'. In 1678 the reprinting of texts from the Civil War period draws attention to the paral-lel.[51] The polarized arguments about religion which were to underpin the Whig–Tory divide were already in place in the late 1670s.

The dramatic language of anti-Catholicism is a *political* lan-guage. Settle's *The Female Prelate* has been called simply anti-Catholic and not political or partisan,[52] even though it has an epistle dedicatory to the Whig leader, Shaftesbury, which explic-itly vindicates the Whig opposition (and it is well known that Settle, like Shadwell, wrote Whig propaganda), and despite the fact that Settle's portrayal of the crimes of papists in *The Female Prelate* is an exact mirror image of Whitaker's royalist anatomization of rebellion in *The Conspiracy.* Moreover, Settle uses exactly the same tropes as Marvell's *An Account of the Growth of Popery and Arbitrary Government.* Both stress the importance of the 'established Protestant Religion' and say that true loyalty means being a friend to English Protestantism in its time of danger (Settle, sig. A1ᵛ, Marvell, 1). Settle shows papists as beyond the pale of civilized humanity and guilty of fanatical cruelty. So does Marvell (5, 9). Settle shows that the Pope and

---

[51] An example of a royalist reprint is Robert Sanderson, Bishop of Lincoln, *Episcopacy (as Established by Law in England) Not Prejudicial to Regal Power.* An anti-papist example is *The Grand Designs of the Papists* (1678). This is a reprint of *Rome's Masterpeece; or, The Grand Conspiracy of the Pope and his Jesuited Instruments to Extirpate the Protestant Religion* (1643), variously attributed to Ondrej Haberveslz Habernfeldu, trans. Sir William Boswell, and to William Prynne.

[52] See n. 49 above.

cardinals place themselves above the law. So does Marvell (10). Settle's Pope Joan manipulates a religious discourse she does not believe in (4. 4. p. 55): her religion is a fraud. For Marvell popery is an impious 'imposture' (5). For Marvell the Roman Church is riven by 'Ambition' (10). Joan is ambition incarnate.

The Roman Church's confiscation of Saxony's property, and its attack on his liberty and sovereignty, represent in dramatic form exactly what Marvell says in political prose: the Roman faith is innovative, not traditional; it involves an attack on property (6, 13); and on sovereignty: 'He by his dispensation annuls Contracts betwixt man and man, dissolves Oaths between Princes, or betwixt them and their People, and gives allowance in cases which God and nature prohibits' (8). This argument was central to the move to exclude James. The Pope sets himself up 'as God and not as man', and claims that 'his Power is Absolute, and his Decrees Infallible' (7–8). Joan boasts that she can make and unmake saints and kings (3. p. 30), just as the Pope in Marvell's account claims 'That he is still Monarch of this World and that he can dispose of Kingdoms and Empires as he pleases' (8). As for the murders of Saxony and his father before him, the belief that the Pope would sanction the murder of 'sovereigns' was central in opposition propaganda, countering royalist accusations that agitation against popery and arbitrary government would culminate in a repeat of the regicide of 1649.[53] Marvell says papists foster rebellion: 'their whole People, if of the *Romish* perswasion' are 'obliged to rebel at any time upon the *Popes* pleasure' (10). Settle shows the rabble running amok, incited by the papists to murder a duke.

For good measure Settle follows the example of the more lurid anti-papist pamphlets in including criticism of 'the Roman Altars Luxury' and 'the rich Churches Riot' (1. 1. p. 2; cf. 1. 2. p. 6), in associating popery and diabolism (1. 2. p. 5; 4. 3. p. 50; 5. 2. p. 69), and in making Rome a centre of hypocritical secret

---

[53] In addition to Marvell's *Account*, see a speech of Pope Sixtus V published in 1678 under the title *The Catholick Cause; or, The Horrid Practice of Murdering Kings, Justified and Commended by the Pope*. Thomas Shipman's play on the same subject, *Henry the Third of France, Stabb'd by a Fryer, With the Fall of the Guise* was probably first performed in 1672. It was published in 1678 and may have been performed then too: see Zimansky and Hume, 'Thomas Shipman's *Henry the Third of France*: Some Questions of Date, Performance, and Publication'.

lust as well as female monstrosity.[54] Other anti-Catholic plays also share the oppositional language of political prose; for example, Shadwell's *The Lancashire Witches* shares Marvell's insistence on the superior liberties enjoyed by English Protestant subjects as compared with Catholic countries.

The Coronation of Queen Elizabeth has exactly the same nexus of attitudes and associations as *The Female Prelate*. Defence of Protestantism is synonymous with the good of the nation. Pope and cardinals revel in 'Blood and Murthers' (1. 1. p. 2), plot to murder the sovereign, and relish their superiority to mere monarchs. They see religion as something to exploit in others rather than to believe in themselves (2. 3. p. 12) and are openly in league with the Devil, to whom the Pope's soul is pledged. The highlight of the third act is a moralized spectacle, as the Devil tells the Pope he was 'once thy Servant, and now thy Master' and 'The Scene suddenly draws off, and discovers Hell full of Devils, Popes and Cardinals' (3. 2. p. 19). Lust is there too: the Pope's downfall comes about because he seduces a nun whose father is a cardinal. This seems fanciful, but the oppositional resonance is clear. The papists pose a real threat: they historicize themselves by revelling in the cruelties of Mary's reign. All Elizabeth's speeches in the play are drawn from the published speeches of the real Elizabeth, so that although the result is heavily ideological, it is an ideology rooted in history. The play follows in the long tradition of criticizing the Stuarts obliquely by praising their predecessor. Elizabeth is shown as one who 'maugred all the Plots and dire Conspiracies of *Rome*' (sig. A2ʳ). This means tackling the enemy within (Catholics at court, the treacherous French ambassador) and without (the Spanish). She expresses humility before God in speeches which seem to criticize Stuart divine right: 'I must refuse that Worship which the Immortal Powers have only bidden to themselves' (1. 1. p. 1).[55] As noted above, she is grateful to her loyal subjects and rewards them. Criticism of the present monarch is implicit,

[54] Cf. *The Plot Discover'd; or, A New Discourse Between the Devil and the Pope*; *Il Putanismo di Roma*. The Pope was associated with the Devil in numerous cartoons and broadsides as well as in the Pope-burning processions.

[55] See Perry, *Elizabeth I, the Word of a Prince*, 311 for Elizabeth I's 'Golden Speech' made to Parliament in 1601 and much reprinted into the 18th-cent., in which she stresses her love for her subjects, her loving subjection to God, and the accountability of princes to him.

as it was in Pope-burnings on the anniversary of Elizabeth's accession, 'which implied a deep criticism of the court as falling far short of Elizabethan perfection'.[56] This play was performed not in the theatres but at Bartholomew and Southwark Fairs in summer 1680. It shares the subversive vitality and comparative freedom from restriction of this plebeian dramatic outlet.[57]

I hope I have demonstrated the oppositional resonance of anti-Catholic plays. It is necessary to add that Tory plays depict religion differently. Tory plays have an uneasy attitude to popery, not excusing but minimizing it. Since Whigs exploited the Popish Plot scare, Tories expressed scepticism about it from the earliest stages.[58] The Whigs made capital out of the king's lukewarm attitude to pursuing the alleged plotters, which was widely supposed to be due to Catholic sympathies.[59] So popery and anti-popery were problematic themes for Tories. Tories deal with the problem of Whig anti-popery in several ways. Firstly, they shift the focus: dissenters become the main threat. They are castigated as descendants of Civil War religious radicals and as Whig supporters: hypocritical, canting puritans are associated with citizen Whigs and satirized in Tory comedies like D'Urfey's *Sir Barnaby Whigg* and Crowne's *City Politiques*. Secondly, Tories draw a parallel between popery and dissent. This parallel originated in the early Stuart period, and, indeed, was being trumpeted loudly in royalist propaganda in the late 1670s.[60]

---

[56] Miller, *Popery and Politics*, 185. As part of the pageantry preceding the 1679 Pope-burning, 'A great statue of Elizabeth was decked out with Magna Carta and the Protestant religion and the Pope was made to bow before it' (ibid.).

[57] Rosenfeld, *The Theatre of the London Fairs in the Eighteenth Century*.

[58] In the 1678–9 season see e.g. Dryden's prologue to *Caesar Borgia* and epilogue to *Troilus and Cressida*, and Behn's prologue to *The Feign'd Curtizans*. Even before the plot scare Nalson claimed in *The Countermine* that 'Enemies of the Church and State' used 'the old Strategem of Fears and Jealousies of Popery' to foment rebellion (sig. A3ʳ). See also Kenyon, *The Popish Plot*, 121.

[59] Price, *Cold Caleb*, quotes the Whig supporter Ford Grey: 'all thinking men did believe the King to be in all parts of the Popish Plot except the murder of himself, which he did not think was intended, knowing the papists were well assured of his zeal to their religion'. Price comments, 'The duplicity of the King's methods and his supposed partiality for the papists had cost Charles the nation's confidence.'

[60] Nalson, *The Common Interest of King and People*, 240 and *The Countermine*, ch. 15. Cf. *A Parallel Betwixt Popery and Phanaticism*. Nalson makes many of the same charges against dissenters that the opposition made against papists, for example that they place themselves outside the law (*Countermine*, 49) and that they are associated with the Devil (ibid., ch. 7). For a survey of Tory pamphlets which

Thus, in *The Royalist*, the plotter Jonas pretends to be a Jesuit, to test the hero, Kinglove, revealing in the process the kinship between papists and puritan 'fanatics': 'They are both the necessary Tools we work with, and indeed the chief Implements of our Trade' (3. 1. p. 22). Thirdly, Tories satirize Whig anti-popery directly: credulous citizens believe ridiculous tales of monstrous happenings which portend the advent of popery in *The Revenge* (2. 3. p. 23) and Otway's *The Souldier's Fortune* (2. 142–50). The abuses of the Popish Plot investigation and injustice of the trials are also brought out (*Revenge*, 5. 4. pp. 59–60; *Souldier's Fortune*, 3. 447–51). Fourthly, Tories try to expose 'Loyal Protestantism' as disingenuous: the Whigs' professed concern for religion conceals a 'real' aim of rebellion for its own sake or for reasons of personal ambition. 'Underneath' they are guilty both of religious hypocrisy and of secret atheism. Thus, in *The Conspiracy* the rebels arrogantly assume heaven is on their side (e.g. 4. p. 34), but also admit their own hypocrisy: 'I yield our Religion is the way to sin'; and atheism: 'one Mute [i.e. assassin] I Can all the wayes of Providence confute' (1. p. 7). Whitaker also works hard to challenge the Whigs' association of superstition and credulity with popery: the rebels sneer at the royalists as cowards 'Whom you might fright to death with shows and Charms' (5. p. 51), but they are lying when they say their enemies have destroyed themselves with 'meer imagination' (ibid.). With heavy irony the rebels are then themselves superstitiously terrified by the appearance of Ibrahim's ghost. The implication is that the 'rebels' of 1679 are lying about who is really guilty of superstitious error.

It remains to consider Dryden's treatment of religion, as I think it has caused some confusion. In the early stages of the Exclusion Crisis it seems as if Dryden's plays are anti-clerical, and this contributes to the view that he was 'slow to enlist as an active Tory partisan'.[61] Anti-clericalism is a frequent, almost stock theme in early Restoration drama, but it becomes problematic for Tories in the crisis as attacks on priests come to seem Whiggish. Whitaker in *The Conspiracy* pointedly repudiates anti-clericalism by including a virtuous and loyal priest. How-

associate rebellion and diabolism, see Miller, 'Political Satire in the Malicorne–Melanax Scenes of *The Duke of Guise*'.

[61] Harth, 'Dryden in 1678–1681', 71.

ever, Dryden in the aftermath of the Popish Plot scare seems in no hurry to relinquish anti-clericalism and seems prepared to get a cheap laugh from sneers at priests. In *Troilus and Cressida* in the 1678–9 season he inserts attacks on priests throughout the play in the form of humorous jibes by Pandarus and more sustained diatribes by Troilus and Thersites. Calchas becomes a 'fugitive Rogue Priest' (4. 1. 16), where Shakespeare merely has a reference to Cressida's father. When Troilus thinks he is betrayed, he curses 'That I shou'd trust the Daughter of a Priest!' (5. 2. 157).

However, it is notable that the first of Troilus' diatribes is an attempt to dismiss bad omens before battle which are actually accurate; and that the second is based on a betrayal which has not actually taken place. For those who are prepared to think a little more carefully, anti-clericalism is shown to be over-hasty and misplaced.[62] In *Oedipus* in the same season Dryden also problematizes hasty anti-clericalism. The good priest Tiresias conjures up the ghost of Lajus to reveal the truth, which leads to an anti-clerical outburst from Oedipus: 'O why has Priest-hood privilege to lye, | And yet to be believ'd!' (3. 1. 434–5). The villain Creon adds, 'Priests, Priests, all brib'd, all Priests' (line 456) and identifies the real threat to Thebes as the foreign prince Adrastus. The audience knows the priest has not lied and that Creon represents the real danger. We are left with a sense of the dangers of facile anti-clericalism, of 'knee-jerk' patriotism, and of not knowing who the king's enemies really are.

To perceive the dangers of anti-clericalism in these plays involves care and thought, and Dryden twice requests such careful reading for *The Spanish Fryar* in his dedication (sig. A2ᵛ). At a superficial level the play might seem Whiggish because of the anti-clericalism of the Friar Dominic scenes. It has a similar resonance to the anti-papist clowning in the anonymous *Rome's Follies; or, The Amorous Fryars*, a play performed privately in the next theatrical season which can clearly be

---

[62] However, I would not go as far as Lewis Moore, who thinks in Calchas Dryden 'specifically attacks Titus Oates, the priest who represented the most danger to the state' (102). This seems to me specious. Oates was not a priest in 1678–9. He took holy orders in 1669, but was quickly dismissed from his living for drunkenness and heretical opinions. He was expelled from the Jesuit seminary at 'St Omers' and was never in Catholic orders (Kenyon, *The Popish Plot*, 54, 57–8). Attacks on a treacherous priest were more likely to have an anti-papist resonance in this period.

identified as Whig.[63] Dryden himself said he had offered something 'to the people' in *The Spanish Fryar*;[64] and this is hardly surprising since it was performed in the 1680–1 season, at a time of apparent Whig ascendancy and during the sitting of the 'Exclusion' Parliament. However, the careful reader can discern that, so far from anti-clericalism in the play having any great force, it is actually questioned. Pedro in Act 1 sneers at the usurper-Queen's prayers and at the priests who will turn victory in war into a miracle; yet the procession of the Queen and choristers is dignified and her piety is one of the good aspects of her contradictory character. She herself turns to anti-clericalism speciously to justify her worst lapse, the sanctioning of old King Sancho's murder (3. 2. pp. 40–1). She is immediately reproached by Torrismond's moving account of the plight of imprisoned majesty. Hysterical anti-clericalism is dangerous in the play, just as royalists thought it was dangerous when Whigs capitalized upon it in the wake of the Popish Plot scare. As I have argued at length in my article 'The Politics of John Dryden's *The Spanish Fryar*', it seems that Dryden's political outlook is fairly consistent, but that he adapts himself to the changing political situation. Here he is going some way to meet the apparently victorious Whigs, but insisting above all on a message of caution, moderation, and reconciliation around the values of 1660.

It is clear that *The Duke of Guise*, produced in the Tory reaction period (November 1682), follows the Tory perspective outlined above. The play offers a very powerful instance of the parallel between popery and dissent. The Catholic extremist French Holy League is portrayed in a way which has clear reference to both interregnum parliamentarians and Exclusion Crisis Whigs: 'Our Play's a Parallel: The Holy League | Begot our Cov'nant: Guisards got the Whigg' (prologue). The parallel is made forcefully and repeatedly, and there is also a strongly emphasized association of both Guisards and Whigs–dissenters

---

[63] In the dedication to Shaftesbury the author, who signs himself 'N.N.', clearly identifies himself as a Whig supporter. He likens his own play to *Caesar Borgia* and *The Lancashire Witches* as being both anti-papist and oppositional, and suggests that this is why his play has to be performed outside the theatre (the tide was turning against the Whigs in autumn 1681).

[64] Dryden, Preface to *De Arte Graphica*, in *Works*, xx. 76.

with the Devil throughout the play.[65] However, Dryden's Tory intentions are clear, and he reiterates them in his defence of the play in *The Vindication*, attacking 'Loyal Protestantism' as a blatantly disingenuous front for rebellion: 'some of them are *Atheists*, some *Sectaries*, yet ALL *True Protestants*. *Most* of them love *all Whores*, but her of *Babylon*' (23).

There are two problems with Dryden's treatment of religion in *The Duke of Guise* which are problems for Tories in general. The first is that they are sometimes forced to abandon the defence of Protestantism to the Whigs, leading to weak or equivocal arguments. In chapter 15 of *The Countermine* Nalson's critique of Calvinism shades into criticism of Protestantism itself, especially since the beleaguered French and Dutch Protestants whom Parliament wanted Charles to aid were strongly Calvinistic. This fits ill with his earlier claim that dissenters are bad Protestants who have themselves opened the door to the threat of popery (16). Similarly, in his *Vindication* of *The Duke of Guise* Dryden is forced by his Toryism into the position that defence of Protestantism must take second place to obedience: absolute loyalty comes before religion. This effectively concedes a Whig accusation that must be denied, that the threat to English Protestantism was not being taken seriously enough.

Secondly, there is an inherent difficulty in the exercise of focusing on popish cruelty as a way of getting at the Whigs, as the author of one of the pamphlets attacking the play points out:

[Dryden] has so reviv'd the Storyes of the Parisian Massacre, and the memory of the Barricaders most damnable Contrivances against their Soveraign, that he has put new life into the drooping Credit of the Popish Plot, rais'd almost from the Grave the Horror of Popish cruelty and disloyalty, destroyed all that R[oger] L['Estrange] has been labouring to make good almost these two twelve months, and may truly be said to be another Titus Oates, bringing new Lights into the World, and new Discoverys of Jesuitical Massacre and Treason.[66]

Tories were put in a difficult position by their monarch and his heir. Under a loudly and unequivocally Protestant king like

---

[65] Cf. Dryden's epistle dedicatory, sig. A3ʳ and Otway's epistle dedicatory to *The Atheist*, in *Works*, ed. Ghosh, 294–5. The association is reversed in *Some Reflections Upon The Pretended Parallel*, where Dryden is identified as Satan (2–3).

[66] *The True History of the Duke of Guise*, sig. A4ᵛ.

James I, the line that popery and presbytery were equally devilish was a strong position. But Charles II's known advocacy of toleration for Catholics, and his brother's known Catholicism, meant that to damn popery too strongly was to strengthen the arguments of the opposition. On the other hand, to damn only presbytery would incur suspicion of popery. Charles's character and James's religion drove a wedge between Tories' monarchism and their commitment to the Established Church. The problem was to become acute in and after 1688. For the present, one leg of the equation—anti-popery—had to be weakened, and the argument tended to stagger.

Class

If defence of Protestantism was rather a weak point for Toryism, class was a somewhat stronger point. I do not mean strong in any absolute or moral sense; but that the argument carried conviction in terms of values about which there was still assumed to be a consensus. So those advancing the argument were on the offensive, not the defensive.

Tory mockery of the Whigs has three aspects. First and foremost is satire of Whig rabble-rousing, a charge which raises the spectre of 1641. The difference between the Whig and Tory rhetoric of class is expressed in the fact that Marvell evinces a concern for the nation as a whole, and for the poorer people (e.g. 3, 14, 76), whereas L'Estrange accuses Marvell of vulgarity and of stirring up the rabble (4, 14–15, 47).[67] Similarly, in *The Duke of Guise* Dryden uses the mob to show the dangers of disloyal agitation. Danger emanates from those who 'Court the Crowd' (1. 2. p. 8). The role of seditious sheriffs is also stressed, reflecting the Whigs' role in the City of London.[68] Rabble scenes such as 3. 1 and 4. 4 give a stark depiction of the combination of populism and contempt for the masses which characterizes

[67] Cf. Nalson, *Countermine*, chs. 6 and 15, in which the same accusation is levelled at dissenters.

[68] Cf. Tate's *Ingratitude of a Common-wealth*. Where Shakespeare refers to the election of five tribunes, Tate names four: Brutus, Sicinius, Cornicius, and Bethellius. The last two refer to Henry Cornish and Slingsby Bethel, radical dissenters who had been elected sheriffs of London in 1680 by a substantial majority, despite government opposition: Haley, *Shaftesbury*, 582.

rebel leaders, and the volatility and illogic of the plebeians. There are frequent references throughout the play to the dangers of the 'Herd' (4. 1. p. 39), the 'Rebellious Rabble', and 'all the Vermin of the vile *Parisians*' (1. 3. p. 8). The rebels are constantly likened to monsters and devils, and the people are rats, bats, curs, dogs, vipers, asps, adders, and even snails (3. 1. p. 23). The Whigs' very real popular support is countered by the depiction of popularity as a suspect and seditious criterion. A rebel cleric argues: 'Rebellion is an Insurrection against the Government; but they that have the Power are actually the Government: Therefore if the People have the Power, the Rebellion is in the King . . . what they call the Lawful Government, | Is now the Faction; for the most are ours' (1. 1. p. 2). Similarly, in 4. 4, a devil in the guise of a fanatic preacher persuades the rabble that the majority, having numbers on their side, can insist that white is black if they wish. In an image familiar in royalist propaganda since before the Civil War, rebellion means 'The World's turn'd upside down' (5. 1. p. 55); or, as Grillon suggests, ''tis downside up'.

Exclusion Crisis adaptations of Shakespeare make alterations and additions to Shakespeare to show the dangers of populism and the mob and to make the citizens seem more like the Whig trouble-makers of contemporary Tory propaganda: we see this in *The History of King Richard The Second*, *The Ingratitude of a Common-wealth*, *The Misery of Civil-War*, and *Caius Marius*. The artisan class is invariably presented as stupid, greedy, illogical, and prone to rebel, and any endearing or redeeming features are eliminated. The disloyal noblemen who raise the mob are always cynical and treacherous, motivated by malice, envy, and ambition. Rebels always fall out among themselves, because once loyalty is breached, treachery and disorder know no bounds. In the mob scenes in *The Young King*, *The Spanish Fryar*, and *The Loyal Brother* we find the message that it is better not to stir up the rabble even in a good (royalist) cause: quiet is best and right will prevail.

Whigs have two different responses to the charge of rabble-rousing. In plays written for the theatre such as *The Female Prelate* and *The Massacre of Paris* the charge is reversed. Papists are the rabble-rousers and heroic anti-papist noblemen the victims who suffer torture and death at the hands of a mob which has no respect for liberty and property. In drama produced outside the theatres there is a positive attitude to the lower classes and the sort of concern for the commonwealth as a whole expressed by Marvell. This is very clear in Jordan's Lord Mayor's Shows; and even more strongly in *The Coronation of Queen Elizabeth*. Obviously it partly reflects the fact that there was a greater preponderance of lower-class spectators in the theatre of London street pageantry and fairs. In *The Coronation* we find a reversal of the theme of mob violence: the artisans are the custodians of order. The play dramatizes the political vigilance of the lower classes as necessary, a direct reversal of the royalist idea of political interest as 'busy' and 'improper'. The nation's leaders are busy fighting the Armada. Their eyes cannot be everywhere. The Pope, who has fled to England, is captured by the trusty artisans whose native British honesty enables them to see through his lies. The artisans then burn the Pope, making a dramatic reality of the annual, symbolic Pope-burning processions. The good order which was reportedly kept at the processions, despite government fears, is reflected in the artisans' first asking the Queen's permission to burn the Pope and her reply that they should do it 'with discretion, without Riot or Tumult' (3. 2. p. 22).

The commoners are depicted as victims: under Mary they suffered papist atrocities, were persecuted as heretics for ridiculous reasons, had their wives and daughters raped and murdered by cardinals. They are sometimes funny and foolish, but the laughter is with the people and against the Pope, whom they are able to outwit. The artisans are good-natured, stout-hearted, full of native common sense, and ultimately the best defenders of the faith and of the realm. Here is no dangerous 'rabble', but the commonalty of England. The harmony of the commonwealth is symbolized by the dance which concludes the piece. There is a lesson here for the monarch who mistrusts his Loyal Protestant subjects and so rules over a divided kingdom.

The second aspect of the Tory rhetoric of class is satire of the citizen-merchant class who had formed a base of support for parliamentarians in the interregnum and now played a central role in opposition to the monarchy in the Exclusion Crisis.[69]

---

[69] See Brenner, *Merchants and Revolution*.

This explains what would otherwise seem an extraordinarily vindictive attitude towards rich citizens in plays, prologues, and epilogues. In *The Revenge*, as in the source play Marston's *The Dutch Courtesan*, there is satire of citizens as a class. Capitalist methods are deplored, and the vintner is shown to deserve his fate of being tricked, robbed, and imprisoned simply for carrying on a thieving trade. In *The Revenge* Marston's satire is given political force by the association of these class faults with anti-papist scaremongering.[70] In *The Souldier's Fortune*, the heroes, the disbanded soldiers Beaugard and Courtine, voice disgust at citizens as a class (e.g. 1. 205–8). Political animus against the citizenry paves the way for the cuckolding plot. Sir Davy Dunce deserves to be cuckolded not only because he is a fool, but also because he supports the opposition (1. 462–6). The theme of cuckolding the Whig is a common one in Tory comedy; indeed, by the height of the Tory reaction in 1682, the association of citizen, Whig, and cuckold had become so axiomatic that in *The Duke of Guise* the word 'cuckold' is used throughout instead of 'citizen' or 'rebel'. In plays like *Mr. Turbulent*, *Sir Barnaby Whigg*, and *City Politiques* citizens are depicted as knaves and fools, guilty of treasonable factionalism, dissent, vulgarity, philistinism, hypocrisy, and overweening presumption in poetry, love, religion, and politics. Such plays aim to place the entire citizen class beyond the pale. Only outside the theatre in the Lord Mayor's Shows do the moderation and centrality of the City continue to be asserted. The Whig Shadwell in *The Woman-Captain* satirizes foolish citizens as part of his quasi-Jonsonian anatomization of the follies of the times, even though his main satiric focus is on dissolute aristocrats and rakes.[71]

The third aspect of the Tory language of class concerns the treatment of the aristocracy. The corollary of the view that the social order is a natural one is that the upper class have a natural nobility and superiority, just as the king possesses inherent

---

[70] The characterization of Diana's lovers is more politically pointed in *The Revenge*. The humours characters Tysefew and Caquetuer, who court Crispinella, become an upstart knight, Sir John Emptie, who is foolishly anti-papist (5. 4. p. 64) and a newsmonger (5. 2. p. 55), and Mr Shatter, a boorish 'cit'.

[71] Danchin takes a disparaging reference to 'men of business' in the prologue to mean citizens, but this is more likely to mean men engaged in public affairs than men engaged in trade (*OED*, citing Burnet).

royalty. Thus Kinglove in *The Royalist* is virtuous, wise, and honourable, and his enemies' moral inferiority to him is signified by their class position: Jonas is 'below a Gentleman's revenge' (3. 1. p. 24); Justice Eitherside's mother was an apple-seller; Oldcut enriched himself among other means by 'Plebeian Tally-mans Extortion' (1. p. 9); the tenants are ignorant and unreliable country fellows who need Kinglove's good government, though they treacherously spurn it. The interregnum is a time when the social and moral order is inverted: 'the most ignorant have wit enough to be rogues, and get estates from those that are wiser' (1. p. 4); and when 'one knows not now who's the Landlord, nor who's the Tenant; which is the King, and which the Cobler. They are both equal now as things are order'd' (3. 2. p. 26). The coffee-house in 4. 2 is 'the Epitome of Hell, where all sorts of male-contented Fiends are in office' and 'the Mart of the Mobile, and throng'd by people of all sorts and qualities, where your Mechanick may vent Sedition at an easie rate, and look as big as your Alderman or Grandee' (4. 2. pp. 46, 47).

The idea of inherent social superiority means that Toryism privileges upper-class bonds over national ones. In Dryden's and Lee's *Oedipus* and Tate's *The Loyal General* class loyalty between the king and a foreign prince is privileged over civic and national bonds. It is rebels who talk of patriotism. In *The Ingratitude of a Common-wealth* Tate alters Shakespeare to emphasize patrician virtue across national boundaries, as a counterpart to plebeian vice.[72] In *The Feign'd Curtizans*, produced early in 1679 in the heat of the Popish Plot furore, Behn seems to be making a political point of her play's conventional Italian setting. Her prologue condemns those who would say, 'This [play] must be damn'd, the Plot is laid in Rome' (sig. A4ʳ). Although the play's plot is set in Rome, there is no Popish Plot there. The play opens with hospitable exchanges between the Italian and English gentlemen, and the latter proceed to court

---

[72] Tate expunges Coriolanus' blame of the Roman patricians in 4. 1, and emphasizes that the people are the enemy. In 4. 3 he deletes the bad behaviour of the Volscian senators in scorning Menenius, possibly for reasons of economy, but perhaps also because his class perspective at this point overrides patriotism. A similar effect is achieved in 1. 3 where Tate shows Rome's enemy Aufidius as braver and tougher than the rank-and-file Romans. Here aristocratic virtue is valued at the expense of consistency: Tate retains Shakespearian material which contradicts his later portrayal of Aufidius as a torturer and rapist.

Italian ladies. Upper-class wit and good taste cross national boundaries.

Class is more important distinction than nationality. There is satire of the Englishman Sir Signall Buffoon, who boorishly apes Italian manners and language, though his father sent him to Italy with a puritan chaplain as a safeguard against 'the eminent danger that young Travellers are in of being perverted to Popery' (1. 1. p. 5). This puritan father is 'a fool and knave' who 'had the attendant blessing of getting an Estate of some eight thousand a year' (1. 1. p. 5), so presumably he is an upstart, sequestrating puritan of the type satirized in *The Royalist*. The tutor, Tickletext, is tasteless and mercenary, making his pupil trade in gloves, stockings, and pins on the Grand Tour. He is also crudely anti-papist and foolishly proud of being English. Yet he is hypocritically glad to exploit Roman custom to get a whore, justifying himself with a legalistic quibble (1. 2. p. 6). Tickletext's faults are generic: 'we have a thousand of these in *England* that go loose about the streets, and pass with us for as sober discreet religious persons' (4. 1. p. 45). Behn thus satirizes the mercantile middle class through an association of anti-popery and patriotism with hypocrisy, folly, pretension, legalism, and low-class money-grubbing.

The play is not doctrinaire: there is also some criticism of the Italian customs of arranged marriage and condemning girls to nunneries: the women plot successfully to get choice and some respect in marriage. There is light-hearted criticism of the worst excesses of cavalier behaviour, as when the libertine Galliard is tamed and married off. However, in the end, *The Feign'd Curtizans* celebrates a mythologized, upper class 'good Nature' (5. 1. p. 70) across national boundaries. Tickletext is taught tolerance, and Sir Signall has the last word in the play to tell him, 'And Governor, pray let me have no more dominering and Usurpation! But as we have hitherto been honest Brothers in iniquity, so let's wink hereafter at each others frailties!' (5. 1. p. 71). Behn suggests that this advice might also hold good for those who criticized the morals of the king and court.

The Whig Shadwell has no sense of the inherent virtue of the nobility: rather the reverse, to judge by his excoriation of upper-class vice in *The Libertine* (1675). In *The Woman-Captain* he depicts the great falling off in manners and morals in recent years, and his primary focus is upon the modern aristocratic 'degenerous Youth' (sig. A2ᵛ). His Sir Humphrey Scattergood is such a youth. Two young gallants, Bellamy and Wildman, encourage Sir Humphrey in excess. These cavalier rakes are the same dramatic types as the heroes in plays by Etherege, Otway, Behn, and others, but Shadwell depicts them negatively. They show their true colours in Act 5, when, after accepting the hospitality of the now ruined Sir Humphrey, they ignore his distress and talk of whores. It is a sign of the times that the custodians of real gentlemanly virtue are a servant and a woman.

Tory dramatists do depict aristocratic vice, but they associate it with corrupt 'great men' (like the Whig leaders) who foment rebellion. These men show the type of class treachery of which the king notoriously accused Thomas Thynne.[73] A notable example is the Constable in *The Ambitious Statesman*. The patrician Metellus in *Caius Marius* is another. The pointed assertion of his class superiority makes Metellus' behaviour seem all the worse. In Tory terms, he does not have the excuse of low birth and ought to set an example. It is unlikely that Metellus personates any particular nobleman;[74] rather, he represents the misleadership and rottenness in high places which unleashed chaos in the 1640s and seemed likely to do so again. The play's moral is 'Be warn'd by me, *ye Great ones*, how y'embroil | Your Country's Peace' (5. 477–8, my emphasis).

The Tory language of class had considerable force. Every problem could be overdetermined by the great spectre of mass revolt. Moreover, the Whigs were vulnerable to the charge of rabble-rousing because they did not really wish to unleash the

---

[73] 'Tom of Ten Thousand', the wealthy owner of Longleat, presented a petition of 30,000 Wiltshire signatures to Charles in Jan. 1680 and was accused by the king of being a traitor to his class: Haley, *Shaftesbury*, 563

[74] As a patrician, Metellus seems a better candidate to represent Shaftesbury than the plebeian Marius, with whom a parallel has been suggested by Murray, 'The Butt of Otway's Political Moral', 49, Warner, *Thomas Otway*, 34, Pollard, 'Shakespeare's Influence on Otway's *Caius Marius*', 541, and, with reservations, by Munns, 'Dark Disorders', 349. However, I do not think there is any sustained portrait of Shaftesbury, or even that there is a split portrait of him, as critics have suggested there is in *Venice Preserv'd*: firstly, personation is a risky business; secondly, more general political reference can be more effective; and thirdly, there were lots of Whig noblemen. Sixteen peers signed the first Whig petition in 1679 (Haley, *Shaftesbury*, 560). Why always Shaftesbury?

danger from below: they had learned that lesson in the 1640s. Whig emphasis on the whole commonwealth and criticism of dissolute aristocrats was not intended as criticism of the existing social order. Yet since the Whigs actually did rely on a base of support among the citizens of London, and since they did engage in populist demagogy and in crowd politics, it was easy for Tories to argue that they posed a threat to the social order in reality, whether they said so or not. However, the Tory class paradigm had its flaws. In particular, it increasingly seems to abandon the middle ground. In plays of the Tory reaction period like *The Duke of Guise* Toryism begins to sound both shrill and élitist. Just as law, patriotism, and Protestantism are abandoned to the Whigs, so is any claim to represent the whole polity.

CHAPTER 5

The Dramatic Language of Sexual Politics

I WANT now to consider the dramatic language of sexual politics, focusing on the interface between party politics and questions of gender and sex. There has been a wealth of recent criticism which has focused primarily on gender; and there are still traditional accounts of literature and politics being produced which take no account of questions of gender at all.[1] My goals are limited and precise: to reinstate gender in the language of 'high' politics, and also to put down some markers about what the dramatic language of sexual politics did and did not say. As in the rest of this book, my aim is to clarify political difference, not to deconstruct it; to examine what the Tory and Whig languages of sexual politics really said, how they were the same and how they were different, and what real contradictions there were. I want to consider the rhetorical use of gender issues in party politics. This is not in the least to devalue the work of those whose focus is on fractures and liminal spaces which open up for women; nor does it mean that I think women's issues are subordinate: I don't. I do think that discourses of party and gender are interpenetrated in this period, and that studying this interpenetration aids our understanding of both gender issues and the language of politics.

Since this is a contentious (and growth) area, let me make clear my critical assumptions. Firstly, like Janet Todd, 'I have followed Behn's lead and not attempted to separate female writing from the web of male- and female-authored works that form the literature of a period'.[2] This is not to say that there is no value in considering women's writing separately or primarily

---

[1] For work on gender, see below. For a 'gender-blind' account, see e.g. Downie, *To Settle the Succession of the State*.
[2] Todd, *Sign of Angellica*, 2.

in relation to other women's writing from different periods; but women were 'political animals' in the Restoration,[3] and I think we can learn something from considering Behn's work within the network of political and ideological assumptions with which it was engaged. The counterpart of considering women's work separately is often that they are *not* considered in the context of 'high' politics, and this impoverishes our understanding.

Secondly, I do not believe that references to sex and gender are depoliticizing or that they always necessarily assert the concerns of a 'private' sphere which is opposed to the political sphere.[4] Conversely, I think the language of sexual politics is part of the language of politics, but not the whole of it. In this my approach differs from, for example, that of Richard Braverman, whose *Plots and Counterplots: Sexual Politics and the Body Politic in English Literature 1660–1730* starts from the political language of patriarchalism and reinterprets the drama and the politics in terms of a master theme of sexual politics.

I think it is possible to overstate the importance of patri-archalism. Although it had real force, it was the force of an ideology which was being shrilly reasserted in an attempt to browbeat those who did not believe in it: 'Filmer marks not the triumphant ascendancy of patriarchal thought, but its demise as tacit knowledge, the fact that it is in crisis'.[5] Moreover, as Stephen Flores puts it, 'patriarchal ideology tends to produce the social, political, and sexual struggles for power it purports to control'.[6] On the other hand, some recent criticism over-emphasizes the extent to which Restoration texts undermine 'patriarchy'. In relation to sexual politics, as with the language of politics generally, it is necessary to stress both sides of the contradiction: the conservatism *and* the seeds of the new within the old.

---

[3] Todd, *Sign of Angellica*, 8.
[4] See my 'Interpreting the Politics of Restoration Drama'.
[5] McKeon, 'Historicizing Patriarchy', 296.
[6] Flores, 'Patriarchal Politics under Cultural Stress: Nathaniel Lee's Passion Plays' (11). However, I disagree with his view that 'Lee maintains ... a largely non-partisan though politically conservative stance' (20), as will be clear from my reading of Lee's work below and in Ch. 8. Also I do not think he distinguishes adequately in this essay between Stuart patriarchalism and patriarchy in the modern sense.

In order to get this right, it is important to distinguish between Stuart patriarchalism and patriarchy in the modern sense:
'historicizing patriarchy', as Michael McKeon puts it in his essay
of that name. A text may challenge patriarchalism in the sense of
the authority of the father–king without necessarily challenging
patriarchy in today's sense of male supremacy: Shadwell's *The
Lancashire Witches* is a good example, as we shall see below. It
is also necessary to recognize that the subordination of women
in late Stuart England did not rest upon patriarchalism alone,
but on a wider and more diffuse Restoration 'patriarchy'. For
example, libertinism has to be understood in its Restoration
context. It is not the same as sexual freedom. In the scene in *The
Rover* in which Angellica gives herself to Willmore, Behn may
(momentarily) celebrate woman's uninhibited sexual pleasure.
She does not offer an 'idealization of libertinism'.[7] Hypocrisy,
bad faith, double standards, predatoriness, and sexism are at
the heart of libertinism.[8] The rake is a Machiavellian and
Hobbesian figure;[9] there is also some continuity with Renaissance Ovidian libertinism.[10] The libertine is opposed to marriage
and marriage is a 'come-down' for the rake. Misogyny and fear
and dislike of women's sexuality permeate the libertine writings
of Rochester and others. Libertinism cannot, therefore, be considered beneficial for women in any simple sense, though it may
open up a space for female sexual desire. The expression of such
desire, for example, in Behn's plays is very exciting but always
problematic. Todd historicizes Behn's treatment of women's
sexual pleasure neatly when she says: 'The implied message is
not the twentieth-century one of liberation, nor the eighteenth-
century one of necessary virtue or chastity, but the Restoration
one of social common sense. Free sexual activity might be pleasant, but it leads women to ostracism or the convent' (82).

A careful and historicized reading of the dramatic language of
sexual politics must also include an understanding of its relationship to the language of party politics. To take the example
of libertinism again, it has been assumed that satire of rakish-

---

[7] Copeland, ' "Once a whore and ever": Whore and Virgin in *The Rover* and its
Antecedents', 24.
[8] See e.g. Goreau, *Reconstructing Aphra*, 177–84.
[9] Weber, *The Restoration Rake-Hero*, 53.
[10] See Shepherd, *Amazons and Warrior Women: Varieties of Feminism in Seventeenth-Century Drama*.

ness could be satire of Whigs and Tories equally.[11] But libertinism tends to be associated with the court and with Toryism,
and personified in 'gallants' who are cavalier in every sense of
the word. The association of libertinism with the court and
with royalism was obvious to contemporaries. Whig critiques of
court and Tory debauchery, the counter-example of the exemplary Protestant couple, the emphasis on the liberties of the
female Protestant subject, and so on had considerable force at
the time.

Most recent treatments of Restoration sexual politics have
followed Catherine Gallagher in positing a symbiosis between
royalism and feminism.[12] However, it is important to distinguish
between what Behn may have thought or intended and the wider
picture. As Todd judiciously notes: 'Royalism was not necessarily allied to women's creative writing or to feminist awareness'
(16). Todd points out that the dominance of royalism in Restoration women's writing 'may simply emphasise the importance of
access to print' (16) and that the prominence of 'a few notorious
women' after 1660 coincided with the suppression of the socially and politically radical voices of puritan women. The fact
that women like Behn and Astell genuinely experience royalism
as empowering does not mean that we should indulge in
a kind of latter-day Jacobitism, ignoring or romanticizing the
reality for women of both the Filmerian ideology of female
subordination and the libertine 'rip-off'. Moreover, Behn's relationship to Toryism was deeply contradictory. Feminism and
Toryism tend to be hard to reconcile in her work, as I have
argued at length in my ' "Suspect my loyalty when I lose my
virtue": Sexual Politics and Party in Aphra Behn's Plays of the
Exclusion Crisis'.[13]

Similarly, there is a need for a nuanced view of the relationship of sexual politics and Whiggery. The corollary of the correl-

---

[11] Brown, 'Nathaniel Lee's Political Dramas', 46; Hume, 'The Satiric Design of
Nat. Lee's *The Princess of Cleve*'.

[12] See also (before Gallagher but less well known): Kinnaird, 'Mary Astell and the
Conservative Contribution to English Feminism'. Gallagher, 'Embracing the Absolute' and 'Who was that masked woman?' Cf. Hutner, 'Revisioning the Female:
Aphra Behn's *The Rover*, Parts I and II', in Hutner (ed.), *Re-reading Aphra
Behn*.

[13] Cf. (from a different perspective) Copeland 'Who can . . . her own wish deny?'
and Kubek, 'Night Mares of the Commonwealth'.

ation of Toryism and feminism is that everything got worse after 1688; but this is not the case in any simple sense. To be sure Locke, as feminist critics have asserted, confines women's role to the family.[14] However, he also denies the father's absolute patriarchal authority in the family. Contractual thinking enabled women's equality to begin to be conceptualized. Just as Mary Wollstonecraft acquired radical ideas about women's equality from French revolutionaries who had no such intention, so, a century earlier, late seventeenth-century Whig thought did not mean to include women in its notion of equality of individuals, but:

What it did do was create a new spectre of equity entitlements which, however unreal, was effective in undermining the paternalistic system of customary entitlements that followed in hierarchical tradition, from the basic assumption of inequality . . . over the long term, the principle of equality in difference has been institutionalized in a network of reforms that are undeniably real and important—universal 'manhood' suffrage, equal opportunity legislation, the reform of the marriage law, etc.[15]

Moreover, as various critics have argued, the Lockean ideology of women's separate sphere was not necessarily culturally disempowering for women in any straightforward sense. The early eighteenth century sees the relocation of ideas of honour and personal worth from the aristocracy to the virtuous woman; the rise of the cult of sensibility and of female-authored sentimental literature gave women a voice and a certain moral authority, despite the need for framing moral protestations; and eighteenth-century notions of the feminine played a strong role in developing ideas of modern subjectivity.[16] As McKeon notes, change for women occurred in a fashion which was gradual, uneven, incomplete, and contradictory. It is one thing for royalist women's writing to employ nostalgic

[14] See e.g. Perry, 'Mary Astell and the Feminist Critique of Possessive Individualism', 444–57.

[15] McKeon, 'Historicizing Patriarchy', 315–16, McKeon anachronistically uses the word 'Liberal' instead of 'Whig', which is perhaps a sign of how hidden from history the real rhetoric and importance of Whiggery has become.

[16] Todd, introduction to *The Sign of Angellica*; Armstrong, *Desire and Domestic Fiction: A Political History of the Novel*.

fictions in the face of the new; another for us to partake of the same fiction.[17]

In the rest of this chapter I shall show that the dramatic language of politics does invoke patriarchal family ideology, though it shows it as an ideal under threat. The political role and personal behaviour of the Stuarts has implications for the ideal of patriarchalism (and vice versa); and this in turn affects the construction of masculinity in the drama. From women's perspective there is conservatism but also radicalism, sometimes in unexpected places. It is far from being the case that Toryism goes hand in hand with feminism and Whiggery with sexism. The picture is more complex, and I shall attempt to show the nuances and contradictions as far as possible in the space available, bearing in mind that my aim in this chapter is to explore the nature of the dramatic language of politics.

The Family

Order and hierarchy in the family or its absence is a major dramatic preoccupation, and an important way in which dramatists engage with the problem of order and disorder in the state.[18] The politically good are those who try to hold the family together. Because of Charles II's libertinism, marriage can be a problematic value for Tory dramatists, but Whitaker manages in *The Conspiracy* to present the violation of marriage with powerful political effect through his portrayal of an exemplary royal couple. Ibrahim and the Young Queen resemble Charles I and Henrietta Maria as seen through royalist eyes. Here it is rebellion which threatens to divide the couple and destroy the family. Family values are a strong component of the loyalty which defeats rebellion, preserves the royal family, and restores the young king. A similar emphasis on the exemplary couple is apparent in *The Ingratitude of a Common-wealth*. By strengthening the role of Virgilia and sentimentalizing her relationship

---

[17] Todd offers a nuanced account of the pluses and minuses of the changes in women's position in the interregnum, the Restoration, and the rampant capitalism after 1688.

[18] The analogy between family and state of course pre-dates and goes beyond Filmer: see Staves, *Players' Scepters*, ch. 3; Schochet, *Patriarchalism in Political Thought*.

to Coriolanus, Tate emphasizes his hero's role as a family man, as opposed to those who would destroy the national family by fragmenting the state. In the April epilogue to *Venice Preserv'd* Otway refers to Mary of Modena's pregnancy, and to the forthcoming Stuart family reunion, as James brings his family out of exile. The '*Infant Prince* yet lab'ring in the womb' is 'a *Medicine* fit to aswage | A peoples *folly*, and rowz'd Monarch's *rage*'. Family values lend an aura of sanctity to the reconsolidation of Stuart political authority, which is portrayed as the reuniting of the national family: loving father-king and future king(s), and obedient subjects. Emphasizing James's role as a family man was an ideological counter to his reputation as a libertine. The admonitory tone of this piece, with its recurring imperatives— 'See, see, the injur'd PRINCE', 'Cast, cast your Idols off', and so on—reveals the constructed nature of this great edifice of wishful thinking. Even royalists feared that James was not the type to hold the national family together. The unconscious irony of Otway's prayers and prophecies was brought out in August when Mary gave birth to a daughter.

Tories show the family violated by rebels and ambitious plotters. Perhaps the most graphic example is the spectacle in *The Ambitious Statesman* of the disloyal Constable torturing his own son on the rack. He also plots to turn the king against his son and vice versa, and to destroy his son's relationship with the woman he loves. The Constable's violation of the family reinforces the monstrosity of rebellion. Louize makes the link when she calls him 'Unnatural Tyrant!' (5. p. 77). In *Caius Marius*, family values are threatened by faction and the republican mentality. The young lovers embody the natural affection and filial piety which is disastrously lacking in the republican state. This is paradigmatically illustrated by Lavinia's tending of her father-in-law, Marius Senior, in Act 3. Thus, when he murders her father in Act 5, he is guilty of ingratitude as well as cruelty.[19] Marius' repentance has a political force lacking in Capulet's in the source play:

---

[19] Wallace, 'Otway's *Caius Marius* and the Exclusion Crisis'. Munns, 'Dark Disorders' is correct to draw attention to the tormented masochism of the lovers which prefigures *The Orphan* and *Venice Preserv'd*; but her discussion of the lovers' psychological dependency misses the fundamental role played by the value of filial piety here and hence the lovers' role as an embodiment of natural virtue.

> We might have all bin Friends, and in one House
> Enjoy'd the Blessings of eternal Peace.
> But oh! my cruel Nature has undone me.

(5. 466–8)

In fact bad fatherhood is a general phenomenon in Otway's Roman republic. It is a characteristic of the patrician Metellus as well as the plebeian Marius. Amongst the omens foretelling the former's downfall is the following:

> Three Ravens brought their young ones in the streets,
> Devouring 'em before the people's eyes,
> Then bore the Garbage back into their Nests.

(1. 421–3)

There is a message in the play about the dangers of division in the national family as well as the domestic one.

However, bad fatherhood can be a problematic theme for Tory dramatists, especially when it is associated with bad monarchical government as in Tate's *Lear* and Otway's *The Orphan*. There are three reasons why this is the case. Firstly, Toryism drew its strength from demonizing the faults of rebellious subjects; but bad fatherhood is a theme which focuses on the faults of the ruler, so the message is the wrong one from the Tory point of view. Secondly, bad fatherhood in the microcosm of the family can draw attention to misgovernment in the macrocosm. A third and connected point is that the theme inevitably resonated uncomfortably for Tories because Charles could be seen as a bad father: it was his failure to father legitimate offspring which had caused the problem about the succession, while his littering the kingdom with bastards and his perceived over-indulgence of the most rebellious of these bastards, Monmouth, was seen as a political as well as a moral problem. I shall consider this further in relation to my reading of *Lear*, *The Orphan*, and other royalist plays in Chapter 7.

Whigs have a range of responses to patriarchalism. At what might be called the more conservative end of the range, the patriarchal premiss may be accepted but the threat to the ideal reversed so that the family is violated by tyranny and popery. Thus, for example, in *Caesar Borgia* popish and machiavellian ambition leads to arbitrary cruelty, and a series of unnatural acts which violate the family and young love, from Orsino's tyranny over his daughter Bellamira in Act 2 to Borgia's eventual murder of both brother and wife and Ascanio's of Borgia's bastard son. Another approach which challenges Stuart libertinism but not patriarchalism is to make use of the Protestant marriage as an ideal. In *The Female Prelate* Saxony and Angeline are an exemplary couple, whereas the papists are guilty of rampant and unnatural lust. In *The Massacre of Paris* the Admiral and Antramont are an idealized Protestant couple. In both plays tyranny and popish cruelty threaten the family and separate the couple. At what we might call the most forward-looking end of the range, patriarchalism may be challenged. In Shadwell's *The Lancashire Witches* Isabella, daughter of the Whig country gentleman Sir Edward, asserts her right to choice in marriage in Whiggish terms: 'For my part I am a free English woman, and will stand up for my Liberty, and property of Choice' (1. p. 111). Her friend Theodosia agrees: 'And Faith, Girl, I'le be a mutineer on thy side; I hate the imposition of a Husband, 'tis as bad as Popery' (ibid.). Yet the women reject the suitors their fathers have chosen without displaying the unfilial disrespect for the older generation which characterizes rakes and 'gay heroines' in Tory comedies. There is no need for revolt because Sir Edward is not patriarchal: he respects his daughter and gives her choice his blessing. It is the same with his other dependants: he disapproves of the man the maid Susan has chosen to marry, but he respects her choice and even gives her financial support. Whereas the patriarchal family is usually in crisis in the drama, Shadwell's non-patriarchal family operates in harmony.

Masculinity and Effeminacy

Ideas about masculinity and heroism can be as problematic and contradictory for Tory dramatists as the question of fatherhood. Manliness is associated with heroism, often in a military context. Unmanliness is often associated with 'effeminacy' in the Restoration sense: subordination to unruly passions and excessive preoccupation with women. The amorous Charles was criticized for effeminacy, which was perceived as associated with political aloofness and irresponsibility.[20] He was also un-willing to respond to parliamentary pressure for military action. So manliness, like patriotism, tends to be problematic for Tories and useful to Whigs.

The heroic plays had included both sentimental and 'huffing' heroes: these types are notoriously parodied in Prince Prettyman and Drawcansir in *The Rehearsal*. In the Exclusion Crisis the Drawcansir prototype becomes useful as an oppositional figure in Whig plays.[21] Thus Lee in *The Massacre of Paris* makes a Protestant hero out of a tough soldier who forces a Protestant policy on the king by military action. Similarly, Saxony in *The Female Prelate* is a 'manly man' who is not afraid to fight for what is right. In Lee's *Theodosius* the kingdom is handed to a 'manly man' from a king who resembles Charles both in his inappropriate withdrawal from the concerns of his kingdom and in his tendency to give way to his passions. In *The Lancashire Witches* Sir Edward's manly vigour stands out against the politi-cal supineness, foppery, and cowardice of the papists and their apologists; while Bellfort and Doubty (i.e. Doughty), in addition to being honest patriots and good Whigs, are 'real men'.[22]

The Prettyman prototype develops into the passive heroes of Tory quietist plays, such as Vendosme in *The Ambitious States-man* and Theocrin in *The Loyal General*. These masochistic, self-stifling, 'emasculated' men are pitiable, but rather unsatis-factory as heroes. Otway tends to introduce manly and decisive soldier characters as a contrast to his suffering, sentimental heroes. For example, the vigour and courage of Chamont in *The Orphan* points up by comparison the peculiar and troubling plight of Castalio and Polydore, who are forced into social and political passivity by their royalist father's cynicism and so turn their active energies inward and destroy the family.

Tory dramatists treat royal effeminacy in different ways, each of which poses its own problems. In *The Young King* Behn uses

[20] See Hutton, *Charles the Second*, 334–7. Criticism of Charles's submission to his mistresses was widespread, but Marvell adds a new twist, hinting at Charles's 'effeminacy' in being influenced in foreign policy by his sister (*Account*, 19).

[21] Braverman, *Plots and Counterplots*, argues that the 'civic mode' of opposition to royalist dogma employs 'a persona whose stoic masculinity answers the excesses of the Stuart court' (p. xv).

[22] An exception is *Caesar Borgia* where excessive preoccupation with manliness is associated with tyranny and popery.

royal unmanliness to offer an anti-Exclusion message, by suggesting that Orsames' unnatural exile has emasculated him and
made him passive and unfit to rule. If the masculinity of a
Cleomena is easily reversible, Orsames' isolation and powerless-
ness is not.[23] However, this presents certain problems because,
as we have seen, there is an association between the exiled
Orsames and James. There is a problematic resonance in the
spectacle of Orsames' weakness at the end of the play that is
enhanced by his unmanliness. His passivity means that he will
take advice on how to rule from his country's former enemy, the
king of Scythia, a most disconcerting parallel with the Stuarts
and Louis XIV. His effeminacy means that he will be ruled by
his wife. Behn thus arouses pity at the expense of respect, and
our lack of respect has an anti-Stuart dimension. In *The Loyal
Brother* Southerne palliates royal effeminacy by showing it as a
temporary aberration and by depicting Whig masculinism as
worse. At first the ruler Seliman is 'unmanly' in his prostration
before Semanthe's beauty. His lust leads to his unnatural exclusion of his brother and gives rebels an opening. The resonance of
this is most unfortunate for royalism: the kingdom is jeopard-
ized by the sovereign's 'rebel passions' (3. 4. 216). In the end
Seliman becomes 'man | Agen' when he learns to be 'merciful
gentle as the first' (3. 4. 195). This kind of manliness is contrasted with the negatively depicted 'rugged' manliness of the
villain Ismael, which resembles that of Whig heroes:

> Ambition is our Idol, on whose wings
> Great minds are carried only to extreams;
> To be sublimely great, or to be nothing:
> And he who aims his actions at this mark,
> Must rush *with Manly resolution* on,
> Stopping at nothing when he has begun.
>
> (1. 1. 469, my emphasis)

Yet the attempt to construct a paradigm of manliness based on
mercy and brotherly love, though compatible with the play's
anti-Exclusion message, is problematic too. Seliman feminizes
himself in repentance. The ruler who leans his 'beaten mind' on

---

[23] Pearson says love reveals Orsames' 'innate kingliness and manliness' (*The
Prostituted Muse*, 159), but this ignores residual contradictions (which she notices in
the case of Cleomena).

his brother's breast (5. 3. 250) is not a very inspiring figure, and he seems as intemperate in repentance as he did before in passion and rage.

Dryden in *Troilus and Cressida* is quite sharply masculinist, making various additions to Shakespeare which suggest that women are bad for heroes, and that 'effeminacy' or excessive preoccupation with women and love are incompatible with affairs of state. In his preface, Dryden observes that: 'Friendship is both a virtue, and a Passion essentially; love is a passion only in its nature, and is not a virtue but by Accident; good nature makes Friendship; but effeminacy Love' (*Works*, xiii. 247). In the play effeminate love is repudiated. Andromache is heroic when she urges Hector to send a challenge to the Greeks against the promptings of her love and womanhood:

> I would be worthy to be Hectors wife:
> And had I been a Man, as my Soul's one,
> I had aspir'd a nobler name, his friend.   (2. 1. 143–5)

Hector's response is:

> Come to my Arms, thou manlier Virtue come;
> Thou better Name than wife!
>
> (2. 1. 156–7)

When Hector later delays fighting in response to the promptings of love he becomes ashamed, for compared with 'superstition' as a reason for not fighting, 'fondnesse of a wife' is 'The more unpardonable ill' (5. 1. 132–4). It is the shame of having a woman (Polyxena) beg his life from Achilles which finally goads him into battle. The morally compromised character of Paris is eliminated, but it is clear from what others say about him that in jeopardizing his country for a woman he has committed an act of the deepest dishonour (2. 1. 53, 167–72).

Hector is the noblest character in the play, and his manliness is a sign of his true royalty. He has moral authority in 3. 2 (a scene added by Dryden to Shakespeare) when he argues that for 'the general state, | And all our common safety' (288–9), Troilus should put aside his irresponsible love:

> If parting from a Mistriss can procure
> A Nations happiness, show me that Prince
> Who dares to trust his future fame so farr

> To stand the shock of Annals, blotted thus,
> *He sold his Country for a womans love!*[24]

These words, ringing out in the theatre, like the italicized line in the text, must surely recall the king's violently unpopular French Catholic mistress. As Maximillian E. Novak points out in his headnote to the play, Troilus resembles James as he exclaims, 'The publick, is the Lees of vulgar slaves' and asserts 'an Eagles life ǀ Is worth a world of Crows' (3. 2. 305, 309–10). He is not allowed to get away with this. Hector rebukes him by, as it were, making Ulysses' speech on degree from the other direction:

> And what are we, but for such men as these? . . .
> Ev'n those who serve have their expectances,
> Degrees of happiness, which they must share,
> Or they'll refuse to serve us.

> (3. 2. 313, 317–19)

Dryden's masculinism in this play and his criticism of selfish passion in princes cannot but reflect badly upon England's 'effeminate' and self-centred royal brothers.

The problem of royal effeminacy for royalist dramatists is most successfully tackled, in my opinion, in three plays in particular. It should come as no surprise by now to learn that these are the vigorously Tory *The Conspiracy*, *The Ingratitude of a Common-wealth*, and *The Duke of Guise*. In *The Conspiracy* Whitaker reverses usual associations once again, making the rebels themselves 'effeminate'. The Grand Vizier is led into treachery by his love for the would-be usurper, Flatra, and is unmanly in his cringing devotion: 'you can never have, ǀ A more submissive, or more grateful Slave' (1. p. 9). Similarly, Oglar's unruly passion for the Queen allows the rebels to manipulate him.

In *The Ingratitude of a Common-wealth* and *The Duke of Guise* the problems are surmounted by the adoption of a method which works because it embraces contradiction. In the

---

[24] 3. 2. 295–9. In his discussion of the play, Winn states that Dryden 'recognized that if Charles gave up his Catholic mistress as a direct result of public or Parliamentary pressure, he might next be asked to abandon his Catholic brother, Dryden's patron' (*John Dryden and his World*, 319). However, there is no suggestion in the play that Troilus is wrong to put his country before his love: he is heroic in doing so, a legitimate object of pity and pathos.

former Tate makes various alterations to Shakespeare to emphasize his hero's manliness and martial courage; but he also gives him a suffering sensibility, especially where his wife and son are concerned. This 'feminine' is the positive version of 'effeminacy'. It is as if Tate has blended Antony and Ventidius in Dryden's *All For Love*, or Castalio and Chamont in Otway's *The Orphan*, into a single character. At the same time, Aufidius is made less than manly, weakened by an excess of sensibility which degenerates into hysteria and spite, and, simultaneously, by an excessive concern about his manhood: the villain Nigridius inflames and unhinges him by telling him that Coriolanus' rivalry has rendered him 'Less than Man' (4. 1. p. 42). There is also a suggestion that witchcraft must be responsible for the destructive alliance Aufidius has made with his old enemy, which conveys the idea that Aufidius has been emasculated and tainted with the feminine. So Tate manages to combine real manliness and sensibility in his hero, and at the same time to problematize excessive concern about masculinity, of the kind which might be said to characterize some Whig dramatists, and to show that it easily leads to the opposite: hysterical unmanliness.

In *The Duke of Guise* the rebellious citizens are unmanly, being both cowards and henpecked cuckolds (4. 4). The eponymous villain is both masculinist in a bad way (2. 2. pp. 16–17; 4. 3. p. 44) and unmanly in his subjection to destructive passions. Royal effeminacy is palliated: love is godlike (2. 1. p. 16) and effeminacy or love-sickness, like mercy, emanates from a royal sensibility which contrasts favourably with rebel ambition. In the role of Marmoutier, the heroine, there seems to be a positive focus on love and the feminine: the king's susceptibility to women makes him responsive to Marmoutier's counsels of continence. Rebels, in contrast, mistrust love as detrimental to political ambition: 'to a Politician, | All Passion's bane, but Love directly death' (1. 3. p. 7). Guise, of course, is a 'True Polititian' (5. 1. p. 73). Love does not unman the king. Instead, what really emasculates him is his humiliating subjection to capricious parliaments. Henry's progress towards firmness against the rebels is associated with a growth of manly resolution and a casting off of 'Womanish tameness' (4. 1. p. 39). The depiction of the king as both effeminate and manly, and of rebels as both unmanly

and excessively manly, is a clever piece of ideological mystification and erasure. The disjunction between patriarchal ideology
and Stuart practice opened up fractures and inconsistencies,
but it was sometimes possible to paper over the ideological
cracks.

Femininity and Female Transgression

Both Whigs and Tories use a rhetoric of good femininity and
female monstrosity. Feminine women arouse pity and horror in
the face of atrocities. Angeline in *The Female Prelate* is a Whig
example. On the Tory side, a good example occurs in *The
Ingratitude of a Common-wealth*, where the victims are the
sentimentalized Virgilia and a Volumnia who is made to feel
'Womans Tenderness... | The Mothers Fondness, and her
panting Fears' (3. 2. p. 36). Valeria, in contrast, becomes a
humorous character (played by a male comic actor) whose self-
professed loyalism thinly veils political opportunism and the
inappropriate and presumptuous 'busyness' about state affairs
for which Whig citizens were criticized. In *Troilus and Cressida*
Dryden's innocent, weak, womanly, and victimized heroine becomes the daughter of a priest, and is in part a tool to teach a
lesson about the dangers of over-hasty accusation at the height
of the Popish Plot scare.

Female monstrosity is also used in a similar way by Whigs and
Tories. Women's unnatural ambition is used to demonize popery in the figure of Joan in *The Female Prelate*, and rebellion in
the Queen Mother and Flatra in *The Conspiracy* and Sunamire
in *The Loyal Brother*. There is always a virtuous feminine
woman for contrast who is on the side of right: Angeline in
Settle's play, the Young Queen in Whitaker's, Semanthe in
Southerne's. Behn also uses female monstrosity for the purposes
of Toryism sometimes, however unpalatable this may be to
modern feminists—and however much it may contradict the
more liberated treatment of women elsewhere in her *œuvre*. In
The Young King the convention of good femininity and its
monstrous inversion is used to exemplify the folly of interfering
with the succession. The Queen exiles her son and heir, training
her daughter to rule in his stead, and this is referred to clearly in

the subtitle as 'The Mistake'. Sexual inversion and unnatural motherhood are associated with Exclusion, and family values invoked against exclusionists: the Queen is unnatural, as Charles would be unnatural if he excluded his own brother.[25] A symbol of the restoration of the natural order is Cleomena's awakening through love to her true womanly nature, so that amazonian ambitions are brushed aside.

Behn also deploys female monstrosity in *The Round-heads*. In Lady Lambert and Lady Cromwell she makes conservative use of the figures of the shrew and the upstart woman aping the great lady. Lady Lambert beats up and bosses her husband, and interferes in political meetings. Lady Cromwell is jealous of her dignity, and indignant when other women encroach on what she calls 'our Royal Family' (5. 2. p. 49). The gender transgression reinforces the social presumption, typifying a world upside-down. Lady Lambert's capacity for love eventually restores her to the 'sanity' of political and sexual submissiveness. Behn also adds a comic interlude of a Council of Ladies, infiltrated, and satirized 'aside', by the heroes in drag. Here she constructs a paradigm of presumptuous folly and impropriety which both reflects and typifies the rebel world; she also focuses on a peculiarly female propensity for pettiness. She shows women in power behaving in a way which anti-suffragists were to depict two centuries later, elevating private grievances, bitchy, competitive, and silly. Behn's habitual—and liberating—portrayal of women who are wiser and wittier than their husbands coexists in this play with a conventional Tory rhetoric of gender difference and female subordination.

More positively, from women's point of view, there are some instances where an explicit focus on women's liberties is used politically. I am talking here about the use of a kind of feminism as part of the dramatic language of politics, and not about other aspects of the drama which are important for modern feminism, for example ways in which a space is opened up for women through contradiction. In Behn's *The Feign'd Curtizans* and *The Revenge*, as I have shown at greater length in my article ' "Suspect my loyalty when I lose my virtue": Sexual Politics and Party in Aphra Behn's Plays of the Exclusion Crisis', feminism coexists

---

[25] In *The Case Put, Concerning the Succession* L'Estrange argues that Charles would be violating 'Natural Affection' if he excluded a brother and friend (p. 17).

with Toryism. In *The Feign'd Curtizans* the satire of upstarts and patriotic puritans coexists with sympathy for women denied sexual expression and marriage choice, and for prostitutes as victims of unfair social arrangements. In *The Revenge* Behn makes a significant change to her source material which suits both Toryism and feminism. Marston's courtesan Franceschina is set apart by a ridiculous foreign accent, but the prostitute Corina in *The Revenge* is not foreign. The ending is altered to permit her to repent of her revenge and be married off. The sympathy for Corina makes all the starker the contrast with the treatment of the tradesman, for whom there is no sympathy at all until he has been stripped of everything. Marston's foreigner is made a native and brought within the fold, but the anti-papist citizen is beyond the pale. This emphasizes the royalist message that the threat is not the foreigner, but the Whiggish 'enemy within'. In other plays, a positive focus on women's liberties takes the form of the wife's rebellion against the Whig-citizen-cuckold. Examples are Behn's own *The Round-heads*, Otway's *The Souldier's Fortune*, Ravenscroft's *The London Cuckolds*, and Crowne's *City Politiques*.

Whigs sometimes present women's liberties as an advantage of English Protestantism, as in Shadwell's anti-patriarchal *The Lancashire Witches*, cited above. In *The Woman Captain* also, as Richard Bevis notes, 'Shadwell has something to say about male misbehaviour and woman's liberation' (p. 93): Mrs Gripe, dressed as a man, teaches all the degenerate men in the play a lesson in moral and 'manly' behaviour, and also in patriotism and courage: with the help of her military brother's sergeant, she puts them through a drill and threatens to send them to Flanders, where they should be fighting the Protestant fight. She exemplifies the connection between Whiggery and a more enlightened view of marriage: she tries to teach her husband a lesson, and when she realizes he is unreformable, forces him to sign an agreement to give her dowry back or pay separate maintenance. The Tory revenge option of cuckolding is explicitly spurned. In *The Lancashire Witches* Shadwell even gives some sympathy to seriously unruly women: the witches are comic pranksters rather than terrible figures, and those (papists) who persecute a 'poor old woman' (1. p. 115) for witchcraft are cruel and shameful.

In Mrs Gripe Shadwell exploits for political purposes the festive potential of female cross-dressing which Behn often uses to quasi-feminist effect.[26] Cross-dressing can also have a more conservative force, as in *The Female Prelate*, where it emphasizes the monstrosity of Pope Joan.[27] In *The Royalist* D'Urfey makes female cross-dressing work for Toryism. Philipa is 'A young Lady that follows Kinglove in Mens Cloths through all his troubles'. She even fights alongside him at the Battle of Worcester. Of course there is the inevitable undercurrent of titillation here, but there is also something touching and heroic. For Philipa, cross-dressing is a sacrifice. Like Shakespeare's Jessica in *The Merchant of Venice*, she blushes to be in 'this strange disguise' which 'these Tempestuous Times' have forced her to assume 'Against my sex, my Honour, and my Birth' (1. p. 2).

Sexual Themes

In some ways Tory and Whig treatment of sexual themes is symmetrical, in others not. Some tropes of the dramatic language of sexual politics are treated in an equal but opposite way, and some relate particularly to one faction or another. Thus, both Tories and Whigs use rampant and unnatural lust to demonize either rebellion or tyranny and/or popery. This had already become a common theme in the pamphlet war in the late 1670s,[28] and was entered into with relish by the drama-

[26] Of course female cross-dressing is extremely common and is by no means always or even mainly used for political effect. One titillating purpose was to show actresses' legs: Howe, *The First English Actresses*, 56.

[27] For the debate about the multiple and contradictory resonances of cross-dressing, see Ferris (ed.), *Controversies on Cross-Dressing*.

[28] In Marvell's *Account* popish clergy are sexually unnatural, and 'either frustrate humane nature if they live chastly, or, if otherwise, adulterate it' (11); see also, for example, *Il Putanismo di Roma*. For the association of voracious and unnatural lust with rebellion and dissent, see e.g. *An Account of the Tryal of That Most Wicked Pharisee Major Thomas Weir, who was Executed for Adultery, Incest and Bestiality,* appended to *Ravillac Redivivus* (1678), an account of the trial of Scots dissenter James Mitchell. We learn that Weir, a Civil War rebel associated with the current (1678) rebellion in Scotland, is guilty of incest, paedophilia, adultery, and bestiality with horses and cows, as well as sorcery and diabolism. Moreover, he is typical of 'the Whigs' (72).

tists.[29] Sexual 'perversion' is a sign of the times.[30] This applies to homoeroticism: in *Caesar Borgia* the 'effeminate Villain', Cardinal Ascanio Sforza (1. 1. 13–14), is also bisexual (1. 1. 21–3). On the Tory side, in *The Souldier's Fortune* the voyeurism and bisexual innuendo of the pimp, Sir Jolly, are a symptom and a symbol of corrupt times in which pardoned rebels and citizens prosper at the expense of the king's loyal subjects. In the second epilogue to *The Duke of Guise*,[31] Dryden has the actress speaker accuse the Whigs of both homosexuality and impotence. Titus Oates's homosexuality becomes a useful theme for Dryden in *The Vindication* (11, 22). It also applies to other forms of sexuality which are perceived as unnatural: in *Rome's Follies* the papists absolve a man who has had sex with a goat (2. 3. p. 20). In *Venice Preserv'd* a republican senator, Antonio, is a sado-masochist whose cringing before his mistress lends force to Otway's negative portrayal of republicanism in power.

Both Whigs and Tories use rape as a trope of the monstrous, associated by Tories with rebellion, and by Whigs with popery and arbitrary government. The virtuous female victim represents the natural at war with the monstrous, as I have shown in my article ' "He that should guard my virtue has betrayed it": The Dramatization of Rape in the Exclusion Crisis'. In *The Female Prelate* both Saxony and his wife are sexually violated. In *Lucius Junius Brutus*, the rape of Lucrece by the lustful Tarquins is a 'public wound' (2. 149); the rape of citizens' wives by princes and courtiers has been common (2. 51–60), and royalist plotter Tiberius looks forward to ravishing the daughters of commonwealthsmen (4. 67), as well as massacring the fathers. Dryden parodies this in *The Duke of Guise*, having the citizens in 4. 4 ridiculously cry on seeing the royalist Colonel

---

[29] For Whig depiction of lustful papists, see e.g. *The Female Prelate*, *The Coronation*, and *Rome's Follies*; and of lustful courtly villains, *The Massacre of Paris* and *Lucius Junius Brutus*. On the Tory side, for lustful rebels, see e.g. *Oedipus*, *The Conspiracy*, and *The Duke of Guise*.

[30] For an account of Rochester's earlier association of sexual perversion and the unnatural political condition of England, see Elias, 'Political Satire in *Sodom*', and Staves, *Players' Scepters*, 267.

[31] Printed second, but written first: 'Intended to have been Spoken to the PLAY, before it was forbidden last Summer' (i.e. July 1682). The prohibition was lifted on 29 Oct. 1682.

Grillon, 'He that devours our Wives, and ravishes our Children' (p. 49). In *Venice Preserv'd* rape typifies the disorder of the republican condition. In Ravenscroft's *Titus Andronicus* the rape of Lavinia is an 'Invasion on a Princes right' (2. p. 16) by plotters, and the day when it happens 'the day of Doom for *Bassianus*' (p. 20).

In many respects, then, Whig and Tory treatment of sexual politics is equal and opposite. However, there is one area in particular where it becomes asymmetrical and unequal. This concerns the issues of royal sexual impropriety and of libertinism. Whigs could make devastating use of the theme of royal lust. Prior to the Exclusion Crisis Lee had offered a critique of tyranny in association with rampant and unnatural royal lust in *The Tragedy of Nero* (1674), and had critically portrayed homoeroticism and 'effeminacy' at the centre of power in *The Rival Queens* (1677).[32] In *Lucius Junius Brutus* the ravening lust of the Tarquins is shown as responsible for their well-deserved overthrow. The subversiveness of this carried extra force because the story was already prominent in oppositional verse and prose admonishing the Stuarts.[33] John Ayloffe's poem 'Marvell's Ghost' (1678) concluded with the warning that England would 'to those resentments come | That drove the Tarquins out of Rome'.[34] Whig depiction of royal lust could therefore have explosive force.

Whigs could also satirize royal and court libertinism to powerful effect, drawing on dissatisfaction which had existed since 1660, expressed in a wide range of texts from Pepys's diary to pamphlets to verses to poems such as Marvell's *Last Instructions to a Painter*.[35] Tories countered by depicting rakishness as a positive theme of class superiority, or offering friendly teasing of rakes rather than hostile satire. We may illustrate this by examining Behn's response in *The City Heiress* to a revival of Shadwell's *The Libertine* during the Tory reaction period in

[32] Barbour, 'The Unconventional Heroic Plays of Nathaniel Lee'; Kastan, 'Nero and the Politics of Nathaniel Lee'; Flores, 'Patriarchal Politics under Cultural Stress: Nathaniel Lee's Passion Plays'.

[33] See my ' "Partial Tyrants" and "Freeborn People" in *Lucius Junius Brutus*', 463–4, for a detailed account.

[34] *Poems on Affairs of State*, i. 286.

[35] See Hammond, 'The King's Two Bodies'.

1682.[36] Some of Behn's plays contain a feminist critique of the predatory aspects of libertinism. In *The City Heiress* she offers a sympathetic view of the rake. I think this might be to do with the fact that she reverses Shadwellian tropes. Whigs had difficulty in getting new plays performed at this time, and the revival of *The Libertine* was the next best thing, since criticism of court libertinism and attacks on the royal mistresses were powerful weapons in the Whig arsenal. Behn is no different from other Tory dramatists in giving urgent and overriding priority to the need to rebut the Whigs at this time.

The libertine in *The City Heiress* is allowed his sexual triumphs. Rather than being obliged to undergo reformation before marriage, the chief rake, Tom Wilding, is allowed to complain that his former mistresses have betrayed his love by marrying other men. It is no accident that these exculpated rakes are labelled by the Whig, Sir Timothy, 'Tarmagent Tories' (1. p. 2). The phrase 'Tory-rory' (1. p. 6), applied to the Tory knight, Sir Anthony, denotes a certain rollicking and roistering mentality, as in Dryden's *The Kind Keeper* (1678). Behn seems concerned to suggest that Tory libertinism is something jolly, wild, and cavalier, and preferable to whey-faced Whiggery and puritan sexual hypocrisy.

The attitude which has authorial sanction in *The Libertine* (disgust at the promiscuity and venereal disease which lurks beneath the façade of nobility), is satirized in Behn's play in Mrs Clacket, 'A City-Bawd & Puritan' (actors' names), and a 'true Protestant' (2. 1. pp. 12–13). In *The Libertine*, rape is a serious threat and women resist it, by suicide if necessary. In *The City Heiress*, Lady Galliard is a willing participant in her own seduction, putting up the expected token resistance, but willingly won over by libertine arguments. In *The Libertine* irreligion is a serious sin, punished by death and damnation. In Behn's play, Tories are cheerfully irreligious. Behn predictably levels the charge of sexual hypocrisy at the godly, whereas in Shadwell's Act 3, the libertines' attempt to label a virtuous man a hypocrite

---

[36] As discussed in the Appendix, *The City Heiress* probably had its première in late April or early May 1682. Shadwell's play was revived on 18 May. My argument stands if Behn's play went on first: the intention to revive Shadwell's play is not likely to have been secret.

and a godly whoremaster is simply monstrous. Behn has venal and ridiculous servants; Shadwell has a serious critique of corruption in great men for its downward ramifications: ' 'Tis true, my Master's a very *Tarquin*; but I ne'r attempted to ravish before'.[37] Behn also reverses other Shadwellian themes. Her play opens with a satirical depiction of the Oliverian Sir Timothy foolishly objecting to his nephew and heir, Tom Wilding, being corrupted by fun-loving Tory rakes: 'Before he fell to Toryism, he was a Sober civil Youth, and had some Religion in him' (1. p. 2). This seems like a direct reversal of the opening of *The Woman-Captain*, where Sir Humphrey abandons the decent ways of his puritan father to devote himself to pleasure and association with Tory rakes. Sir Timothy's lament seems ironically to echo the reproach of the old steward in Shadwell's play: 'I would have you cleanly, and serve God as my old Mr. did' (1. p. 2). Under the influence of his burgeoning Whiggery Shadwell shifts in *The Woman-Captain* to emphasize anti-court aspects of his social satire: in *The Virtuoso* (1676) he had mocked in the person of Snarl an 'old fashion'd Fellow' (*Works*, iii. 115) who hankers after the morals and fashions of the 1640s while hypocritically keeping a whore.[38] Similarly, Behn's treatment of libertinism in the Tory reaction period seems to have shifted to outright indulgence, in the face of Whig disapproval.

Libertinism is cheerfully palliated in countless Tory prologues and epilogues, in opposition to Whig-citizen sexual impotence and hypocrisy. Just one example is the prologue to *The Royalist*, where Whig sexual potency is impugned in the epithet 'Rigling', while Tories are predisposed to 'kind intrigue'. Three farces for courtiers performed at Newmarket in autumn 1679, and published together under the title *The Muse of Newmarket; or, Mirth and Drollery*, cheerfully, even proudly associate the court with libertinism. Extenuation of libertinism may also extend to homoeroticism, as in *The Royalist*, where Kinglove calls Philipa, who is disguised as a youth, 'little *Ganymed*' (1. p. 5). There is a cheerful polymorphous perversity about Heartall's suggestion

---

[37] *The Works of Thomas Shadwell*, iii. The speaker is Jacomo, 4. 2. p. 78.

[38] He shifts again in *The Lancashire Witches*. In *The Woman-Captain* he had included citizens in his inclusive social satire; by 1680 Tory satire of 'cits' made that ineligible, and Shadwell focuses on celebrating the Whiggish country gentry in opposition to the court.

that the 'youth' might be both the product and the object of uncontrolled male desire: 'Nay, you have reason to be fond of him, if this be not a Slip of your own Grafting I am mistaken: I fancy he's like you.—He looks as if he were begot in a Riot of Appetite. The Youth may come to preferment in time; for to my knowledge there's many a *Noble Peer* in this Country would give 100 Guineys for such a Page' (1. p. 5).[39] The play associates royalists with good living, which includes drinking and whoring, but also, simultaneously, with sexual continence: they are falsely and ridiculously accused of rape, and they sacrifice love to loyalty (1. p. 6). Rebels are impotent, but also associated with sexual incontinence and irregularity: Sir Oliver has 'not bin a man [in bed] this 20 years' (5. 2. p. 60), but encourages his friends to kiss and fondle his wife in a speech which carries overtones of sexual perversion, voyeurism, pimping, and vulgarity (2. 1. p. 12). The roundheads also display homoerotic interest in the 'youth' in 4. 1, and here homoeroticism is made to seem both hypocritical and distasteful. Tory plays often depict as ridiculous in lower-class characters the libertinism which can be indulged in upper-class ones.

D'Urfey's treatment of libertinism is by no means atypical. In fact exactly the same constellation of ideologically powerful contradictions is employed in Behn's *The Round-heads*. As in D'Urfey's play the royalist heroes are both sexy and sexually active; yet (also as in *The Royalist*) the wife of a parliamentarian virtuously refuses to cuckold her husband, even though he deserves it (4. 1. p. 33). This is a mirror image of Shadwell's depiction of Mrs Gripe. Meanwhile, the parliamentarians' neglect of their wives' sexual needs is combined with secret lust hypocritically concealed beneath puritan cant.

So the refraction of libertinism in the language of party is not equal and opposite: Whig criticism of royal and court libertinism is countered by Tories with a combination of indulgence and erasure, and refocusing of the charge upon the opposition. It is also necessary to complicate slightly the Whig side of the

---

[39] The homoeroticism of the references to the youth as a 'page' may be seen from other analogous, but more explicit, references, e.g. Crowne, *Sir Courtly Nice*, 4. 1; Rochester: 'There's a sweet, soft page of mine | Does the trick worth forty wenches' ('Song: Love a Woman! Y'are an Ass', in *Poems*, 25, lines 15–16); also, 'And missing my whore I bugger my page' ('Régime de Viver', in *Poems*, 130, line 11). For the controversy over authorship of the latter, see *Poems*, 310.

argument, firstly with an exception to the usual critique of
libertinism and secondly with a qualified instance. An anomalous Whig treatment of libertinism occurs in *Rome's Follies*. The
author succeeds in associating not merely lust but rampant
libertinism with the Roman Church, the friars being rakes and
masters of libertine ingenuity: so far so conventional. Yet the
treatment of libertinism seems quite indulgent as well as satirical. The impotent, foolish husband deserves to be cuckolded and
the 'gay heroine' who couples with the friar is sympathetic. The
audience is rendered complicit in libertine jests. Two things are
happening here, it seems to me. Firstly, there is a conscious
reversal of the paradigm of Tory libertine comedies, mirroring
Tory dramatists' deliberate reversal of Shadwellian themes and
tropes. Secondly, the author is appealing to his presumably
upper-class patrons at the private house where the play was
performed. By using the same tropes of upper-class libertinism
as Tory plays, he implicitly denies the social marginality and
class inferiority with which Tories were striving to taint the
Whigs when they presented them as stupid, lewd citizens worthy
only of being cuckolded.

The 'qualified instance' of Whig anti-libertinism is Lee's *The
Princess of Cleve*. The play is qualified not in its indictment of
libertinism, which is searing and comprehensive, but in its
Whiggery. Indeed it has been claimed that the play's satire of
libertinism is aimed primarily at the Whigs.[40] This is not at all
likely. It is true that Lee has moved away from the inspired
Whiggism of *Lucius Junius Brutus* in the direction of cynicism;[41]
but there is only one instance of anti-Whig satire. The rake's
cynical exposé of the lust which permeates all levels of society
concludes with what must surely be a reference to Shaftesbury:
'Does not your Politician, your little great Man of bus'ness, that
sets the World together by the Ears, after all his Plotting, Drudg-
ing and Sweating at Lying, retire to some little Punk and untap
at Night?' (2. 3. 43–5). Shaftesbury was small and had a tap in
his side as a result of an operation to treat an illness wrongly
said by his detractors to be venereal in origin. However, the
satire here is perfunctory and entirely fleeting: the politician in

---

[40] Hume, 'The Satiric Design of Nat. Lee's *The Princess of Cleve*'.
[41] Ibid. Hume plausibly argues that the play is transitional between the Whiggism
of *Lucius Junius Brutus* and the Toryism of *The Duke of Guise*.

the speech is a cipher, mentioned in passing in a catalogue of the corrupt which also includes priests. The only other thing in the play which could be taken as anti-Whig satire is a reference to the fact that, when in England, the foolish cuckold Poltrot fraternized with the Lord Mayor and Common Council (1. 2). This jibe at the City seems to be a very mild sop to Tories. If the play was written during or after the Tory backlash of autumn 1681, it is the very minimum of what could be considered *de rigueur*, and, moreover, the Lord Mayor in question would have been the Tory supporter Sir John Moore, whose election was a triumph for the government.[42] The passage includes satire of all levels of society, but principally, it seems, of England as the home of cuckoldry. What seems more significant in Lee's treatment of the cuckolds Poltrot and St Andre is the absence of anti-Whig reference. Hume implies that they are 'cits', but the historical figures were noblemen.[43] Lee could have altered history and made them cits, but he doesn't. Their social character is that of hangers-on at court.

This brings me to the main thrust of the play's satire of libertinism. The satire is definitely not indulgent, like that in Tory prologues and epilogues, or court farces such as *The Muse of Newmarket*, but is as savage as that in Shadwell's *The Libertine*. Moreover, that the main force of the attack is directed at the court is constantly stressed. The Vidam utters the 'Rosidore is dead' speech, which all critics agree satirizes Rochester, in response to a request by Nemours to know 'the bus'ness of the Court' (1. 2. 83). Rosidore, says the Vidam, has been the life and soul of the court's pleasures, and the place is dismal without him. Poltrot is prepared to abuse his friend and his wife to be in fashion at court. It is made clear that the court is the site of the Princess's guilty passion, as she begs her husband, 'Take me from Paris from the Court' (2. 3. 128). She tells him, 'the Court has Charms' and he echoes, 'Because there is some cursed Charm at Court, | Which you love better than me and all the World' (131, 134–5). The 'cursed Charm' is the arch-libertine Nemours, thus identified as belonging to the court. Nemours is guilty of amoral animalism, bisexuality, sexual predatoriness,

---

[42] If the play belongs to 1682–3 the Lord Mayor would have been Tory Sir William Pritchard. For the problem of dating, see the Appendix.

[43] Armistead, *Nathaniel Lee*, 151.

grotesque double standards, and irresponsibility with property. He resembles not so much the indulgently portrayed rakish cavaliers of Tory plays as Shadwell's Don John. Libertinism in this play and generally is a disease of the court. In his 1689 dedication Lee claims to outstrip even the Whig Shadwell in his exposure of the rake as a ruffian. *The Princess of Cleve* was written after *The Massacre of Paris* was banned and 'this Farce, Comedy, Tragedy or meer Play, was a Revenge for the Refusal of the other; for when they expected the most polish'd Hero in Nemours, I gave 'em a Ruffian reeking from Whetstone's-Park'.[44] Lee satirized libertines as an act of revenge on those who had *The Massacre* banned. Of course he is trying to curry favour with his dedicatee, Dorset, as Lord Chamberlain, and with William, whom he praises in his prologue. The point is that he considers it plausible to assert that an attack on libertinism is an appropriate revenge on the government and the frivolous, Francophile court of Charles II.[45]

With sex and gender, then, as with other aspects of the dramatic language of politics, the two sides sometimes deploy the same tropes with opposite associations, while some tropes become the particular property of one side or the other. In the next chapter we shall see how the struggle to appropriate particular tropes developed into a pitched battle.

---

[44] Dedication to *The Princess of Cleve*, in *Works*, ii. 153.

[45] *The Massacre* was said by Dryden in *The Vindication of The Duke of Guise* to have been banned at the instigation of the French ambassador: Lee, *Works*, ii. 3.

CHAPTER 6

Themes and Tropes Reversed

At this point I think that it will clarify our understanding of the dramatic language of politics to examine the way in which Shadwell and his Tory opponents deploy its themes and tropes in opposite ways. The deliberate reversal of themes and tropes illustrates the way in which these function as a political language through which the dramatists can engage, in effect, in a political dialogue with each other and the audience.

In Chapter 5 I discussed Behn's reversal in *The City Heiress* of Shadwell's attack on libertinism in the recently revived *The Libertine*. Other Shadwellist themes receive pointed reversal by Tory dramatists. In *The Woman-Captain* Shadwell satirizes a dissolute aristocrat's over-indulgence in fine food and drink, in contrast to the plain fare of his decent, puritan father. Tories retaliated by portraying cavalier drunkenness indulgently;[1] and by satirizing Whig citizens' greed and predilection for plain food. Behn satirizes Whig gluttony in the prologue to *The False Count*. In D'Urfey's *The Royalist* Kinglove says of his hardships: 'Besides, is not this better than to lie for a well-dress'd dish of Wild-fowl, or pawn my soul to the Devil, or forfeit my Honour and Loyalty for a Fricasee or a Ragoust? I have known a Roundhead do it for a dish of butter'd Eggs!' (2. 2. p. 16). The height of Oldcut's aspiration, having obtained £2,000 a year from Kinglove's sequestered estate, is 'a whole Shoulder of Mutton to morrow Dinner, and some Butter in my Cabbage' (2. 1. p. 13).

In *Mr. Turbulent* food is a dominant motif. Firstly, there is satire of the citizenry's predilection for plain English meats and

---

[1] In *The London Cuckolds* one rake's response to another's telling him he has been saying the 'love litany' to his mistress is 'Spoke like a cavalier, egad! If thy inclination did but lie a little more to the bottle, thou wouldst be an admirable honest fellow' (1. 1. p. 45). There is some mockery of Tory rakes here, but it is indulgent. See also the discussion of *Sir Barnaby Whigg* below.

ale, which acquires political resonance in the context of opposition criticisms of court self-indulgence, and also opposition to
French imports, especially of wines and spirits. Thus Friendly
mocks Fairlove: 'who is it you are in quest of, that has so strong
a Cart-Rope, as to draw thee from all the fine things in the Mall,
to these stinking Tents of Bottle Ale and rusty Bacon? sure
'tmust be some rare piece: Or art thou cloy'd with Partridge and
Pheasant, and long'st after Hung-Beef, musty Swines-flesh, or
Rashers on the dirty Coales?' (1. p. 3). Secondly, food is a source
of over-indulgence for Turbulent. His overeating is diagnosed as
a symptom of his madness, and he becomes unhappy in Bedlam
only when he remembers that lunatics are starved for their own
good. Besides signifying a self-indulgence which is hypocritical
in a 'railer' against degenerate times, Mr Turbulent's overeating
is a signifier of excess and impropriety. It may also associate him
with Shadwell, whose obesity was satirized by his enemies, most
notably Dryden in *The Vindication*.[2] The prologue also uses
overeating as a metaphor for lack of critical discernment: 'you
come with Stomachs, as if full, | Tast nothing, but cry out, the
Poets dull'. The audience's appetite is 'sick and squeamish' (sig.
A3^r) and must be tempted by sensational novelty.[3]

The theme of criticizing the times in *Mr. Turbulent* may be
intended as a direct satire of Shadwell, who is much given to
moral indictment of the times in his prologues and epilogues,
and in his humours comedy. A humorous example occurs in
Act 3:

TURBULENT. The Villanies, the Whoredoms, the Fornications, the
   Adulteries, the Pride, Folly, and Vain-glory of this Age.
HANGBY. This wanton, luxurious, exorbitant, abominable, scurrilous,
   cheating, bribing, cousining, and treacherous Age—
TURBULENT. This libidinous, licentious, lascivious, lying, lazie, latitu-
   dinarian Age—   (p. 39)

Railing against the times is more than just a choleric humour:
it is given explicitly treasonable colouration: 'This Mr *Turbulent* is one that is still Railing against the Times, the Court, the
King, the Church, the Government, and almost every thing that
stands in his way, loves to speak Treason privately, and has a

---

[2] Shadwell is accused of being fat at 25, 40, and 49; he is also a drunkard (25).
[3] Cf. Dryden's prologue to *The Loyal General*, lines 21–7.

great delight and faculty that way' (1. p. 5). The bogus arrest which undoes Turbulent at the end is for precisely this offence of railing against the times, 'As good Drinking. Whoreing, Cheating Times, as any ever were since the Creation' (4. p. '59' [51]).[4] Thus, in Mr. *Turbulent* the weapon of Jonsonian humours comedy is used against Shadwell, its chief Restoration exponent.

Now I want to look at the language of politics in Shadwell's *The Lancashire Witches and Tegue O Divelly the Irish Priest*, a play considered by contemporaries (though not by modern critics) to be a provocative piece of Whig propaganda. Then we will see how Tory dramatists responded to Shadwell's play by 'shouting louder'. giving sharper expression to the themes and tropes of Toryism. The main example of this will be D'Urfey's *Sir Barnaby Whigg*.[5] That *The Lancashire Witches* was perceived as provocatively Whiggish in its own time is clear. In the preface Shadwell complained that the Tories were determined it should fail:

they came resolved to hiss at it right or wrong, and had gotten mercenary Fellows, who were such Fools they did not know when to hiss and this was evident to all the Audience. It was wonderfull to see men of great Quality and Gentlemen, in so mean a Combination. But to my great satisfaction they came off as meanly as I could wish. I had so numerous an assembly of the best sort of men, who stood so generously in my defence, for the three first days, that they quash'd all the vain attempts of my Enemies, the inconsiderable Party of Hissers yielded, and the Play lived in spight of them.[6]

The author of *Rome's Follies* comments that the play was badly received for party reasons (sig. A3^{r-v}). As noted in Chapter 1, Shadwell's preface informs us that the play was initially licensed with few alterations, but that the censor deleted substantial sections of the play in response to complaints from Tory sup-

---

[4] After page 24, the page numbers are so muddled as to be almost random, making it difficult to give meaningful references for quotations. I give the correct number in square brackets.

[5] Clearly this statement assumes that Shadwell's play pre-dated D'Urfey's, and D'Urfey's satire of Shadwell strongly suggests this. See the Appendix.

[6] Shadwell, *Works*, iv. 99. I use Summers's text in this instance because his notes on witchcraft are particularly useful, though the lack of references for information given points to the need for caution. The text seems reliable when compared with that of the first edition.

porters in the audience. Shadwell helpfully prints these in italics. However, D'Urfey in the prologue to *Sir Barnaby Whigg* claims of *The Lancashire Witches* that: '*the Mobile either encouraged by their Grandees, or treated by the Poet, shall throng to it with as much zeal, as they once did to the Committee,*[7] *when the scale was turn'd, and Loyalty began to come in fashion*' (sig. A3ʳ). Dryden in *The Vindication of The Duke of Guise* comments that 'the *Lancashire Witches* were without doubt, the most *insipid* Jades that ever flew upon a Stage; and yet even *These* by the favour of a *Party* made a shift to hold up their heads' (p. 5). As much as Shadwell and 'N.N.'s' complaints of politically motivated hissing, these jibes tell us that *The Lancashire Witches* was seen as a controversial Whig play in its own time.

The play's language of politics includes themes of disorder, social class, and sexual politics. Themes of disorder find reflection in the villainous characteristics of changeability, self-interest, and flexibility of conscience. Reversing Tory association of these qualities with rebels, Shadwell attaches them to the papist Tegue. When the witches counteract Tegue's charges with accusations that he is a fornicating popish priest, he cunningly swears an oath of loyalty, with a 'Mentall reservation', a deception which his Church allows (p. 183). He also has a dispensation to give answers pleasing to Anglicans when Sir Edward cross-examines him on articles of faith. The play also includes topical references to court corruption and folly, rather boldly in a play set in England. An example is Sir Timothy's unmerited knighthood. Isabella remarks, 'I am sorry the king bestowed Honour so cheaply' (1. p. 110). Sir Timothy's reply casts further aspersions, both sexual and financial at the court of Charles: 'Nay, not so cheaply neither; for though my Lady Mother had a dear Friend at Court, yet I was fain to give one a Hundred pounds, besides my Fees' (ibid.). One of the king's noblemen sold him a sword to be knighted with, for they will 'sell that or anything else at Court' (ibid.). Sir Timothy says of this man, 'I am sure he was a great Courtier, he talked so prettily to the Kings Dogs, and was so familiar with them, and they were very kind to him, and he had great interest in them: He had all their

---

[7] Howard's *The Committee* (1662) was a dramatic satire of interregnum parliamentarians, puritans, and sequestrators.

names as quick, and *Mumper* and I don't know who, and discours'd with them, I protest and vow, as if they had been Christians.' Charles II's excessive fondness for dogs was a subject of contemporary criticism.[8]

The central feature of *The Lancashire Witches* is Shadwell's appropriation of the themes of class superiority, more frequently used by Tories, for his Protestant country gentry, and application of the themes of class inferiority—philistinism, credulity, etc.—to popish and crypto-popish bigots. We see Shadwell's paradigm of order exemplified in the first scene in the confrontation between Sir Edward Hartfort[9] and his chaplain, Smerk.[10] Most of the exchange is italicized, indicating deletion by the censor.[11] Smerk's insistence on knowing the cause of his master's distress is made the occasion for several speeches by Sir Edward in which we may find the tropes of Whig conservatism in more elaborate form than in *The Female Prelate*. Smerk is advised to acquire '*Sence and Good-manners*' and to remember that '*Your Father is my Taylor, you are my Servant*' (p. 106). Social hierarchy is asserted against clerical presumption. Sir Edward then denounces the mischiefs caused by domestic priests in the best English families, as they usurp men's authority over their wives and children. This modulates into an attack on clerical sexual hypocrisy and on Anglicans whose '*furious zeal*' leads them to '*Foam at the mouth when a Dissenter's nam'd*' (p. 107). Such fury is portrayed as disloyal to a king who is '*renown'd for Grace and Mercy, | Abhorring ways of Blood and Cruelty*' (ibid.). Sir Edward insists, '*I will have moderation in my House*' (p. 108).

---

[8] Summers, in *The Works of Thomas Shadwell*, 397. Critical comments on Charles and his dogs may be found in Pepys's *Diary*, viii. 420–1 (1667) and *The Diary of John Evelyn*, iv. 410 (1685). Pepys's editors also cite Rochester, 'The Restauration': 'His very dog at Council Board, | Sits grave and wise as any Lord.'

[9] 'A worthy Hospitable true English Gentleman, of good understanding, and honest Principles' (dramatis personae), a living embodiment of the ideals represented by the deceased older generation in *The Woman-Captain*.

[10] 'Foolish, Knavish, Popish, Arrogant, Insolent; yet, for his Interest, Slavish' (dramatis personae). Marvell had written *Mr. Smirke; or, The Divine in Mode* in response to Francis Turner's *Animadversions Upon a Late Pamphlet Entituled The Naked Truth*, an anti-dissenting tract which was itself a response to a pro-toleration piece by Bishop Herbert Croft. This suggests a proto-Whiggish antecedent for the satirical use of the name; though there is a Smirk in Etherege's *The Man of Mode*.

[11] See Shadwell's preface to the reader, *Works*, iv. 99.

Shadwell thus reverses Tory satire of dissenting hypocrisy and extremism. For Shadwell it is not Whiggery, but the Tory reaction of fanatical anti-dissidence which is the problem. With the dignity of a Protestant gentleman, Sir Edward promises to forgive if Smerk will know his place, stop trying to confess his employer, and refrain from 'controversial Sermons' (p. 108). However, Smerk's fanaticism reaches new heights in Act 3: told that his disbelief in the Popish Plot is 'great Impudence, after the King has affirm'd it in so many Proclamations, and three Parliaments have voted it, Nemine contradicente', he replies by scorning Parliament itself (p. 144). Shadwell returns upon (Tory) Anglicans the charge of meddling in state affairs which were so often levelled at Whiggish citizens:

> No meddling with Government; y'are ignorant
> O'th Laws and Customs of our Realm, and should be so.
> The other world should be your care, not this.
> A Plow-man is as fit to be a Pilot,
> As a good Clergy-man to be a States-man, Sir.

> (p. 108)

Tories deployed the notion of presumptuous 'meddling' in association with the idea that the Whigs represented the 'worse sort' of people. It is not surprising that Shadwell's depiction of the 'better sort' reproaching clerical impropriety made Tories angry. Shadwell is careful to make in the play the statement which he reiterates in his preface, that Smerk is not typical of the Church, but 'a Rascal conceal'd in the Church, and is none of it' (3. p. 144). 'All the Eminent men of the Church of England believe the Plot, and detest it with horrour, and abominate the Religion that contriv'd it' (ibid.). However, the portrayal of an Anglican priest saying to a Catholic one, 'For my part, I think the Papists are honest, loyal men, and the Jesuits dyed innocent' (3. p. 143) is inflammatory. The same can be said of the passage in Act 4 in which Smerk praises the Roman Church and tells Tegue he might even accept the idea of purgatory since priests get paid to pray for souls there, though he balks at transubstantiation.

Sir Edward's moderation reverses the charge of cruelty levelled at Whigs, for example in Ravenscroft's epilogue to The Conspiracy where those who gloat over the Popish Plot executions are accused of barbarism. Shadwell displaces cruelty on to

Smerk and Tegue, who relish the prospect of Presbyterians burning at Smithfield (3. p. 143). Cruelty is also attributed to Sir Jeffery, who describes in detail the tortures he will inflict on Mother Demdike, who has been guilty of harmless pranks. Meanwhile, Sir Edward offers a running commentary, in which sympathy for the 'poor old woman' (1. p. 115) mingles with disgust at Sir Jeffery's methods. In Act 3 we see Sir Jeffery's rough justice in action.

In order to sustain the model of country Whig dignity and humanity, it is necessary for Sir Edward to be a wise defender of Protestant tradition, rather than a keen anti-papist. Popery must be made to look ridiculous and must be self-defeating. Sir Edward speaks of a Catholic neighbour without hostility (3. p. 138). His reaction to Tegue's avowed intention to take the antipapist oaths and be excused by his Church is sardonic, not horrified: 'Excellent Principles!' (3. p. 138). Tegue implies that he is Kelly, murderer of Godfrey, and says his right name is 'O Devilly', or son of the Devil (ibid.); but he is not portrayed as a monster. Instead his accent is meant to be ridiculous and his attempts to exorcise the witches with holy water and relics comic and futile. He is not worried about dying because he thinks he will be a saint, and 'besides shome great people will be nameless too' (3. 138–9). Shadwell thus writes out Protestant vindictiveness and combines the idea that 'the damn'd Plot' (3. p. 138) is real and serious with the suggestion that foolish papists put their own necks in the noose for reasons of self-glorification.

Shadwell reverses the cavalier comic paradigm of Town rakes gulling country dolts. Rural idiocy is a real phenomenon: Sir Edward's son is a fool who delights in country sports to the exclusion of all else, falls asleep when paying court to a lady (2. p. 126), and goes hawking on his wedding morning. However, the country gentry are the embodiment and the custodians of English Protestant tradition. The heroes, Bellfort and Doubty (i.e. Doughty), respect Sir Edward's 'country' values and are themselves of the country gentry and worthy of respect.[12]

Whiggery is associated with culture and common sense. Shadwell concludes the preface with a discussion of the witches,

[12] 'Two Yorkshire Gentlemen of good Estates, well bred, and of good Sense' (dramatis personae).

saying he has portrayed them as real for fear of being thought atheistical, though he himself is *'somewhat costive of belief'* (p. 101). He thus assumes the mantle of rationality and also of kindliness towards *'poor old Women'* hanged from superstition (ibid.). He then associates witchcraft, devil worship, and popish ceremonies.[13] Shadwell also says that the witches are the sort of entertainment a man of sense must resort to in an age which cannot bear to have its follies anatomized (the proper business of comedy). It is clear that urbanity is to be the note struck, rather than the horror and hysteria of other anti-papist plays such as *The Massacre of Paris*, *The Female Prelate*, and *Henry the Sixth*. This urbanity works to suggest that Whiggery is based on common sense and English tradition. In the play Shadwell plays down the threat of disorder which emanates both from the witches and from the persecution of them in his major source, *The Late Lancashire Witches* (1634) by Heywood and Brome.[14] The Whig gentleman Sir Edward is well educated and rational. His scepticism about witchcraft mirrors that of his author. He is called atheistical by the chaplain Smerk and by the credulous Sir Jeffery Shacklehead, who believes in the danger of witches and in the efficacy of Tegue's popish remedies against them. Sir Edward retorts, ''tis such as you are Atheistical, | that would equal the Devils power with that of Heaven it self' (1. p. 113). Shadwell deflects the charge of atheism from a Whiggish country gentleman to crypto-papists. The charge of philistinism, often levelled against the Whigs, is also reversed: it is Sir Jeffery who cites a work's title as the author's name, and Sir Edward who offers sardonic comment (1. p. 114).

Shadwell has an inclusive social vision. At the end of the play, tenants and country fellows come in and are welcomed: 'These

[13] Burns, *Restoration Comedy: Crises of Desire and Identity*, 99, notes that the witches are both real and unreal, serving Shadwell's dramatic purposes in both aspects. Cf. Brown, *English Dramatic Form*, 107.

[14] A further reason for the simultaneous reality and unreality of the witches might lie in the historical events which were the source for both Heywood's and Brome's, and for Shadwell's play: 'witches' were executed in Lancashire in 1611, but in 1633 several women who had been found guilty were pardoned after the accusations against them were found fraudulent. Credulity coexisted with scepticism in the Restoration: 'witches' were executed in 1665 and 1674, and, for the last time in England, in 1682. The historical literature on witch trials is voluminous; a useful short account focused on this period is Shapiro, *Probability and Certainty*, ch. 6.

honest men are the strength and sinnews of our Country; such
men as these are uncorrupted, and while they stand to us we fear
no Papists, nor *French* invasion' (p. 185). As in *The Coronation
of Queen Elizabeth*, it is the common people's vigilance which is
the kingdom's security, and indeed it is country fellows who
have caught the witches. As in Jordan's Lord Mayor's Shows the
vision is one of the whole English commonwealth.

Social inclusiveness is accompanied by patriotism. In *The
Lancashire Witches*, patriotism is reasonable, moderate, and
traditional. A patriotic exchange in Act 2 (p. 129) is representative. Sir Edward extends his hospitality: 'I knew your Fathers
well, we were in *Italy* together, and all of us came home with
our English Religion, and our English Principles.' Bellfort
praises his generosity and reputation and Doubty agrees: 'A
Character that *England* rings with, and all men of never so
differing opinions agree in'. Sir Edward responds: 'Gentlemen,
you do me too much honour; I would endeavour to imitate the
life of our English Gentry before we were corrupted with the
base manners of the *French*.' Bellfort's reply reinforces the patriotic message: 'If all had had that noble resolution, long since we
had curb'd the greatness of that Monarch [Louis XIV].' In Act
3 (pp. 136–7) there is a further passage in which country values
are given Whiggish and patriotic significance. Bellfort tells Sir
Edward, 'Methinks you represent to us the Golden days of
Queen *Elizabeth*, such sure were our Gentry then; now they are
grown servile Apes to foreign customes, they leave off Hospitality, for which We were famous all over *Europe*, and turn Servants to Board-wages.' Sir Edward responds, 'For my part, I love
to have my Servants part of my Family.' Doubty says admir-
ingly, 'You speak like one descended from those Noble Ancestors that made *France* tremble, and all the rest of *Europe*
Honour 'em.' Sir Edward replies, 'I reverence the Memory of
'em: But our new-fashion'd Gentry love the *French* too well to
fight against 'em; they are bred abroad without knowing any
thing of our Constitution, and come home tainted with Foppery,
slavish Principles, and Popish Religion.' Here we see all the
tropes of Whiggery: Elizabethanism, Protestantism, patriotism,
and manly vigour counterposed to Francophilia, popery, political supineness, and foppery. After further condemnation of
'Foreign Vices and Follies', Sir Edward sums up in an explicitly

Whiggish passage which was deleted by the censor: '*I am a true English-man, I love the Princes Rights and Peoples Liberties, and will defend them both with the last penny in my purse, and the last drop in my veins, and dare defy the witless Plots of Papists.*' After Bellfort has agreed that 'our Gentry are so much poysoned with Forreign Vanities, that methinks the Genius of *England* seems sunk into the Yeomanry', the gentlemen enjoy an Italian song. This is not hypocrisy, but evidence of the ability to discriminate between true patriotism and the philistine rejection of all things continental which is satirized in Tory prologues and plays like Behn's *The Feign'd Curtizans.*

In the field of sexual politics, Shadwell in *The Lancashire Witches* offers a country alternative to the aristocratic debauchery which Tory playwrights frequently palliate, and which Shadwell himself satirized in *The Woman-Captain.* This is a striking reversal of the 'cavalier' portrayal of the country gentleman as a dolt who deserves to be tricked and is unable to succeed sexually. There is nothing callous or cynical about the gallant courtship by Bellfort and Doubty of Isabella and Theodosia, and their intentions are strictly honourable. Predatory amorousness is attributed not to rakish gentlemen, but to the Catholic priest who thinks fornication a venial sin compared with marriage. It is he who, like Behn's Willmore, seeks sexual release regardless of the object, and who ends by copulating with the wrong woman in the dark, in this case one of the witches. Lust is also attributed to Smerk, who courts his master's daughter in Act 2 with the same presumption he showed towards the father in Act 1: in passages deleted by the censor he asserts his clerical authority as overriding her father's and she cries, '*How, Arrogance! Can any power give honour but the Kings? This is Popery, I'll have you trounc'd*' (2. p. 122). Unchastened, in Act 5 he tries to persuade the maid Susan to have sex with him, as '*The Casuists will tell you, it is a Marriage in* foro Conscientiae; *and besides, the Church of* Rome *allows Fornication: And truly it is much practis'd in our Church too*' (p. 173). Also lustful is Lady Shackleton, who shares her husband Sir Jeffery's credulous belief in witches and popish charms against them. Lust is thus associated with popery and superstitious folly.

The sexual politics of *The Lancashire Witches* shows a Whiggish duality. There is emphasis on the liberties of the Protestant

Englishwoman. As I noted in Chapter 5, the heroines express their 'Liberty, and property of Choice' in marriage in Whiggish terms (1. p. 111); they and their servant Susan all win their choice in marriage, and the model of the family is anti-patriarchal. The witches are never the objects of empathy, but have a certain function in exposing depravity and folly. A liberal tolerance and compassion are extended towards them by Sir Edward.

At the same time Shadwell gives expression to the Whig masculinism which I have identified in other plays. Sir Jeffery is ridiculously uxorious, allowing his wife to control the conversation and to help him examine the witches. As she says, 'I assist him very much in his business, or he could never do it' (3. p. 145). Sir Timothy quails before the abuse of the spirited Isabella in Act 2 and whines that he will tell their respective parents, a threat which he carries out in Act 4. In Act 3 she throws stones at him and he runs away, calling for help. He threatens to fight Bellfort for dallying with his 'Mistress' (p. 140), but is easily intimidated by the latter's accounts of his own prowess. Meanwhile, the doltish young Hartfort tells Theodosia, 'I had never so much mind to be Married as now; for I have been so woundedly frightened with Witches, that I am affraid to lye alone' (pp. 142–3). In addition to being honest English patriots and traditionalists, Bellfort and Doubty are 'real men'.

The Lancashire Witches ends on a note of harmony. Sir Edward sets an example to Sir Jeffery by forgiving his daughter's secret marriage with his usual generosity and good sense. The final speech by Sir Edward strikes a note of religious humility:

> How shallow is our foresight and our prudence!
> Be ne're so wise, design what e'er we will,
> There is a Fate that over-rules us still.

> (5. p. 188)

This seems to combine constructive self-criticism of his own misguided marriage plans with the wise Protestant caution which has been consistently counterposed to popish and misguided Anglican fanaticism.

How do Tory dramatists respond to Shadwell's play? Whereas in many Tory plays the primary goal is to cuckold the citizenry, in *Mr. Turbulent* the gallants take on the mantle of decency and good sense which Shadwell in *The Lancashire*

Witches drapes around the shoulders of the country gentry. Fairlove is determined upon marriage and has withdrawn into the city partly because there is no shame about marriage there (1. p. 4). Rakish values are embodied in the citizen's nephew, Furnish, who despises women who ask him to repay money he owes them, believing they should be satisfied with his sexual services. As we saw in Chapter 5, Behn tackles a similar theme in two opposite ways. In *The Round-heads* she associates royalism with virtue, and in *The City Heiress* she palliates libertinism in what appears to be a response to Shadwell. D'Urfey's *Sir Barnaby Whigg; or, No Wit Like a Woman's* is obviously a partisan play, a Tory satire on the Whigs. I believe it is also a response to *The Lancashire Witches*. There are some specific jibes at Shadwell. Thus in his epistle dedicatory, D'Urfey says of his own play: 'it had the Honour to please one party; and I am only glad, that the St. Georges of Eighty-one got a Victory over the old hissing Dragons of Forty-two; 'tis a good Omen, and I hope portends future successes, though some fat Whiggs of Sir Barnaby's tribe made all the interest they could to cry it down' (sig. A2^r). The reference to fat Whigs seems clearly to be a reference to Shadwell, whose obesity is also mocked in Dryden's *Vindication*. The fact that the fat Whigs are said to be 'of Sir Barnaby's tribe' alerts us to the fact that D'Urfey's Sir Barnaby might well be a portrait of Shadwell.

Shadwell, himself a Lancastrian, has Whiggish Lancastrian country gentlemen who support traditional Protestant and parliamentarian values. D'Urfey has Sir Walter Wiseacre as 'An Opinionated Fool and Cuckold: | A Lancashire-Knight' (dramatis personae). Sir Walter is a 'scowrer', a type frequently satirized by Shadwell. The opinionated Sir Barnaby may well be a caricature of Sir Edward Harthouse in *The Lancashire Witches*, who is fond of explaining the problems of his times, and of Shadwell himself, who excoriated his times in Jonsonian fashion. There is also satire of Shadwell in the description Benedick gives of Sir Barnaby as 'a huge fat fellow' (1. p. 9). Sir Barnaby's obesity and greed are also mocked in 2. 1. p. 19, 4. 1. p. 41, and 5. 1. p. 49. In 2. 1 we learn that Sir Barnaby is, like Shadwell, an opposition pamphleteer. Wilding calls him 'an audacious and impudent Libeller' (p. 19). It seems clear that in *Sir Barnaby Whigg* D'Urfey intends to counter Shadwell. Whig patriotism and Francophobia are mocked. In 2. 1 Sir Barnaby cries: 'the Turk, the French, the Moors, nay the very Devil will have us: Oh, that ever the Noble family of the Whiggs should live to see this day—we are beset, the Enemy is coming—and yet we are asleep: we are surrounded, and shall be confounded' (p. 18). Fear of the French is made ridiculous, as in the first prologue where the poet satirizes 'City-friends' who 'fear the *French* should come and eat 'em up' (sig. A4^r). The Tory trope that rebels can flourish because the king is too merciful can be found in a speech of Wilding's in the same scene: 'Villains, that can rail at Monarchs, and not blush, upbraid him by whose Clemency you live, that fearless lets you indulge your horrid Treasons, nourish the musty seed of Old Rebellion, so sure a guard is Sacred Royal Vertue' (p. 19).

Class themes in *Sir Barnaby Whigg* inversely reflect Shadwell: the men 'of sense' are the young cavaliers (5. p. 61). Partisanship is skilfully grafted on to existing tropes and devices of Restoration comedy: the team of light-hearted rake and 'railing' misogynist is familiar, and the latter is well suited for adaptation to vituperative railer against Whig traitors. Whiggery is skilfully presented as a Jonsonian or Shadwellian 'humour'. It is the citizen dissenter not the Anglican who is a presumptuous upstart. Sir Barnaby combines the pious zeal attributed to the Whigs in the first prologue with the self-interest alluded to in the epilogue, and later in the epistle dedicatory. So he praises 'zeal' in the face of popery and is presumptuously busy about the affairs of the nation: 'I can tell you, that if our soul-saving Party do not settle the Nation, I say 'twill crack, 'twill unhinge—whip you're gon, old Antichrist will have your Lands and Bodies, and the Devil your Souls' (1. p. 10). This ridiculous puritan rhetoric is intended to recall the interregnum. Sir Barnaby's generic forebears are the civil war parliamentarians. He is described in the dramatis personae and by Benedick in Act 1 as 'one of Oliver's Knights' (p. 9) and himself refers to 'the blessed year of 48' (1. p. 11). The government chooses to ignore the dangerous foreign enemies which threaten England, but 'it was not so in Oliver's | time' (2. 1. p. 18). He and his co-thinkers are, in 1640s parlance, 'the Saints' (3. 2. p. 29).

In contrast to Shadwell's cultivated Sir Edward, Sir Barnaby is a philistine with ridiculous aspirations. He shows Wilding a treasonable paper 'with all the Wise mens hands to't', which he thinks shows his 'wit'. Wilding, 'A Loyal and Witty Gentleman' (dramatis personae) responds, 'Wit—why thou double Traytor, dar'st thou assassinate that too—thou contrary to Wit as Loyalty' (2. 1. p. 19). In 2. 2 Sir Barnaby sings a song:

> I got Fame by filching from Poems and Plays,
> But my Fidling and Drinking has lost me the Bays;
> Like a Fury I rail'd, like a Satyr I writ,
> Thersites my Humour, and Fleckno my Wit.   (p. 28)

We are reminded of the references to Shadwell's lute and his drinking in *MacFlecknoe*, and of the accusation of derivative dullness which Dryden levels at him. There is also a foretaste of the accusations of polemical vituperation which Dryden was to make against Shadwell in *The Vindication of The Duke of Guise*.

Sir Barnaby is also credulous and superstitious. He shows his ignorance and credulity by his belief that 'Meteors', 'Comets', and 'Pestilences' are signs of sinful Tory times (1. p. 10). He is scared in Act 1 because his astrologer has told him there is going to be a famine. In Act 5 he thinks he will get away with stirring up sedition, saying, 'I'me sure I'm safe, for my Astrologer has secur'd my life' (5. 1. 50). When he hears he is to be hanged, he says, 'my | Astrologer's a damn'd Dog for telling me I shou'd be a Duke' (p. 51). Moreover, Sir Barnaby is not merely a butt of satire, but also a demon villain like the Constable, Guise, and others. He plans, like Marlowe's Barabas, to sell his city to the Grand Turk. This is expressed in terms of a Tory caricature of what are supposed to be Whig methods: 'I'le go presently and corrupt my Men; some with bribes, some with promises and fair words, others with preferments: Then sow Sedition 'mongst the Mobile, win 'em with Pots of Ale, and Peny-Loafs, to commit Ryots, Murders; there's your Policy!' (5. 1. p. 50).

This villainy is also reflected in changeability, hypocrisy, and underlying atheism. Before we meet Sir Barnaby, Benedick says that 'In all turns of State, [he will] change his Opinion as easily as his Coat, and is | ever zealous in Voting for that party that is most Powerful' (1. p. 9). Wilding comments: 'They of his Tribe say, theirs is the Church-Militant; but I say Money is both their God and King, and the greatest Zealot amongst them for the sake of the Popes Golden Slipper, shall not only kiss his Toe, but eat it, as the story goes of the hungry Spaniel' (ibid.). An unprincipled willingness to change becomes the central aspect of the section of the comic plot that concerns Sir Barnaby. First he turns his coat from fear when Wilding tells him the government has 'an Army raising, and 20000 in Arms already' (2. 2. p. 29). He becomes a royalist at the end of Act 2, and by 4. 1 has impeached his 'late friend and brother Sir Miles Mutinous' (4. 1. p. 48), who will hang at the next sessions, and joined the Church of England. We find him singing a Tory song, 'Let the Round-heads Plot on'. In Act 5 greed becomes the spur, as Wilding's man, disguised as a Dominican, tells Sir Barnaby that he may marry an heiress if he turns Roman Catholic. Sir Barnaby immediately exclaims, 'I'me no Protestant; not I, nor never was, nor never I will be, not I—'sbud Ten thousand pounds' (5. 1. p. 49). Then a letter, purporting to come from the uncle of the imaginary heiress, says the marriage depends on Sir Barnaby's turning Muslim. He responds: 'Turk! Well, well, since it can't be help't, I'le turn Turk, man, Jew, Moor, Graecian, any thing: Pox on't, I'le not lose a Lady, and such a sum for the sake of any Religion under the Sun, by Mahomet not I. . . . Why you old fool, our Conscience is our Interest always, and I have not been a Rebel so long sure to have any squeamish fits at these years' (5. 1. p. 50). Sir Barnaby is portrayed as atheistical beneath his outward zeal, and as changeable in matters of religion.[15]

As regards sexual politics, libertine amours are viewed indulgently, and are associated with the court: Sir Walter's wife, Livia, says of a lucky escape during her intrigue with Townly, 'Some Courtly God looks down and lends us chance' (3. 3. p. 45).[16] 'Courtly' values demand rejection of puritan morality. Drinking and swearing are even *de rigueur*. At the end of Act 1 Wilding and Benedick force the reluctant Sir Barnaby with threats of violence to drink the king's health. He responds: 'Well, I acquiesce: I am silent: you will awake when the Sword's at your throats; you will I say, and repent this prophane drinking of Healths' (1. p. 11). As in *The Revenge* and Dryden's

---

[15] Christopher Wheatley argues that this might be a reference to Shadwell: *Without God or Reason*, 92–4.

[16] The page numbers in the first edition are faulty, leaping from 35 to 44. I give the page numbers as they are in the text.

prologue to *The Loyal General*, there is satire of the Whig boycott of French wines and spirits: at the end of 2. 1 the Captain invites Sir Barnaby to drink punch with brandy and is told: 'Not I sir, I hate all Heathen Liquors' (p. 20). In Act 4 Sir Barnaby is learning to swear as befits a royalist: 'I can't mouth an Oath worth a farthing, for I have bin so us'd to uds-nigs, uds-chitterlings, and the like, that my mouth is quite spoil'd for Swearing; but I don't doubt in a little time' (4. 1. p. 48). The cavalier code opposes cheerful debauchery to puritan morality, the discourse of upper-class wit to the language of upstart zeal. Wilding ends the play on a typically libertine note with a warning to women against pride:

> Fools may love Pride, and a coy face adore;
> Just Spaniel-like, though beaten, cringe the more.
> To such be proud and vain, but shun th'Offence,
> If you wou'd e're attract a man of Sence.
> Pride hinders there the Joys his Love wou'd bring,
> As Storms and Frost keep back the kindly Spring.
>
> (5. p. 61)

The fools in the play are the Lancastrian knight Sir Walter, who loves only women who are unavailable and despises the lovely Millicent because she is his wife, and the Captain, who falls for Townly in drag.

Themes of order and disorder find inverse reflection in Shadwell's plays and those of his Tory opponents. The ideal for Shadwell, threatened by popery and the Tory faction within the Church of England and the court, is a hierarchical society based upon English Protestant and parliamentary tradition. For Tory dramatists the ideal, threatened by upstart cits who want to meddle in affairs of state and either ape or interfere with the sexual pleasures of their betters, is a society based upon the hegemony of royal rule and aristocratic taste. The charges of credulity, superstition, hypocrisy, changeability, and monstrosity, applied by Tories to rebels, are associated by Shadwell with papists and their apologists.

In terms of the treatment of social class, Shadwell extols the country gentry, whose reputation for parliamentary opposition had resulted in the coining of the term 'country party' in the

1660s. This also counters the Tory claim to represent the 'better sort' (a claim which was itself a counter to Whig popularity). D'Urfey responds with aristocratic rake heroes and by sneering at cits harder than ever. D'Urfey's elevation of the aristocratic élite and denigration of the citizenry reflects the way in which Toryism in the reaction period increasingly relies on élitism and suppression, leaving the middle ground to the Whigs. Shadwell's social vision of an English Protestant society is more holistic. As regards sexual politics, Shadwell extols the Protestant companionate marriage and women's right to choose a marriage partner. At the same time, he gives positive expression to Whig masculinism and scorns effeminacy. D'Urfey condones courtly libertinism and mocks puritan morality.

Shadwell's Whiggish vision was provocative to Tories because it was a comprehensive reworking and reconceptualizing of the dramatic language of politics and the social vision behind it. It provoked Tory dramatists into a sharper and shriller reiteration of the themes and tropes of Toryism.

Having shown that there were separate Tory and Whig rhetorics and 'situated' these in relation to one another, I want now to consider Tory plays more fully, in relation to their moments of paralysis as well as to the powerful aspects of their dramatic and political discourse. With the language of Toryism identified, we will be able to see what contradictions there were: not a meaningless muddle of contradiction which deconstructs or obscures partisanship and political meaning, but genuine sites of awkwardness, tension, and fracture.

CHAPTER 7

Tory Plays: The Contradictions of Royalism in Crisis

IN this chapter I want to challenge the view of the drama of the Exclusion Crisis as simply 'Royalism's Last Dramatic Stand'. Douglas Canfield, in particular, has argued for the tenacity of Stuart ideology and of aristocratic themes and tropes in the drama.[1] This perspective is purveyed less consciously in the mass of recent articles on gender in Restoration drama, with their unthinking references to a Stuart 'patriarchalism' which is assumed to be hegemonic. However, even when dramatists eagerly profess loyalty or Toryism in prologues, epilogues, prefaces, and dedications, there is often a disjunction between the professions and what is achieved in the plays. I believe there are inherent problems with the royalist–Tory paradigm which the process of dramatization tends to exacerbate. In particular, it is hard to dramatize Tory quietism convincingly. However much moral and political force the idea of absolute loyalty is felt to have, there is something unconvincing about the spectacle of 'quiet' heroes. The heroes of avowedly royalist or Tory plays are often masochistic, passive, and paralysed by a sense of the difficulty of right action. The problem of Restoration heroism is not new;[2] but it gains an extra dimension in the drama of the Exclusion Crisis.

---

[1] See Canfield's 'Royalism's Last Dramatic Stand' and 'Dramatic Shifts: Writing an Ideological History of Late Stuart Drama'; also Wikander, 'The Spitted Infant'.

[2] Newman, 'Irony and the Problem of Tone in Dryden's *Aureng-Zebe*', argues 'Restoration heroism generally is connected with the fundamental irony that self-denying behaviour is so lacking in the world that its appearance must be described in rarefied terms that arouse admiration and wonder and suggest that a virtuous person is more like a god than a man' (446). West, 'Dryden and the Disintegration of Renaissance Heroic Ideals' argues that Dryden offers 'an intelligent and painstaking analysis of the bankruptcy of heroic values in the late seventeenth century' (218). Hughes, *Dryden's Heroic Plays*, argues that Dryden made 'the disparity between heroic art and mortal life' the mainspring first of comedy, later of tragedy (152).

Moreover, if absolute loyalty is to be heroic, it must be tested and found true even in the face of vitiated kingship; but there is also something troubling from a royalist point of view about the spectacle in play after play of royal faults. Nor are these faults random: they correspond with the faults of the Stuart brothers as even the most tolerant contemporaries perceived them. Thus we find royal lies, ineptitude, passivity, misrule, 'effeminacy', and excessive mercy towards the kingdom's enemies, which are all failings for which Charles was criticized; arbitrariness, rage, and self-centredness, considered to be faults in James; and lust and (quasi-)Catholicism, perceived faults of both. Court corruption and sexual rivalry between prince and subject also have a disquieting resonance. The heroism of Vendosme in Crowne's *The Ambitious Statesman* involves loyalty to an ideal of kingship, but this ideal is compromised by the Dauphin's abuse of power to steal his mistress while the king stands impotently and obliviously by.

Whitaker in *The Conspiracy* responds to contemporary anxieties about royal immorality and intemperance by wishing away royal faults and reverting to the idea of inherent royal superiority in the heroic plays.[3] As we saw in Chapter 4, he also contains and assuages anxieties about court corruption and the king's inability to reward loyal service and punish rebels. However, for others the contradictions often loom too large. There are times when the assertion that the monarch will rule well if the people will be quiet and courtiers constant rings distinctly hollow. There is little scope for heroism when the Vendosmes and Theocrins must annihilate themselves in conformity with the ideal of absolute obedience and the Castalios and Polydores are destroyed before their life is begun. If the radical alternative was unthinkable for loyal playwrights, conformity is a bleak prospect too, especially for Otway, whose plays offer little more reassurance than that misfortune might possibly be endured.

As we saw in Chapter 5 royalism can make powerful use of family themes, drawing upon the Filmerian political association of absolute monarchy and patriarchal authority. However, the

---

[3] As Staves points out, the depiction of imperfection in the true king, rather than in a usurper, is a break in dramatic continuity with the heroic plays: *Players' Scepters*, 85. I feel this would give added force to the dramatic representation of royal faults.

spectacle of bad fatherhood in the microcosm, even if intended to dramatize the evils of republicanism, as in Otway's *Caius Marius* and *Venice Preserv'd*, can resonate uncomfortably for royalists. The Exclusion Crisis was a crisis of fatherhood: Charles had no legitimate son and was considered to have scattered his seed irresponsibly throughout the land and to be over-indulgent towards his illegitimate son, Monmouth. Royalist dramatists try to contain and assuage such anxieties, either by exculpating the father-king or by putting all the social responsibility upon the son-subject. In *Absalom and Achitophel* Dryden strives, in the Tory cause, to 'Extenuate, Palliate, and Indulge'[4] the father-king's moral deficiencies, as well as Monmouth's as a son and subject. In her dedication of *The Round-heads* to Charles's bastard son Henry Fitz-roy, Duke of Grafton, Behn admonishes her patron about his father's virtues and his own duty of filial obedience, and covertly criticizes Monmouth in the process: 'Oh what Son can desert the Cause of an Indulgent Parents (*sic*), what Subject, of such a Prince, without renouncing the Glory of his Birth, his Loyalty, and good Nature' (sig. A3ʳ).

Nevertheless, as Paul Hammond demonstrates in 'The King's Two Bodies', the language of patriarchalism had been undermined following the execution of Charles I in 1649. Problems were posed for the Stuarts by the disparity between Filmerian ideology and the perceived reality: Charles I was virtuous but impotent, so unable to be a good father to the nation, and Charles II was unable to be a good father literally in terms of securing the succession with a legitimate son, or figuratively in his conduct as leader of the nation. Moreover, the representation of crisis in the family can work not to shore up authority relations by analogy with the macrocosm of kingly power, but to foster an all-pervading cynicism in the face of complete social breakdown. As we shall see, this is very apparent in Otway's *The Orphan*. The treatment of division in the family is fraught with contradiction.

In plays with a royalist slant the pathetic portrayal of division in the family reflects neither (anachronistic) emphasis on an apolitical private sphere, nor (or at least not simply) the meta-

---

[4] Preface to *Absalom and Achitophel*, in *Works*, ii. 4.

phorical reflection of social breakdown, but the literal absence of the very qualities of natural affection, duty, and piety which are necessary in the state. However, unlike propaganda, drama shows us the human cost with which the attempt to be dutiful is fraught. There seems to be a semi-conscious awareness in royalist dramas like *The Loyal General* and *The Orphan* that ideology is a construct: the characters moralize themselves and others into 'correct' attitudes which are completely at odds with their own human desires. An ideology which is revealed as constructed must by definition lose force and become fragile.

It might be argued that, since drama is not propaganda, there are contradictions in all plays: why are the contradictions in royalist and Tory plays particularly significant? In fact the nature and extent of contradiction in Whig plays seems different. The most notable contradiction in plays such as *The Massacre of Paris* and *The Female Prelate* is that the heroes' hotheadedness makes the assertion that 'Loyal Protestantism' is compatible with loyalty—or even epitomizes it—seem questionable. However, on the whole the greater robustness of the heroes of these plays carries conviction. Plays in which contradiction is all but eradicated may create their own doubts: in *The Conspiracy* and *The Coronation of Queen Elizabeth*, for example, internal cohesion is purchased at the price of a blatant contradiction with perceived social reality, resulting in an entire absence of realism. Restoration audiences were well aware of the disparity between prevailing social mores and any kind of idealized noble or self-sacrificing behaviour. Ironic attention was continually being drawn to this disparity in the indulgent teasing of the audience for immorality and witlessness in prologues and epilogues. However, such plays might inspire or even mobilize people politically, overriding doubts and contradictions. In this limited sense they may be said to resemble propaganda, as found in pamphlets and broadsides. So, as with Whig plays, there is a robustness and an agitational force which is simply lacking in the royalist and Tory dramas which I shall consider below.

I shall illustrate these remarks with a reading of seven plays: *Oedipus* by Dryden and Lee (1678), Tate's *The Loyal General* (late 1679), Otway's *The Orphan* and *The Souldier's Fortune* (both 1680), Tate's *The History of King Richard the Second* and

The History of King Lear (both late 1680 or early 1681), and Otway's *Venice Preserv'd* (1682). I shall consider the plays in chronological order, in so far as this can be determined. Crowne's *The Ambitious Statesman*, discussed in Chapter 3, is also an excellent example of the kinds of difficulties and contradictions which I shall talk about in this chapter.

Oedipus

I want to draw out three political and moral themes in *Oedipus*: exculpation of royal impropriety; a sense that problems of vitiated kingship are outweighed by the supreme danger of rebellion; and the dangers of hasty judgement. Then I will examine a negativity which undercuts the play's loyalism.

Oedipus is exculpated in three ways. Firstly, he is made a better man than his counterparts in Sophocles, Seneca, and Corneille.[5] Even the ghost of wronged Lajus says he is possessed of 'Temperance, Justice, Prudence, Fortitude, | And every Kingly vertue' (3. 1. 364–5). He fights bravely for his country, firmly suppresses rebels, but is also merciful, as when he spares the plotter Alcander. Thus, though he does not represent Charles or James, he has the positive qualities of both as contemporaries perceived them: mercy and military heroism respectively. Secondly, the love interest is enhanced to arouse pity. The incestuous passion is given prominent and sentimental treatment, mother and son even yearning for an embrace after the awful truth is known (5. 1. 220–5). This accords with the aesthetic notions of Dryden,[6] who 'drew the *Scenary* of the *whole Play*'.[7] Thirdly, a royal heroine who also suffers in love is created. Princess Eurydice loves Prince Adrastus and shuns the rebel leader to whom her parents betrothed her as a baby. Even

---

[5] Dryden states in the preface that they have improved on the Oedipus of Corneille, who 'miserably fail'd in the Character of his Hero: if he desir'd that Oedipus should be pitied, he shou'd have made him a better man' (*Works*, xiii. 115).

[6] 'Then we are not touch'd with the Sufferings of any sort of Men so much as of Lovers; and this was almost unknown to the Antients; so that they neither administred Poetical Justice (of which Mr. Rymer boasts) so well as we, neither knew they the best common Place of Pity, which is Love' (*Heads of an Answer to Rymer*, in *Works*, xvii. 191).

[7] Dryden, *The Vindication*, 42. Dryden also says he wrote the first and third acts.

though Adrastus is virtuous and suitable where the rebel leader is a murderer and rapist, Eurydice is in breach of a moral absolute, curtly expressed by the priest Tiresias: 'She broke her vow | First made to *Creon*' (3. 1. 257–8). The princess and her lover must die. The effect of this is to evoke a general sympathy for royal love beset by religious restrictions. Dryden similarly creates sympathy for Anthony and Cleopatra in *All For Love* and indulgence of David's scattering of his seed in the opening lines of *Absalom and Achitophel*. Eurydice's response to the revelation of Oedipus' crime is to tell her lover:

> 'Tis true, a Crown seems dreadful, and I wish
> That you and I, more lowly plac'd, might pass
> Our softer hours in humble Cells away.
>
> (5. 1. 93–5)

This emphasis on the burdens rather than the faults of princes is a recurring royalist theme.

Royal lust is further palliated by stressing the danger of rebellion as the greater evil. Creon is turned into a ranting villain who works on the real or imagined grievances of the people to try to overthrow the king. His deformity may recall Shaftesbury, now crippled by ill health, his impiety may recall Shaftesbury's supposed atheism, and his lechery royalist slanders of Shaftesbury's morals. However, there is more here than a possible personal parallel. By having the rebel leader contemplate rape and murder in a temple, the authors associate sacrilege and sexual disorder with disruption of the social order. By making the lust of Creon incestuous, as Eurydice is his niece, they also further exculpate by comparison the hero's unwitting sexual crimes.

Creon instructs his cronies to 'insinuate | Kind thoughts of me into the multitude; | Lay load upon the Court; gull 'em with freedom' (1. 1. 98–100). This abuse of libertarian rhetoric works because for the rabble, 'the last man ever speaks the best reason' (1. 1. 301). They are ungrateful for Oedipus' good government, and fickle; they want a new king so they can 'see another Coronation!' (1. 1. 242) and to 'satisfie our Consciences'. The latter reason refers to superstitions about the cause of the plague in Thebes and may satirize puritan interpretation of the plague and fire of 1665–6 as divine retribution for court immorality. Thus we find in *Oedipus* what was to become the conventional Tory treatment of rebellion, embracing sexual monstrosity, specious populist rhetoric, and a fickle and credulous mob.

Associated with the theme of rebellion as rampant villainy is a rather more subtle treatment of the difficulty of understanding appearances, leading to the necessity of quietism. Dryden was to return to this theme two years later in *The Spanish Fryar*. Lee's Act 2 is permeated by a sense of the difficulty of knowing what is right, what heaven intends, how the king should act. The whole play is fraught with the difficulty of interpreting signs and prodigies. Premature application of reasoning to events is condemned by Tiresias:

> But how can Finite measure Infinite?
> Reason! alas, it does not know it self!
> Yet Man, vain Man, wou'd with this short-lin'd Plummet,
> Fathom the vast Abysse of Heav'nly justice.
>
> (3. 1. 240–3)

Meaning is extracted from complexity by a judicious mixture of active seeking after truth and being quiet and waiting for revelation. Oedipus several times prays for enlightenment. In Act 2, when his prayer is answered by a prodigy of himself and Jocasta, figured in the sky, Adrastus cautions, ''Tis wonderful; yet ought not man to wade | Too far in the vast deep of Destiny' (2. 1. 68–9).

Act 3 opens with a comprehensive indictment by Creon of folly; but misdirected reason is the real danger. Adrastus offers an alternative definition of folly when he says that anyone who does not learn from Oedipus' fate will be an 'inconsiderate and ambitious Fool' (5. 1. 90). The opposite qualities would be thoughtfulness and humility, not cleverness. It is important to learn the lessons of history when these are clear, but to be cautious when the way is dark. Superficial appearances should be mistrusted.

The theme of the dangers of hasty action and the need for quiet is linked to two other royalist themes: the importance of class distinction and the dangers of patriotism. The rebels are guilty of a false interpretation of the plague: '*Oedipus* pollutes the Throne of *Lajus*, | A stranger to his Blood' (1. 1. 297–8). Creon should rule because he is '*Theban* born' (1. 1. 56). Oedipus has faults, but they are not what the rebels think. Their inversion of the truth poses dangers to Thebes. Tiresias, who has moral authority, confidently quells the mob in the name of the 'lawful King' (1. 1. 324). The rebels also attack Adrastus as 'a Foe to *Thebes*' (1. 1. 96); but the foreign prince is brave and honourable. Eurydice loves him and Oedipus has more in common with him than with his own people. Thus Dryden and Lee vindicate love and friendship across national boundaries, just as they problematize the collapse of class distinction in their depiction of Creon's over-familiarity with the mob. Social distance is one of the stable referents in the midst of darkness and difficulty. Patriotism is shown as a facile misreading of appearances, and that political action based on the false reasoning which results from such misreading is a real danger.

Above all, through the misguided actions of Oedipus, and Lajus before him, as well as in its depiction of the rebels, the play offers the lesson that it is futile and dangerous to interfere in the destiny of kings, or in the business of the gods. Human attempts to interfere with the ordained succession are based on ignorance and tragically misguided. There is a clear royalist message here.

However, two factors undercut the play's loyalism. The first is tainted heroism: Alcander, ironically, is right when he warns of Oedipus, '*Thebans*, behold | There stands your Plague' (4. 1. 138–9). We wince as we see the people waving branches before Oedipus, as the priest praises him as 'a visible Divinity' (1. 1. 411). The love scenes with his mother seem in bad taste. Dryden later saw the moral problem: 'perhaps I have made him too good a man'.[8] A second, associated problem is the lack of any positive values: vitiated kingship is better than rebellion, though it still causes a plague. Douglas Canfield argues that nothing can be deduced from such darkness of tone: 'Quite often tragedy portrays a fundamental mutability of things that teaches the lesson of *contemptus mundi*, and yet as often it paradoxically at the same time reaffirms the threatened social order.'[9] My point is that the authors are straining every nerve to affirm the threatened social order, but that they do not succeed in making this

[8] Dryden, *De Arte Graphica*: 'Preface of the Translator, With a Parallel, of Poetry and Painting', in *Works*, xx. 70.
[9] Canfield, 'Royalism's Last Dramatic Stand', 262–3.

affirmation inspiring. There is no sense in *Oedipus* of a special providence in the fall of a sparrow, or the fall of a king. Oedipus curses the gods over the bodies of his children, stabbed by Jocasta (5. 1. 445–9). He then commits suicide in what a loyal functionary calls, 'O curs'd Effect of the most deep despair!' (5. 1. 463). There is no counterpoint to Creon's atheistic defiance of fortune and reliance on 'the God, Ambition' (5. 1. 393) and his own right arm. There is no one left alive to receive Oedipus' 'dying voice' or to obey the weight of the sad time and care for the kingdom. There is no transcendence in death: Jocasta foresees reunion in the grave, but she has been shown throughout as given to foolish interpretations and wishful thinking. Oedipus foresees weeping spirits greeting him as he goes 'downwards, to the darker Sky' (5. 1. 461). There is no reversal of the darkness of vision with which the play opened, 'Methinks we stand on Ruines' (1. 1. 1), echoed by the opening words of Act 2, 'Sure 'tis the end of all things!' (2. 1. 1). Tiresias pronounces the dismal moral 'Let none, tho' ne're so Vertuous, great and High, | Be judg'd entirely blest before they Dye' (5. 1. 469–70). If there is another lesson it is that the pursuit of love regardless of obligation leads to disaster. This message is incompatible with the exculpation of the royal hero and must also be productive of uneasiness for royalists, since it accords so closely with what the opposition was saying about the king.

The Loyal General

Tate's title is politically suggestive, but he does not himself invite a royalist interpretation. His epilogue and epistle dedicatory eschew the connection between aesthetic and political falling-off in Dryden's prologue. However, in his play he does make effective royalist use of themes such as rebellion and civil war, faction and ambition coupled with female impropriety and unnatural parenthood, exemplary loyalty, and virtue as its own reward. On the other hand, the characterization of the king and prince, and the fate of the hero and heroine, have a problematic and contradictory resonance.

As the memory of the English Civil War overshadowed the Exclusion Crisis, so the spectre of Argaleon's rebellion hangs

over the play. Almost the first words we hear in the play are 'The
Rebels have the Royal Troops in chase' (1. p. 1). Even after the
victory of the loyal general Theocrin, pockets of resistance flare
up and have to be quelled, creating a nightmare spectacle of
danger and disorder which renders all rejoicing premature. Fear
of civil war is exploited by Theocrin's enemies in Act 3 to
discredit him with the king: '*Theocrin*'s grown Popular, | And
Heads our Army' (p. 21). The king fears civil war as a threat to
peace, the family, law and established religion:

> Now Lords as you do prize your Countreys Peace,
> Your Ages ease, your Wives and Childrens Safety;
> Ply your best Skill and Bank against the Deluge!
> Methinks I see our *Greece* again embroil'd
> And Slaughter's bloody Sluces drawn anew;
> Our Laws disarm'd, and holiest Rites profan'd,
> Our Streets alarm'd with Tumults, Rapes and Fire,
> And all the Terrors of *Argaleon's* War.

> (3. p. 20)

The deluge was a common image of successful rebellion in the
Civil War period and afterwards. This image is reflected through
the play in a repeated association of the villains with images of
sea and tempest.[10]

There is no 'rabble-rousing' in this play. Instead Tate
demonizes faction and ambition in the arch-rebel Argaleon, who
never appears and thus remains a stereotypical ambitious plotter. We learn that, like Shaftesbury, he was formerly favoured
with high office, and is thus guilty of ingratitude (1. p. 6). The
chief villain, however, is Escalus, who plots against Theocrin:

> Three Factious Stout Repiners at the State
> (Of Bank'rupt Fortunes) I have Brib'd already.
> To swear this Charge, a Circumstance or two,
> Neatly devis'd and plausibly alledg'd,
> Will make th'Impeachment pass.

> (3. p. 22)

The reference to corrupt witnesses suggests Whig exploitation of
the Popish Plot scare, while the word 'impeachment' brings

---

[10] The Queen at 1. p. 3, Escalus at 2. pp. 19, 20, 3. p. 32, and 5. p. 52. Cf. the
use of sea imagery to indicate court changeability as against Protestant fidelity in *The
Massacre of Paris* (2. 2. 59) and court corruption in *Virtue Betray'd* (3. p. 40).

immediately to mind the impeachment of Danby. Escalus' ambition unleashes ramifying villainy. Like the Shaftesbury of royalist propaganda he is continually shifting allegiance, as 'interest' prompts him. Escalus has a female counterpart in his sister, Myrrhoe:

> She's a Projector too,
> Lur'd on by Interests resistless Charms;
> The vig'rous Spring that sets all Plots adrift,
> From Womens Projects to th'Intrigues of State.

(3. p. 22)

The women's projects overlap with the men's, but also show the reflection of disease in the body politic in the domestic sphere: Myrrhoe supports Escalus' intrigues, but also plots against Theocrin's fiancée, Princess Arviola. Myrrhoe induces Arviola to doubt Theocrin's fidelity, just as his loyalty is unfairly doubted by the king. The association of rebellion and female monstrosity is also exemplified in the adulterous queen, who plots 'to blast the Kings Succession' (2. p. 10). She supports the rebellion which leads to the death of the king's sons in battle, and plots to replace Arviola with her own daughter, Edraste. She is thus a wicked stepmother as well as a bad wife. As in *The Young King*, the destruction of the succession is associated with the perversion of 'natural affections'. The queen's destructive energy is reminiscent of Crowne's Constable, as she tries vainly to instil her own 'active Blood' into her unwilling and virtuous daughter (1. p. 3).

Exemplary loyalty is personified in Theocrin and Edraste. Theocrin stands firm even when slandered and dispossessed. Like the Admiral in *The Massacre of Paris*, he rebukes his supporters, who rightly fear the outcome of his summons to court, asserting his trust in the king and Arviola (4. pp. 38–9). Like Vendosme in *The Ambitious Statesman*, he tells his faithful officers to remain loyal to the king even when he himself has been reduced to the lowest pitch of suffering by the failure of the king and his own mistress to believe in him (5. p. 47). If Theocrin resembles Vendosme here, elsewhere he is less passive, a military hero and an inspiration to the nation, especially in Act 2 when he single-handedly overcomes the despair of the king and his advisers. It is Edraste who, like Vendosme, suffers a paralysing conflict between filial duty and loyalty as a subject and friend: 'I must unnat'ral or disloyal prove!' (1. p. 4). Both Theocrin and Edraste, like Vendosme, suffer unrequitable love for the object of a royal superior's affections. Edraste loves Theocrin, fiancé of her royal mistress and sworn friend, Arviola, and Theocrin suffers rivalry from the arrogant Thracian prince, Arbardanes. Edraste utters loyal sententiae and, like Eurydice in *Oedipus*, informs us of the cares that beset the monarch: 'The rightful Crown at best uneasie sits, | But sinks the crusht Usurper to the Ground' (1. p. 3). The king utters similar sentiments: 'Friendship's the privilege | Of private Men, for wretched Greatness knows | No Blessing so substantial' (3. p. 20).

Theocrin and Edraste show constancy against a background of changeability, shifts, and overturns. Theocrin is described as a strong tree (4. p. 41). The moral contrast between Theocrin and Escalus is nowhere more apparent than in relation to the question of reward, which Tate treats in a more 'sound' way from the royalist point of view than Otway, who is constantly bemoaning the lack of reward for loyal service. Escalus at first offers misplaced loyalty to the queen in exchange for social and sexual 'Preferment' (1. p. 1), then switches to the king's service, then to that of Arbardanes because:

> Mid'st all my busie Zeal,[11] this stupid King,
> As yet no mention of Reward has made!
> And rates my Service as a Subjects Duty.
>
> (3. pp. 31–2)

Desire for reward leads logically to aspiring to the crown itself. The futility of this overreaching is shown as Escalus goes to execution, happy in 'that minutes Pride' (5. p. 59) when his plots culminated in his being hailed as heir to the throne.

Theocrin is loyal without hope of reward: 'What I perform'd was but a Subjects Duty' (2. p. 13). At first the king rewards him for saving the nation with his daughter and his crown, because 'Thou merrit'st Both: Though not from Kings descended, | Thou art by Vertue to the Gods Ally'd!' (2. p. 13). When the promised reward is unjustly withdrawn, Theocrin endures voluntary exile,

---

[11] The word 'zeal', with its puritan overtones, is associated with misdirected political and sexual energy throughout the play. See e.g. 1. p. 3; 2. p. 10.

sacrificing his happiness for the general good. In this he has a female parallel in Edraste, who makes the same sacrifice. In Act 3 Theocrin, in anguish, wishes to be annihilated for the good of his beloved and the state: 'Fate wills, and 'tis expedient that I die!' (3. p. 25). In Act 4 he tells the prison guards to kill him, and in Act 5 he goes into the desert and takes poison, refusing even to let his officers give him a funeral so that he might be remembered after death.

However the depiction of loyalty is not ideologically unproblematic. Theocrin's loyal desire for self-obliteration has an element of masochistic excess. Moreover, Theocrin's downfall results from self-confessed royal ineptitude. This tends to arouse our anger on his behalf. As in *The Ambitious Statesman*, the hero is destroyed because of the king's inability to see clearly or judge rightly. In Act 1 the king's behaviour is characterized by querulous distraction and indecision (1. p. 2). There is some resemblance to King Charles in Lee's Whig play *The Massacre of Paris*. For much of the play Tate's king dithers; then in Act 5 we see him in a weak man's rage, taking an unseemly revenge on innocent priests for Arbardanes' abduction of his daughter during sacred rites. This punishment of the innocent is matched by preferment of the guilty: he has only himself to blame for the rebel successes which have caused the succession to become endangered, for he has forgiven rebels when he could have conquered them, and bestowed favour where he should have punished:

> Were you as quick to punish a Delinquent
> As to reward the smallest Worth, your Throne
> Had still been fixt.   (1. p. 6)

This reminds us of the complaints of royalists from 1660 onwards about Charles's excessive mercy to former parliamentarians.

The play's king, like Tate's own, is unable to counteract the corruption of his court. The courtiers are cowardly and self-seeking, giving the king bad or useless advice which he cannot see through. Theocrin moralizes on their changeability, as their sycophancy towards him is abandoned in his misfortune: 'Th'are Weather-cocks of time, and face about I To ev'ry veering Wind!' (4. p. 39). The king ends by retiring to a hermit's cell. He says he wishes to subordinate his appetites to his reason (5. p. 59), but he is really motivated by an impulsive and belated access of mortification at his own failures. Theron calls it a 'rash resolve' (5. p. 59), and it is indeed politically disastrous as the realm is left leaderless. The theme of inappropriate royal withdrawal recurs in Lee's *Theodosius*, where, as we shall see in the next chapter, it may well refer to Charles's perceived aloofness from his subjects' anxieties.

If the king is weak, Arbardanes has all the intemperance of Crowne's Dauphin. Like James, he is feared as a possible source of war. The king's advisers warn the king to give him what he wants, which is the princess, even though she is already promised to Theocrin. Arbardanes is also a powerful foreigner who might threaten the kingdom. There is some ground for these fears, as Arbardanes is arrogant and high-handed. Like Adrastus in *Oedipus*, he believes in ruling-class solidarity: he comes to help against the rebels, 't'uphold the Rights of Majesty, | Whose Dignity's the Common Cause of Kings' (2. p. 17). Unlike Adrastus, he thinks his royal blood entitles him to behave as he pleases. In particular he rides roughshod over Arviola in courtship and ultimately abducts her. It is the low-born Theocrin who behaves nobly, wishing to fight for his country to prove himself worthy of his love and offering to die for her. Arbardanes sneers at Theocrin's prior claim to the lady and flaunts his own royal birth:

> Dar'st thou, poor Sprout of obscure Growth, presume
> To be ingrafted to the Royal Stock,
> And stain with Peazant Blood the Race of Kings?
>
> (4. pp. 40–1)

He uses the same argument to defend to the king his attempted abduction of Arviola (5. p. 54). The rivalry between Arbardanes and Theocrin thus places assertive royalism in direct contrast with merit.

The attempt to write a 'loyal' play is fraught with contradictions: vitiated centres of power, masochistic self-destruction of the loyal hero, a thread of world-weariness running through the play and culminating in a bleak and unsatisfactory ending. The playwright is loyal, but blind loyalty is, in the end, a sterile value when there is little positive sense of worth in what it upholds.

The Orphan *and* The Souldier's Fortune

Tragedy in *The Orphan* ensues when Acasto's sons, Castalio and Polydore, both desire his ward, Monimia. Fearing his father's displeasure, Castalio marries her secretly. Polydore observes her tenderness towards Castalio and thinks her a whore, so he seduces her in the dark, pretending to be his brother. As in *Troilus and Cressida*, truth is found too late. Monimia takes poison, Polydore falls on his brother's sword, and Castalio also commits suicide after cursing creation. The domestic tragedy results directly from injustice at the centres of power and inability to reward loyal service.[12] In Otway's play the unjust exile dramatized by Crowne and Tate in *The Ambitious Statesman* and *The Loyal General* has already come about. Acasto is unfairly out of favour. Like Theocrin, he has often fought successfully 'against the rebels' (1. 10), but he has been overlooked in a corrupt court, which he now hates (1. 20–4). Yet Acasto remains loyal to his king, 'Nor ever names him but with highest reverence' (1. 26). This beleaguered loyalty associates him with Crowne's Vendosme and Tate's Theocrin, but also, as the play's modern editor points out, with the old cavaliers who were passed over at the Restoration.[13] It also connects him with his author, himself an old soldier who persistently complained of lack of reward as a soldier, son, lover, poet, and loyal subject.[14] Otway also resembles his heroine: we learn in the opening scene the reason why Monimia is dependent on Acasto, and why she is an ineligible bride: Bohemia has been riven by 'late and civil discords' (1. 56) in which her father (like many old cavaliers) was ruined. Otway was to say in the epistle dedicatory to *Venice Preserv'd* that 'a steady faith and loyalty to my prince, was all the inheritance my father left me' (pp. 3–4).

The epigraph of *The Orphan* is from the *Satyricon* of

---

[12] I disagree with Tumir's perception of the relationship between the father and king as merely a metaphorical and symbolic equation, and also with her view that the 'victimization' of the family group 'appears entirely self-inflicted' ('She-Tragedy and its Men', 418).

[13] Taylor, introduction to *The Orphan*, p. xxvii.

[14] Prologue and epilogue to *Caius Marius*, epilogue to *The Souldier's Fortune*, dedication to the Duchess of York and epistle to Bentley, the publisher of *The Souldier's Fortune*. For Otway's suffering in love, see Ghosh, in *Works of Thomas Otway*, i. 13–14.

Petronius, and concludes with a passage which translates as 'eloquence alone shivers in rags and cold, and calls upon a neglected art with unprofitable tongue' (p. 2, translated p. xvi). Lack of reward is thus foregrounded thematically in the way in which political disloyalty was foregrounded in the epigraph of *Caius Marius*. Loyalty is fraught with contradiction when the king is surrounded by corruption and unable to protect the loyal subject against it. Acasto's consistent exculpation of his monarch seems like an effort of will and recalls the parliamentary tradition of describing Stuart kings as 'badly advised' as a politically expedient euphemism. Acasto is a bad father in an opposite way to Marius Senior and Metellus in *Caius Marius*, whose ambition destroys their children's happiness. Acasto destroys his children through lack of ambition. The young-love plot is punctuated by diatribes expressing the father's comprehensive world-weariness which embraces most of society and both sides of the political divide. He attacks 'Corruption, envy, discontent, and faction' (2. 59) in the army. He condemns 'the factious fool', 'knaves of conscience', 'Atheists' who 'make use of toleration', and those who call 'saucy loud suspicion, public zeal' (3. 79, 95, 93, 82). However, he also inveighs against the court at every opportunity and is reinforced by Chamont, who loathes the Court (2. 113–17) and the hypocrisy of priests (3. 194 ff.).

Acasto's sons become his victims. Like Otway's own father, he has nothing to offer them except his loyalty. His cynicism keeps them at home, forcing their active desires inward and turning them sour. Predatory lust in the private world becomes a substitute for action in the vitiated political sphere. This is clear in the terms in which Polydore describes his lust for Monimia:

> Now by my great soul,
> M'ambitious soul, that languishes to glory,
> I'll have her yet, by my best hopes I will.

> (3. 15–17)

Contrary to Stuart quietist ideology, the stifling of 'ambition' is seen as unnatural. Darkness and difficulty in private reflect the paralysis which afflicts the loyal subject in public. The contradictions in society are internalized in the family and the self and become self-consuming. The mistrust of Acasto and Chamont for their society generates a pervasive atmosphere of mistrust. Castalio and Monimia mistrust the institution of marriage and the possibility of happiness; all the main characters mistrust one another. Acasto has tried to withdraw into the retirement and private virtue praised in loyal subjects since the reign of James I.[15] However, his attempts to seal off his domain from corruption misfire, and he complains: 'In my house | I only meet with oddness and disorder' (4. 263–4). The Stuart ideal of 'quiet' is an illusion.

The stifling of natural ambition leads to unhealthily heightened sexual desire, the thwarting of which is itself disastrous. The characters moralize themselves into correct attitudes based on duty to friends or parents, or to socially correct ideals like primogeniture and advantageous marriage for the good of the estate; then they behave in a contradictory way, impelled by overmastering desires which have become warped through suppression. Restraint and self-denial breed not harmony, but tragic misunderstanding. This is made clearer by the introduction of the character of Chamont. In contrast to the neurotic inhabitants of Acasto's house, this character has some of the positive qualities of soldier characters such as Ventidius in Dryden's *All For Love* and of the 'manly' heroes of Protestant plays such as *The Massacre of Paris* and *The Female Prelate*. Chamont is a 'hot-brained, boisterous, noisy ruffian' (5. 496); but he is 'noisy' to some purpose: he wants to protect his sister and get at the truth. Because he courts Acasto's daughter Serina with openness and determination, he wins her. Either Otway is ineptly reinforcing here the oddity of Castalio's secrecy, which many critics have found a structural weakness,[16] or, more probably, he is drawing attention to a tragic anomaly. The self-tormenting heroism of the loyal son is vitiated, and the hothead who despises the court and rides rough-shod over obstacles to his own desire succeeds. In the contrast between Chamont and Castalio Otway enhances the pathos of self-defeating conformity.

The young victims of political, social, familial, and emotional

---

[15] For the influence on literature of James I's attempt to banish the gentry to their estates, see Turner, *Politics of Landscape*, 86 ff. See also the discussion of retirement in Ch. 4.

[16] See Taylor, introduction to *The Orphan*, pp. xviii–xxi.

repression yearn for the comparative freedom of a state of nature (1. 356–60; 5. 20–2, 25, 27). In Act 4 Polydore and Monimia revel in their exclusion from the moral order and devise tortures for each other. Despite horror at their sin, there is a sense of relief at not having to strive any longer to conform to impossible ideals. Pure self-hatred is easier than the struggle for a happiness which an all-pervading cynicism has vitiated in advance.

The tone of the play's ending is bleak and pessimistic. The moral is:

> 'Tis thus that Heaven its empire does maintain;
> It may afflict, but man must not complain.
>
> (5. 542–4)

The word 'empire' suggests cold power, naked domination. Authority must be suffered without complaint, though the result be terrible affliction. God must be served as Acasto has served the king, loyally, but without hope of joy or reward. The dying Polydore is as careful to excuse heaven of responsibility for his crimes as his father is to excuse the king from any responsibility for the state of society. The fact that the speaker of the play's last words is Chamont emphasizes the sense of unfairness. The failed conformist, Castalio, ends cursing, like Dryden's Oedipus:

> Confusion and disorder seize the world,
> To spoil all trust and converse amongst men;
> 'Twixt families engender endless feuds;
> In countries needless fears; in cities, factions;
> In states rebellion; and in churches, schism:
> Till form's dissolved, the chain of causes broken,
> And the Originals of Being lost.
>
> (5. 516–22)

In a sense this has already been fulfilled. Castalio's curse is a way of making sense of the political and familial division he has already experienced and associating it with chaos in the universal order of things. What is significant is the association of chaos with royal and heavenly authority which is absent or remote, with power which is badly or negligently exercised.

In *Caius Marius* Otway associated bad fatherhood and faction, moral deficiency and the republican condition. *The Or-*

phan cannot replicate this ideologically convenient paradigm. There is a sense in both plays that more trust, communication, and mutual confidence would be a good thing in family and nation, but what *The Orphan* primarily dramatizes is a family destroyed by social injustice in a kingdom in which loyalty is not rewarded. Whatever his intentions, the main force of Otway's play is to suggest that his society is one which destroys its best men and women. I shall argue in relation to *Venice Preserv'd* that it is anomalous to 'read back' an emphasis on a privileged, apolitical private sphere, characteristic of post-1688 domestic tragedy. However, the belated popularity of *The Orphan* in the eighteenth century may be due to the fact that this idea is embryonic or emergent within the play, such is the weight of cynicism expressed about the public sphere. Otway has not abandoned the Stuart 'patriarchal' idea of the family as microcosm of kingly power in favour of a 'bourgeois' idea of the family as economic and emotional unit; rather the reverse. The family offers no escape from the contradictions of the political macrocosm. Yet there is a troubling sense that in foul times openly seeking to fulfil personal desires is all that makes sense.

The theme of lack of reward for loyal service is a central one in *The Souldier's Fortune*. As the heroes comment on passers-by in Act 2, we see that former rebels prosper, while ''Tis as unreasonable to expect a man of Sense should be prefer'd, as 'tis to think a Hector can be stout, a Priest religious, a fair Woman chast, or a pardon'd Rebel loyal' (2. 371–4). Otway strives for humour, yet sometimes cuts rather close to the bone. The plight of the disbanded soldiers (of whom Otway himself was one) cannot help but raise political questions.[17] Thus Courtine com-

---

[17] These soldiers were victims of the vicissitudes of Stuart foreign policy. Their presence in the city streets in spring–summer 1679 was a threat to public order and a political problem linked to the crisis of confidence in Charles's government. Prior to 1678 Charles had both fostered the French alliance and used Danby to further the appearance of a Protestant foreign policy involving overtures to William of Orange. By 1678 public opinion had moved from hostility to the Dutch as trading rivals to fear of French Catholic expansionism. Under pressure Charles moved to support the beleaguered Dutch while he still had some soldiers serving with Louis. In Feb. 1678 Parliament voted £1 million for war with France, but Charles never declared war. Some troops were sent to Flanders to help in the fight against France (referred to in *The Woman-Captain*), but most never saw action, instead being wasted by disease and suffering in one of the worst winters of the century. In autumn 1678 Parliament voted money to disband the army, following the peace treaty of Nymwegen in

plains to Beaugard, ''twas your fault we left our Employments abroad to come home, and be Loyal, and now we as Loyally starve for it' (1. 11–13). Beaugard's reply links the sufferings which result from the vagaries of contemporary foreign policy with the injustices of 1660: 'Did not thy ancestors do it before thee, man? I tell thee, Loyalty and Starving are all one: The old Cavaliers got such a trick of it in the Kings Exile, that their posterity could never thrive since' (1. 14–17). The problem of the king's inability to reward loyal service recurs, here with little attempt at containment or mitigation. Tension is defused by the comedy and direct political criticism is avoided, though sometimes this very avoidance seems pointed, as when complaints which might well be directed against the government are directed instead, rather sarcastically, at the perversity of fate: 'Fortune made the peace just when we were upon the brink of a War; then Fortune disbanded us, and lost us two Months pay: Fortune gave us Debentures instead of ready Money, and by very good Fortune I sold mine, and lost heartily by it' (1. 188–92). In reality the soldiers 'have forsaken considerable advantages abroad in obedience to publick Edicts' (4. 39–41).

In *The Souldier's Fortune* there is an even stronger focus on the futility of royalist endeavour than in *The Orphan*. Despite the satire of anti-papist citizens, there is no reverential royalism in the play. Courtine sings a snatch of a royalist song when drunk, then mocks himself: 'I am mighty loyal to Night' (4. 543). As a comic dramatist Otway is a shrewdly cynical observer of a world vitiated by corruption, both sexual and political. Yet the tone is never moralistic or corrective. The lesson which the gallants draw from their anatomization of the evils of the age is to get what pleasure they can. It is the foolish citizen, Sir Davy, who moralizes in Shadwellian vein about the state of the times (4. 417–18, 422–3). Even he ends by laughing good-naturedly at the cuckolding trick which has been played on him, his futile self-righteousness abandoned. He too has discovered adversity and realized that the only thing to do is to laugh in its face. The play has no other moral than the wisdom of smiling in the face of misfortune. There is no justice in society as it exists,

Aug. Charles did not disband them until spring–summer 1679, leading to fears of a military coup: Childs, *The Army of Charles II*, chs. 9 and 10, app. E; Miller, *Popery and Politics*, 152–3.

and no valid alternative. Despite jibes at rebels and plot-mongers, the play is ultimately apolitical in the sense that belief in political solutions involves some faith in human nature and collective social potential. Any such belief is entirely lacking in the play. The servant Fourbin sums it up: 'Pox o' the times, the times are well enough so long as a man has money in his Pocket' (4. 419–20).

The History of King Richard the Second

Like Crowne in *The Misery of Civil-War*, Tate alters Shake-speare to emphasize the horrors of rebellion. Crowne foregrounds and sharpens the scenes involving Cade and the rebels. Tate similarly adds a mob scene (2. 4) in which a levelling crowd led by 'Revelation Stitch' who has 'born Commission with *Watt Tyler*' (p. 21) announce their intention of taking advantage of the king's absence to make, and if necessary unmake, a leader of their own choosing. They are manipulated by the usurper-to-be, Bullingbrook, through typically specious appeal to their 'Liberty and Rights' (p. 22). As in Crowne's play, there is a deliberate attempt to recall the English Civil War. Like some radical sectary, Stitch has experienced and communicated revelation about 'the Poyson of the Whore and the Horns of the Beast' (p. 23). Bullingbrook demonstrates his acumen and op-portunism by persuading the mob to hang their own leader. We see the internecine viciousness and dangerous volatility of the lower orders, unleashed when there is discord among those who should know better.

A number of changes successfully criminalize Bullingbrook. In Act 1, where Shakespeare's banished Bolingbroke exits de-claring his love for his country, Tate's is machiavellian:

> A Beam of royal splendor strikes my Eye,
> Before my charm'd sight, Crowns and Sceptres fly;
> The minutes big with Fate, too slowly run,
> But hasty Bullingbrook shall push 'em on.

> (1. 3. p. 11)

In Shakespeare Bolingbroke is described as 'Bereft, and gelded of his patrimony' (2. 1. 237). The word 'gelded' implies that not only his honour, but his manhood, is at stake. In Tate 'the Kings pleas'd | To have occasion for his temporal wealth' (2. 2. p. 15).[18] It is a forced loan, not an expropriation. In Shakespeare the barons recount legitimate grievances of the nobles and commons. These grievances, together with all the references to the king's rapacity, extravagance, and bankruptcy, are eliminated by Tate, who shows disgruntled trouble-makers overreacting to the king's need for a loan and over-ready to make mischief. In Shakespeare's 2. 4 there are accounts of unnatural prodigies, foretelling or reflecting Richard's downfall. Tate instead puts the language of prodigy self-damningly into the mouth of a rebel, Willoughby:

> Nature her self of late hath broke her Order,
> Then why should we continue our dull Round?
>
> (2. 2. p. 16)

Shakespeare's lords want to restore the order of things which the king has violated:

> Redeem from broking pawn the blemished crown,
> Wipe off the dust that hides our sceptre's gilt,
> And make high majesty look like itself.
>
> (2. 1. 293–5)

Tate's lords are typical ambitious plotters wishing to push forward to glory, or 'make our selves a Sea and fail in Blood' (2. 2. p. 16). Overtones of the 1640s and the recent Exclusion Parliament are added, by references to Bullingbrook's parliamentarianism. While the latter is waiting for Richard to descend from the castle walls in 3. 4, Tate interposes a hasty order to Northumberland to ride to London and 'Summon a Parliament i' th' Commons Name' (p. 34). In 4. 1 Aumerle expostulates:

> To call a Senate in King Richard's Name
> Against King Richard, to depose King Richard,
> Is such a Monster of curst usurpation,
> As nere was practis'd in the barb'rous Climes.   (p. 35)

---

[18] 2. 3. begins on p. 18. Where 2. 2. begins is not indicated, but it must either be on p. 12 as the king, queen, and nobles enter to York and Gaunt, or on p. 15 after the king, queen, et al. exeunt and before S. D. Manet, [N]orthumberland, Piercy, Ross, Willoughby. The latter would be my choice, as there is a natural break when news arrives of the death of Gaunt (who exited on p. 14).

Later in this scene, Richard refers to 'Th' usurping House' (p. 39).

Condemnation of rebellion is unequivocal at the end. Shakespeare's Bolingbroke merely regrets Richard's death. Tate's repents his usurpation and is filled with 'tort'ring Guilt' (5. 5. p. [55]). Shakespeare's Bolingbroke thinks he will expiate his guilt by a visit to the Holy Land. Tate's says that neither he nor the kingdom can be at peace and wishes that he lay in the coffin in Richard's place. Tate also enhances the play's royalism by making Richard a noble martyr. Reference to Richard's complicity in Gloucester's murder is omitted. His misleadership is palliated by Gaunt, who says his 'easie gentle Nature has expos'd | His unexperienced Youth to flatterers frauds' (2. 1. p. 12). Tate's Richard listens with dignity and courtesy to Gaunt's criticisms and is even self-critical:

> Nor shall we be unmindful to redress,
> (However difficult) our States corruption,
> And purge the Vanities that Crown'd our Court.

> (2. 1. p. 14)

Tate strengthens Richard's character, removing the weakness which would be problematic from a royalist point of view. In 3. 1, where Shakespeare's Richard is too despondent to fight, Tate's is merely keen to act according to law, and to keep the peace: 'Move we secure then in our Royal Right, | To th'Traytors Executions, not to Fight' (p. 25). Where Shakespeare's Richard gives in to Bolingbroke, saying 'I must not say no' (3. 3. 208), Tate has Richard give a less conciliating response, appropriating lines which in Shakespeare belong to the Bishop of Carlisle at the end of Act 4:

> And yet I cannot chuse but weep to think,
> That whilst you press and I permit this Scorn;
> What Plagues we heap on Children yet unborn.

> (3. 4. p. 35)

In 4. 1 Tate has Richard say that he is resigning the crown to spare his subjects further bloodshed.

However, a contradiction arises from the fact that Tate also tries, as he says in his dedication to his friend George Raynsford, to emphasize Richard's misfortunes to show 'Extremity of Distress' (sig. A2ᵛ). Making Richard pitiable, the victim of events rather than the culprit, is achieved by sentimentalizing. Tate brings forward the garden scene in Act 3 to before Richard's defeat, thus eliminating a central metaphor: in Shakespeare, a gardener tells the queen that

> Bolingbroke
> Hath seized the wasteful king. Oh what pity is it
> That he had not so trimmed and dressed his land
> As we this garden!

$$(3. 4. 54-7)$$

In Tate's version the scene becomes one more instance of the queen's grief, increasing pity for Richard. Tate adds an exchange between king and queen (3. 3) in which they lament their fate and affirm their loyalty to each other. In 4. 1 Tate has Richard enter 'in Mourning' (p. 37), thereby assuming the mantle of the series of suffering victims who populate the play: the Duchess of Gloucester, the dying Gaunt, the sorrowing queen. Tate puts back the parting scene between king and queen in Act 5 until after the scene in which York describes Richard's humiliation at the hands of the populace, so that we can actually see him besmeared with dirt. All this is affecting, but tends to work against the desire to increase Richard's nobility and strength of character. The dramatic method involved cuts across the adherence to Rhymerian principles referred to in the dedication: 'Nor cou'd it suffice me to make him speak like a King (who as *Mr. Rhymer* says in his *Tragedies of the last Age considered*, are always in Poetry presum'd Heroes) but to *Act so too*, viz. with *Resolution* and *Justice*' (sig. A2ʳ). A virtuous but impotent king is not as bad as a corrupt king, but is nevertheless politically problematic, given widespread anxiety about Charles II's failure to act decisively to secure the succession.

Moreover, though Tate works hard to palliate the seizure of the Lancastrian revenues, transforming this into a forced loan serves only to increase the resemblance to Charles II. The insertion of promises made by Richard to Gaunt that he will redress corruption in court and state has the unfortunate result of making it seem as though amendment is a question of the king's will; something which Whigs asserted, but which a royalist would fiercely deny. Sometimes it seems, ironically, as if Tate's very amelioration of Richard is an implicit criticism of Charles, as when he stresses Richard's marital fidelity, or adds material to emphasize his patriotic defence of his country against its enemies (2. 1. p. 15).

In his dedication Tate says that in order to make Richard 'a Wise, Active and Just Prince', he has removed all 'Detracting Language' against him, even in the mouths of conspirators. He then quotes a passage from Shakespeare in which disgruntled nobles condemn Richard's predilection for the advice of unsuitable companions, his financial impositions and extravagance, and his refusal to fight his country's enemies. This begs the question why remove such aspersions in the mouths of villains, unless it is because they touch a raw nerve, as they so obviously do? Unfortunately Tate's alterations expose the anxieties they attempt to assuage and make explicit what Tories might have preferred him to have left unsaid. In detailing in the dedication his efforts to turn Richard into 'a Wise, Active and Just Prince', in defiance of his source, Tate lays bare the fact that the virtue of the king and loyalty of the Duke of York are authorial constructs, differing from known reality. Royalism is thus seen to stand on shaky foundations.

This brings me to a second reason why the play fails as Tory drama: the nature of the story. The play was banned without even being examined by the Lord Chamberlain (sig. A2ᵛ): that an English king should be unable to resist the combined challenge of strong noblemen and the discontented people is disturbing, and was so even in Shakespeare's time.[19] It was particularly disturbing at a time when Whigs resurrected the story of Richard II in the pamphlet war as a legal precedent for parliamentary alteration of the succession.[20] In this context the amelioration of the monarch's moral character is irrelevant. Moreover, the very act of making alterations to render the play acceptable emphasizes the possibility of contemporary application. The particular interest and relevance of English history is acknowledged in the dedication, where Tate says that when he transformed his characters into Sicilians in an attempt to evade

---

[19] See Dover Wilson's introduction to the old Cambridge edition of Shakespeare's *Richard II*, pp. xxx–xxxiv.

[20] See e.g. Somers, *A Brief History of the Succession*, 6–7.

the censor,[21] he 'might as well have made 'em Inhabitants of the *Isle of Pines*, or, World in the *Moon*, for whom an Audience are like to have small Concern' (sig. A2ᵛ–A3ʳ).

Tate strongly denies topicality in his dedication, but this is unconvincing: there are striking historical parallels in the story. The play opens with the vexed question of who among the king's relatives is and is not a traitor. Subsequently at every stage we are confronted by the same tension between private and political loyalty which was the key issue in the Exclusion Crisis: should the king put loyalty to James before Protestantism, should he deal firmly or leniently with Monmouth? In the play's opening scene, Richard tells Mowbray that there will be no more favouritism:

> Were he my Brother, nay my Kingdoms Heir,
> Our Blood shou'd nothing privilege him, not bend
> Our upright Soul from Justice. (p. 3)

This derives from Shakespeare, but the words heard in the theatre must have hit close to home. This is exactly the statement the Whigs wanted Charles to make. In the next scene York tells the grieving Duchess of Gloucester that one should not mourn a traitor: 'I hate a Traytor more than I love a Brother' (1. 2. p. 6). Presumably intended to demonstrate York's loyalty in Tate's play, this addition has the effect of foregrounding the issue of patriotic versus familial—and specifically brotherly— duty. Tate does nothing to disguise and even reinforces the fact that one of the play's central themes is also the central obsession of 1680.

Most bizarre is the fact that, at the same time as demonizing rebels, Tate makes his ultra-loyal York into a fat buffoon, and does nothing to palliate the fact that he is a cruel father. Thus from a political point of view there is something in the play to offend everyone. The play does not succeed as Tory drama and it is not surprising that it was banned.

The History of King Lear

Tate's alterations to Shakespeare's *Lear* are notorious, particularly the happy ending and the addition of a love plot between

---

[21] See Van Lennep *et al.* (eds.), *The London Stage*, 293.

Edgar and Cordelia. Some of them seem to be dictated by taste, but others have a political resonance. It is partly true that the political implications are Tory, as some critics have commented.[22] The loyal brother (Edgar) is, like James, maligned, then vindicated. We gradually see through the seeming loyalty of Edmund, who is referred to in the text as 'Bastard', as if to emphasize a resemblance to Monmouth. Edmund's political ambitions are stressed: 'Thus wou'd I Reign cou'd I but mount a Throne' (3. 2. p. 25).

Usurpation is demonized by Goneril's and Regan's misuse of power:

> The Riots of these proud imperial Sisters
> Already have impos'd the galling Yoke
> Of Taxes, and hard Impositions on
> The drudging Peasants Neck.   (ibid.)

Tate also develops the triangular lust and intrigue between Edmund, Goneril, and Regan. Thus wrongful power, baseborn ambition, 'Cromwellian' tyranny, presumption, machiavellianism, ingratitude, and women out of place are associated. The sexual politics of the play are strongly royalist. We are told that 'The Commons repine aloud at their female Tyrants' (3. 2. p. 26). The idea of 'female Tyrants' is supposed to carry an oxymoronic force of peculiar unnaturalness. Cordelia, pursued and threatened with rape and imprisonment, seems to represent the suffering kingdom. Thus female lust and ambition on the one hand, and feminine virtue on the other, are both mobilized for Toryism. The moral is the need for strong kingship: a good lesson from a Tory point of view.

The potentially embarrassing French invasion is removed, and the native hero, Edgar, substituted for Shakespeare's king of France. As in *The Conspiracy*, we are presented with a compelling spectacle of loyal heroism in Edgar, Kent, and Gloster, the basis for which was present in Shakespeare. The gods are on the side of 'the King's blest Restauration' (5. 4. p. 62). In 4. 4 Cordelia prays to the 'never-erring Gods' to recognize Lear's cause as their own: 'Revenge your Selves, and right an injur'd

---

[22] Hume, *Development*, 350; Wallace, 'Otway's *Caius Marius* and the Exclusion Crisis', 363–4.

King' (p. 53). After Lear's restoration, she moralizes, 'Then there are Gods, and Vertue is their Care' (5. 4. p. 62). The play concludes with Edgar's assertion, reminiscent of *The Conspiracy* and *The Spanish Fryar*, '(Whatever Storms of Fortune are decreed) | That Truth and Vertue shall at last succeed' (5. 4. p. 67).

However, there is an important difference between Tate's play and Dryden's. Tate's old king is not so much the victim of usurpers as of his own folly. Lear's faults have unleashed the forces which devastate England. Lear is a bad father and a bad king: a combination which is intensely problematic for Tory patriarchalism. As in Shakespeare, what is portended by 'These late Eclipses of the Sun and Moon' is division in both family and nation: 'In Cities mutiny, in Countrys discord, | The bond of Nature crack't 'twixt Son and Father' (1. p. 9). Tate adds anxiety about the misrule of 'the King who comes resolv'd | To quit the Toils of Empire, and divide | His Realms amongst his Daughters' (1. 1. p. 2). The reference to daughters emphasizes the fact that, as in Lee's Whiggish *Theodosius*, power is being inappropriately handed to women. With equally embarrassing topicality, Tate has Kent say, 'I grieve to see him | With such wild starts of passion hourly seiz'd, | As renders Majesty beneath it self' (ibid.). The royal intemperance and the royal ineptitude which were divided between two characters in *The Loyal General* are combined in Lear. Tate keeps the reference to the 'unbounded Riots' of Lear's entourage (1. p. 11). As in Shakespeare, his knights are 'Men so debaucht and bold that this our Palace | Shews like a riotous Inn, a Tavern, Brothel' (ibid.). The association of corrupt court and vitiated majesty had been made by Tate himself in the dedication to *Richard II*, where it is also given the force of topicality (sig. A2ᵛ).

It might seem as if Tate, like Whitaker in *The Conspiracy*, is shaping the action of his play according to the providential pattern of seventeenth-century history: decline and fall of the monarchy, followed by miraculous rise; or that, as in Dryden's *The Spanish Fryar*, he is positing regroupment around the triumphant values of 1660. However, like the king in *The Loyal General* and Lee's Theodosius, Lear ends by retiring 'to some cool Cell' to reflect upon events, while others more suitable rule the kingdom (5. 4. p. 67). Lear's abdication in favour of his daughter and her husband suggests the possible accession of William and Mary which some Whigs were already contemplating.[23]

The loyal heroism which is so inspiring from a Tory viewpoint also has problematic aspects. Perhaps Tate is trying to reclaim for Toryism the kind of vigorous, manly, and patriotic hero we find in Protestant plays like *The Massacre of Paris* and *The Female Prelate*. He uses old-fashioned tropes, such as decency, charity, and national pride, which we find in Shadwell. Thus he keeps in Gloster's speech, 'So Distribution shall undo Excess' (4. 2. p. 43), although he deletes the reference to 'the superfluous and lust-dieted man' (Shakespeare, 4. 1. 67), which might seem Whiggish or anti-court and draws a moral pointed at rich citizens: 'Thus let the griping Userers Hoard be Scatter'd.' Even so, there is perhaps too much egalitarianism for Tories' comfort. Tate keeps the 'Let copulation thrive . . . | To't Luxury, pell mell' speech (4. 3. p. 48); though the application to the Stuart court is infelicitous. He keeps in modified form the speech about the interchangeability of justice and thief and the observations that 'a Dog's obey'd in Office', and that 'Robes and Furgowns hide | All' (4. 3. p. 49). By 1681 such references had acquired Whiggish overtones. To Shakespeare's Lear's 'I will die bravely, | Like a smug bridegroom' (4. 6. 199–200), Tate adds, 'flusht and pamper'd as a Priest's Whore' (4. 3. p. 50). Perhaps, like Dryden's low plot in *The Spanish Fryar*, this is a sop to the popular preference for anti-popery which accompanied the Whig ascendancy in the 1680–1 season around the time of the second Exclusion Parliament.

Equally problematic is Gloster's rabble-rousing. It is Regan who speaks of 'this Monster of Rebellion' and Gloster who raises 'Mutiny' (4. 1. p. 41). Gloster speaks of showing his injuries to 'Enflame' the crowd to 'Revenge' and 'Glorious Mischief' (3. 4. p. 39). Tate deploys the tropes of Whig dramatists in a way which resonates uncomfortably for Tories and uses the key Tory trope of rebellion in a way which backfires upon the king's party. Added to the spectacle of royal irresponsibility and bad fatherhood, these factors render the play's apparent royalism uncertain.

[23] Cf. Maguire, 'Nahum Tate's *King Lear*: "The king's blest restoration"', 39.

The Politics of Pain in Venice Preserv'd

This is a Tory play which also shows that anxieties and contradictions within Toryism persisted in the Tory reaction period, in spite of the reconsolidation of Stuart ideology which accompanied the king's use of French subsidies to rule without Parliament. The play problematizes rebellion, in keeping with Tory advocacy of non-resistance, and also problematizes republicanism in power, but it does both with only limited success. Otway's Toryism is clear in the various prologues and epilogues and the circumstances surrounding their composition and delivery. The February prologue questions the existence of the Popish Plot, while the epilogue makes an explicit application of the play's conspiracy to Whig factionalism. Following the première, probably in February 1682, the play was specially performed before royalty in April, when James returned from exile to London. Another performance in May celebrated the return of the Duchess of York.[24] Dryden and Otway wrote special loyal prologues and epilogues respectively for these occasions, which were published as broadsides. Otway's Tory intentions, then, seem not to be in doubt.

Yet the witty and cynical tone of the prologues and epilogues gives us pause. In the April epilogue Otway unabashedly prostitutes his art:

> No more let *Bout'feu's* hope to lead *Petitions*,
> *Scriv'ners* to be Treas'rures; *Pedlars*, Politicians;
> Nor ev'ry *fool*, whose Wife has *tript* at Court,
> Pluck up a spirit, and turn *Rebell* for't.

The association of Whigs and cuckolds was a common feature of Tory comedy. Some violence is done to our sensibilities by the implied attribution of this character to Jaffeir and Pierre, the former prompted to rebellion against the government by his wife's sufferings, and to rebellion against his friends by her attempted seduction; and the latter prompted to revolt by the theft of his mistress. Otway's feelings about his own text are not

---

[24] As Danchin points out, the *Newdigate Newsletters* give the performance to which the May prologue and epilogue refer as *The Royalist*. However, Luttrell's copy of the broadside bears the note, 'At ye Dukes theater at Venice preserv'd &C Acted 31 May 1682' (Danchin, *Prologues and Epilogues*, vol. ii, pt. 2, p. 413). Quotations from the later prologues and epilogues are from Danchin's text.

so fastidious. He evidently does not mind about the ironic comment he has supplied upon his own characters.

As a poverty-stricken playwright, Otway is ready to place his play at the disposal of the dominant political faction, distressingly willing to admit positively facetious applications in the various prologues and epilogues. The February prologue opens with the author's mockery of his own motives:

> In these distracted times, when each man dreads
> The bloody stratagems of busy heads;
> When we have feared three years we know not what . . .
> What makes our poet meddle with a plot?
> Was't that he fancied, for the very sake
> And name of plot, his trifling play might take?
>
> (p. 5)

No doubt the intention in subtitling the play 'A Plot Discover'd' was, as these lines might cynically imply, to give rise to all sorts of interesting speculation in the light of the accusations and counter-accusations of plotting which had been flying between the factions for at least the previous eighteen months. The mocking and jaundiced tone alerts us to the dangers of assuming that it is a sincere and straightforward statement of dramatic intent.

Moreover, prologues and epilogues may be unreliable guides to plays, especially in this period when they were published separately as interventions in the pamphlet war. Partisan prologues or epilogues may be affixed to plays which have little or no Tory content: in August 1682 Behn and Lady Slingsby were imprisoned for writing and speaking respectively an epilogue to *Romulus and Hersilia* which was considered critical of Monmouth. The play itself seems innocent of any such political intention. It is also a period in which it is impossible to take at face value what an author says about his own and other authors' texts, as is clear from the frankly disingenuous nature of some of Dryden's arguments in *The Vindication of The Duke of Guise* and the attacks to which it was a reply.

In the play itself there is a similar undercurrent of doubt beneath the surface Toryism. To illustrate I want to look first at the significance in the text of the sexual impropriety so flippantly referred to in the April prologue, and then at the question of vitiated fatherhood. Satire of republicanism in power is a familiar Tory theme; so is the demonizing of rebellion. Otway links both republicanism and rebellion with sexual monstrosity. The sexual perversion of Senator Antonio and the allusions to Shaftesbury in the 'Nicky-nacky' scenes have received substantial critical attention already. I shall content myself with stating that I do think that Antonio's behaviour reflects adversely upon the republican senate, of which he is a member.[25] I refer not only to his sexual masochism, which is portrayed in a ridiculous way, but also to the fact that he has stolen Pierre's mistress. At the same time, the attempted rape of Jaffeir's wife, Belvidera, by the rebel leader, Renault, is used to demonize rebellion.[26]

Belvidera's repeated assertion of her near-rape's political importance is not an insistence on the primacy of an apolitical private sphere at the expense of a public political sphere. She mobilizes her chastity and her sense of violation in the interests of loyalty to the established order and 'non-resistance' (3. 2. 179 ff.; 4. 1. 63–6). The connection is as obvious to her as the contrary connection between rebellion and rape. At the same time, the fact that Jaffeir's impulse to conformity is motivated by response to this event, and the absence from his thought of political reasoning about the public good and the wrongness of rebellion, serve to deprive the republican government of legitimacy.

However, Jaffeir is never whole-hearted about betraying his friends 'In fond compassion to a woman's tears' (4. 1. 16), and ultimately he deserts Belvidera to die with Pierre on the scaffold. The fact that the importance of the near-rape is contested contributes to our sense of ambivalence about the play's success as Tory drama. Rape is associated with rebellion, but Belvidera's ultimate lack of success in asserting the validity of her experience partially forestalls the horror and revulsion with which we are encouraged to distance ourselves from rebellion in other plays. Moreover, the near-rape taints the opposition with the lust and perversion which is associated with the government and

[25] A rather obvious point, which Harth repudiates, 'Political Interpretations of *Venice Preserv'd*', 356.

[26] See my ' "He that should guard my virtue has betrayed it": The Dramatization of Rape in the Exclusion Crisis'.

thus engenders a sense of universal nastiness which almost prevents our pity.

Let us now look at the issue of fatherhood. In his April prologue to *Venice Preserv'd*, Dryden uses indulgent fatherhood as an image for the royal mercy that can facilitate the re-establishment of order:

> Yet, late Repentance may, perhaps, be true;
> Kings can forgive if Rebels can but sue:
> A Tyrant's Pow'r in rigour is exprest:
> The Father yearns in the true Prince's Breast.

This is Tory patriarchalism at its most persuasive. *Venice Preserv'd* is about bad fatherhood, but because the bad father is a republican senator, Otway avoids the painful and problematic aspects which the theme had in *The Orphan*.

It is clear from the first lines that the issue of bad fatherhood is a central one. The play opens with a row between Jaffeir and Belvidera's father, Priuli. Jaffeir's bitterness over Priuli's neglect and his own and Belvidera's resulting poverty and social exclusion provides the fertile ground for Pierre's words of rebellion to grow in. Priuli is also guilty of ingratitude. Jaffeir has saved Belvidera's life, which Priuli himself endangered:

> Your unskilful pilot
> Dashed us upon a rock; when to your boat
> You made for safety, entered first yourself;
> The affrighted Belvidera following next,
> As she stood trembling on the vessel side,
> Was by a wave washed off into the deep—
> When instantly I plunged into the sea,
> And buffeting the billows to her rescue,
> Redeemed her life with half the loss of mine.

> (I. I. 33–4)

It would hardly be over-subtle to discern some allusion here to political misleadership. In Behn's dedication to *The Round-heads* it is asserted that Charles II 'will like a skilful Pilate, by the wreck of one Rich Vessell [Charles I], learn how to shun the danger of this present Threatning and save the rest from sinking' (sig. A3ʳ). We may compare the political use of similar imagery in *Absalom and Achitophel*, where Shaftesbury is described as

A daring Pilot in extremity;
Pleas'd with the Danger, when the Waves went high
He sought the Storms; but for a Calm unfit,
Would Steer too nigh the Sands, to boast his Wit.

(159–62)

The republican senator Priuli is cowardly and incompetent, rather than fanatical, like Shaftesbury, but both are equally unfit to steer the ship of state. The theme of bad fatherhood, then, seems to contribute to problematizing republicanism in power. The play offers us a spectacle of a father failing to protect his loyal daughter, and of the republican government of which he is a member failing to honour its word, adopting the 'rigorous' course which Dryden associates with tyranny in the April prologue. This is further suggested by the fact that the play ends not, like royalist plays set in monarchies, with moralizing against rebellion and legitimization of the established authority, but with Priuli's regrets about his own bad fatherhood:

Sparing no tears when you this tale relate,
But bid all cruel fathers dread my fate.

(5. 4. 36–7)

The substitution of the father-senator's regret for the rhetoric of governmental self-justification with which plays such as *The Royalist* and *The Loyal Brother* conclude deprives the government of legitimacy. It is quite possible that Dryden intended his prologue to counterpose Charles's indulgence as a father and mercy as a king to the spectacle of bad fatherhood associated with tyranny in the play.

The theme of vitiated fatherhood is also used to demonize rebellion, and to offer a message of quietism. For Belvidera filial obligation to her cruel parent is an aspect of political conformity. It is a component of her attack on Jaffeir's rhetoric of rebellion in 3. 2, an explicit counter to his intoxicated references to glorious ruin and impartial slaughter:

Murder my father! Though his cruel nature
Has persecuted me to my undoing,
Driven me to basest wants, can I behold him
With smiles of vengeance, butchered in his age?

The sacred fountain of my life destroyed?
And canst thou shed the blood that gave me being?

(3. 2. 154–9)

This carries considerable rhetorical force.

However, as I have already noted, bad fatherhood is an awkward theme from a Tory point of view because of the anxieties arising from the disparity between the ideology of Filmerian patriarchalism and the reality of royal misbehaviour. The play depicts abrogated fatherhood leading to personal bitterness and political rebellion by a character with whom we sympathize. This is not as politically problematic in a republican context as in *The Orphan*. There can be no comparison between the republican senator Priuli, a cruel father, and Charles, a notoriously indulgent one. Yet the moral of *Venice Preserv'd*, that bad fatherhood should be avoided, is the wrong one from the Tory point of view. Toryism puts the onus of political responsibility upon the son (or subject), not the father.

Furthermore, as I have repeatedly argued, loyalty to a bad father—or to an unsatisfactory ruler or regime—can be productive of bitterness, pessimism, or self-destructiveness in the child or subject, rather than inspiring tragic heroism. In *Venice Preserv'd*, as in *The Orphan*, the characters try to moralize themselves into 'correct' attitudes, and struggle with desires and perceived ideals and obligations which are contradictory. In *Venice Preserv'd*, as in *The Orphan*, self-denial breeds tragic misunderstanding. Jaffeir's abandonment of his beloved wife to the conspirators, supposedly a gesture of noble trust and friendship, recalls Castalio's self-sacrificing friendship in allowing his brother to woo his wife-to-be. This raises disastrous false hopes in Polydore and leads Monimia to doubt his love, just as Belvidera doubts Jaffeir.

Just as Monimia and Polydore masochistically enjoy devising tortures for each other after their act of incest, Jaffeir likens himself to a sacrificial lamb, who 'hardly bleats, such pleasure's in the pain' (4. 1. 94). To win Pierre's forgiveness he will 'Lie at thy feet and kiss 'em though they spurn me' (4. 2. 235). When Pierre is on the scaffold, Jaffeir asserts, 'stripes are fitter for me than embraces' (5. 3. 34). Sado-masochism in Jaffeir, as in Monimia and Polydore, is associated with self-loathing. This shades into a deep personal bitterness and utter negativity. Jaffeir's speech, 'Final destruction seize on all the world!' (5. 2. 93), recalls Castalio's demented, suicidal curse: 'Confusion and disorder seize the world' (5. 516). The character's self-disgust has its parallel in the author's lack of esteem for his suffering characters. This is apparent in the parallel between Jaffeir's masochism and the sexual sado-masochism of the obnoxious Antonio.[27] This may be compared with the violence Otway does to his text in the April prologue. All this reinforces the pervasive atmosphere of pessimism which *Venice Preserv'd* shares with *The Orphan*, and which has its comic parallel in the 'hard-boiled' cynicism of *The Souldier's Fortune*. The outlook is too close to nihilism to be compatible with fervent Toryism.

As in *The Orphan*, there is a 'tough' character who stands in opposition to the suffering characters. This is Pierre, who partakes of some of the positive connotations of the soldier character.[28] On the scaffold his tears are the more moving because 'I never saw thee melted thus before' (5. 3. 70). He wrings Jaffeir's sensitive heart with the words:

> Is't fit a soldier, who has lived with honor,
> Fought nations' quarrels, and been crowned with conquest,
> Be exposed a common carcass on a wheel?
>
> (5. 3. 75–7)

In fact, what Pierre ultimately offers his friend is not hope, but defiance in the face of despair. Of their double suicide, Pierre asserts, 'This was done nobly' (5. 4. 99), and Jaffeir's responds, 'Bravely' (line 100). The Officer comments: 'Heav'n grant I die so well' (line 111). However, the suicide does not offer hope of any kind of transcendence. The 'heroic' alternative to masochism is simply a more defiant self-destruction. 'We have deceived the Senate', says Pierre (line 99), and he dies laughing.

In the republican setting, the contradictions posed for royalism by corruption and injustice are neatly expunged. The counterposition of bad government and bad rebellion leads to a lack of heroic options. However, the sense of bleakness, of a lack of viable alternatives, remains. Rebellion is no solution: it

---

[27] See also Hughes, 'A New Look at *Venice Preserv'd*', 437.
[28] See also Teeter, 'Political Themes in Restoration Tragedy', 182 ff.

never is, even in the royal cause, which the conspiracy in *Venice Preserv'd* obviously is not. There is no monarchist alternative in the Venetian state. This also makes it harder to demonize republicanism by specific reference to the form of government than it is in plays set in the English interregnum: there is no glorious counter-revolutionary future. It is also a paradox that the republican setting makes it impossible to engage convincingly in the moralizing against rebellion on which other Tory plays rely for their effect. Otway has eliminated one set of contradictions, only to find himself confronted with another.

Amongst critics, the troubled and fractured nature of the play's Toryism has been obscured by a strange and regrettable gulf between a rather limited kind of political reading in terms of spotting topical allusions and parallels, and more thematically oriented apolitical readings. For example, Harry M. Solomon has little patience with the darkness of tone and moral difficulty noticed by 'apolitical' criticism: 'This depoliticizing of *Venice Preserv'd* is an interpretative technique for turning perceived dramatic inconsistencies and inadequacies into rich ambiguities.'[29] Solomon strives for 'an interpretation that incorporates the author's known political opinions and the immediate audience's response' (p. 294). He follows Zera S. Fink in suggesting that the Venetian senate in the play is the Whig ideal discredited.[30] It had previously been suggested that the senate represented the English court,[31] or, alternatively, the English, Whig-dominated Parliament.[32] Solomon also expresses in sharper form an idea put forward by Fink and Ham that the conspiracy against the senate represents a Whiggish plot. David Bywaters countered with the suggestion that the conspiracy represents the Tory idea of the Popish Plot as hollow and silly,

---

[29] Solomon, 'The Rhetoric of Redressing Grievances', 294. Those castigated include Rothstein, *Restoration Tragedy*, Warner, *Thomas Otway*, Waith, *Ideas of Greatness: Heroic Drama in England*; Parker, 'The Image of Rebellion in Thomas Otway's *Venice Preserv'd* and Edward Young's *Busiris*'. Solomon's extraordinary subtitle is 'Court Propaganda as the Hermeneutical Key to *Venice Preserv'd*'. The idea that we can decode, unlock, or solve the mystery of the text by reference to court propaganda seems dubious in terms of literary critical method, and simplistic in political terms.

[30] Fink, *The Classical Republicans*, 124–48.

[31] Summers, in *Complete Works of Thomas Otway*, vol. i, p. lxxxviii.

[32] Moore, 'Contemporary Satire in Otway's *Venice Preserv'd*', and Ham, *Otway and Lee*.

while the senate represents the Whig leadership of the City of London.[33] This is supported by Judith Milhous and Robert D. Hume.[34] Jessica Munns accepts the identification of the senate with the City Whigs, but insists that the conspiracy is real, dangerous, and Whiggish.[35]

Political criticism has much to learn from the many apolitical readings of the play. A good example of such a reading is Schille's 1988 piece 'Reappraising "Pathetic" Tragedies: *Venice Preserv'd* and *The Massacre of Paris*'. Schille reads the play as a kind of 'pathetic tragedy' in which 'emotionalism does not devolve on pitiably distressed individuals, but on that sense of a disordered, disorienting, and insidious existence which the plays urge us to share' (p. 34). Such insights have much to offer, but we need to ask ourselves why a political play might engender a sense of disorder, and what the significance of the characters'— or the audience's—disorientation might be. An exception to the tendency to see political allusion in narrow terms is Staves, who, in *Players' Scepters*, sees Jaffeir in the framework of her broader argument, according to which our sympathy for those who suffer and rebel in a corrupt society points to the need for the new political order after 1688. A similar view is put forward by Laura Brown.[36] This interpretation has been largely ignored by subsequent critics.[37]

---

[33] Bywaters, 'Venice, its Senate, and its Plot in Otway's *Venice Preserv'd*'.

[34] Milhous and Hume, *Producible Interpretations*, 173–6.

[35] Munns, ' "Plain as the light in the Cowcumber": A Note on the Conspiracy in Thomas Otway's *Venice Preserv'd*'.

[36] Brown, *English Dramatic Form*, 94.

[37] Harth, 'Political Interpretations of Venice Preserv'd', claims to offer a different kind of political reading from those who see the play as a precise allegory of English political events. However, his method is to return to Otway's source in Saint-Réal's *A Conspiracy of the Spaniards Against the State of Venice*, in order to suggest that 'Otway did not enjoy the freedom of the allegorist' (347), and that the play offers a historical parallel rather than an allegory. This 'parallel' is open to all the criticisms which Harth levels at others. His argument that the conspiracy must represent a parallel with the Popish Plot is no more plausible than Solomon's contrary argument that it represents a Whig plot. Moreover, parallelism, like looking for allegories, involves distortions in the interests of consistency: the parallel consists of the existence of a plot against the state. So, according to Harth, the government cannot be Whiggish, and the corruption which numerous 'political' and 'apolitical' critics have felt to inhere in the Venetian government must be explained away. However, Harth plausibly questions the double identification of Shaftesbury as Antonio and Renault which has become almost axiomatic. There is no evidence that Renault is Shaftesbury apart from a reference in the Feb. prologue which is clearly flippant and facetious.

The fact that the play remains comparatively popular when other tragedies of the period are forgotten is probably partly due to its potential for contradictory interpretations. Politically, these contradictions are suggestive. Although he has tried to problematize both republicanism and resistance, Otway has not produced a totally satisfying Tory play. The inability of the dramatists to produce satisfying Tory drama is not so much their problem as a problem of Toryism. Throughout the Exclusion Crisis period, loyalty is seldom characterized by glad submission, and is more likely to be characterized by pain than pleasure. Otway strives to avoid some of the worst dilemmas and contradictions by placing *Venice Preserv'd* in a republican context, but he is less successful in finding positive Tory tropes. In the end, Toryism has as little to offer the dramatist as Charles had to offer the old cavaliers in 1660, or as James was to have to offer to his Tory supporters after he came to the throne.

CHAPTER 8

Whig Plays: Vitality in Opposition

THIS chapter addresses two major critical misapprehensions. The first is the belief that there are no opposition plays in the early stages of the Exclusion Crisis because everyone uses anti-popery equally and indiscriminately. As Richard E. Brown remarks: 'only as the Whigs began to wonder aloud who would have followed Charles to the throne if the Popish Plot against his life had succeeded, did objections to the Catholic Duke of York concentrate anti-Catholic feelings on the Whiggish side'.[1] Susan Staves expresses a more general belief that anti-Catholicism is not necessarily Whiggish. She says of *Caesar Borgia*, *The Massacre of Paris*, and *The Female Prelate*: 'it would be more to the point simply to call these anti-Catholic plays. They contain none of the abstract political theorizing that characterizes a genuine Whig play like Lee's *Lucius Junius Brutus* or Rowe's *Tamerlane*'.[2] The second critical assumption I wish to challenge is the idea that the differences between Whig and Tory plays later in the crisis are minimal, and that therefore, by implication, Whiggism has little separate cultural identity and vigour.[3] This latter misconception may sometimes be associated with the mistaken belief that the Whigs were an extremist minority in the Exclusion Crisis.

I have already begun to demonstrate the vigour of Whig ideology in my discussion of the oppositional character of anti-Catholic plays in the section on religion in Chapter 4, and in my discussion of *The Lancashire Witches* in Chapter 6. I want now to examine plays whose Whiggishness has been doubted or questioned, or not perceived by modern critics. I have chosen a selection of plays which are oppositional in different ways, in

---

[1] Brown, 'Nathaniel Lee's Political Dramas', 45. Cf. Hume, *Development*, 342.
[2] Staves, *Players' Scepters*, 79.
[3] See e.g. Brown, 'Nathaniel Lee's Political Dramas' and 'The Dryden–Lee Collaboration'.

order to show the range as well as the vitality of Whiggish drama. Plays which work mainly through anti-popery are Lee's *Caesar Borgia; Son of Pope Alexander the Sixth* (1678–9) and *The Massacre of Paris*.[4] Plays which dramatize republican virtue are Bancroft's *The Tragedy of Sertorius* (1679) and Lee's *Lucius Junius Brutus* (1680). Then there are more coded discussions of bad kingship and loyal opposition: Lee's *Theodosius; or, The Force of Love* (1680) and Settle's *The Heir of Morocco, With the Death of Gayland* (1682). Finally, there are plays which draw on British history: Banks's *The Unhappy Favourite; or, The Earl of Essex* (1681) and *Verture Betray'd; or, Anna Bullen* (1682).

Caesar Borgia *and* The Massacre of Paris

That *Caesar Borgia* was perceived as oppositional in its time is suggested by Lee's difficulties in getting a licence for it.[5] In this play Lee associates popery, machiavellian ambition, and the abuse of power in a way which was unlikely to have been taken as politically innocent. The central figure was probably the most notorious perpetrator of papist atrocities in the seventeenth-century English Protestant mind, with the possible exception of the Duke of Guise. The fact that Machiavelli praised Borgia in *The Prince* would have damned him further, and Lee has Machiavelli himself in the play encouraging Borgia to commit further atrocities. The subtitle of the play, 'Son of Pope Alexander the Sixth', foregrounds that Pope's sexual impropriety. Lee further associates the Roman Church with lust and sexual perversion, and also with arbitrary cruelty and the violation of the family. For example, the corrupt and ambitious Cardinal, Ascanio Sforza, is also shown to be bisexual, as I noted in Chapter 5. He plans revenge on his rival Borgia with an arbitrary savagery which violates the family: 'His little Bastard, |

---

[4] There is no disagreement about assigning *Caesar Borgia* to the 1678–9 season. The date of composition of *The Massacre of Paris* is doubtful because the play was banned, and only acted and published after 1688 (a fact which critics who see no Whiggishness in the play find of no significance). I discuss the problem in the Appendix and tentatively follow the editors of Lee's *Works* and Anthony Hammond in assigning the play to 1679.

[5] Mentioned in the dedication to *Rome's Follies*, sig. [A3]ʳ.

Because he doats on him, shall strait be mangled' (1. 1. 504–5). This is the sort of thing popish ambition leads to, and it sets the tone for the unnatural acts which are to follow, from Orsino's tyranny over his daughter, Bellamira, in Act 2 to Borgia's eventual murder of both brother and wife.

There are pointed similarities in Act 5 between the way in which Borgia murders his brother and the circumstances of the death of Sir Edmund Berry Godfrey as contemporaries understood them. In 5. 1 Borgia has his brother tortured to death in a chair. In his epilogue Lee refers to the murder of Sir Edmund Berry Godfrey in terms of 'the horrid Chair the Mid-night show' (145). Act 5, scene 2 sees the disposal of Gandia's body in a river, and the murderers' plan to deal with the natural revulsion of their comrade: 'Strangle him in some Corner, lest he prate' (5. 2. 21). Ascanio refers to this in terms which have little relevance to the play's love and revenge plot, but seem to allude to the time of 'Universal Consternation' (dedication, 71) in which the play was first performed:

> If a man cannot speak his mind of
> State Affairs,—but he must streight be
> Dogg'd by Hell-hounds, Blood-suckers, Decoyers,
> Rascals, that watch to throttle him in some
> By-corner, then quoit him like a Cat into
> The River, 'tis very fine.
>
> (5. 3. 159–64)

Political topicality is also apparent in 5. 3 as Borgia defies death and claims that he will:

> Brittain attempt, though her most watchful Angel
> Saves the Lov'd Monarch of that happy Isle,
> And turns upon ourselves the plotted Wound,
> That sinks me to the Earth.
>
> (5. 3. 345–8)

Lee, like Whig propagandists, is making emotive use of fears about popery in Britain. These fears are connected in the play to questions of government: earlier in the same scene Lee has Borgia defy fortune in terms which seem to allude to Danby's notorious attempts to buy support in the Cavalier Parliament: 'The Gentry are all mine | For ever, gain'd by Presents and

Preferments' (5. 3. 24–5). We are reminded of Marvell's attack on corrupt office-holders and court faction 'yes-men' in what he calls 'this House or Barn of Commons' which has become 'a meer property to the Conspiratours' (*An Account*, 74–81, 149, 150).

What Borgia stands accused of is, precisely, 'abitrary government' or tyranny (e.g. 1. 1. 206; 5. 1. 121). Tyranny and popery are quite explicitly associated. After Borgia's death, Machiavel is left to draw the moral:

> No Power is safe, nor no Religion good,
> Whose Principles of growth are laid in Blood.
>
> (5. 3. 371–2)

Lee's difficulties in getting a licence for this play seem scarcely surprising. Lee's editors suggest that 'Charles himself could not have looked with favor on a play which attacked the Catholics so violently', and they plausibly hypothesize that this violent attack was the reason for the harsh criticism which Lee complains of in his dedication.[6] As I noted in the section on religion in Chapter 4, Charles and his court were sceptical about the Popish Plot from the earliest stages, and there was a widespread belief that the king was doing nothing about the plot. It seems extremely unlikely that Lee's play could have been taken as politically neutral.

Both Dryden's prologue and Lee's epilogue to the play assume that it has political meaning. Indeed, Dryden tries to reverse Lee's own interpretation of his play's political significance. Dryden attacks newsmongering and sneers at credulity:

> You love to hear of some prodigious Tale,
> The Bell that toll'd alone, or Irish Whale.
>
> (p. 74, lines 18–19)

The citizens of London are looking for 'Entertainment' (line 30) in the Plot scare, but Dryden adds, 'we dare engage | To show you better Rogues upon the Stage' (lines 32–3). The implication is clearly that the real villains in the play have no parallel in the times, except in the overheated imaginations of sensation-seekers.

---

[6] Introduction to *Caesar Borgia*, in *Works*, ii. 67.

Lee's epilogue, however, has a different political slant. Lee associates superstition and credulity with Roman Catholicism and compares a catalogue of pernicious popish practices to the ill-informed criticism which has contrived 'To damn this Play about the Court and Town' (p. 145, line 8). He suggests that such criticism is misdirected, and might have been justified if he had been trying to perform 'But half those Miracles they do at Rome' (line 6). He concludes with a reference to the king's former mistress, Barbara Villiers, Countess of Castlemaine and Duchess of Cleveland:

> High English Whores, that have all Vices past,
> Shall cease to turn true Catholicks at last,
> When Poets write, tho by exactest Rules,
> And are not judg'd by Knaves, and damn'd by Fools.
>
> (37–40)

The word 'English' might well evoke the thought of a 'whore' still in favour at court who was not only Catholic, but French. Attacks on the king's French, Catholic mistresses were fuel to the Whigs' fire. The epilogue as a whole associates the play's malicious critics with court circles where Catholicism is condoned. Thus although we do not find at this point the polarization of the later Exclusion Crisis, we do find political partisanship, and we cannot say that a sustained attack on Catholicism was politically innocent. Some playwrights, such as Dryden and Crowne, had already found a royalist trope in the association of ambition with rebellion. Lee, like Marvell before him, associates 'popery' and 'arbitrary government', and shows the threat of popular discontent emanating from popery and bad government rather than from rebel agitation.

The Massacre of Paris, the first play to be banned during the crisis, is even more clearly political than *Caesar Borgia*. Canfield dismisses Staves's view of the play as merely anti-Catholic for exactly the wrong reasons: 'I would argue that it *is* a substantively political play exhibiting *royalism* . . . Lee portrays a weak king . . . but the play is definitely not therefore antimonarchal. Despite Charles IX's weakness and his actual complicity in the plots against Chastillon, the Admiral of France and champion of the Huguenots, Chastillon, like Crowne's Vendosme and Glocester, remains absolutely loyal' (p. 247).

However, the choice in 1679 was not between royalism and anti-monarchism. The opposition professed themselves 'Loyal Protestants'. The professed loyalty of Lee's Admiral might be said to increase his resemblance to opposition politicians, especially since it sometimes wears thin: the Admiral's loyalty is not of the supine kind shown by the masochistic royalist heroes like Crowne's Vendosme, considered above, but includes taking up arms to safeguard Protestantism and force a Protestant foreign policy on the king.

Canfield points out that the play concludes with the king's guilty horror at the massacre of the Protestants, his sense of impending doom, and the criticism of posterity: 'Thus the violated code is still the standard, and its violation will be divinely punished. Not even kings are exempt from *that* justice' (p. 248). However, the Protestant message that God will punish kings who lend themselves to popish brutality was scarcely royalist in 1679. As Candy B. K. Schille comments, 'the King's last speech is more panicky than restorative; and a vision of moral order restored which is delivered only in the final moments of such a play, by one who has been a participant in the devastation, can hardly relieve the weight of the poetry and action of five acts'.[7]

Richard E. Brown sees the play as less Tory than *The Duke of Guise* only on a few points, 'clearly anti-Catholic, but not so clearly anti-monarchist'.[8] However, the notion of anti-monarchism is unhelpful, and, as already noted, bears no relation to Whig protestations of 'Loyal Protestantism'. Whigs professed to be the best loyalists, not afraid to advise the king for his own good because they cared about his interests. The oppositional force of *The Massacre of Paris* is increased by the spectacle of a weak king called Charles regretting that he did not stand out against popish cruelty. Brown describes the Admiral as monarchist because he is 'heroically devoted to the Protestant monarch whom he chiefly recognizes, the Queen of Navarre'; but it was subversive to offer to any rival claimant the allegiance due to the sovereign, whether the rival be Navarre in sixteenth-century France, or Monmouth or William in the England of

[7] Schille, 'Reappraising "Pathetic" Tragedies: *Venice Preserv'd* and *The Massacre of Paris*', 38.
[8] Brown, 'The Dryden–Lee Collaboration', 22.

1679. For all the chivalry and courtesy of his speech to the queen of Navarre in 2. 1, the Admiral actually expresses loyalty to the Protestant 'cause' and to 'Liberty of Conscience and Religion' (106–7). Plays with a royalist slant give a rebel colouration to exactly this sort of phraseology.

Let us look briefly at the values which are heroic in the play, then at the rottenness at the centres of power to which they are counterposed. The Admiral and his wife, Antramont, are an exemplary Protestant couple, possessed of Roman virtue, whose devotion and decorum contrast with the histrionic extremism and verbal excesses of Guise and Marguerite. The Admiral possesses courage and military heroism, instigating a 'correct' Protestant foreign policy in the form of war with Spain. He also fights corruption, spots dissimulation in Guise, but loyally gives the king the benefit of the doubt, telling the lying Cardinal, 'I must not doubt your Oaths, | But with implicite Faith believe the King' (2. 1. 158–9).

The Admiral is, precisely, a 'Loyal Protestant' hero whose virtues are continually contrasted with Guise's Catholic vices. The Admiral is a good Calvinist: 'There is a Providence that over-rules: | Therefore submit' (5. 2. 21–2). In 4. 1 Guise utters the words 'My Lord, I yield' (line 73) to acquiesce for reasons of ambition in the king's sordid plans for Guise's mistress, Marguerite. The Admiral echoes these words emotively in the next scene:

> But, if the Will of Heav'n has set it down,
> That all this trust is deep dissimulation,
> That there's no Faith nor Credit to be given
> To the inviolable Royal Word;
> . . . If this be so, I yield, I yield to die.
>
> (4. 2. 45–50)

Protestant readiness for death shames Catholic hypocrisy. Whereas the Cardinal claims to be sent from Heaven, the Admiral appeals to his and the king's private relationship with God: 'He then, to whom our hearts are free and open, | Be judge betwixt his Majesty and me' (2. 1. 147–8).

There is a further contrast in the play's treatment of revenge. Guise is determined to seek revenge on the Admiral for the instigation of his father's murder, even though the Admiral's

agreement that the murderer of his father is a villain suggests
that the accusation is untrue. The massacre of the Protestants
is portrayed as an act of revenge which dissolves the moral
order:

> The King has giv'n his Warrant for my last;
> His Vows, his Oaths, and Altar-Obligations
> Are lost: the Wax of all those Sacred Bonds
> Runs at the Queens Revenge, the Fire that melts 'em.
>
> (5. 4. 3–6)

The Admiral is also the custodian of law and the liberty of the
subject:

> If that a great Man's breath can puff away
> On every Pet the Lives of Free-born People;
> What need that awful General Convocation,
> Th' Assembly of the States? nay, let me urge,
> If thus you threat the Venerable Beza,
> What may the rest expect? (4. 2. 172–7)

Guise's reply is, 'What if I could, I They should be certain of;
whole Piles of Fire' (177–8). Lee twists Guise's pursuit of his
father's murderer into a scenario in which fire, the stereotypical
papist threat, is counterposed to Parliament and the whole legal
system. Thus the play shows a hero who is prepared to die for
the rule of law, morality, and the true religion. His willingness
to act against the government if necessary to this end is presented heroically. In a discussion with his followers in 2. 1, he
justifies having been in arms against his sovereign in terms of the
atrocities and disorders of popery (49–53). The Queen Mother's
proclamation of the Admiral as a traitor, which we might feel
was natural in the circumstances, is described as 'that start of
open vengeance' (line 46), and the play bears out the Admiral's
assessment of her as 'a Serpent equal to the first' (2. 1. 11). The
play thus sanctions the Admiral's subordination of reasons of
state to Protestant truth.

In contrast, the court is a milieu in which authority is corrupt
and unnatural relationships flourish. The king's subjection to his
mother is a paradigm of perverted authority relations. The love
plot between Guise and Marguerite focuses important themes:
the verbal falsity and duplicity of the court milieu are introduced
in the opening scene, as Marguerite says of Guise, 'With a Court

Metaphor, he Vows he loaths me' (1. 1. 14). Marguerite stops Guise swearing his love, 'For Perjury so necessary seems | To great Men's Oaths, thou must of course be damn'd' (1. 1. 19–20). Later we see the Cardinal, the queen, and the king himself perjuring themselves to swear that the Admiral and his friends will be safe at court. Guise is forced by the king literally to break his contract with Marguerite by tearing it up, a gesture of almost purely political significance: Richard Ashcraft has shown how Whig ideology was constructed around the idea that 'natural law requires the keeping of agreements and contracts'.[9]

The love plot also reveals the decadent sensuality and hunger for power of the court; Guise experiences his love consciously as merely sensual, describing Marguerite's white breasts against black sheets. He affects a libertine misogyny, countering Marguerite's every insult with 'Woman' and 'Woman still' (3. 2. 96–7). Like Borgia, he subordinates love to ambition, sacrificing Marguerite to the queen's plots. His subsequent confused torment is an indictment of libertine values. Libertinism and ambition are associated with popery, as the Cardinal tells Guise, 'I had rather you should Whore a thousand Women, | Than love but one, tho' in a lawful way' (1. 1. 87–8). Guise becomes the product of his milieu; once he capitulates to ambition, he degenerates into a monster:

> The old gray Sire, the Dam, and little Babes,
> I'le take 'em all together in the Nest,
> And pash 'em till they Sprawl.
>
> (5. 3. 29–31)

To the Admiral's restraint and Protestant commitment are counterposed intemperance and ambition, not only in Guise, but also in the queen, 'an absolute Murderer and Dissembler; | Who that proceeds on such black principles, | That thinks there is no God above Ambition' (2. 1. 18–20). In justifying her plot against the Protestants to Charles, the queen pronounces the royalist rationale:

> If, Sir, you fear it,
> Why give it o're, and let the Admiral Reign,
> Call in the Hugonots, and drive your Friends,

---

[9] Ashcraft, *Revolutionary Politics and Locke's* Two Treatises of Government, 190 ff.

Banish your Blood, and the Establish'd Peers,
Forget the long Succession of your Fathers,
The Throne of Kings, forget the Laws, Religion,
Cut off the Noble Spirits from your Council;
And from the Dregs of this Heretical Faction
Compose a Bastard Cabinet-Election,
Let Knaves in Shops prescribe you how to Sway,
They read your Acts, and with their hardned Thumbs
Erase them out, or with their stinking Breath
Proclaim aloud they like not this or that;
Then in a drove come lowing to the Louvre,
And say, they'l have it mended, that they will,
Or you shall be no King.

(1. 2. 81–96)

This is a comprehensive piece of royalist argumentation with sundry topical allusions, notably to the exile of James, the proposals to alter the succession, and the taking of opposition supporters on to the Privy Council in 1679. It is therefore extremely significant that Lee has it voiced by an evil mouthpiece. Her claim to stand for law and religion is utterly specious: as we have already seen, these fall before her 'Revenge'. Moreover, the accusation that Protestantism means populism does not hold up: various nobles, including the prince of Navarre, support the 'Heretical Faction'. The Admiral is no inciter of the rabble. It is the royalist-backed, extremist-inspired popish massacre that rouses the people, so that at the end of the play we hear with horror that the Admiral has been dragged off and mutilated by the mob (5. 5. 4–8). This is especially horrific since the Protestants have offered no provocation. As the opposition claimed in the Exclusion Crisis, there is no Protestant plot.

At the end the piling-up of horror and pity in the interests of Protestant sympathy is almost reminiscent of a propaganda piece such as Dryden's *Amboyna*. By the end we have neither the energy nor the inclination to feel much sympathy for Charles. Indeed it is hard to see why Brown thinks Charles a 'sympathetic figure'.[10] The periodic qualms which Charles smothers, culminating in guilty self-disgust, are a mechanism for distancing and revulsion. He knows the course of action in which he has let his mother embroil him is 'Barbarous', 'unworthy of a King', and

---

[10] Brown, 'The Dryden–Lee Collaboration', 22.

'damnable' (1. 2. 23, 24, 80), yet he still proceeds in it. In a king this weakness is inexcusable: he is, or should be, responsible. The Admiral must believe that he is true to 'the Reform'd Religion' (4. 2. 41). The alternative is too horrible to contemplate. The point is hammered home repeatedly in 5. 2: 'Once more I say, my Fate is in the King' (36). The relevance to Lee's own king, whose dissimulation and religious ambivalence aroused widespread mistrust, is obvious.

The play's Charles is a vacillator: 'I know not what to say, whom to accuse, | Or where to turn my self' (3. 2. 253–4). Where Guise shows a destructive self-mastery, and where the Admiral shows exemplary stoicism, the king is incapable of self-control: 'O, I could rave! | Our hearts are Rebels to our Bosom Councils' (3. 2. 239–40). He lashes himself into a weak man's rage (3. 2. 278–86), but never uses his kingly power for good. Instead he alternates between plotting and manipulating and complaining, and tries to find reasons of policy to mitigate his mother's violence (5. 1. 73 ff.). He violates sovereignty as his mother violates motherhood and womanhood. Lest we should be in any doubt, the king's Genius appears to warn him before the massacre:

> But Charles beware, oh dally not with Heav'n,
> For after this no Pardon shall be giv'n.

> (5. 1. 28–9)

Lee, then, has written a play about the disastrous results which ensue when a sovereign surrounded by an ambitious, decadent, popish court lacks firmness of moral and religious purpose. The logic of Catholic absolutism is ruthlessly exposed and the sense that the catastrophe could have been averted if those in authority had behaved in a responsible way has clear topical application. The play asserts the importance of Protestantism in a manner just as militant and emotive as that in Whig propaganda.

The Tragedy of Sertorius *and* Lucius Junius Brutus

Like Lee's anti-Catholic plays, Bancroft's *The Tragedy of Sertorius* problematizes tyranny and makes a Whiggish distinction between good rebellion and bad. In *The Massacre of Paris* the Admiral had to take unilateral military action to safeguard Protestantism; in *The Tragedy of Sertorius* Sertorius must resist Sulla's tyranny. Bad rebellion, in contrast, is shown in Perpenna's revolt against Sertorius' good government. Sertorius is a conquering hero, exiled from ungrateful Rome at the instigation of Sulla. Sulla is a notorious tyrant. Like Lee's Guise, his tyranny takes the form of attacking Parliament: 'Slaughter, big with blood, | In Sanguine hue, and a Tyrannick pace, | Sweeps, like a Plague' through '*Rome's* Senate' (1. 1. p. 1). Bancroft deploys Whiggish tropes of parliamentarianism and tyranny virtuously resisted.

Douglas Canfield argues that the play is '*fundamentally* an attack on rebellion, for it focuses on the Italian Perpenna's revolt against Sertorius . . . Whether Sertorius is a king or not, the patriarchal hierarchy is reaffirmed'.[11] He points out that Pompey asserts at the end that Sertorius' fall is a divine judgement for rebellion against the fatherland. However, Pompey's speech in 5. 10 has no moral authority: Pompey is no hero and his pronouncement of Rome's 'Vengeance' (5. 10. p. 59) comes across as a statement of naked force. His injunction to the 'whole World' to 'Submit to *Rome*, as to her Emperor' rings hollow: Pompey is for the moment 'of *Sylla's* Faction' (dramatis personae), but Sulla 'both hates and fears' him (4. 5. p. 42). On this basis Sertorius' rebellious allies calculate on an alliance with Sulla, and Sertorius' friend Bebricius joins Pompey against them. History sanctions the view that Pompey's obedience to the tyrant is purely a matter of temporary expedience.

Moreover, the play can scarcely be primarily an attack on rebellion if Sertorius is a hero, which does not seem to be in dispute. In fact the play shows us tyrannical qualities both in power (Sulla) and in opposition (Perpenna). Disorder can emanate from rulers as well as subjects: Rome's Emperor is 'the source of Civil War, | *Sylla*' (2. 10. p. 19). Sertorius and Perpenna are examples of good and bad rebels. What distinguishes them is their values. Thus the play dramatizes the kinds of distinction which informed political debate before 1660. The pervasive influence of Milton on Bancroft's style might support

[11] Canfield, 'Royalism's Last Dramatic Stand', 239.

this assertion.[12] We may compare the distinction made between Cromwell and the radical sectaries in Marvell's *The First Anniversary of the Government Under His Highness the Lord Protector*. Cromwell is the champion of 'sober liberty' (line 289). The radicals crave an excess of liberty. Cromwell brings order, the radicals chaos.

Sertorius is a tragic hero who speaks of 'our just Cause'[13] and says, 'We fight for Liberty, and for our Gods' (1. 2. p. 4). Extraordinary as it may seem, he is a positive version of Tory drama's Whig rebel with overtones of a Civil War parliamentarian. His emphasis on liberty and godliness as the grounds of good government resembles Algernon Sidney's.[14] He sees himself as fighting for peace, and disruption as emanating from Sulla, just as Marvell had portrayed the threat to stability as emanating from the corrupt centres of power. He is a good parliamentarian, seeking 'parliamentary' sanction for his actions from the exiled senators as a matter of principle. He is activated by desire to restore the glories of 'Old *Rome*' (1. 2. p. 5), recalling Whigs who spoke of the ancient constitution, and seeks the sanction of historical precedent to justify his claim that he represents a continuity which the tyrant has violated:

> *Sertorius* says,
> When barbarous *Gaul* sack'd *Rome* and lay'd it wast,
> *Camillus* unto *Vei* made retreat,
> Gave out, that *Rome* it self was thither mov'd;
> And, for the confirmation, added this:
> 'Where e're the Senate was, there *Rome* was still.'

The idea that the state was in any strong sense in the Parliament was a very radical one after 1660.[15] Yet the speech is not meant to seem specious. It is Perpenna whose self-confessed hypocrisy devalues meaning. This is clear from his blatantly false description of Sertorius as a tyrant just like Sulla (3. 6. p. 41). Perpenna

---

[12] For instance Perpenna uses language similar to Milton's Satan (e.g. 2. 5. p. 13) and compares his former supremacy to 'Paradise that's lost' (2. 6. p. 15).

[13] The word 'cause' in Exclusion Crisis propaganda usually refers to interregnum parliamentarians, and, by association, Whigs. Cf. Dryden's reference to 'The Good old Cause reviv'd' in *Absalom and Achitophel* (line 82). The subtitle of Behn's *The Round-heads* is 'The Good Old Cause'.

[14] See the discussion of this aspect of the *Discourses Concerning Government* in Scott, *Algernon Sidney and the Restoration Crisis*, 214–20 and ch. 10 *passim*.

[15] 4. 5. pp. 39–40. Cf. Western, *Monarchy and Revolution*, ch. 2.

misuses libertarian rhetoric, inducing the conspirators to stab Sertorius with shouts of 'Liberty, Freedom, Liberty!' (5. 6. p. 54); but really the freedom he wants is freedom from any restraint upon the free play of his destructive passions. He also abuses the language of belief, claiming a revelation that 'Gods have decreed the fall | Of proud *Sertorius*, and have chose thee out | To free the *Romans* from their Slavish State' (4. 5. p. 42). Like Crowne's Constable, he revels in chaos and destruction. We might say that where Sertorius has a parliamentarian idea of liberty, he has an antinomian one.

Unlike the rebels of royalist plays, Sertorius is not motivated by personal ambition. He rejects the sort of flattery which is acceptable to Dryden's Oedipus. He accepts his role as agent of heavenly justice, but refuses to usurp the attributes of divinity:

> We're Men, *Perpenna*; Men, by Fate chose out
> To launch through all the Terrors of the World;
> Frail, mortal Men, subject to every Chance:
> And while we praise our selves, we rob the Gods.

> (2. 10. p. 19)

Perpenna, in contrast, is ambitious, blasphemous, and atheistic.

Sertorius treats his subordinates well and wins loyalty. He is deeply concerned for 'the safety of this Common-wealth' (3. 5. p. 30) and the people love him. Sertorius is governor of Lusitania by popular acclaim, and the foundation of his rule is merit. This accords with Sidney's notion that it 'is the fundamental right of every nation to be governed by such laws, in such manner, and by such persons, as they think most conducing to their own good'.[16] We see him resisting bribes, confirming the territories of tributary kings, but also safeguarding 'what the *Romans* won by force of Arms' (3. 5. p. 30). He defends the interests of the country which has rejected him, and does the job which Sulla neglects. In this he might be said to resemble the parliamentary patriots of 1679 who saw themselves as defending tradition in the face of misrule. In a Tory play such qualities would be denigrated.

---

[16] Sidney, *Discourses Concerning Government*, 462.

Like *The Massacre of Paris*, this play also depicts courtly values negatively. The courtly decadence of Perpenna's wife, Fulvia, and her admirers is contrasted unfavourably with the married love of Terentia and Sertorius, and courtly language is condemned as an excess. When Sertorius greets Terentia, she tells him to 'Leave . . . this Courtly Stile' (1. 6. p. 9) and bid her a plain welcome. Bebricius warns Fulvia, 'Yet Truth and Honesty, absent from Courts | Where gaudy Birds with borrow'd Feathers wing, | Dwells in my language' (3. 2. p. 24).

Loyalty in the play does not mean fidelity to existing alliances, but to certain principles and values: virtue, peace, the common good, honourable love and friendship, truth, sincerity, law, beneficent authority, honour even in enmity. It is in royalist plays that loyalty and non-resistance are upheld at all costs. For Bancroft, whether rebellion is a fault depends on circumstances. The play's Horatian epigraph, 'Invidus alterius rebus macrescit opimis' (one who is envious of another grows thin on rich things) might be taken to apply to the rebellious mentality in general, but the only person in the play to whom it can be related is Perpenna; the 'rebus opimis' from which he is unable to profit must be Sertorius's good government and moral example. The royalist paradigm is that rebellion breeds rebellion, but we cannot read this play as an indictment of one rebellion creating another: before Sertorius' popularity coerces him into alliance, Perpenna is thriving as 'General of the *Italian* bands: a Villain' (dramatis personae). Sertorius does not corrupt him. If anything he temporarily civilizes him. The play belongs within the framework of opposition sentiment, as it is informed by a political outlook involving support for constitutional forms, the liberty of the subject, and the need to resist tyrants for the sake of the common good and the defence of traditional liberties. The virtuous hero who defends these principles inspires others, even after death. Canfield's statement that 'Whether Sertorius is a king or not, the patriarchal hierarchy is reaffirmed' blurs all valuable political distinctions. It is like saying that praising Cromwell is no different from praising Charles I.

Lucius Junius Brutus is, in a certain sense, the most obviously oppositional play of the entire crisis: a play which dramatizes the expulsion of a corrupt dynasty and the formation of a republic, and which was banned after a few days' performance for 'Scandalous Expressions & Reflections upon ye Government.'[17] Like Bancroft in *Sertorius*, and Sidney in *Discourses Concerning Government*, Lee uses the Roman republic to legitimize parliamentary institutions and the rule of law against the strong trend of patriarchalist monarchism in Tory argument and drama. The play is, however, 'more than merely a party piece',[18] and as a result of its complexities some recent criticism has attempted to revise the traditional understanding of its Whiggishness. I have argued at length elsewhere that this revisionist approach does not succeed.[19] Here it is sufficient to note three points.

The first is that, like *Sertorius*, *Lucius Junius Brutus* offers a distinction between good resistance to tyranny and bad rebellion. Here, however, the bad rebels are self-styled 'royalists' (4. 53) who, like courtiers in 1680, 'scorn the late election' (3. 2. 34). Brutus himself is a hero of the type of the Admiral in *The Massacre* and Sertorius. He is pious and chosen by the gods, public-spirited, but firm; his Whiggish philosophy is presented in a positive way. The royalists, by contrast, are characterized by oratorical hollowness and barbarity, delighting in rape and slaughter; they are associated with priests who gleefully torture citizens.

Secondly, the commoners are foolish and rough, but differ significantly from the 'rabble' in other plays in not yearning for change and destruction for their own sake. Brutus does not so much engage in rabble-rousing as mobilize the people for a worthy goal: the expulsion of tyranny and the founding of Rome's greatness. This contrasts sharply with the strong class hostility and demonization of the mob seen in many Tory plays, and also used for Whiggish purposes in *The Massacre of Paris*.

Thirdly, the sufferings of the young lovers play a markedly different role in the play's drama from the apparently analogous sufferings of young love at the hands of ambition and faction in, for example, *The Ambitious Statesman* or *Caius Marius*.

[17] Public Record Office, LC 5/144, 28, cited by Loftis, in introduction to Lee, *Lucius Junius Brutus*, p. xii.

[18] Loftis, in introduction to *Lucius Junius Brutus*, p. xix.

[19] Owen, ' "Partial Tyrants" and "Freeborn People" in *Lucius Junius Brutus*'.

Theodosius *and* The Heir of Morocco

Both these plays offer more coded political interventions: the focus is on bad rule and the possibility that subjects may criticize their ruler and yet be loyal. Lee's *Theodosius* followed serious difficulties with the censor, which, as he clearly states in the epistle dedicatory and epilogue, forced him to express himself more guardedly. Lee says that he had tried to overcome the 'ungovern'd Fancy' of his youth (p. 238). He no longer dares to rail against the French or the Roman Catholic menace. His meaning is to be a matter of interpretation and there will be something for everybody. Yet he feels that he is prostituting himself. In the epilogue we hear that young writers are like some new 'Captain of the City Bands' who cries 'Pox o' the French-King' (p. 304). Apparently a conventional sneer at cits, this in fact conceals the less palatable meaning that the responsibility for defence of the realm against the French is being ignored by the government and upper classes. Older poets, like ageing mistresses, do not dare to be so bold. They must flatter all, in 'City, Town, and Court', and 'you may turn 'em ev'ry way for pleasure' (ibid.). The poet is poor and getting old. His lack of means has forced him to be cautious. Younger, bolder men are mocked, but also seen as 'Thrice happy' (ibid.).

J. M. Armistead convincingly argues that Lee offers in his depiction of Theodosius critical allusions to Charles II's effeminacy, possible Catholicism, and irresponsible withdrawal from politics at Windsor in the summer of 1680.[20] The reputed chastity of Lee's dedicatee, the Duchess of Richmond, finds reflection in that of Pulcheria and Athenais in the play, suggesting a critique of Charles and his court.[21] The abdication of Theodosius in favour of his sister, Pulcheria, and her husband, the martial hero, Marcian, may allude to the plan of some Whigs to replace an excluded James with William and Mary. Richard E. Brown, on the other hand, thinks that 'The play divides its criticisms between Whig and Tory positions without ever achieving a fully unified perspective.'[22] However, Brown

---

[20] Armistead, *Nathaniel Lee*, 128–9. Hutton notes: 'It was in Charles's nature not merely to continue the pursuit of pleasure during difficult times, but to accentuate it' (*Charles the Second*, 232).

[21] Armistead, *Nathaniel Lee*, 127.

[22] Brown, 'Nathaniel Lee's Political Dramas', 47.

plays down the significance of some of his own insights, particularly the perception that the ruler's being subjected to candid criticism has a peculiar force in a rapidly polarizing political environment.

Marcian makes pointed topical criticism of the weak ruler, corrupt court, and inequitable society: parasites disport themselves, while poor soldiers starve, and preferment is given to knaves while real heroes are slighted. Marcian's obstinate paganism and tendency to ranting excess might distance the audience; but he also has the traditional appeal of the soldier-hero and 'manly man'. Moreover, he is vindicated: Pulcheria banishes him for traitorous talk, but it is quite clear that she loves him and intends to forgive him, as when she forgets his banishment and confides her secrets to him in 4. 1, or hints in 5. 3 that she has meant all along only to teach him a lesson: 'I must no longer lose him; | Lest he should leave the Court indeed' (lines 2–3).

Most importantly, like the Admiral in *The Massacre*, Marcian is a loyal subject who is not afraid to criticize the ruler for the good of the nation. Thus he dissuades Lucius from raising the soldiers in Act 2 and in 4. 1. In 4. 2 he confronts Theodosius and even fights with him. Yet the scene ends not with an absolutist withering of the presumptuous subject, but with mutual pledges, of loyalty on Marcian's part and of renewed vigour on Theodosius'. Marcian's apologies represent not retraction of the criticisms made, but courtesy and compassion for the wounds inflicted. Theodosius accepts criticism, and is not above correction. Instead of the royalist theme that the king will rule wisely if only subjects will be quiet, we have the more radical alternative that the subject will restrain himself if the king will see sense. As in Settle's Whiggish dedication of *The Female Prelate* to Shaftesbury, loyalty is seen as courageous determination to advise the erring monarch for the good of the kingdom.

Brown objects that 'Marcian does not sound like a perfect Whig. Instead of Parliamentary government or a Shaftesburian oligarchy, he advocates that Theodosius become a strongman like Nero (4. 2. 81–109)—or Brutus' (p. 47). However, what Marcian says is that Theodosius' sloth is worse than Nero's cruelty and that at least Nero had spirit whereas Theodosius is 'A pretty Player, one that can act a Heroe, | And never be one' (4. 2. 98–9). There is clearly an allusion here to Charles II's lifelong preference for the theatre, reputedly at the expense of state affairs. We do not need to see Marcian as 'a perfect Whig' to discern some radical political resonance here. The play offers a critical depiction of corrupt and effete monarchy that is, in the light of the difficulties with *Caesar Borgia* and *The Massacre of Paris*, surprisingly unconciliating.

Satire of the 'Phanatick Knave' in the prologue might at first suggest that Lee has abandoned his hostility to Rome. The opening scene might, too, appear to glorify ritualistic religion. We are presented with the spectacle of 'A stately Temple, which represents the Christian Religion, as in its first Magnificence: Being but lately establisht at Rome and Constantinople. The side Scenes shew the horrid Tortures with which the Roman Tyrants persecuted the Church' (1. p. 241). The beauty of the religious ritual and the pastoral overtones of the religious retirement which tempts Theodosius and even Varanes may have been responsible for the play's success at court.[23] Yet in fact this early Church embodies a purity which Protestants saw themselves as continuing. 'Roman Tyrants', applied in the above quotation to pagan emperors, also suggests the Catholic Church, often described in similar emotive phraseology. Lee's treatment of religion is more subtle than in his previous two plays, in keeping with the caution and restraint announced in the epilogue and epistle dedicatory, but it is absolutely clear that the Emperor has been led astray in matters of religion. As Varanes says, 'drawn by Priests, and work'd by Melancholly, | Thou hadst laid the golden Reins of Empire down' (1. 268–9). The ruler's misdirected religious impulses have their parallel in his lovesickness, which leads Marcian to exclaim, 'you do not know | The wounds which rage within your Countries Bowels' (4. 2. 177–8). Lest we should doubt the authority of Varanes and Marcian, further proof of the disastrous nature of Theodosius' inattention to duty is supplied by the fact that Pulcheria can get him inattentively to sign the death warrant of his beloved Athenais. There is no motive for this, and it is clumsily introduced, merely serving to exemplify the point. Religious retirement is all very well for the Emperor's sisters, but it will not do for the ruler himself. Moreover, its topicality

---

[23] Downes, *Roscius Anglicanus*, cited in Lee, *Works*, ii. 231; epistle dedicatory, 237. Purcell's music also ensured success.

is marked. Rather than showing in Theodosius a 'wan
monasticism' which is 'a satiric reversal of Charles's libertine
pursuits' (Brown, p. 47), Lee depicts a ruler whose susceptibility
to feminine charms reflects a temperament which also renders
him vulnerable to the appeal of ritualistic religion. Even the
High Priest thinks Theodosius' religious resolve is motivated by
'disgust and melancholly bloud, | From restless Passions' (1. 41–
2). The alarming contemporary application is obvious.

Brown finds Marcian's paganism, which 'distinguishes him
from the intense Protestantism of many Whigs', a 'surprising
inconsistency' (p. 47). However, Whigs were also associated
with secularism and anticlericalism. In Marcian irreligion is
associated with an aggressive, empire-building foreign policy
(2. 102); and with manliness and the right order of things.
He criticizes 'our Female Court' (2. 17) and even though he
loves Pulcheria, he says, 'forgive me, | If with reluctance I behold
a Woman | Sit at the Empires Helm, and steer the World' (2.
130–2). Marcian is battling for nothing less than the stability
of the entire social fabric. This is clear as early as Act 2, when
he gives point to his criticisms of the corrupt court with this
warning:

> If things are suffer'd to be thus, down all
> Authority, Preeminence, Degree and Vertue.   (2. 78–9)

The play's conventional sexual politics reinforces the message.
The contradiction between essential feminine passivity and the
need for a wise woman to act when her menfolk fail is expressed
by Pulcheria in an image of maidenly confusion, as she tries to
manœuvre to bring about her marriage to the strong man she
knows both she and the country need:

> O help me forth, lost in this Labyrinth;
> Help me to loose this more than Gordian Knot,
> And make me and your self for ever happy.
>
> (5. 3. 80–2)

Upon her marriage in the following scene, the image is appropri-
ated and reversed by Atticus, reflecting the restoration of the
right order of things: 'The more than Gordian knot is ty'd, |
Which Deaths strong Arm shall ne're divide' (5. 4. 1–2).

In contrast to Marcian and Pulcheria, religious and lovesick Theodosius lets his sister rule while he mopes about the palace. As the philosopher Leontine says:

> You know that Theodosius is compos'd
> Of all the softness that should make a Woman,
> Judgement almost like Fear fore-runs his Actions;
> And he will poise an injury so long,
> As if he had rather pardon than revenge it.
>
> (1. 52–6)

The mercy and toleration which exasperated royalists in Charles, even while they praised him for it, is here associated with effeminacy and cowardice as Theodosius is damned with faint praise. Theodosius' heroism is of the theatrical kind which belongs in the heroic play and is disastrous in reality. He precipitates the catastrophe by honourably encouraging his friend and rival to approach his fiancée. The same theme occurred in *The Orphan*, but here it seems clearer that such worthy posturings lead directly to disaster. Theodosius is weak. He has good qualities: he unhesitatingly risks all for love, which is possibly why the play was popular with the ladies.[24] He is too good a Christian to kill himself (5. 4. 85–7). His virtues are not those of an efficient ruler. Perhaps, like Crowne's Henry VI, he is too good to rule, though there is also a touch of the culpable ineptitude of King Charles in *The Massacre*. In the end, Theodosius passes judgement on himself by abdicating in favour of worthier rulers.

Theodosius does have certain 'native', quasi-Protestant attitudes which are positively valued in contrast to Varanes. It is the foreigner who (like Louis XIV) is arrogantly obsessed with the honour of his throne. Whether to avoid a pointed parallel, as an exhortation, as a pointed contrast, or as an act of wishful thinking by the playwright, royal licentiousness is displaced on to Varanes. Also displaced on to Varanes is typically royalist whining about the cares of kings, as when he laments that 'Princes are barr'd the Liberty to Roam' (1. 388), as for them love is 'clogg'd with Scepters, and to Crowns confined' (1. 393). As with Crowne's Dauphin, the impression given is negative.

[24] Downes, cited in Lee, *Works*, ii. 231.

Similarly, it is Varanes who indulges in pastoral self-pity: 'Oh that I had been born some happy Swain' (3. 2. 387).

Like Jane Austen's Mr Darcy, Varanes eventually proposes in spite of himself: 'tho' to my Confusion | And everlasting shame; yet I must tell her, | I lay the Persian Crown before her Feet' (4. 2. 387–9). Athenais, who is virtuous, lowly born, and well educated (l. 68), seems to have no doubts that a prince should marry for love. Theodosius likewise has no hesitation in proposing to her, and he believes she should be free to choose as well. This Protestant, bourgeois ethic ultimately triumphs in his mind, as the ethos of the heroic play finds its ludicrous and painful culmination in 'honourable' suicide, and he reproaches the dying Athenais:

> Thy choice without this cruel act of Death
> I left thee to thy will, and in requital
> Thou hast murder'd all my Fame.   (5. 4. 62–4)

The facile solutions of the royalist heroic play in which the unsuitable object of desire invariably turns out to be disguised royalty have no place here.

The Heir of Morocco is another example of covert or coded Whiggery. It was difficult for an obviously Whiggish play to be performed in the theatres in the Tory reaction period, though we have seen in Chapter 7 that contradiction and doubt persist in the drama. In the prologue, Settle facetiously suggests that he might have written a Tory play:

> How finely would the Sparks be catch'd to Day,
> Should a *Whig*-Poet write a *Tory*-Play?
>
> (sig. A2ᵛ)

However, he goes on to attack Dryden for being a court pensioner, and to comment sarcastically, though without political statement, on the murder of the Whig Thynne. The epilogue concludes with an apparently light reference to the departure for France of the violently unpopular royal mistress, the Duchess of Portsmouth.[25] The play is dedicated to Monmouth's mistress, Henrietta Wentworth. The epistle dedicatory alludes to the loyal

---

[25] See e.g. the broadside, *A Dialogue Between The Dutchess of Portsmouth, and Madam Gwin, at parting*, cited in Danchin, *Prologues and Epilogues*, vol. ii, pt. i, pp. 382–3.

service of her ancestors in the Civil War, with a sly allusion to the fact that their loyal service received no reward from the king (sig. A2^r). In the play, lack of reward for loyal service has more serious consequences. The play ostensibly offers a message of loyalty to the king at all costs, whilst deploying similar themes and tropes to *The Ambitious Statesman* and *The Loyal General* in a more Whiggish configuration. In order to perceive the differences, it is essential that we rid our minds of the notion that loyalty and Whiggery are incompatible.

The play focuses on a loyal hero, Altomar, who bears a considerable resemblance to Crowne's Vendosme and Tate's Theocrin, but there are several significant differences of tone and emphasis. Firstly, the focus on royal ambition and ingratitude is stronger, and bad fatherhood seems to be the author's primary target. The contradictions always present within the paradigm of loyalty to vitiated kingship are so great as to rupture the fabric of quietism. Secondly, the 'manly' hero and self-confident heroine defy the king, and bear more resemblance to Settle's anti-papist hero Saxony in *The Female Prelate* than to the self-annihilating quietist heroes and heroines of Tory drama. Their resistance to tyranny is sanctioned. Moreover, a distinction is made, as in *Sertorius*, between real rebels and noble resisters:[26] the former must be destroyed, while the latter stand up to the king and argue for justice, but are not really traitors. Thirdly, there is some evidence that the treatment of love in the play stands for the liberties of the subject in general. I shall elaborate upon these points in turn.

Like the king in *The Loyal General*, Settle's Albuzeiden at first promises that the young lovers can marry as the just reward for Altomar's loyal service (1. p. 4). The king's subsequent insistence that the princess marry Gayland, motivated, as he repeatedly says, by 'Ambition', thus renders him guilty of flying in the face of justice and breaking his promise. Whereas the caprice of Tate's king in *The Loyal General* is born stoically, Settle draws out the fact that the king is a contract-breaker, an impious violator of sacred bonds, guilty of ingratitude, and motivated by pride and ambition. These are the qualities Whig propagandists

[26] In keeping with this interregnum-style distinction between good and bad rebels, Settle, like Bancroft, uses Miltonic imagery, for example, of angels, creation, and the war in heaven. See e.g. Act 1, pp. 2, 5; Act 2, p. 20.

attributed to popish princes. Moreover, like contemporary Whigs, Altomar claims that it is possible for the king's actions to nullify his royal authority: 'Oh hold, let not the Breath of Majesty | Pronounce those barbarous words as will Un-king you' (1. p. 8).

The Tory model is that the king is the supreme authority, possessor of divine power. In Settle's play such notions come across as machiavellian rant, and not only in the usurper Gayland, but also in the true king, Albuzeiden. Both men are referred to as tyrants. In this play, it is clear that there is a power above earthly monarchs. As Altomar warns, 'Ah Royal Sir, take heed how you resolve | What Heaven and Justice must forbid' (1. p. 6).

The king's inability to protect the loyal subject is extreme in this play, and more wilful than in *The Ambitious Statesman* or *The Loyal General*. He is motivated in his torturing to death of Altomar, 'A Deed below the worst of Savages' (5. p. 44), not only by ambition, but also by cowardice and supineness in the face of the country's enemies (the army of Gayland whom Altomar has slain in self-defence). Thus the king is inadequate as father of the nation. Bad fatherhood is a central theme: we repeatedly hear associated with Albuzeiden phrases such as 'a harsh, severe, imperious Father' (1. p. 4), 'Tyrannick Father' (3. p. 39), 'Oh Bloody Tyrant Father' (4. p. 40), and 'Inhumane, bloody, Savage, Tyrant, Father' (5. p. 45). The play's moral in the last lines is: 'See here the dire Effects of unkind Parents' (5. p. 51).

The king repents of slaying Altomar not from conscience, but only because Altomar is revealed to be a prince, 'That could have made me great' (5. p. 48). This is regret for the sanctity of royal blood, not for the goodness of a loyal subject or the bravery of the nation's military saviour. Artemira's judgement on this has moral authority:

> Could nothing but an Empire make him mine?
> Oh the ill judging World! . . .
> Has he more Love, more Charms, more Hearts to give me,
> Because he's Heir t' a Crown. Ah no, he was
> To me my King, my World, my Heaven before,
> And Crowns and Empires could not make him more.

> (5. p. 49)

It is only after Artemira has stabbed herself that the king is truly mortified. He stabs himself, then commands that his body be laid in the grave beneath Altomar's feet. This is marvellous theatre, but it is also a gesture of histrionic extremism which onlookers stigmatize as 'rash', and which leaves the country leaderless.

Altomar resembles Tate's Theocrin in that he is a warrior hero who is unjustly punished despite saving his country. Like Crowne's Vendosme, he is literally tortured. Like both Theocrin and Vendosme, he counsels his supporters to remain loyal to the king, despite his own sufferings (4. p. 41). Like Dryden's Torrismond in *The Spanish Fryar*, he is unknowingly the heir to a throne currently occupied by a usurper. In theory, all this offers considerable scope for a quietist message. However, there is a difference between Altomar's demeanour and the neo-stoicism of Vendosme and Theocrin, or that of Torrismond, who counsels patience and reconciliation, and rebukes precipitate action by the royalist hothead Raymond. Altomar knows what is right and nothing can stop him speaking and acting accordingly. In Act 3 he defends his own worth against the 'Dross' and 'baser Mould' of Gayland (p. 36), even though he still thinks at this stage that he is a commoner, whilst his rival is a prince. There is a Whiggish suggestion that true royalty is not necessarily synonymous with rank, and princes must win and merit respect, rather than being entitled to receive it automatically.

A most significant exchange takes place after Altomar's killing of Gayland. Altomar defends his action as self-defence, arguing that Gayland was a 'Tyrant' and that his behaviour in attacking an unarmed man was base and 'unmanly' (3. p. 37). Resisting tyrants is both legitimate and courageous, and is associated with real manhood, and with true nobility of character, as opposed to hollow insistence upon rank. The king's absolutist response is meant to sound ridiculous:

> Better a thousand low-born Souls like thine
> Should float in Shoals through Tides and Seas of Blood,
> Than the least Vein of Majesty should bleed,
> Or a Crown'd Head but ake.

> (3. p. 37)

This is the occasion for a denunciation by Altomar of the notion that royalty must always be respected no matter how corrupt:

> A Crown'd Head! so at that rate a Villain
> May be an Emperor at his Coronation.
> Murder and Hell held up the Canopy,
> Whilst Blood and Treason dyed his Royal Purple.
> No Voice of Majesty, no Sound of Glory;
> But Massacre, Rebellion, Desolation.   (ibid.)

The king's response is that this is 'Blasphemy' and that princes are entitled to stab unarmed subjects, just as 'angry Gods | Strike impious Men' (ibid.). This naked assertion of divine right is quite clearly intended to sound not merely ridiculous, but villainous. The torturing of Altomar on the rack is the occasion for many pathetic and harrowing speeches by the lovers, arousing pity. Crowne's Vendosme was also racked by an unnatural father, the villainous Constable. Settle's king takes on the mantle of that other ambitious and ungrateful villain, with shocking effect.

Nowhere is the difference between royalist and Whig heroism more apparent than in the contrast between Vendosme and Altomar, whose fate is similar. Crowne's hero is so passive that the villain accuses him of being feminine: 'To glory thou art a Girle, but to a Woman | Thou art a vig'rous Man!' (5. 1. p. 72). Vendosme's bride is actually stolen from him by a violent, lustful prince. Yet he regrets his attempt to defend Louize against the prince's murderous rage with his dying breath: 'I lifted up my Arm against the *Dauphin*, | It ought to have dy'd and rotted in the Air' (5. p. 86). Altomar denounces the cruelty of those who would attempt to punish him for killing the prince thus:

> I kill'd him nobly, bravely kill'd him, King.
> No grapling *Roman* in *Romes* Amphitheater
> Took an encountring Lion by the Throat,
> And tore his heart out with a Rage more manly.
>
> (3. p. 38)

In contrast to Vendosme, who foresees no prospect of reunion or transcendence in death, but only chaste proximity in the grave, Altomar is confident of meeting again after death (4. p.

40): love will find a way around arbitrary royal prohibition. Even the message of loyalty to the soldiers seems different in Settle's play:

> But now with my last breath I must conjure you;
> Let not my ghastly Fortune fright you from
> Your dearest Loyalty. Fight on my Souldiers;
> Fight for your Royal Lord; go on till you
> Have won him Trophies numberless as Stars,
> And Glory dazling as the Sun: And then expect
> The brave Reward of all your Noble Toyls:
> For he's a King so just, a King so generous,
> A King so merciful—he can be cruel
> To nothing but to *Altomar*; unkind
> To nought but *Altomar*.
>
> (4. p. 42)

The inflated implausibilities of the first part of this speech are punctured by the last three lines, with the words 'cruel' and 'unkind' emphasized at the ends of lines, and the repeated focus on the name of the suffering hero who has not been so rewarded given extra emphasis in the short, climactic line. The speech says more about the speaker's nobility of character than about the king. It is the occasion for comment by admiring onlookers about the brightness of his mind and honour, and the sadness of his fate, and for further speeches by Altomar to the effect that he suffers only because of the undeserved and shameful name of traitor, that he is a soldier and will not shed an 'unmanly Tear' in spite of 'Tyranny, | Ingratitude, Death, Tortures, Infamy', and that his love gives him the strength to be calm (ibid.). Here we seem to have the capacity for feeling of Otway's Jaffeir, combined with the 'manly' courage of his Pierre: the best qualities of both and the worst of neither. In death Altomar is spoken of in language usually applied to Charles I: 'God-like Martyr' (5. p. 44), 'Sacred Martyr' (5. p. 47), 'martyr'd Saint' (5. p. 49).

A real rebel, Meroin, is introduced as a contrast to Altomar and to provide him with an opportunity to show his loyalty, thus clarifying the point that he is no traitor. Maddened by lack of reward for his military service, and by Princess Artemira's scorn of his love, Meroin tries to murder both king and princess in Act 3. Altomar interposes and saves the day. This occasion also reinforces the king's ingratitude, already clear in Act 1. There he owed his throne and security to Altomar; now he owes his life. Yet his response is to animadvert churlishly upon Altomar's low birth, and to insist upon the superiority of 'Descent, Nobility, Birthright and Power' (3. p. 28). This notion of royal ingratitude is Whiggish. As I noted in Chapter 4, Whigs argued that the king owed a debt of gratitude to his people, who had placed him in power.[27]

The heroine is defiant without being presented as undutiful. Settle forgoes the pathetic possibilities of conflict between love and filial duty, and offers us a character who is both morally superior and self-confident. Like Eurydice in *Oedipus*, Edraste in *The Loyal General*, and Eugenia in *The Injur'd Princess*, Artemira yearns for the simple life, but there is a difference between the plaintive, pastoral effusions of these other heroines and her forceful and politically pointed outburst:

> Nurs'd in a Palace, and a King my Parent,
> And yet thus wretched! would I had met my *Altomar*
> In some hospitable Desart born:
> What tho' we lived with Brutes and Savages,
> They would be kinder than inhumane Fathers.
>
> (2. p. 16)

Artemira's and Altomar's defence of true love against royal and parental tyranny seems to have wider libertarian implications. The king calls his daughter a 'rebellious Syren' (1. p. 7). The young lovers are 'wanton Traytors' who engage in a 'dark Cabal' (ibid.). This misapplication of precisely the terminology used against the Whigs seems pointed. It is repeatedly made clear that heaven is on the lovers' side in the fight against the king's pride, worldly ambition, and venality. It is common for choice in marriage to be a positive value. However, in this play the arranged marriage, to which true love is counterposed, is not simply the product of parental caprice, but is associated with a whole perverted system of dynastic and monarchist values according to which royalism is more important than truth and justice. Instructing Artemira to be false to Altomar, the king explains:

[27] See e.g. *A Just and Modest Vindication of the Proceedings of the Two Last Parliaments*, 29.

> 'Tis then thou'rt false when thou lovest *Altomar*;
> False to thy Blood, thy Honor, and to me,
> To love below the Daughter of a King . . .
> All my Ambition bounds in this Alliance.

(2. p. 15)

It is quite extraordinary to find the familiar Tower of Babel image, associated with machiavellian villains throughout Renaissance and Restoration drama, here used to express the king's desire for an alliance through marriage with a powerful foreign power:

> Heavens! I was raising her
> A Pile of Majesty, so high, so lofty,
> On whose Imperial Towers she might shake hands
> With Gods: But angry Love, that envious Deity,
> Confounds the Languages of Power and Glory,
> And stops the rising Fabrick.

(3. p. 22)

Later in this scene, the king is inspired by Meroin's suggestion that he should order the priests to preach Artemira into submission. There is surely a topical resonance in this spectacle of tyranny employing the Church to counsel subjection. The role of the Church in the Exclusion Crisis had already been satirized by Shadwell in *The Lancashire Witches*.

It seems clear, then, that Settle's moral against bad fatherhood is also a warning against royal pride and absolutism; but the message is presented indirectly and through an appropriation of the theories of suffering loyalty in the face of bad kingship characteristic of Tory drama.

The Unhappy Favourite *and* Vertue Betray'd

Banks is known as the master of the sentimental.[28] He chooses stories with great political potential, but often collapses political into sentimental effect. Yet Banks had three plays banned: *Cyrus the Great* (1681), *The Innocent Usurper* (1683), and *The Island*

---

[28] Hume calls him 'The real champion of the pathetic'. He says of *The Unhappy Favourite*, 'the play lives on whopping infusions of emotion', and calls *Vertue Betray'd* 'a bathetic tearjerker' (*Development*, 351).

Queens (1684). In *The Unhappy Favourite* he excels at the depiction of emotional conflict, but there is also a political message against the disastrous results of intemperance and the need for reconciliation between sovereign and subject. There is an attempt at balance: on the one hand, there may be criticism of the Whigs in the depiction of Burleigh as ambitious, as leading 'Factious members of the House' (1. p. 5), and as having 'Brains | Stufft with Cabals, and Projects for the Nation' (1. p. 6). However, this characterization is not consistently sustained. Essex may represent Monmouth: he returns to court to justify himself despite royal prohibition and, when deprived of his offices, he associates with 'Rebels' in an 'unjust Assembly' and goes to the City to complain of his wrongs and raise 'the stinking rabble' (4. pp. 44–5). Like Dryden's Achitophel, he is the victim of an ambitious schemer. Topicality is enhanced by the fact that the Restoration Earl of Essex voted for Exclusion and was dismissed from the Privy Council a few months before the play was produced.[29] However, the play's Essex is also a warrior hero, intensely pitiable, and ultimately loyal: he goes to his death calling on heaven to protect Elizabeth, even though he wrongly believes she has spurned his request for forgiveness.

On the other hand, the play seems quite sharply critical of Charles. The similarity between Essex and Monmouth foregrounds the comparison between Elizabeth and Charles. It is a comparison which favours Elizabeth. In Act 1 the queen joins with Burleigh and Southampton in recalling the defeat of the Armada and abusing popery and a foreign Catholic power. This resembles the recalling of Elizabeth's victories in *The Coronation* as a device for focusing on Charles's inactivity against both popery and France. The scene continues with the queen giving audience to MPs in tones very similar to those used by the character of Elizabeth in *The Coronation*:

> Welcome my People, welcome to your Queen,
> Who wishes still no longer to be so
> Than she can Govern well, and serve you all;
> Welcome again, dear People; for I'me Proud
> To call you so, and let it not be Boasting

[29] Hutton, *Charles the Second*, 398.

In me, to say, I Love you with a greater Love
Than ever Kings before showr'd down on Subjects,
And that I think ne're did a People more
Deserve, than you. Be quick,
And tell me your Demands; I long to hear:
For know, I count your wants are all my own.

(I. p. 10)

The people's proposed measures 'for the safety of your Crown and Life' (p. 11) are greeted with a gratitude which was conspicuously absent from Charles II's response to similar concerns during the Popish Plot scare. An attempt by the MPs to impeach Essex calls forth severity: they become 'Ingrateful People', a 'Factious Crew' with 'Impudent Petitions' (p. 12). This seems anti-Whiggish. However, Elizabeth's noble struggle to subdue her unruly passions offers a favourable comparison with Charles, who was notorious for giving way to his.

In *Vertue Betray'd* Anna is a sentimentalized, suffering victim. Act 4 especially is full of histrionic high-flights, struggles between duty and pity, appeals to heaven, self-conscious references to the suffering heart. Yet the play is by no means politically innocent. There is enough loyal statement to enable Danchin to read it as 'a markedly loyal' one.[30] There is a potentially Tory treatment of the preoccupation with the nature of royalty. Royalty consists not in merit, but in blood. Anna's brother Rochford, foreseeing disaster from her marriage, offers what could well be a Tory response to the pretensions of the son of Lucy Walter:

> Thrones are severest Touch-stones;
> And, like the Emblem of their Guard, the Lyon,
> All but of Royal-Blood they will destroy.   (I. p. 2)

We find the doctrine of non-resistance in Act 4, as the wrongly accused Anna counsels submission to her brother: 'No more, Dear Brother; let us both submit' (p. 59).

However, there are also strong and numerous Whiggish elements: Banks's Anna is an English Protestant martyr, undone by the diabolical papist machinations of Wolsey, who hates to see

---

[30] Danchin, *Prologues and Epilogues*, ii. 387.

'A *Lutheran* Queen upon the Throne of *England*!' (1. p. 3). As Diane Dreher puts it:

Banks's anachronistic representation of Wolsey cannot be attributed to a historical oversight; Cavendish's *Life of Wolsey* made the story too familiar for that. By combining the villainy of Wolsey with that of Thomas Cromwell and further emphasizing his degeneracy by giving him a liaison with [the king's cast-off mistress, Lady Elizabeth] Blunt and proud ranting speeches in which he boasts of his ability to manipulate the King, Banks made the Cardinal an evil caricature of the Catholic Church itself. Blunt's speeches associate the Cardinal with Alexander VI, the notorious Borgia Pope, intensifying the villainous caricature yet more.[31]

Wolsey is associated with the Devil, and Blunt uses hellish arts to further their joint plots (3. pp. 30–1, 38–9; 4. pp. 55, 57; 5. p. 63). Like the priests in *Lucius Junius Brutus*, he is much given to false oaths and assurances.

The common theme of the 'wretched state of Princes' here receives a Protestant gloss: Anna's elevation forces her into contact with court falsity, and compromises 'my Liberty of Thinking' (1. p. 9).[32] As in *The Heir of Morocco*, for Anna, for her friend Diana, and also for Piercy, love stands in opposition to *realpolitik*. Anna's role as a martyred monarch, and the mother of a monarch, is stressed in a Protestant context: at the end of the play there is a prophetic speech by Anna, foreseeing her daughter Elizabeth's triumph over the Pope,

> That holy Tyrant,
> Who binds all *Europe* with the Yoak of Conscience,
> Holding his Feet upon the Necks of Kings.
>
> (5. p. 74)

Just before this, Banks violates logical constraints of time to bring in the emotive Protestant figure of Princess Elizabeth herself. The little child has an instinctive mistrust of Wolsey: 'He looks for all | The World, just like a Picture of the Pope' and she

---

[31] Introduction to facsimile reprint of the first edition of 1682, p. vi.

[32] The imagery Anna uses to describe the court recalls that used by Marguerite in Lee's Protestant and Whig play *The Massacre of Paris*: 'this place is Hell; | Vipers and Adders lurking under Smiles, | And flatt'ring Cloths of State: Oh! do not tread here; | Under this Mask of Gallantry and Beauty, | Is a rude Wild; nay, worse, a dangerous Ocean, | Into whose Jaws, Love, like a Calenture, | Will tempt us, where we both must Sink and Perish' (3. p. 40; cf. 3. 2. 59).

does not love the Pope (5. p. 67). She movingly begs her father
to save her mother's life:

> Father, will you not let your *Betty* kiss you?
> Why do you let 'em pull me from you so?
> I ne're did anger you:
> Pray save my Mother, Dear King-Father do;
> And if you hate her, we will promise both,
> That she and I will go a great, huge way,
> And never see you more. (5. p. 68)

However, she sees that she is doomed to failure because Henry
is in thrall to the 'Devil' Wolsey.

Henry sees through Wolsey at the end and vows to 'break the
Yoak' of popery and rule alone, stressing the dangers to England
of royal subordination to popish control (5. p. 79). In the epistle
dedicatory, Banks praises Elizabeth, Duchess of Somerset,
for her Protestant commitment, exemplified in her marriage:
'England adores you for it; the Protestant Religion blesses You
. . . and the Chief of all, young *Edward*, its great Establisher,
looks down with Joy to see his happy Successor lye in your
Arms' (sig. A2ᵛ–A3ʳ). Such a strongly Protestant statement is
'against the stream' and potentially oppositional in its resonance
in 1682. It is also politically suggestive that another prologue to
the play is extant, written by the Whig Shadwell.

There are numerous references to 'unhappy England'. At the
end of Act 4 Anna, who is much given to historicizing herself,
sees herself in a line of royal martyrs, but begs heaven that
England be unpunished for her wrongs. There is a sense in
which Anna represents England. At the beginning of Act 5,
Wolsey asks Blunt: 'Is she Condemn'd? Shall *Rome* be Abso-
lute? | Shall Woolsey Reign, and shall my *Blunt* be Queen?'
Blunt replies: 'These Eyes saw the bright *English* Sun Eclips'd'
(p. 62). This English heroine is destroyed through a combination
of papist villainy and royal lust (for Jane Seymour). As in *The
Heir of Morocco*, there is a Protestant critique of royal high-
handedness in matters of the heart: 'What would the Tyrant be
a God? | To take upon him to dispose of Hearts!' (3. p. 41). The
presence of an ambitious former royal mistress (Elizabeth Blunt)
who conspires with papists enhances topical resonance. Henry
has the predatory amorousness of James Stuart and perhaps

resembles him also as he offers rage where Anna anticipated mercy. In Act 5, scorning mercy, he is said to have 'Deny'd all *Englands* Prayers, and Tears of Angels' (p. 65).

Bad fatherhood is prevalent. Northumberland thwarts the true love of Anna and his own son Piercy through trickery (because he wants to marry Piercy to an heiress). He swears falsely that Anna will be safe (4. p. 57). After Anna's death Piercy comments: 'And my hard hearted Father too was there' (5. p. 65). Anna has also been let down by her own ambitious parents: 'Parents Threats and Kings Authority, | Rent me, like Thunder, from my fixt Resolves' (1. p. 10). When she is condemned, 'The Cruel Duke of *Norfolk*, her Relation, | As Steward for the Day, pronounc'd the Sentence' (5. p. 65). Worse, 'Her own Father, | The Earl of *Wiltshire*, sate amongst her Judges' (ibid.). There is an explicit association between unnatural parents and the king: Piercy proclaims that tigers, wolves, and panthers 'are more merciful than King or Parent' (5. p. 77). This seems Whiggish.

Banks disavows political alignment in the prologue and epilogue, deplores faction, and pleads for moderation. However, the prologue also has a Whiggishly patriotic tone, emphasizing the need for English unity. It concludes by noting that the author's heroes are the brave English:

> He brings no Foreigners to move your pity,
> But sends them to a *Jury of the City*.   (36–7)[33]

This is a telling contrast to the anti-Whig reference to ignoramus juries common in 1680. There may be an allusion to the German assassin of the Whig Thomas Thynne, also referred to in Shadwell's prologue and the broadside epilogue. In the epilogue both parties are condemned and 'loyalty' is seen as being as bad as 'faction'. Banks appears to be allying himself with advocates of moderation such as Halifax, whose *Character of a Trimmer* was in circulation in manuscript well before the king's death in 1685, and Dorset, a patron of both Dryden and Shadwell. In a poem circulating by 1682, Dorset states:

---

[33] I use Danchin's text, which usefully compares the various broadside and quarto texts. In the quarto, but not the broadside, the prologue is said to be by 'a Person of Quality'.

After thinking this Fortnight of *Whig* and of *Tory*,
(This to me is the long and the short of the Story)
They're all Fools and Knaves; and they keep up this pother
On both sides, designing to cheat one another.[34]

However, Trimmers were regarded as being as bad as Whigs in
1682, as Dryden says in his epilogue to *The Duke of Guise*.
Vertue Betray'd warns against both royal and papist intemperance. It has a fervent commitment to Protestantism and patriotism, without going as far as to sanction resistance to tyranny.
This is about as oppositional as it is possible to get in the Tory
reaction period.

Whiggism was not an unambiguously radical, democratic, and
innovative politics, but appealed to ideas which were in a sense
conservative against what were seen as undesirable innovations.
These circumstances have led critics to perpetuate the winner's
history of the early 1680s by writing out, or down, oppositional
plays and the force of their ideas. In reality the division of the
political nation did find forms of expression in the drama.
Oppositional force could be given to drama in various ways:
anti-popery, seen in *Caesar Borgia* and *The Massacre of Paris*,
as well as in *The Female Prelate*, *Rome's Follies*, *The Coronation*, and *The Lancashire Witches*; an appeal to law and liberty
based on English tradition (*Lancashire Witches*) or ancient
Rome (*Sertorius* and *Lucius Junius Brutus*); an appeal to sexual politics which dramatizes bad kingship as effeminacy
(*Theodosius*) or as bad fatherhood (*The Heir of Morocco*); and
an appeal to British Protestant tradition as in *The Lancashire
Witches* and Banks's plays. The plays considered in this chapter
deploy the full range of Whig tropes outlined in Chapters 4–6
and, as we have seen, make use of similar themes to opposition
and Whig propagandists. Lee's experience with *The Massacre*
and *Lucius Junius Brutus* indicates that opposition needed to
be more coded than royalism. However, in some respects,
oppositional playwrights had less difficulty in dramatizing their
ideas than royalists. Patriotism and resistance to tyranny can be
more uplifting than passive obedience to corrupt kings. Whig
dramatists have access to themes of masculinity and martial

[34] Winn, *John Dryden and his World*, 387.

heroism, where Tories have self-emasculating, quietist heroes, destroyed by the ideal they serve. It is always easier to be fervent in opposition than to defend a flawed regime; and Whig plays have the vitality of an ascendant ideology. It is time to put Whig drama back on the cultural map.

CHAPTER 9

City Drama: Thomas Jordan's Lord Mayor's Shows

A CONSIDERATION of the Lord Mayor's Shows, performed each year on Lord Mayor's Day, 29 October, will enrich, complicate, and clarify our view of drama and politics and will provide a counterweight to satire of factious 'cits' in the theatres. The published texts of Jordan's shows are entertaining accounts of what was both formal pageantry, meticulously planned down to the last piece of visual symbolism, and live spectacle, involving all sections of society. Jordan takes care to satisfy, interact with, and include his audience, and the shows provide a fascinating insight into differences in taste and outlook between theatre and city audiences. The shows are characterized by vitality, enthusiasm, inclusiveness, and scrupulous attention to detail, and combine pomp and ceremony with affection for the humblest revellers and children.

John Patrick Montano has argued that in the 1670s 'these pageants began to promote government propaganda directly . . . Lord Mayor's Day Shows were designed to bring an oral and emblematic version of government policy onto the streets for the ideological consumption of the London populace. The reason for this was a desire to consolidate belief in a national consensus supporting the restored monarchy.'[1] In my opinion, this is the opposite of the truth. Jordan's shows exhibit genuine concern about the growth of popery and arbitrary government. As in most Whig texts, so in the shows, opposition to royal high-handedness or government policy is expressed through conservative tropes of 'Loyal Protestantism'. It becomes clear from reading the Exclusion Crisis shows that influential

---

[1] Montano, 'The Quest for Consensus: The Lord Mayor's Day Shows in the 1670s'.

citizens and merchants, quite contrary to the satirical depiction in Tory drama, were cautious and conservative and feared disorder and disruption. Jordan is no radical. He has an enduring commitment to sovereignty, moderation, peace, trade, colonialism, the city, the national interest, Protestantism, and the whole commonwealth. Yet, as we have seen, such a configuration of values came to seem *Whiggish* in the Exclusion Crisis, especially in the extremist Tory reaction period. Jordan's moderation is similar in character but very different in perspective from that of Dryden, discussed in Chapter 4. The need for a careful reading of the shows is posed by an apparent contradiction: Jordan, like the theatre dramatists, was sensitive to changing times, adapting his shows to the political situation and to each different Lord Mayor. However, there is also a sense in which Jordan stays the same while society changes around him, inspired by and expressing an unchanging core of recurring themes and values which seem moderate, even conservative, at one moment and inflammatory the next. City support for the Whigs was based upon alarm over the apparent threat to stability posed by popery and royal high-handedness, and over the lack of Protestant leadership shown by the king. Jordan's Protestant, patriotic traditionalism is the same as that of moderate Whigs who were outraged by the government's 'extremist' violation of traditional parliamentary and Protestant liberties. The fact that Jordan stresses the need for unity to face the popish threat should not obscure this;[2] nor should the fact that he consistently employs a rhetorical strategy of legitimizing authority and bolstering sovereignty.[3] Moreover, the nature of the shows as popular spectacle opened up space for a carnivalesque challenge to authority: as Benjamin Klein has pointed out, 'an active relationship existed between the ruler and the ruled, spectacle and spectator, actor and audience'.[4] The Pope-burnings were an unambigu-

---

[2] See e.g. Harris, *London Crowds*, 123.

[3] Cf. other Whig 'Loyal Protestant' texts such as Settle's dedication to *The Female Prelate*.

[4] Klein, 'Between the Bums and the Bellies of the Multitude', 20. In contrast to Klein, Montano seems to have a conspiracy theory of culture, stating that the Lord Mayor's Shows had 'a unity of thematic content which resulted in a type of sermon' (36) and that the outdoor staging enabled the message to reach 'those officially excluded from the political nation' (38). He acknowledges disunity in *government* (39–40), but seems to think culture has more cohesiveness than political history,

ously Whig spectacle which asserted loyalty as well as Protestantism; and the crowd joined in by drinking the king's health in conjunction with that of Monmouth, and uttering Whiggish cries such as 'No popery, God Bless the King, Protestant Religion, The Church and Dissenting Protestants, both of whom God unite'.[5] This provides a context for our reading of the politics of the shows. As the clamping down on the shows in the reaction period demonstrates, the shows offered a threat both to public order and to royalist ideology.[6]

The Triumphs of London (1678)

There are three aspects to the show's political outlook: civic pride, Protestantism, and loyalty.

The City's importance is stressed in two ways. The first is its social inclusiveness: the procession contains all strata from poor pensioners to civic dignitaries. Here and in all the pageants the participants carry banners of the king, the Lord Mayor, the City, and the Grocers' Company, this year's sponsors. In the processions we also find the banner of the Duke of York. Secondly, the City is the centre of the nation's prosperity. Jordan's epistle dedicatory to the Lord Mayor praises the role of merchants in colonialism and social progress. The three pageants celebrate England's colonial power, based on the City. The First Pageant has an Indian boy on a camel, the Grocers' emblem, with hampers full of fruits and spices. A Fortress of Government displays 'a very large Banner of the *Grocers*' (p. 4). The boy is flanked by figures representing Industry and Fortune, carrying the Grocers' and Lord Mayor's banners. Other figures are Fidelity, Loyalty, Vigilancy, Justice, Constancy, Wit, Concord, Reli-

---

rather than being a site of contestation, contradiction, or fragmentation. This is in striking contrast to MacLean's excellent introduction to the volume. To support his argument Montano's quotation is selective and his coverage ends in 1678, presumably because the 1679 and 1680 shows so clearly contradict his point.

[5] Harris, *London Crowds*, 109, 159, 163.

[6] For further reading on the shows see: Fairholt, *The Lord Mayor's Pageants*; Williams, 'The Lord Mayor's Show in Tudor and Stuart Times'; Withington, *English Civic Pageantry*; Morrissey, 'English Street Theatre'; and (though not dealing with Jordan) Richards, 'The Restoration Pageants of John Tatham'; and Tumbleson, 'The Triumph of London'.

gion, Union, and Truth. In the Second Pageant, an Indian temple contains 'an *East-Indian* Deity called OPULENTA, a Representative of all the Intrinsic Treasure in the Oriental *Indies*', flanked by black princes, Animalia, Vegetabilia, and Mineralia, each bearing a golden key 'to all the Treasuries of *India*, and generally to all Human Nature; Comprehending the diversities of Traffick and several Commodities, which our Noble *English* Merchants bring from *India* to *England*' (p. 8). Representatives of six Indian cities pay tribute, literally and figuratively, to the Lord Mayor. The Third Pageant features an Indian plantation, rich in spices and jewels, and featuring happy labourers and Aromatorio, the 'Governour', flanked by Toyl, Traffick, Treasure, and Triumph. Again the power of the City and its leader is celebrated in a speech.

Together with colonial pride goes Protestant humility. Fidelity's speech in the First Pageant, admonishing through praise, tells the Lord Mayor that 'The faithful *Fortress* of *Just Government*' in the tableau resembles his own rule: 'The Adamantine Rock 'tis built upon, | Merits the Name of *True Religion*' (p. 6). She urges him to be 'a faithful *Governour*' (p. 7). Opulenta's speech in the Second Pageant concludes:

> You do adore a Power greater than Mine,
> A *God*, that doth all other Gods excell,
> Imitate *Him*, and you will *Govern* well.   (p. 10)

This emphasis on the ruler's subordination to God is Whig not Tory. A Protestant work ethic combines with celebration of colonialism, as the plantation workers sing a song on the theme 'What a Life of Delight do we Labourers live?' (p. 13). City puritans were satirized for mirthlessness in the theatre (and in the etymology of the word 'Whig'), but here Protestantism is combined with pleasure in singing and dancing and the concluding 'Drolleries' include comic characters trading insults, such as 'Sheep-biter', 'ship-shiter', and 'Crablouse' (16–17).

Civic pride and Protestantism are associated with loyalty. In the Second Pageant we learn that the 'good Lord Mayor's Power doth Spring, | From *Honour's Fountain*, in my Lord, the King' (p. 10). This emphasizes both the Lord Mayor's importance in the scheme of things and his service to the monarch. The figure

of Loyalty in the First Pageant bears a shield with the motto
'Fear God, Honour the King' (p. 4). The loyalty of the citizens
is more pointedly stressed in the planters' song, as though in
answer to criticism:

> For *London's* great *Grocers* we Labour and Work,
> No Plots against Princes in our Heads do lurk:
> We Plant, Set, and Sow, likewise for the Physician,
> But Plant no Rebellion, and Sow no Sedition.
> The *Grocers* and *Merchants* are Men of Renown,
> They are just in their Trading, and true to the Crown.
>
> (p. 14)

The chorus combines pride, devotion, and duty: 'Let's Pray for
King *Charles*, and his Brethren, the *Grocers*' (ibid.). Whatever
royalist propagandists might assert, it is clear that Jordan does
not see the term 'Loyal Protestant' as either disingenuous or a
contradiction in terms.

Though the tropes of civic pride and Protestantism distinguish
Jordan from the authors of the contemporaneous *Oedipus*, he
concludes with a similar theme:

> Want of Amity
> Breeds calamity,
>   We are too much divided;
> By Atheistick persons too,
>   Religion is derided.

However, Jordan's motivation is different. He thinks peace is
better for trade:

> Since Union and Concord bring Plenty and Peace,
> And Amity is the kind cause of Increase:
> Let Love from Division our fancy's release,
> And all our Dissentions ever cease.   (p. 20)

Religious turmoil and political division are as uncongenial to
the wealthy and cautious citizen as to the royalist, whatever
Tory dramatists might assert. However, Marvell's defence of
precisely the same values of Protestantism, prosperity, patriotism, and trade had marked him as oppositional the previous
year and placed him on a collision course with the royalist
L'Estrange.

London in Luster *(1679)*

Jordan reiterates themes from the 1678 show with some new emphases. He celebrates the political centrality of the Lord Mayor, with a new stress on his key role in the troubled times. He gives loyalty a more overtly anti-papist slant than in 1678, though with a cautionary stress on moderation. The popular revels which conclude the festivities indicate a social inclusiveness absent from Tory drama in the theatres.

For Jordan the Lord Mayor's importance derives firstly from his relationship to the king. This is clear in the description of the inaugural procession:

> Where having took an Oath that He will be
> Loyal and faithful to His MAJESTY,
> His Government, His Crown and Dignity,
> With other Ceremonials said and done,
> On Order to his Confirmation;
> Sealing of Writs in Courts, and such-like things,
> As shew his power abstracted from the King's.   (p. 3)

Lord Mayor Clayton is rather like a king, as he processes with quasi-regal pomp and ceremony. After swearing his oath of loyalty he proceeds 'To th' Water-side, and having given at large | To th' poor of *Westminster*) doth Re-imbarge' (ibid.). The association of bounty and royalty is drawn out in the First Pageant in the figure of September, whose 'purple Robes sheweth how she reigneth like a Queen above other Months, abounding with plenty of things pleasant and necessary for Man's life' (p. 6). It must be recognized that all this functions not so much to buttress authority in any abstract sense as to underscore the fact that 'Loyal Protestantism' really is loyal and to emphasize the importance of the City in the face of attempts by royalists to satirize, scorn, and socially and politically exclude it.

Secondly, the importance of the Lord Mayor derives from the City's central role in the scheme of things. There is less emphasis on colonialism than in the previous year, presumably because it is less relevant to this year's sponsors, the drapers. However, as before, the social inclusiveness of the procession is minutely detailed: ushers of the King and Duke of York are followed by

civic dignitaries, companies, artisans, apprentices, and pensioners. The figures in the pageants hold banners of the king, Lord
Mayor, City, and Drapers' Company. The speech in the Second
Pageant spells out the inclusive social significance of the Lord
Mayor's 'government'. The speaker is a 'Royal Shepherd' (p. 11)
who identifies himself with the biblical King David, and who is
to be associated not with King Charles, but with Clayton.[7] With
a familiar admixture of praise and good advice, he addresses the
Lord Mayor as follows:

> This *little* Scene, and I, do represent
> A Model of Your *greater* Government.
> For you present a *Shepherd*, This great Town
> Infolds your Flock, (a Plain of great renown)
> You do present a *Souldier*, when, by Law,
> You fit and Act in the *Militia*.
>   In your distinct Capacities, Men know
>   You are *tam Marti quam Mercurio*.
> You do present a *Judge*, when you dispence
> *Guerdon* to Guilt, *Succour* to Innocence.
> You'r a *Musician* too, in the Consent
> And Harmony of well tun'd Government.
> You do present a *King*, in this degree,
> For you present His Sacred MAJESTY.

> (pp. 12–13)

The pageant of shepherds usurps courtly pastoral for Clayton's
greater glory. Jordan's concentration of the Lord Mayor's social
and political centrality serves to demonstrate both his potential
usefulness to the king, and his strength, at a time when the king
was showing an increasing tendency to try to interfere in the
affairs of the City and ride roughshod over its leadership.[8]

Jordan also seems anxious to warn Clayton himself that he
has a particular role to play in the current crisis. A speech in the
Third Pageant concludes:

[7] Charles had often been identified with David from 1660 onwards. See Dryden,
Works, ii. 231 and Hammond, *Dryden: A Literary Life*, 96 and 178 n. 4.
[8] Charles interfered in the 1679 Common Council elections, ordering the reintroduction of the disused anti-puritan oaths. In Jan. 1680 he reportedly intimidated
Common Council members by declaring that if they petitioned for Parliament to
meet, he would dissolve it next day, and if a civil war ensued, he would declare they
had begun it. In summer 1680 he tried unsuccessfully to overturn the election of the
republican Slingsby Bethel and the puritan Henry Cornish as sheriffs: Haley,
Shaftesbury, 562, 564, 582.

Y'have gain'd the Love of LONDON, o're which, *Fate*,
Merit, and *Choice*, have made you Magistrate,
The *great* and *good* Lord Mayor, in such a Season
As will require your most refined Reason,
Authority, and Judgement, (all the Town
Is big with Expectation) . . .

(p. 15)

Jordan's epistle dedicatory to Clayton offers the same combination of praise and warning. His breadth of legitimacy gives the
Lord Mayor an authority which has never been more necessary:
'By Divine Manuduction, Ability, Opportunity, Legal Election,
and Regal Authority, you are invested and confirmed a Vice-
regent over the most Celebrious City of all *Europe*, LONDON;
yet at such a *Season*, when the *Trouble* of the Times will prove
the *Trial* of the Magistrate' (sig. [A1]ʳ). The emphasis on merit
and legal election as well as royal and godly authority as the
basis for Jordan's power seems Whiggish, as does the Jordan's
repeated insistence on Clayton's accountability to his people.
He also tells him how to exercise his responsibility, advising
'an even Carriage may render you a good Governour, of great
Circumspection'. Similarly, the speech of Opportunity in the
First Pageant counsels justice and moderation:

> But when *Extremes* on either hand do sway,
> 'Tis safest sure to chuse the *Middle*-way.
> Extremes are dangerous, and apt to hurt us,
> We read, *in medio consistit Virtus*. (p. 8)⁹

The good government and order necessary to preserve the city
are associated with Loyal Protestantism. It is made clear that the
threat to the city comes from the Popish Plot. The paired shepherds and shepherdesses in the Second Pageant are called
'Vigilius & Precaria, Canonicus & Evangelia, Orthodoxus &
Protestantia, Fidelius & Bonopera' (pp. 10–11). The speaker is
Loyalty, 'A young Man of Heroic Aspect' (p. 13):

> That I appear thus Arm'd with Shield and Sword
> Is proper, my Name's LOYALTY, My Lord.

---

⁹ Clayton was in fact a moderate in office, though this did not stop royal
interference in the City government (Haley, *Shaftesbury*, 559–60, 564, 568). In
the Tory reaction he helped Whigs safeguard their fortunes: Melton, 'A Rake
Refinanced'.

True *Loyalty*, without Schism or Rent,
For th'King, my Country, and The Government,
Against all those that hatch'd the late damn'd Plot
As black as Hell, and would have been as hot,
If *Providence* and *Loyalty* had not
Discover'd it; who will as long as able
Persist with Spirits indefatigable.
Except true *Concord* be amongst us bred,
We shall be *ruin'd*, as your Lordship said.
I do, my Lord, the more insist upon't,
'Cause y'have declar'd for a True *Protestant*;
For so am I, a Vessel of such Rate
As ventur'd against *Spain* in *Eighty Eight*:
According to that Church, i' th' Life and Death
Of peaceful, blessed, Queen *Elizabeth*—[A good Pause].

(p. 15)

The speaker's motto is 'Pro Rege, Lege & Grege'.[10] The combination seems Whiggish. Protestantism is associated with unity and stability, which are also the names of two of the figures attending Loyalty, the others being Equity, Verity, Fidelity, and Magnanimity. Popery and its apologists are the main threat. There is no sign of the ebbing of belief in the Popish Plot apparent in more elevated social and theatrical circles.[11] The 'good pause' after Elizabeth's name dramatically emphasizes the distance between the past security of established Protestantism and the troubled present. The silence after 'peaceful, blessed, Queen *Elizabeth*' carries the burden of omission. Where are the efforts of the present monarch to protect his people and safeguard Protestantism? The task must be assumed by 'the great and good Lord Mayor', who is the focus of the town's hopes for peace and security.

Jordan's 'Loyal Protestantism' in *London in Luster* is associated with a striving for moderation and (in the speech of Loyalty) with criticism of disturbers of the peace. Nevertheless, the show is more oppositional in its context than it might seem at first glance. The reference to Queen Elizabeth would inevitably

---

[10] For King, Law, and Flock, 'Grege' may mean 'people' or 'corporation'. Uses of 'grex' applied to humans, including a troop, band, or company.

[11] The reality of the Popish Plot was questioned in this season of 1679–80 in *The Revenge* and *The Souldier's Fortune*. In the previous season see e.g. Behn's prologue to *The Feign'd Curtizans* and Dryden's prologue to *Caesar Borgia*.

recall the Pope-burning processions organized by the Whigs, and the way in which Whig propagandists made political capital out of Elizabeth's defence of Protestantism.[12] Jordan's protestations of loyalty resemble those of Whig proponents of 'Loyal Protestantism'. Despite his appeal to a place in the hierarchical order of things, his show is oppositional *de facto*, because of its anti-popery and because of its contradictory relation to dominant cultural themes. For example, at a time when playwrights demonized the 'rascal rabble',[13] Jordan continually stresses the Lord Mayor's relationship with his people. In a passage which has no parallel in previous or subsequent years, the watching crowd become not merely spectators, but spontaneous participants in the pageantry, and part of its written record:

But in brief they were Shows to one another, the disorder'd People below in the Street was an excellent Scene of confusion to the Spectators above in the Balconies, who like waves of the Sea, did in continual agitation, roul over one another's necks like Billows in the Ocean, and the Gallantry above were as pleasurable a sight to the Spectators below, where hundreds of various defensive postures were screw'd, for prevention of the fiery Serpents and Crackers that instantly assaulted the Perukes of the Gallants, and the Merkins of the Madams.   (p. 16)

There are two things to stress here: firstly, the people are far from being passive consumers of authoritarian ideology; and secondly, Jordan's attitude is not authoritarian anyway. The people's fun and games at the expense of the gallants and madams is productive of sympathetic amusement, and we are struck by the author's generous appreciation of the populace as spectacle.

The Fourth Pageant celebrates the people at work and at play. While some demonstrate the making of cloth, others dance, sing, and tumble about, for 'the Excellencie of this Scene doth consist in confusion' (p. 17). A shepherd and shepherdess sing a duet about how 'Divine History dignifies Shepherds' (p. 18), in which kings are mocked for the humble shepherd's greater glory. In this song King David is yoked with Tamburlaine as an illustrious shepherd and gently mocked through a jocular refer-

---

[12] Popes were burnt in 1673, 1677, 1678, 1679, 1680, and 1681. See Miller, *Popery and Politics*, 182–8, and Williams, 'The Pope-Burning Processions of 1679, 1680 and 1681'.
[13] *Absalom and Achitophel*, line 579.

ence to Bathsheba. The self-pity of courtly pastoral is satirized in glib rhyme: David was happier as a shepherd than as a king, because 'His days of delight | Were trouble and fright' (p. 17). If there is a half-serious jibe at Charles here, there might also be mockery of the royalist case against Exclusion and a trivializing of arguments about natural affection in the following passage:

PASTORA. Just *Abel* 'tis said,
  A Shepherd by Trade,
  Did dye the first Martyr that ever was made.
OPILIO. And by his own Brother received his Doom,
  Although their Formation were both in a Womb.
PASTORA. This Example may teach us, if well understood,
  That there's no Infallible friendship in Blood.[14]   (p. 17)

The tone of the Fourth Pageant is light, and 'tongue in cheek': the people are allowed to 'cock a snook' at the great ones as they take their turn, and 'let off steam'. The social inclusiveness which prompts Jordan to assert the importance of the Lord Mayor in the order of things also leads him to view the people as a legitimate part of the commonwealth. It is as ideologically disturbing to Toryism to have the 'rabble' humanized as it was politically disturbing to have them on the streets.

London's Glory *(1680)*

This show is shaped by the same Protestant but cautious vision as *London in Luster*. Jordan's vision is conservative, but also Whiggish in its emphasis on the importance of Protestantism, national unity, and rule by consent, and on the social and economic importance of merchants and craftsmen. However, this year Jordan seems more sharply Whiggish, stressing more strongly the French and popish threat; though there is a warning against popular disorder.

Like Settle in *The Female Prelate* Jordan celebrates sover-

---

[14] Of course it could be argued that the reference to Cain and Abel offers a paradigm of the unnaturalness of Exclusion, but it seems to me that the tone is flippant and irreverent, serving to debunk the arguments of L'Estrange and others about the sanctity of brotherhood: see e.g. L'Estrange, *The Case Put, Concerning the Succession*, 17.

eignty, and also order in the senses of both social hierarchy and public peace. As in *London in Luster*, there is emphasis on the role of the Lord Mayor as the king's representative, 'his power abstracted from the King's' (p. 3). The Lord Mayor resembles a monarch as he processes with his retinue, dispensing largesse to the poor. All are included, from representatives of the king, City, and guilds, to poor pensioners.

The pageant also provides potent emblems of the context in which sovereignty, who sits enthroned in the first pageant, can be respected. No one is exempt from social obligation; and secondly, all in the commonwealth have their place and deserve respect. Just as no section of society was excluded from the procession, the tableau is socially unifying. Depressing pretension, the figure of Nobility bears the motto 'Virtue is the true Nobility', and Honour, in Protestant vein, the motto 'Honor solus Dei est' (Honour belongs only to God) (p. 6). Literally and symbolically central in the tableau is Integrity. This figure 'which sitteth in the middle, with both Arms extended, is in a Posture to Unite, into one Principle of Loyalty, and Fidelity, his two next Neighbours, Gentility and Commonal[t]y, and is thus adorned, as an emblem of Court, City and Country. On a long curled brown Hair, he weareth the Coronet of an Earl, for the Court, a loose Robe of Scarlet-coloured Silk for the City, under which, he wears a Close Coat of Grass-green Plush, for the Countrey' (ibid.). The social inclusiveness celebrated in the procession and first pageant is reflected in the basis of the Lord Mayor's power, elevated as he is 'by timely Succession, Unanimous Election, Popular Approbation, and Regal Consummation' (sig. A2). An unfavourable comparison with royal high-handedness may well be implicit.

Jordan's attitude to the people is carefully balanced. On the one hand he celebrates the contribution to society of the citizens and artisans who are mocked and feared in plays written for the theatre. The First Pageant is introduced by figures glorifying the Merchant Taylors and by characters such as Diligence, Industry, Ingenuity, and Success, carrying banners of the City and company as well as of the Lord Mayor and king. The speaker in the First Pageant who represents English tradition is 'an ancient *English Hero*, habited in Antick Habiliaments of War, such as were worn by the Chief Commanders: under the Conduct of

Edward the Third, when he conquered *France*, whose Name was Sir *John Haukwood*, a *Merchant-Taylor*' (p. 6). The Haukwood figure offers a compelling patriotic response to the taunts of royalist prologues against popular Francophobia:

> I flourish'd in those daies *Edward* the Third
> Did conquer *France*, with his Victorious Sword.
> He purchas'd Fame, Wealth, Honour in that Nation,
> But all the purchase now, is a new *Fashion*.
> What your Fore-Fathers gain'd by Blood and Sweat
> Is now exchang'd for a *French* Flagellet.[15]   (p. 7)

England's now threatened greatness was rooted in the blood and sweat of people like the very Merchant Taylors who are sponsoring this year's show. We are reminded that the Merchant Taylors made the robes of royalty and the nobility, which is not only a celebration of the craftsman's useful role, but also a reminder of the material basis of power. This theme is continued in the Third Pageant, which celebrates the economic and political centrality of the Merchants in colonialism and trade, and then, in a lighter vein, the antiquity and importance of the tailor's profession. Finally, Jordan extends his commitment to inclusiveness and co-operation to his own role as artist in his concluding words: 'To close up all, the Artists and Artificers, (the Builders, Painters, and Shipwright, each of them deserving Commendations) bid you all Good Night' (p. 16).

Both the patriotism of the Haukwood speech and the celebration of the people are Whiggish. However, it is a moderate, not a radical, Whiggery. There is mistrust of popular recklessness and disorder. There is no celebration of the crowd's informal revels as in *London in Luster*. Harmony, the speaker in the Second Pageant, protests, 'For Petty Niceties ye disagree, | 'Tis neither Piety, nor Policy' (p. 9). *The Protestants Exortation*, which concludes the festivities, contains the warning:

> Let us not mingle our
>   Faith with our Fancies,
> And leave the Substance for
>   Small Circumstances;
> Let love and Reason work
>   In us and on us,

---

[15] A flagellet, or flageolet, is a small wind instrument.

> Serpents in secret lurk
>   To over run us;
> Their stinging Pens are free
>   To raise Conspiracie,
> Which will be foil'd if we,
>   *Love one another.*   (p. 14)

Jordan's commitment is to the peace which enables rich merchants and civic dignitaries to thrive. The Second Pageant emphasizes this: 'a Chariot of Ovation, or peaceful Triumph' drawn by 'a Golden Lion and a Lamb' (p. 8) is flanked by the figure of Concordia, who bears the Merchant Taylors' motto: 'by Concord small things increase' (ibid.). Unanima bears the same motto and is accompanied by Pacifica, Consentania, Melodia, Benevolentia, and Harmonia. Peace and harmony are to be guaranteed by moderation: the speech of Harmony praises Sir Patience Ward's 'Moderation, Judgment, and good Parts' (p. 10) and advises him to temper vigilance with mercy and discretion. The figure of Mediocrity[16] in this pageant bears the motto '*In medio consistit virtus*', a phrase which also occurred in the First Pageant of *London in Luster*. Jordan takes the same tone in his epistle dedicatory:

And I heartily wish that the Persons which you are to govern this Year, may be no less flexible to your Commands, than your self hath been to the dictates of Religion and Reason; then I hope we shall enjoy two great Virtues, which have been great strangers to us, *Union* and *Concord*: It is your turn to be at the Helm when the turbulent Billows of the common Enemy to our Religion and Laws are in so high Commotion; But I foresee, your Prudence will so qualify your Government, with Justice, Moderation, and Impartiality, that the good shall be confirmed, and the bad converted.   (sig. A2ʳ)

The 'common enemy' here must be popery, and in the pageants themselves, the dangers of popery are far more strongly stressed than in the previous year. In the First Pageant Haukwood incites war with France. In the Second Pageant Harmony warns:

> Divide them, and destroy them, is the Pope's
> *Maxim*, and ready road to all his Hopes,
> The work of *Jesuits* . . .   (p. 10)

---

[16] Here used in a non-pejorative sense which was current in the period together with the pejorative sense (*OED*).

This is more overt than anything in the 1679 show. Whereas the banquet concluding last year's festivities was accompanied by a drinking-song, this year the dignitaries feast to the accompaniment of *The Protestants Exortation*, followed by *The Plotting Papists Litany*. The refrain of the *Exortation* is 'Love one another'. The song warns against conspiracy, but also unequivocally claims that the greatest threat to peace is from the papists, *'England's* Enemies', who are 'driving on that Plot | (They think we have forgot)' (p. 14). Division between the English and the Dutch while *'French* laugh at 'um' is lamented (ibid.). The populace is urged to 'Joyn all our forces, | Against the Romish Bands' (ibid.) and to 'let true Protestants | *Love one another'* (ibid.). Papists are beyond the pale, outside the community which it has been Jordan's concern to celebrate and perpetuate. It is notable that this year's opening procession excludes the representatives of the Duke of York who marched in 1679. The conclusion of the *Exortation* unambiguously supports the Exclusion Parliament:

> Our Unanimity
> > I' th' late Election,
> Shew'd that we well agree
> > In our Affection,
> Where all Men did consent,
> > Without resistance:
> 'Twas a good Argument
> > Of God's Assistance.
> When Men so well agree,
> And so concordant be,
> 'Tis a plain sign that we
> > Love one another.   (p. 15)

In its overall effect, and because it ends on this note, the song is almost inflammatory. In *The Plotting Papists Litany* the singers invoke various notorious pagan and Catholic plotters past and present, including defendants in the Popish Plot trials, and gleefully accept responsibility for the death of Justice Godfrey.

Jordan may well be adapting to the Whiggery of Sir Patience Ward, who was more militant than his predecessor, Clayton.[17] It is also likely that feelings in the City were running higher,

---

[17] Haley, *Shaftesbury*, 600.

following the king's interference with the Common Council, one aspect of which had been to reimpose much-resented anti-puritan oaths. The king's refusal to call Parliament, despite elections, had also caused much resentment. Jordan may just be giving his audience what they wanted to hear. It also seems likely that the hardening of the opposition emboldened people to take a firmer stand, whilst it was not yet clear that there was nothing to be gained and much to be lost by doing so. This may have been Ward's own view. He was no hothead, as is shown by his initial reluctance to call a Common Council in April 1681 to petition for a Parliament after the dissolution of the Oxford Parliament.[18] Yet he courageously defended the City's rights and privileges against royal encroachment.

Jordan stresses the importance of consent: 'Without consent, no true content' (p. 9), as the motto of Consentia in the Second Pageant puts it. He sees that 'all Men did consent' (p. 15) in the recent elections and is by implication critical of the king's refusal to rule by consent. This is brought out by his celebration of the importance of the City throughout the show and by the positive value he places on the whole community. The City corresponds to the alternative social model which Jordan is proposing in its exemplary yoking of disparate elements in useful work and mutual respect. If the qualities Jordan values—moderation, prudence, and integrity—can exist anywhere, it is in the City leadership as it balances between disastrous extremes; but like Settle's and Shadwell's, his moderation can emerge in Whiggish form as the powers in the land become prepared to sacrifice Protestantism to order.

London's Joy (1681)

Ward's replacement, Sir John Moore, was, though not a Tory, supported by and more amenable to the court.[19] We might therefore expect a more royalist tone to the festivities. In fact, this is what we do find. However, it is not the same sort of tone as that of Tory plays, being couched in terms of commitment to moderation and peace rather than 'reaction', and coupled

18 Haley, *Shaftesbury*, 638.
19 Ibid. 668.

with emphases on religious observance, colonialism, trade, and social inclusiveness. This is very different from the tone of the theatrical backlash against the moderation and outright Whiggery of the 1680–1 season which began in autumn 1681.

The ushers of the Duke of York, present in 1679 and absent in 1680, are absent again this year, but a new feature is the 'Company of Artillery-men' representing 'the Military Glory of this Nation' (p. 4). The Honourable Artillery Company, of which James was colonel, had entertained Charles and James to indicate support for the latter in October 1679.[20] The royalism is most obviously apparent towards the end, when the royal family is present, 'nothing being omitted by the City that might express, their Duty to their Majesties, and the humble Sense they had particularly of this gracious Condescension' (p. 15).[21] Accordingly, 'His Lordship beginning the several Healths of his Majesty and the Royal Family, the Hall was filled with the Shouts and Acclamations at the naming of each Health' (ibid.). Then an apparently royalist song is sung. Verse 2 may serve as an illustration:

> Here is never a Pate
> That hath Plots against State,
>   All are pure, and Ingeniously Loyal,
> For it never can be
> That he, or thee, or me,
> Can be righteous, that is not Royal.   (p. 15)

Verse 3 begins, 'Divisions are base, | And of Lucifer's race; | Civil Wars from the bottom of Hell come.' In context this seems royalist, but it is also in accordance with the assertion in the previous year's show that it is not the city which is the source of the nation's troubles.

The second chorus stresses the fact that the Lord Mayor is the king's lieutenant, a point which is also stressed in Jordan's

---

[20] Hutton, *Charles the Second*, 383–4; Kenyon, *The Popish Plot*, 210.
[21] The king had attended in previous years, but this year the feast at the Guildhall which concluded the show was dignified by 'the sacred Presence of the King and Queen, Prince, Arch-Bishop of Canterbury, and all the other bishops (at this time in London,) all the Resident Embassadors and Envoys, all the Lords of the Privy-Council, all the Principal Officers of State, all the Judges and Serjeants at Law, with their Ladies' (p. 15).

account of the oath-taking (p. 3), in the St Anthony's speech in the First Scene, and in the last verse of the song in the Third Pageant.[22] Yet this does more than emphasize the Lord Mayor's loyalty; it reminds us that the king needs the city. The only solution to the nation's ills is a socially inclusive one. The point is brought out more clearly in the final chorus, and especially in the climactic sentence:

> This Land and this Town have no cause to despair,
> No Nation can tell us how happy we are;
> When each Person's fixt in his Judicial Chair,
> At White-hall the King, and at Guild-hall the Mayor,
> > Then let all Joy and Honour preserve, with renown,
> > The City, the Country, the Court and the Crown.

> (p. 16)

Royalism in the drama tends to find articulation through grafting satire of Whigs on to satire of citizens as a class, and denigrating the common people as a dangerous mob. Jordan stresses the role of the whole city in his festivities, from civic dignitaries and guildsmen to poor pensioners and children.[23] For Jordan the people are loyal, turning out in 'most incredible numbers' to greet the king and queen 'with universal Joy and Acclamations' (ibid.).

The show also differs from royalist plays in coupling loyalty with religious observance. Plays such as *Sir Barnaby Whigg* satirize Whig concern with true Protestantism. Whiggery is associated with dissent and tarred with the brush of sanctimonious hypocrisy. The last verse of Jordan's song illustrates the difference in outlook:

> May this Years Mayoralty so happy prove,
> That ye may wallow in each others Love;
> > And every Subject his Endeavours bring

---

[22] In this year's show there is a 'First Scene' (p. 4) similar to the First Pageant in previous years, a 'Second Scene' (p. 8), and a third 'pleasant Pageant' (p. 11).

[23] Civic plurality and unity are celebrated in the initial procession, which includes as usual king's ushers, civic dignitaries, guildsmen, doctors of divinity, and poor pensioners, 'In amicable measure, more like Friends | Fill'd with one Joy' (p. 2). The children who sit in the pageants are mentioned at the end, as Jordan tells us, with his characteristic care and attention to detail, that they will also get refreshment. As in previous years, unity is suggested by the fact that the allegorical figures in the various pageants carry banners of the king, City, and sponsoring company (this year the grocers).

> To the Fear of God and Honour of the King.
> May Trade increase with Piety and Pity,
> (For Traffick is the Sinews of the City.)
> That Fort shall hold out in despite of all weather,
> Where Courage and Conscience are coupl'd together.
>
> (ibid.)

Gone this year, of course, are all overt references to plotting papists. Yet the treatment of religious themes in the show works against ultra-royalism. In St Anthony's speech in the First Scene (pp. 7–8) Moore is praised as the king's loyal representative, but warned against excess: 'Equity brings true Peace, and Peace good Trading.' Moreover, 'We hope the Civil, not the Souldiers Sword, I Shall moderate all feud.' The warning against excessive 'reaction' is couched in terms of the magistrate's holding power in trust, not only for the king, but also for the electorate and for God:

> Y'are one whom all good Citizens Embrace,
> And therefore Gratitude, and what is Just,
> May move you to be true unto your Trust,
> Least God do lay your Honour in the Dust.

The speech of Diogenes in the Second Scene (pp. 9–10) has a similar ambivalence. Diogenes represents 'severity' (p. 9) and speaks in a 'humorous manner'. His sharpness appears to be used both to reflect the current mood of reaction and to warn against it. On the one hand Moore is warned, 'Be Loyal to your Prince, Rebellion's Name, I Like Witchcraft, will destroy both Soul and Fame' and 'Suppress Pamphlet-Contentions, for they are I The Serpentary Seeds of Civil War.' Yet there is also an attack on whores and on court corruption, in accordance with the views of dissenters, and apprentices who were notorious for rioting against brothels:

> Punish all Harlots that are in your reach,
> They Corrupt Prentizes, and bring Disasters
> . . . I can not gild their Crime, a Whore's a Whore;
> Tho ne'r so brave, and count'nanc'd by bad Times,
> Their Grandeur doth not mitigate their Crimes.

There is a reference to the need to suppress 'Privy Conspiracies' and 'Seditious Cabals', for 'The Law doth call them

Conjurations, which | Must needs imply a Plotter is a Witch.'
This recalls the terms in which popish plotters are described by
Whig playwrights and pamphleteers; it could certainly refer
both to popish and to Whig 'plotters'. Furthermore, because
Diogenes is a 'humours' character, he can say that he is sent
to warn, rather than to congratulate. The warning is not only to
be loyal, but to remember that 'There is a See-existent Power
that will | For all your Deeds make you Accomptable.' So
although the surface texture of the speech is almost aggressively
royalist, the emphasis once again is on responsible and godly
government. There is certainly no support for unrestrained Tory
backlash.

There is an equally striking mixture in the First Scene. On
the one hand the emphasis on social inclusiveness recalls previous shows and Whig propagandists' reference to the people's
welfare and the well-being of the whole commonwealth and
differs from the élitism of Tory drama. On the other hand,
inclusiveness overrides national and religious boundaries in a
way which would have been obnoxious to patriots and true
Protestants. In a 'Royal Theatre' we see: 'several Heroic and
victorious persons of Honour, pertinently representing the
Seven Champions of Christendom, (viz.) St. George for England, St. Andrew for Scotland, St. Denis for France, St. Patric for
Ireland, St. David for Wales, St. James for Spain, St. Anthony
for Italy; with five beautiful Ladies, which in proper order
personate the five Senses, Seeing, Hearing, Tasting, Feeling,
Smelling' (p. 5). The suggestion of sensuality, coupled with the
mythical obfuscation of Whig concerns about religion and foreign policy, suggest an attempt to appeal to the court faction.
Yet this is to some extent offset by even broader frames of
reference. Jordan's allegorical representation of the forces centred on London is much more comprehensive geographically,
historically, intellectually, and scientifically than ever before. In
the first scene he has a camel, the grocer's emblem, with a
'young Negro' (p. 4) on its back, representing 'Liberality',
flanked by virgins representing Plenty and Wholesome. This
tableau implicitly represents colonialism. Explicitly, as St
Anthony explains, it shows: 'The Means and Ends of righteous
Government. Industry is the Means, Plenty the Event' (p. 7). The
tableau in the second scene (pp. 9–10) associates the city not

only, as in previous years, with a range of virtues and qualities, but also with architecture, philosophy, science, and the natural world: two stages are surmounted by 'Two Golden Gryphons, the Supporters to the Arms of the worshipfull company of Grocers, on whose backs are mounted Two European Native pretty Boyes, representing Jucundity and Utility'. On two stages are eight figures: 'Power, Prudence, Fate, Fame, Fertility, Integrity, Agility, and Alacrity'. Between the stages is 'another delightful and magnificent Fabrick, according to the Composit Order, which participateth of all the four Orders of Architecture', called 'the Academy of Sciences', sitting on which are Aristotle, Plato, Socrates, Diogenes, and a learned woman, Diotima, 'so famous in philosophy, that Plato and Socrates came to hear her Lectures'. Also there are the four elements, 'Fire, Air, Earth and Water' and 'the Four Complections, viz. Sanguine, Choler, Phlegm and Melancholy', 'personated by eight Virgin Ladies'.

It seems as if Jordan is taking refuge from politics in a display of general knowledge, finding fixity by moving from current sources of pain and insecurity to the gamut of seventeenth-century scholarship. More precisely, present divisions are subsumed in a vision of world unity. This is given more explicit and topical expression in the Third Pageant, which takes place in 'an Indian Garden of Spices' (p. 11) presided over by Fructifera, who makes a speech celebrating colonialism. This is the climactic vision of the show: 'London's the Dining-Room of Christendom.' Jolly black natives then sing and dance: 'We are Jolly Planters that live in the East, | And furnish the World with Delights when they Feast.' The song celebrates peace and prosperity, transforming the reality of colonial exploitation into a happy and spontaneous yielding up of an Indian surplus to merchants like Moore himself, for the greater glory of England's king and the city of London. There are two points to be made here. The first is that in this period a commitment to colonialism was Whiggish rather than Tory.[24] The second is that such commitment links this show thematically with the previous

[24] The foreign policy of the late Stuart monarchy tended to be pacifist rather than imperialist, and the politician most keenly committed to colonialism in this period was Shaftesbury (Haley, *Shaftesbury*, 227, 262–4). Cf. also Brenner, *Merchants and Revolution*.

year's and seems by its fervour to work against and render subordinate more topical political references which are royalist this year.

Jordan concludes on a note which tends to normalize the situation, rather than responding to it with the near-hysteria of some playwrights. He places this year's show in line with those of previous years: 'Thus to their Honours, the Company of Grocers have with indefatigable Industry and Affection, five times been at the Charge of such Triumphs, since the happy Restauration of his Majesty' (p. 16). The Lord Mayor's Show itself becomes an act of loyalty, an annual celebration on Charles's behalf of the spirit of his reign. Contrary to the spirit of Toryism which was rampant in the theatres, Jordan locates loyalty, continuity, and stability in the City and in civic culture.

The Lord Mayor's Show of 1682

Tory Lord Mayor Sir William Pritchard was elected after electoral manipulation and bitter controversy. Perhaps unsurprisingly, the show at his inauguration is minimal, and without a title. Luttrell reported that 'There was little or no show by land.'[25] Considerations of public order as well as ideology must have dictated the necessity of muting the customary festivities this year.[26] The show is attributed to Jordan by *The Short Title Catalogue* and *The London Stage*, but I doubt whether he was the sole author. The absence of his name on the title-page is unusual and might suggest that if he was involved at all, he did not wish to take responsibility for the entire content.[27] The third verse of the opening song advises the Lord Mayor to 'proceed with vigour', which seems unlike Jordan and contrasts with the caution and moderation which is a consistent theme of his, whatever else may vary.

The title-page stresses loyalty: 'The Lord Mayor's Show: Being A Description At The Inauguration *Of the truly Loyal and Right Honourable* Sir William Prichard (*sic*), Kt. . . . With several new Loyal *Songs* and *Catches*'. The opening song is a

---

[25] Cited in Van Lennep *et al.* (eds.), *London Stage*, i. 315.
[26] Jordan was to have shows in 1683 and 1684.
[27] The publisher is Burnet, not Playford as in previous years.

virulently Tory and reaction piece, and gives a partisan account
of the situation in the city:

> LONDON is chang'd, and the Times are turn'd;
> The *Mayor* and *Sheriffs* are brave and true:
> Poor *Whigs*! their Tricks and their Plots are scorn'd;
> The Laws shall be free, and the King have his due.
> What a noise and a din has here bin of late,
> To hinder your Choice with idle debate?
> Yet who can think the *Whigs* so great,
> That only the *Whigs* can govern the State?
>
> Then welcome Great *Monarch*, welcome again,
> The real Joy of all true hearts;
> This day shall shew how great you reign
> In spite of Faction's busie Arts.
> Health to your Princely Brother too,
> As dear to Us, as dear to You;
> Let him appear, and *Whigs* look blew,
> That others can better govern the State.

(sig. A1ᵛ)

References in the second and third verses suggest that the king
and Duke of York were present at the Mayor's inauguration.
The fact that there is no real show 'by land' suggests a very
different audience than in previous years. The reference to
choice in verse 1 seems somewhat problematic, since Pritchard
had been elected with 2,233 votes, as against the Whig candi-
dates, Gold and Cornish, who obtained 2,289 and 2,258 respectively: one wonders what the effect on public order might have
been if the song had been sung more publicly.[28]

The account of the procession is much as usual, except that
representatives (trumpeters) of the Duke of York are restored
alongside those of the king, City, and (Merchant Taylors') company, having been excluded in 1680 and 1681. The queen, who
had been the target of Popish Plot accusations and of proposals
that she be put aside, is also represented in the banners carried
(p. 2) and the healths drunk (p. 6). The description of the
procession differs from before in that prose replaces Jordan's
usual triumphal verse, and that the former sense of pride and joy

---

[28] For an account of Tory electoral sharp practice here and in the Sheriffs'
elections, see Haley, *Shaftesbury*, 699–704, *Poems on Affairs of State*, iii. 297–316,
and the discussion of Crowne's *City Politiques* in Ch. 3.

is lacking. Since there are no pageants, the procession is followed by the 'Loyal Songs' (p. 4) by which the Lord Mayor is entertained at dinner. However, the first of these, 'Let the Traytors Plot on', is a Loyal Protestant song, repeated from a previous year: 'And he that dares hope to change King for a Pope, | Let him dye, whilst *Caesar* lives long' (ibid.). The second song is anti-Whig, but also anti-papist, and perhaps the anti-popery is stronger since it merits two mentions to anti-Whiggery's one (p. 5). The third song, described as a 'new Song, which is set to an excellent Tune by Mr. *Pursell*', is a Tory reaction piece:

> Since the DUKE is return'd we'le slight all the Whigs,
> And let them be hang'd for Politick Prigs;
>   Both *Presbyter Jack* and all the old Crew,
>   That lately design'd *forty one* to renew:
> Make room for the Men that never deny'd
> To God save the *King*, and *Duke* they reply'd;
>   Whose Loyalty ever was fixt with that zeal,
>   Of rooting out Schism and proud Common-weal:
> Then bring up a Bottle each Man in his place,
> 'Tis a health to the DUKE, Boy give me my Measure,
> The fuller the Glass is, the greater the Pleasure.
>
> (ibid.)

A final drinking-song celebrates royalism and quietism:

> Come here's to the Man that lives quiet
>   And follows his own occupation;
> That sawcily dares not to fly at
>   The settled Estate of the Nation.
>
> That never in Faction took pleasure,
>   Nor sign'd a seditious Petition;
> Whose Religion no Int'rest does measure,
>   Whose heart ne're committed Misprision.
>
> But boldly dares own himself Loyal
>   To every Phanatical Rumper;
> And to all of the family Royal,
>   Most freely will take off his Bumper.   (p. 6)

It is not clear who wrote the Tory reaction songs, which are markedly different in tone and content to the Loyal Protestant ones from previous years. The fact that the latter are included in what is otherwise a sycophantically Tory show may suggest that the court needed to present itself as anti-papist in order to work with moderates; or that some sop was needed to palliate the imposition of government policy on the City by dubious means; or perhaps that Toryism wants to present itself as compatible with defence of Protestantism in order to marginalize the Whigs, grafting itself on to existing City traditions through the comparatively uninflammatory medium of drinking-songs sung to people who are in the process of satisfying their appetite. It seems significant, however, that the triumph of Toryism in the medium of the Lord Mayor's Shows could only take place through suppression of the pageantry which made them dramatically interesting and the socially inclusive spectacle which made them politically significant.

Jordan's shows thus move with the times, paralleling shifts in the drama of the theatres. However, there is a stable centre which is closer to Whiggish plays than Tory ones. Constant values are moderation and peace, coupled with Protestantism, patriotism, the promotion of trade, and a socially inclusive vision in which the city and its government have an important role in the nation. Jordan reverses the satire of the city which is central to Toryism.

Appendix: Dating

Except in certain specified cases, I have followed the usual sources: *The London Stage*, as amended by Milhous and Hume, 'Dating Play Premières from Publication Data', and Danchin, *Prologues and Epilogues of the Restoration*. In some cases I have been able to speculate about première dates from internal evidence. I have also a point to add to the observations of Milhous and Hume about erratic publication and a longer gap between première and publication in the Exclusion Crisis: there are several examples of royalist or Tory plays being rushed into print very fast, presumably for political reasons.

1678–1679

Oedipus	September 1678 (see below)
The Triumphs of London	29 October 1678
The Destruction of Troy	Autumn before 26 November
The Tragedy of Sertorius	Early 1679
The Feign'd Curtizans	Early 1679
Troilus and Cressida	Early 1679
The Ambitious Statesman	Spring 1679
Caesar Borgia	May 1679 (see below)
The Massacre of Paris	Not acted until 1689. Written summer 1679? (see below)
Titus Andronicus	Autumn 1679? (see below).

PROBLEM CASES

Oedipus A première date at the beginning of the 1678–9 season is suggested by references in the prologue to the victory at Mons on 17 August 1678 and to the piece as 'The first Play bury'd since the Wollen Act'. On this basis Wilson, in 'Six Restoration Play Dates' (222), and the editors of *The London Stage* suggest that the play might have been the first in the season, in September 1678. Wilson shows that supposed references to Guy Fawkes' night are illusory, so that there are no grounds for an earlier suggestion of a November date. There are no grounds for Novak's suggestion of November (headnote to the play, in

Works, xiii), based upon the play's apparent relevance to the Popish Plot scare (cf. Winn, *John Dryden and his World*, 314, 591 n. 51): the reference in the epilogue to the 'burning of a *Pope*' could refer to the Pope-burnings of 1673 and 1677, or possibly to plans which were afoot in the early autumn to organize a re-enactment of the success of the previous year. The satire of ambition in the character of Creon, possibly referable to Shaftesbury, could date from any time after the latter's move into opposition in 1673–4. The government had been sufficiently worried to imprison him in 1677. He was released in February 1678, presumably shortly before the composition of *Oedipus*. Dryden had attacked Shaftesbury in the Dedications to *Aureng-Zebe* (1676) and *All For Love* (1678). Fear of popery and plots had been a feature of the political situation throughout the 1670s.[1] Moreover, even if we consider only the furore of autumn 1678, we find that this had begun by September. The prime movers of the Popish Plot scare, Oates and Tonge, were meeting in August. They met the king on 13 August and laid before him forty-three articles, including information about a supposed plot to assassinate Charles involving the queen and her physician. Oates made his deposition to the magistrate Godfrey on 6 September. So the September date does not preclude pointed political relevance.

Caesar Borgia The editors of Lee's *Works* are similarly led astray by a reference in the epilogue to burning 'the Pope's Effigies', which they take as a reference to the Pope-burning procession of November 1679. This ignores the fact the popes were burnt in 1673, 1677, and 1678. The play was entered in the *Term Catalogues* in November 1679, and both *The London Stage* (276–7) and Danchin (*Prologues and Epilogues*, vol. ii, pt. 1, p. 169) argue plausibly for a first performance in May. A reference in the epilogue to Father Lewis suggests that the play was performed between his conviction in March and execution in August.

The Massacre of Paris The play was not acted until 1689 or published until 1690. We know that Lee used parts of it in *The Duke of Guise* (1682). Lee's editors think the play was composed 'in the spring of 1679 at the very height of the excitement raging over the Plot and the possibility of massacre' (*Works*, ii. 3). Hume thinks the play may have been written in the spring or summer of 1681.[2] He argues that there are no other instances of major censorship prior to the spate of bannings in late autumn, 1680. However this ignores the difficulties with *Caesar Borgia* (*Rome's Follies*, sig. A3^{r–v}). Hume argues that there

---

[1] Haley, *Shaftesbury*, ch. 17 on fear of popery and politics in 1674 is essential reading in this context.

[2] Hume, 'The Satiric Design of Nat. Lee's *The Princess of Cleve*', 119–23.

is no reason why *The Massacre* should have been singled out as against, for example, Settle's *The Female Prelate*; but, as I argued in Chapter 8, *The Massacre* may be construed as containing criticism of the monarchy, whereas Settle cunningly uses monarchical arguments through the mouth of his noble hero against the Roman Church. Hume suggests that, following the banning of *Lucius Junius Brutus* in December 1680, 'Lee decided to write a propaganda piece whose "loyalty" could not be called in question, but found to his mortification that the French ambassador had enough influence to get the piece stopped' (120). However, such a harmless interpretation of the play is untenable, and it can be argued on the basis of internal evidence that *The Massacre* is a more 'oppositional' play than *Caesar Borgia* (see Chapter 8). Moreover, one could argue that the caution against royal intemperance in *The Massacre* places it later in 1679, when the reaction to the opposition's exploitation of the Popish Plot scare really gained ground. I think the play was probably intended for performance either at the end of this season or at the beginning of the next. All these arguments are extremely speculative, but my view that 1679 is a more likely date than 1681 is shared by Antony Hammond.[3]

Titus Andronicus   The preface to the first edition of 1687 states that the play 'first appear'd upon the Stage, at the beginning of the pretended Popish Plot' (sig. A2ʳ). On this basis it is tentatively assigned to the 1678–9 season by *The London Stage*. However, some slender internal evidence might suggest that it appeared later in 1679, after Monmouth's exile to Holland in September. Ravenscroft's alteration of Shakespeare includes changes in the character of the banished Lucius which may refer to Monmouth. The banishment is foregrounded by reordering and by added speeches such as the moving farewells at the end of Act 4. Instead of leading an army of Goths against his countrymen, Lucius leads a popular uprising with the help of Titus' former legions. Like Charles's 'Loyal Protestant' critics, Lucius and his followers stand opposed to a corrupt ruler and his court.

1679–1680

The Young King	Late September or early October 1679 (see below)
The Woman-Captain	September 1679
The Virtuous Wife	September or October 1679
Caius Marius	October 1679.

---

[3] Hammond, 'The "Greatest Action": Lee's *Lucius Junius Brutus*', 185 n. 11.

The order and proximity of the three plays seems certain: there is a reference in the prologue to D'Urfey's play to Gripe, a character in *The Woman-Captain*,[4] while Mrs Barry, speaking the epilogue to Otway's play, refers to her part in Shadwell's: '*For t'other day I was a Captain too.*'

The Muse of Newmarket	September or October 1679
London in Luster	29 October 1679.
The Loyal General	Early December 1679[5]
The Loving Enemies	January 1680
The Misery of Civil-War	January 1680 (see below)
The Orphan	Late February or early March 1680
Fools Have Fortune	Early February?[6]
The Conspiracy	Late Febrary or early March 1680
The Revenge	Spring 1680
Thyestes	Spring or Summer 1680
The Female Prelate	31 May 1680
The Souldier's Fortune	June 1680
The Coronation of Queen Elizabeth	August 1680.

PROBLEM CASES

The Young King The play was entered in the *Term Catalogues* in November 1682 and published in 1683. However, the epilogue is said to be spoken 'at his Royal | Highness's second Exile in *Flanders*', which would indicate a first performance between 24 September and 14 October 1679. The editors of *The London Stage* state that 'It may have been first acted as early as March 1679, when the political flights of the Duke of York were also a matter of public concern' (281). However, the play's theme is Exclusion, which makes the later date seem more likely. In Parliament 'The case for Exclusion was first openly developed on 11 May [1679].'[7] Behn states in her epistle dedicatory that this was her first play. If so, we might speculate that its performance at this time was due to its potential topicality, and that Behn might perhaps have

---

[4] As Danchin points out, *Prologues and Epilogues*, vol. ii, pt. i, p. 191.
[5] Dryden, who wrote the prologue, was beaten up on 18 Dec. Haley, 'John Dryden: Protestant in Masquerade?', suggests the prologue may have led to the beating, a suggestion I made, coincidentally, in my Ph.D. dissertation.
[6] Milhous and Hume, 'The Prologue and Epilogue for *Fools Have Fortune*'.
[7] Jones, *Country and Court*, 208.

reworked the piece (which does not bear signs of immaturity), enhancing topicality in the process.

The Misery of Civil-War   The play was entered in the *Term Catalogues* in May 1680. *The London Stage* suggests a première no later than February, since Luttrell bought a copy on 22 March (283). Milhous and Hume argue, 'this sets the première too close to publication for this year. A date in November, December, or early January is most likely' (391). However, there is no reason why this play should precede *The Loving Enemies*, which was also entered in the *Term Catalogues* in May, and probably premièred in January.[8] Indeed it seems conceivable that a highly topical royalist play might have been rushed into print faster than a light comedy by a beginner. Moreover, there does not seem always to have been a longer than average gap between première and publication at this time. *The Orphan* was entered in the *Term Catalogues* at the same time as *The Misery of Civil-War*, but Pepys saw it on 6 March, calling it a 'New Play'.[9] The prologue refers to James's return from Scotland on 24 February. A late February or early March première for *The Orphan* seems likely, and this makes a January première for *The Misery of Civil-War* seem perfectly plausible. The gap between performance and publication was clearly erratic. *The Conspiracy*, entered in the *Term Catalogues* in May 1680, was performed, according to the prologue, in Lent, which fell between 25 February and 3 April 1680. Thus a March première, two months before publication, is likely. Both *The Conspiracy* and *The Misery of Civil-War* were fervently royalist pieces which may have been published quickly because they were politically useful to the authorities. *Thyestes* was not entered in the *Term Catalogues* until May 1681. Wilson ('Six Restoration Play-Dates', 222) has argued that a reference in the prologue to the return of young actors from Scotland in February places the première during or near to March 1680. Yet, this was the first play to be performed by the ailing King's Company after a gap of several months. The prologue discusses the theatre's misfortunes and the reference to the actors' exodus and return is part of this: it could well be something which has occurred within recent months, not necessarily the previous month. No one would have had any previous opportunity to mention it, since the theatre had been dark. Internal evidence suggests a date later in the spring or summer, as the play is politically transitional between the vehement Toryism of *The Misery of Civil-War* and the anti-popish *Henry the Sixth*, which is typical of the 1680–1 season.

---

[8] The prologue alludes to the attack on Dryden as to a recent event, and to the Whig petitioning of Dec. and Jan.

[9] Van Lennep *et al.* (eds.), *The London Stage*, 285.

1680–1681

Fatal Love	September 1680 (see below)
Theodosius	September 1680 (see below)
The Spanish Fryar	October 1680
London's Glory	29 October 1680
Lucius Junius Brutus	8 December 1680
Richard II	December 1680 or January 1681 (see below)
The History of King Lear	January 1681? (see below)
The Second Part of The Rover	January 1681
Henry the Sixth	January–March 1680
Tamerlane the Great	Early 1680 before 19 March
The Lancashire Witches	Spring or early summer 1680
The Unhappy Favourite	May 1681
The False Count	Summer 1681 (see below)
The Injur'd Princess	? (see below).

PROBLEM CASES

Fatal Love and *Theodosius*   Milhous and Hume consider it quite possible that *Fatal Love*, entered in the *Term Catalogues* in November 1680, was first performed in early summer rather than in September as suggested in *The London Stage* (391). They put forward a similar speculation in relation to *Theodosius*, also entered in the *Term Catalogues* in November and listed in *The London Stage* under September. Danchin has 'September 1680; or perhaps earlier?' for *Fatal Love* and 'September 1680, or earlier' for *Theodosius*. However, an early summer date for Settle's *Fatal Love* might place it rather soon after his *Female Prelate*, which enjoyed a successful run in London in June and was probably performed by the King's Company when they were in Oxford in July. The evidence available suggests that the ailing King's Company was not putting on as many new plays as the Duke's at this time.

Richard the Second and *The History of King Lear*   *Richard the Second* was banned on 14 December and Tate's prefatory epistle states that it was acted twice, but it is not clear whether this refers to performances in December or to the attempt to revive the play in January under the title *The Sicilian Usurper*. However, it seems clear that the première was in December or January. *Lear* was entered in the *Term Catalogues* in May 1681. Spencer (in *Five Restoration Adaptations of Shakespeare*) suggests a première between March and October 1680, but Milhous and Hume follow Black's 'An Augustan Stage-

History: Nahum Tate's *King Lear*' in assigning a date of late autumn 1680 or early January 1681. There is a reference in the epilogue to fighting at Tangier which took place at this time. Tate states in his preface to *Richard the Second* that *Lear* was written first, but Black argues that *Lear* was performed after *Richard the Second*: 'Tate seems to be so naive in his choice and presentation of *Richard II* . . . and so dextrous about avoiding offence in *King Lear* that there is some reason to believe that he learned caution from the banning of the former play and perhaps was able to make some emendations to his *King Lear* before it was staged' (37). This seems correct in principle (though it may overstate the 'inoffensiveness' of *Lear*: see Chapter 7).

The False Count This play should, in my view, be assigned to the end of the season. The prologue refers to Whig ascendancy, and facetiously affects conversion to Whiggery. This suggests the 1680–1 season, before the Tory reaction of 1681–2. The play itself is strikingly different in tone to Behn's Tory reaction piece *The Round-heads* (December 1682?), being light and comparatively apolitical. Luttrell's copy is dated December, leading Milhous and Hume to the view that 'October is the latest likely première date—and even then the lapse is very short' (394). Danchin points out that the reference to an ignoramus jury in the prologue need not refer to the famous decision in Shaftesbury's trial in November. There had been an ignoramus verdict in the first trial of Stephen College in July.

The Injur'd Princess D'Urfey's adaptation of Shakespeare's *Cymbeline* is a perplexing case. It was entered in the *Term Catalogues* in May 1682, so, on the basis of the usual lapse between première and publication, Milhous and Hume suggest a possible première date of February or March in that year.[10] However, there is such a notable difference between this play and the author's Tory pieces *Sir Barnaby Whigg* and *The Royalist* that I can only assume that the play was composed, at least, at the end of this season, rather than in the Tory reaction period to which *The Royalist* belongs. There are some similarities with Tate's *Lear*.

Thus, there are royalist elements: Cymbeline is given more dignity at the end, and certain alterations stress that he must be served with loyalty, whatever his behaviour. After the queen's death, 'the old King | Comes forward with his Power' (4. 4. p. 43). D'Urfey has Bellarius and the princes assert their determination to fight for 'the King's Party' against the Romans in an added loyal speech, and omits the statement

---

[10] The epilogue, which states that 'this Play was writ nine years ago', pre-dates the play and 'was printed in 1690 to the Earl of Orrery's *Mr. Anthony* (acted 1669) . . . and also in C[ovent] G[arden] D[rolery] 1672' (Danchin, *Prologues and Epilogues*, vol. ii, pt. 1, p. 375). The epilogue of 1669 does not contain the line about the play being written nine years ago, but the 1672 version does.

of Shakespeare's Belarius that 'the King | Hath not deserved my service nor your loves' (4. 4. 24–5). He also cuts the assertion of Palladore–Guiderius that it is 'Better to cease to be' (line 31) than to be excluded from the action, and Arverigus' shame at being 'So long a poor unknown' (line 43). Despite the fact that the speakers' royal blood excuses their urge to be politically involved, it is possible that such statements carried a politically improper suggestion that it was unnatural for men to be inactive in the affairs of the realm: the royalist assumption is that it is natural for men to be 'quiet'.

However, there are significant contradictions.The theme of banishment and exclusion is heightened, with an ultimate message of reconciliation; but so is the theme of royal folly and misrule. This duality is apparent in the play's opening lines, as Pisanio exclaims, 'What Commission from the King to seize and banish my dearest Friend! Who would be good or vertuous if this be the reward! Can it be true?—What banish'd!' (1. 1. p. 1).[11] Added speeches (e.g. in 3. 3) bring out the fact that the banished heir to the throne is fierce and vengeful, which could have a topical resonance embarrassing to James. There is a potential for topical allusion in the king's susceptibility to female influence and (bad) advice. The conclusion that 'The Countrey is not savage but the Court' (4. 2. p. 37) seems justified. In the treacherous Shattilion Shakespeare's Jachimo becomes a Frenchman and 'a most methodical Courtier' (4. 4. p. 43). Courtly libertinism is brought into question both by the negative depiction of Cloten's attempts to be a rake[12] and by the tasteless and cynical discussion of women and wifely virtue, and the nearly disastrous wager which follows. Shattilion, stealing into Eugenia's chamber, likens himself to 'Lewd Tarquin' (2. 4. p. 20).[13] Finally, in opposition to the aristocratic and anti-populist values of Tory drama, Ursaces (Shakespeare's Posthumous) is valued despite being 'mechanick' and 'plebeian' (1. 1. pp. 2, 5). The title of the play at the head of each page of the first edition text is given as The Unequal Match; or, The Fatal Wager, which emphasizes the class issue, and it is made clear that Ursaces is a worthy heir to the throne despite his low birth.

[11] Royal culpability and ineptitude seem the greater as we are immediately in the presence of the injured parties themselves. Shakespeare's two gentlemen discuss the affair in a rather more detached way.

[12] Cloten is more like Shadwell's wolfish Don John in The Libertine or Lee's Nemours in The Princess of Cleve than like the appealing rakes of Tory comedy. Pisanio is given a daughter, so that Cloten can threaten to 'ravish her before his face' (4. 3. p. 39).

[13] Shakespeare has 'Our Tarquin' (2. 2. 12). For the anti-Stuart resonance of references to Tarquin, see my ' "Partial Tyrants" and "Freeborn People" in Lucius Junius Brutus', 463–4.

Above all, the theme of banishment and exclusion resolves itself into a warning against bad kingship and bad fatherhood. Alterations to Shakespeare draw out the fact that Cymbeline is a usually merciful king who is acting with undue severity (2. 1. pp. 11–12). The king's response is 'Paternal Love and Mildness I disclaim' (2. 1. p. 11). Cymbeline banishes a loyal daughter.[14] He also unjustly banishes a baseborn 'son' (Ursaces), which is what Whigs claimed Charles II did in the case of Monmouth. Admittedly the two young princes are 'excluded' by the vengeful action of Bellarius, but Bellarius is an old soldier who has himself been unjustly banished. Like the old cavaliers, his loyal service has received no reward. Ursaces is also a loyal servant of the king whose loyalty is misrecognized, undervalued, and unrewarded. D'Urfey gives him a parting loyal speech after his banishment (1. 1. p. 3). Pisanio is also a loyal character, not afraid of giving the king much-needed, though unheeded, good advice. Both Ursaces and Pisanio are warrior heroes who fight bravely for king and country. Pisanio has all the familiar and likeable characteristics both of the 'bluff soldier' character, and of the hero's friend. Ultimately, like Gloster in Shakespeare's *King Lear*, he has his eyes put out (by Cloten), and becomes the focus of tragic sympathy. The cumulative effect of all this is anti-patriarchal: the focus is on misgovernment and the king's inability to discern and protect. Misuse of power is subject to scrutiny and correction in the macrocosm of the state and in the microcosm of the family.[15]

The themes of bad fatherhood and loyalty to vitiated kingship resonate uncomfortably for Toryism. Moreover, it does seem significant that the direction of Cymbeline's energy is in defiance against the combined 'Powers of *Rome* and *Gaul*' (5. 1. p. 46). There seems to be a Whiggish resonance to some of D'Urfey's added passages: the king urges his troops to 'fight for Liberty, *Cymbeline* and *Britain*' (ibid.). The voluntary submission to Rome at the end is omitted. Bellarius cries, 'haughty *Rome* must bow | To th' *British* Power' (5. 2. p. 48).[16]

---

[14] D'Urfey transforms Shakespeare's Imogen into Eugenia, a typical Restoration heroine with 'panting heart' (1. 1. p. 3) and 'pale and pining looks' (4. 2. p. 35): see Marsden, 'Pathos and Passivity'. This makes her seem pitiable, and makes the bad father-king more culpable.

[15] Jean Marsden in 'Pathos and Passivity' is right to stress Eugenia's wifely subordination, but it is also important to note Ursaces' profound guilt and willingness to be guided in the future by his wife, whom he calls 'my better genius' (5. 3. p. 53).

[16] The division between 5. 1 and 5. 2 is not marked. 5. 3 begins on p. 51. I have taken 5. 2 to begin at the top of p. 48. Shattilion is on-stage with Eugenia just before this, and shortly afterwards re-enters disguised and is convinced by Ursaces that Eugenia is dead. A scene break here would allow a sense of time having passed and make the transition more plausible.

The Frenchman, Shatillion, is a snarling machiavellian to the end, unlike Shakespeare's Jachimo, whose guilt about Imogen impedes his courage. Like Shadwell's Tegue in *The Lancashire Witches*, going cheerfully to the gallows, Shattilion tells Ursaces: 'I'me of a Religion, Sir, that tells me, | My life's not in your power, if taken nobly' (ibid.).

1681–1682

Sir Barnaby Whigg	October 1681 (see below)
The London Cuckolds	October 1681
London's Joy	29 October 1681
Rome's Follies	Autumn 1681 (see below)
Mr. Turbulent	Late November 1681? (see below)
The Round-heads	December 1681
The Ingratitude of a Common-wealth	December 1681
The Royalist	23 January 1682
The Loyal Brother	Early Febraruy 1682
Venice Preserv'd	9 February 1682
The Heir of Morocco	11 March 1682
Vertue Betray'd	Late March 1682
The City Heiress	Late April or early May 1682
Romulus and Hersilia	Early August 1682.[17]

PROBLEM CASES

Sir Barnaby Whigg The play was listed in the *Term Catalogues* in November 1681. *The London Stage* suggests a première in late October 1681, soon after the reopening of the Theatre Royal, where it was performed. Milhous and Hume say 'Either the play was published extraordinarily fast, or it should be dated early summer 1681 . . . from publication lapse usual at this time, a production at the end of the previous season seems likely' (392). However, Danchin makes an argument which I find convincing: 'the Ms. of the second prologue, spoken before the King, presumably for a public performance during the first run of the play, (Bodl.) is dated 'November 1681', which

---

[17] The *Newdigate Newsletters* report that on 10 Aug. Behn and the actress Lady Slingsby were arrested for writing and speaking respectively the epilogue which contained offensive references to Monmouth. Luttrell acquired his copy of the broadside of the prologue and epilogue on 8 Aug.

would confirm a date of late October or early November for the première' (vol. ii, pt. 2, p. 332). It is clear that the play belongs to the period of Tory reaction. Milhous and Hume imply this in considering another Tory play, *Mr. Turbulent*: 'In type, the play belongs with such political productions as *Sir Barnaby Whigg* and *The Roundheads*. October 1681 is a reasonable guess' (392).

Mr. Turbulent The play is dated by Allardyce Nicoll January 1682 (*A History of Restoration Drama 1660–1700*, 205). Nicoll's date is followed by *The London Stage*, but Milhous and Hume consider this very unlikely since the date of 27 January on the British Library MS is 'presumably an acquisition date'. As noted above, they consider October 1681 'a reasonable guess'. I agree that the play belongs to the Tory reaction period from autumn 1681 onwards. On the basis of a reference to 'lustful *Zimri*' (p.'53' [45]), I am tentatively inclined to place it in late November 1681, after the publication of *Absalom and Achitophel* (see line 551). As in the case of *Sir Barnaby Whigg*, this would mean swift publication, a further illustration of the fast publication of Tory pieces.

Rome's Follies Autumn 1681 is a reasonable certainty. The play was advertised in *The Impartial Protestant Mercury*, 30 December 1681–3 January 1682. The title-page states, 'As it was lately acted at a Person of Qualitie's House'. The dedication refers to *The Lancashire Witches* in such a way as to suggest that *Rome's Follies* postdates it (sig. A3ʳ⁻ᵛ). The date of the première of *The Lancashire Witches* (q.v.) was probably early summer 1681. The dedication also conveys a sense that the anonymous author felt beleaguered by political enemies not only at the time of writing, but at the time of performance. He suggests that the play was performed privately because it could not have been performed in the theatre: 'the Subject being not a little Satirical against the Romanists, would very much hinder its taking, and would be far more difficult to get play'd than Caesar Borgio (*sic*) was: or if it should chance to have been played, might have found a colder entertainment than Tegue O Divelly, The Irish Priest, at the Duke's Theatre, merely for the Subjects sake' (sig. A3ʳ⁻ᵛ). The negative view which is taken of Whig fortunes and audience attitudes, particularly when compared with Shadwell's bullish preface to *The Lancashire Witches*, suggests the Tory reaction period, around the time of the spate of Whig-baiting plays in autumn 1681.

1682–1683

The Lord Mayor's Show	30 September
The Duke of Guise	28 November 1682

The Princess of Cleve	Winter 1682? (see below)
City Politiques	19 January 1683
The Restauration	February 1683? (see below)
Dame Dobson	31 May 1683[18]
The Atheist	Spring or early summer 1683.[19]

PROBLEM CASES

The Princess of Cleve   The play was not published until 1689, so all we know for certain about the date of the first performance is that it must have been after the death of Rochester on 26 July 1680 (alluded to in the play) and before December 1682, which is the date of Thomas Farmer's music for the play. Since Lee's output was prolific in autumn 1680, Hume suggests that the play was written in spring or summer 1681 and 'was being prepared for production in December 1682 and was staged a little later that season'.[20] The delay between production and composition was probably due to the fact that the Duke's Company had quite a lot of new plays in production in the 1681–2 season. Thus for Hume, *The Princess of Cleve* marks a transition from the radicalism of *Lucius Junius Brutus*, banned in 1680, and the Toryism of *The Duke of Guise*. My own reading of the play as savagely critical of court libertinism but cynical about the existence of any political alternative tends to support Hume's view of the play as politically transitional. Hume's date is accepted by Danchin, and by Armistead (*Nathaniel Lee*).

The Restauration   There are references in the epilogue to the death of Shaftesbury, which occurred on 21 January 1683, so *The London Stage* and Danchin suggest a première in February, though both say there is no certainty that the play was ever acted: it appears in *The Works of His Grace, George Villiers, Late Duke of Buckingham* (1715), i.

[18] Wilson's suggestion in 'More Theatre Notes from the *Newdigate Newsletters*' that an item on the attendance of the Duke and Duchess of York at a new play refers to this one, since Luttrell's acquisition date of the broadside of the prologue and epilogue is 1 June, seems likely: there are far fewer new plays to confuse the issue in this season than in previous ones.

[19] The title-page is dated 1684. Either this is a misprint, or the play was advertised in error.

[20] Hume, 'The Satiric Design of Nat. Lee's *The Princess of Cleve*', 119.

Bibliography

Here, as in the notes, I have not reproduced eccentric capitalization and punctuation in Restoration titles where to do so without also reproducing unusual fonts etc. would create a misleading emphasis. Pamphlet titles are given in short form. The place of publication is London unless otherwise stated.

ABBREVIATIONS

ECS	*Eighteenth-Century Studies*
HJ	*Historical Journal*
HLB	*Harvard Library Bulletin*
HLQ	*Huntington Library Quarterly*
JEGP	*Journal of English and Germanic Philology*
MP	*Modern Philology*
NQ	*Notes and Queries*
PMLA	*Publications of the Modern Language Association*
PQ	*Philological Quarterly*
RECTR	*Restoration and Eighteenth-Century Theatre Research*
SEL	*Studies in English Literature*
SP	*Studies in Philology*
TN	*Theatre Notebook*

PRIMARY TEXTS

A Just and Modest Vindication of the Proceedings of the Two Last Parliaments (1681). See discussion of authorship in Ch. 3.

A Letter From a Parliament Man to His Friend Concerning the Proceedings of the House of Commons (1675). Signed 'T.E.' but widely attributed to Shaftesbury.

A Letter From a Person of Quality to his Friend in the Country (1675). Attributed to Shaftesbury.

A Parallel Betwixt Popery and Phanaticism (1680 or 1681?).

A Seasonable Argument to Perswade all the Grand Juries in England, to Petition for a New Parliament ('Amsterdam', 1677).

A True Extract Out of the Commons Journal (1678).

An Appeal from the Country to the City, by 'Junius Brutus' (1679).

An Epode To His Worthy Friend Mr. John Dryden, To Advise Him Not To Answer Two Malicious Pamphlets Against His Tragedy Called, The Duke of Guise (1683).

Baker, Aaron, *Achitophel Befool'd* (1678).

Bancroft, John, *The Tragedy of Sertorius* (1679).

Banks, John, *The Destruction of Troy* (1679).

—— *The Unhappy Favourite* (1682).

—— *Vertue Betray'd* (1682), repr. with intro. by D. Dreher (Los Angeles, 1981).

Behn, Aphra, *The Feign'd Curtizans* (1679).

—— *The Revenge* (1680).

—— *The Second Part of the Rover* (1681).

—— *The Round-heads* (1682).

—— *The City Heiress* (1682).

—— *The False Count* (1682).

—— *The Young King* (1683).

—— *The Works of Aphra Behn*, ed. M. Summers (1915).

Buckingham, George Villiers, Duke of, *Buckingham, Public and Private Man: The Prose, Poems and Commonplace Book of George Villiers, Second Duke of Buckingham* (1628–87), ed. C. Phipps (New York, 1985).

—— *The Rehearsal* (1671), ed. D. Crane (Durham, 1976).

Burnet, Gilbert, *History of My Own Time* (1724), ed. O. Airy, 2 vols. (Oxford, 1897).

The Catholick Cause; or, The Horrid Practice of Murdering Kings, Justified and Commended by the Pope (1678).

The Coronation Of Queen Elizabeth, With The Restauration Of The Protestant Religion: Or, The Downfal Of The Pope by 'J.D.' (1680).

Croft, Herbert, *The Naked Truth* (1676).

Crowne, John, *The Ambitious Statesman* (1679).

—— *The Misery of Civil-War* (1680).

—— *Henry the Sixth: The First Part* (1681).

—— *Thyestes* (1681).

—— *Sir Courtly Nice* (1685).

—— *The English Frier* (1690).

—— *City Politiques* (1683), ed. J. Wilson (1967).

—— *The Dramatic Works of John Crowne*, ed. J. Maidment and W. H. Logan, 4 vols. (Edinburgh, 1873–4), not a complete collection and textually unreliable.

The Declaration of the Rebels Now in Arms in the West of Scotland (1678).

Downes, John, *Roscius Anglicanus* (1708), ed. J. Milhous and R. D. Hume (1987).

Dryden, John, *Amboyna* (1673).

—— *Aureng-Zebe* (1676).

—— *The Kind Keeper* (1680).

—— *The Spanish Fryar* (1681).

—— *The Duke of Guise* (1683).

—— *The Vindication [of]* . . . The Duke of Guise (1683).

—— *Letters of John Dryden*, ed. C. E. Ward (1942).

—— *The Works of John Dryden*, ed. E. Hooker *et al.*, 20 vols. (Berkeley, 1956–).

—— *The Poems of John Dryden*, ed. P. Hammond, i: 1649–1681, ii: 1682–1685 (1995).

D'Urfey, Thomas, *The Virtuous Wife* (1680).

—— *Sir Barnaby Whigg* (1681).

—— *The Injur'd Princess* (1682).

—— *The Royalist* (1682).

Evelyn, John, *The Diary of John Evelyn*, ed. E. S. de Beer, 6 vols. (Oxford, 1955).

Filmer, Robert, *Patriarcha and Other Writings*, ed. J. P. Sommerville (Cambridge, 1991).

The Grand Designs of the Papists (1678).

Halifax, George Savile, Marquess of, *Complete Works*, ed. J. P. Kenyon (Harmondsworth, 1969).

Heywood, Thomas, and Brome, Richard, *The Late Lancashire Witches* (1634).

Humfrey, John, *The Healing Paper* (1678).

Hunt, Thomas, *The Great and Weighty Considerations, Relating to the Duke of York* (1680).

—— *A Defence of the Charter, and Municipal Rights of the City of London and the Rights of other Municipal Cities and Towns of England* (1683?).

The Irish Evidence Convicted by their own Oaths (1682).

The Irish Evidence, The Humours of Tiege; or, the Mercenary Whore (1682?).

Jesuitical Aphorisms . . . Extracted out of the Writings . . . of the Jesuits and Other Popish Doctors, Englished by Ezerel [i.e. Israel] Tonge (1678).

Jordan, Thomas, *The Triumphs of London* (1678).

—— *London in Luster* (1679).

—— *London's Glory* (1680).

—— *London's Joy* (1681).

—— *The Lord Mayor's Show* (1682). See discussion of authorship in Ch. 9).

Lawrence, William, *Two Great Questions Determined by the Principles of Reason and Divinity* (1681).

Lee, Nathaniel, *Lucius Junius Brutus* (1681), ed. J. Loftis (Lincoln, Nebr., 1967).

—— *The Works of Nathaniel Lee*, ed. T. Stroup and A. Cooke, 2 vols. (New Brunswick, 1955).

L'Estrange, Roger, *An Account of the Growth of Knavery* (1678).

—— *The Case Put, Concerning the Succession* (1679).

Lloyd, William, *Considerations Touching the True Way to Suppress Popery* (1677). This piece is universally attributed to Lloyd, but the preface states that it is 'by two several hands' (sig. A2^r), the second author contributing 'chiefly from p. 80 till the Conclusion' (sig. A3^v).

Luttrell, Narcissus, *A Brief Historical Relation of State Affairs from September 1678 to April 1714*, 6 vols. (Oxford, 1867).

Maidwell, Lewis, *The Loving Enemies* (1680).

Marston, John, *The Dutch Courtesan* (1605), ed. M. L. Wine (1965).

Marvell, Andrew, *Mr. Smirke; or, The Divine in Mode* (1676).

—— *An Account of the Growth of Popery and Arbitrary Government in England* ('Amsterdam', 1677).

—— *The Poems and Letters of Andrew Marvell*, ed. H. Margoliouth, rev. P. Legouis and E. Duncan-Jones, 2 vols. (Oxford, 1971).

—— *The Complete Poems*, ed. E. Donno (Harmondsworth, 1972).

Milton, John, *True Religion, Heresy, Schism, Toleration: and What May Be Used Against the Growth of Popery* (1673).

—— *Paradise Lost*, in *The Poems of John Milton*, ed. J. Carey and A. Fowler (1968).

Mr. Turbulent; or, the Melanchollicks (1682).

The Muse of Newmarket; or, Mirth and Drollery (1680).

Nalson, John, *The Common Interest of King and People* (1677). See Nalson, *The Project of Peace*.

—— *The Countermine* (1677). See next entry.

—— *The Project of Peace* (1678). I have used the 1678 edn., which reprints the first two of these works and binds all three together.

Nedham, Marchamont, *A Pacquet of Advices and Animadversions Sent From London to the Men of Shaftesbury* (1676).

—— *A Second Pacquet of Advices and Animadversions Sent to the Men of Shaftesbury* (1677).

Oldham, John, *The Poems of John Oldham*, ed. H. Brooks with R. Selden (Oxford, 1987).

Otway, Thomas, *The Complete Works of Thomas Otway*, ed. M. Summers, 3 vols. (1926).

—— *The Orphan* (1680), ed. A. Taylor (1977).

—— *Venice Preserv'd* (1682), ed. M. Kelsall (1969).

—— *The Works of Thomas Otway*, ed. J. Ghosh, 2 vols. (Oxford, 1932).

Pepys, Samuel, *The Diary of Samuel Pepys*, ed. R. Latham and W. Matthews, 11 vols. (1970–83).

The Plot Discover'd; or, A New Discourse Between the Devil and the Pope (1678).

Poems on Affairs of State: Augustan Satirical Verse 1660–1714 (New Haven, 1963–75), i, ed. G. Lord, ii, ed. E. Mengel.

The Poor Man's Cup of Cold Water, Ministered to the Saints and Sufferers for Christ in Scotland, attributed to Robert MacWard (Edinburgh, 1678).

Porter, Thomas, *The French Conjurer* (1678).

Il Putanismo di Roma . . . Written in Italian by the Author of Cardilinismoe Nepotismo [i.e. Gregorio Leti?] *and Made Into English by I.D. Esq.* (1678).

Ravenscroft, Edward, *Titus Andronicus* (1687).

—— *The London Cuckolds* (1682), in N. Jeffares (ed.), *Restoration Comedy* (1974).

Ravillac Redivivus, Being a Narrative of the Late Tryal of Mr. James Mitchel . . . To Which is Annexed, An Account of the Tryal of That Most Wicked Pharisee Major Thomas Weir, who was Executed for Adultery, Incest and Bestiality (1678).

Rochester, John Wilmot, Earl of, *The Poems of John Wilmot, Earl of Rochester*, ed. K. Walker (Oxford, 1984).

Rolle, Samuel, *Loyalty and Peace* (1678).

Romes Follies; or, The Amorous Fryars, by 'N.N.' (1681).

Romulus and Hersilia; or, The Sabine War (1683).

The Roxburghe Ballads, ed. C. Hindley, 2 vols. (1873–4).

Sanderson, Robert, *Episcopacy (as Established by Law in England) Not Prejudicial to Regal Power* (1661, repr. 1673 and 1678).

Saunders, Charles, *Tamerlane the Great* (1681).

The Secret History of the Most Renowned Queen Elizabeth and the Earl of Essex (1680).

Sedley, Sir Charles, *The Poetical and Dramatic Works of Sir Charles Sedley*, ed. V. Pinto, 2 vols. (1928).

Settle, Elkanah, *Fatal Love; or, The Forc'd Inconstancy* (1680).

—— *The Female Prelate* (1680).

—— *The Heir of Morocco* (1682).

—— *A Narrative* (1683).

Shadwell, Thomas, *The Libertine* (1675).

—— *The Woman-Captain* (1680).

—— *The Lancashire Witches* (1682).

—— *The Works of Thomas Shadwell*, ed. M. Summers, 5 vols. (1927).

Shakespeare, William, *Cymbeline*, ed. J. Maxwell (Cambridge, 1960).
—— *Coriolanus*, ed. P. Brockbank (1976).
—— *King Richard II*, ed. A. Gurr (Cambridge, 1984); ed. J. Dover Wilson (ibid., 1939, repr. 1968).
—— *King Richard III*, ed. A. Hammond (1981).
—— *King Lear*, ed. J. Halio (Cambridge, 1992).
—— *The Second Part of King Henry VI*, ed. M. Hattaway (Cambridge, 1991).
—— *Titus Andronicus*, ed. E. Waith (Oxford, 1984).
—— *Troilus and Cressida*, ed. K. Palmer (1982).
Shelton, William, *A Discourse of Superstition with Respect to the Present Times* (1678).
Shipman, Thomas, *Henry the Third of France, Stabb'd by a Fryer. With the Fall of the Guise* (1678).
Sidney, Algernon, *Discourses Concerning Government* (1698), in *Sydney on Government: The Works of Algernon Sydney*, ed. J. Robertson (1772).
Sol in opposition to Saturn. Or a Short Return to a Late Tragedy Call'd The Duke of Guise (1683).
Some Reflections Upon The Pretended Parallel In The Play Called The Duke of Guise (1683).
Somers, John, *A Brief History of the Succession of the Crown of England* (1680).
Southerne, Thomas, *The Loyal Brother* (1682), ed. P. Hamelius (Liège, 1911).
—— *The Works of Thomas Southerne*, ed. R. Jordan and H. Love, 2 vols., i (Oxford, 1988).
Strange News From France (1678).
Summers, Montague (ed.), *Restoration Comedies* (1921) .
Sutherland, James (ed.), *Restoration Tragedies* (Oxford, 1977).
Tate, Nahum, *The History of King Lear* (1681).
—— *The History of King Richard the Second* (1681).
—— *The Ingratitude of a Common-wealth; or, The Fall of Caius Martius Coriolanus*, in R. McGugan, *Nahum Tate and the Coriolanus Tradition in English Drama with a Critical Edition of Tate's The Ingratitude of a Common-wealth* (New York, 1987).
—— *The Loyal General* (1680).
Tatham, John, *The Rump* (1660).
The Term Catalogues, 1668–1709, i: 1668–1682, ed. E. Arber (1905).
The True History Of The Duke Of Guise (1683).
Turner, Francis, *Animadversions Upon . . . The Naked Truth* (1676)
Whitaker, William, *The Conspiracy* (1680).

SECONDARY TEXTS

Altieri, J., *The Theatre of Praise: The Panegyric Tradition in Seventeenth-Century English Drama* (Newark, NJ, 1986).

Armistead, J., *Nathaniel Lee* (Boston, 1979).

—— 'Dryden's Poetry and the Language of Magic', *SEL* 27 (1987).

Armstrong, N., *Desire and Domestic Fiction: A Political History of the Novel* (Oxford, 1987).

Ashcraft, R., *Revolutionary Politics and Locke's* Two Treatises of Government (Princeton, 1986).

—— 'The Language of Political Conflict in Restoration Literature', in R. Ashcraft and A. Roper, *Politics as Reflected in Literature* (Los Angeles, 1989).

Ashton, R., *The English Civil War: Conservatism and Revolution 1603–1649* (1978).

Avery, E., 'The Restoration Audience', *PQ* 45 (1966).

Barbeau, A., *The Intellectual Design of Dryden's Heroic Plays* (New Haven, 1970).

—— 'Free Will and the Passions in Dryden and Pope', *Restoration*, 4 (1980).

Barbour, F., 'The Unconventional Heroic Plays of Nathaniel Lee', *University of Texas Studies in English*, 20 (1940).

Baxter, S., *William III* (1966).

Bevis, R., *English Drama: Restoration and Eighteenth Century 1660–1789* (1988).

Bhaskar, R., *Reclaiming Reality* (1989).

—— *Dialectic: The Pulse of Freedom* (1993).

Black, J., 'An Augustan Stage-History: Nahum Tate's *King Lear*', *RECTR* 6 (1967).

Braverman, R., *Plots and Counterplots: Sexual Politics and the Body Politic in English Literature 1660–1730* (Cambridge, 1993).

Brecht, B., *Brecht on Theatre*, ed. and trans. J. Willett (1964).

Bredvold, L., 'Political Aspects of Dryden's *Amboyna* and *The Spanish Fryar*' (1932), repr. in H. Swedenberg (ed.), *Essential Articles for the Study of John Dryden* (1966).

Brenner, R., *Merchants and Revolution: Commercial Change, Political Conflict and London's Overseas Traders 1550–1653* (Cambridge, 1993).

Brown, L., *English Dramatic Form 1660–1760: An Essay in Generic History* (New Haven, 1981).

Brown, R., 'The Dryden–Lee Collaboration: *Oedipus* and *The Duke of Guise*', *Restoration*, 9 (1985).

Brown, R., 'Nathaniel Lee's Political Dramas 1679–1683', *Restoration*, 10 (1986).

Burns, E., *Restoration Comedy: Crises of Desire and Identity* (Basingstoke, 1987).

Butler, M., *Theatre and Crisis 1632–1642* (Cambridge, 1984).

Bywaters, D., 'Venice, its Senate, and its Plot in Otway's *Venice Preserv'd*', *MP* 80 (1983).

Canfield, J., 'The Significance of the Restoration Rhymed Heroic Play', *ECS* 13 (1979).

—— 'Royalism's Last Dramatic Stand: English Political Tragedy, 1679–1689', *SP* 82 (1985).

—— *Word as Bond in English Literature: From the Middle Ages to the Restoration* (Philadelphia, 1989).

—— 'Dramatic Shifts: Writing an Ideological History of Late Stuart Drama', *RECTR* 6 (1991).

—— and Payne, D. (eds.), *Cultural Readings of Restoration and Eighteenth-Century English Theater* (Athens, Ga., 1995).

Carswell, J., *The Porcupine: The Life of Algernon Sidney* (1989).

Chernaik, W., *The Poet's Time: Politics and Religion in the Work of Andrew Marvell* (Cambridge, 1983).

—— *Sexual Freedom in Restoration Literature* (Cambridge, 1995).

Childs, J., *The Army of Charles II* (1976).

Clark, J., 'A General Theory of Party Opposition and Government 1688–1832' *HJ* 23 (1980).

—— *English Society 1688–1832* (Cambridge, 1985).

—— *Revolution and Rebellion* (Cambridge, 1986).

Coleridge, H., *The Life of Andrew Marvell* (Hull, 1835).

Collinson, P., *The Birthpangs of Protestant England* (Basingstoke, 1988).

Condren, C. and Cousins, A. (eds.), *The Political Identity of Andrew Marvell* (Aldershot, 1990).

Copeland, N., ' "Once a whore and ever": Whore and Virgin in *The Rover* and its Antecedents', *Restoration*, 16 (1992).

—— ' "Who can . . . her own wish deny?": Female Conduct and Politics in Aphra Behn's *The City Heiress*', *RECTR* 8 (1993).

Corman, B., 'What is Restoration Drama?', *University of Toronto Quarterly*, 48 (1978).

Crist, T., 'Government Control of the Press after the Expiration of the Printing Act in 1679', *Publishing History*, 5 (1979).

Danchin, P., *The Prologues and Epilogues of the Restoration, 1660–1700*, 4 vols. in 7 parts (Nancy, 1981–8).

Davis, N., 'Women on Top: Symbolic Sexual Inversion and Political Disorder in Early Modern Europe', in B. Babcock (ed.),

The Reversible World: Symbolic Inversion in Art and Society (1978).

De Krey, G., 'London Radicals and Revolutionary Politics', in Harris *et al* (ed.), *The Politics of Religion in Restoration England*.

DePorte, M., 'Otway and the Straits of Venice', *Papers on Language and Literature*, 18 (1982).

Dobson, M., *The Making of the National Poet: Shakespeare, Adaptation and Authorship 1660–1769* (Oxford, 1992).

Dollimore, J., *Radical Tragedy: Religion, Ideology and Power in the Drama of Shakespeare and his Contemporaries* (Brighton, 1984).

Downie, J., *To Settle the Succession of the State: Literature and Politics 1678–1750* (1994).

Eagleton, T., *Ideology: An Introduction* (1991).

Earle, P., *The Making of the English Middle Class: Business, Society and Family Life in London 1660–1730* (1989).

Elias, R., 'Political Satire in Sodom', *SEL* 18 (1978).

Evans, D., ' "Private Greatness": The Feminine Ideal in Dryden's Early Heroic Drama', *Restoration*, 16 (1992).

Fairholt, F., *The Lord Mayor's Pageants*, 2 vols. (1843–4).

Feiling, K., *A History of the Tory Party 1640–1714* (Oxford, 1924).

Ferris, L. (ed.), *Controversies on Cross-Dressing* (1993).

Fink, Z., *The Classical Republicans* (Evanston, Ill., 1945).

Flores, S., 'Patriarchal Politics under Cultural Stress: Nathaniel Lee's Passion Plays', *RECTR* 8 (1993).

Franceschina, J., 'Shadow and Substance in Aphra Behn's *The Rover*: The Semiotics of Restoration Performance', *Restoration*, 19 (1995).

Fraser, A., *The Weaker Vessel: Women's Lot in Seventeenth-Century England* (1984, repr. 1985).

Fujimura, T., 'Dryden's Changing Political Views', *Restoration*, 10 (1986).

Gallagher, C., 'Embracing the Absolute: The Politics of the Female Subject in Seventeenth-Century England', *Genders*, 1 (1988).

——'Who was that masked woman?', *Women's Studies*, 15 (1988).

Gardner, W., 'John Dryden's Interest in Judicial Astrology', *SP* 47 (1950).

Gibbs, V. *et al.* (ed.), *The Complete Peerage* (1910–59).

Goldberg, Jonathan, *James I and the Politics of Literature* (Baltimore, 1983).

Goldie, M., 'Danby, the Bishops and the Whigs', in Harris *et al.* (ed.), *The Politics of Religion in Restoration England*.

Goreau, A., *Reconstructing Aphra: A Social Biography of Aphra Behn* (Oxford, 1980).

Greaves, R., *Secrets of the Kingdom: British Radicals: From the Popish Plot to the Revolution of 1688–1689* (Stanford, Calif., 1992).

Greenblatt, S., *Renaissance Self-Fashioning from More to Shakespeare* (Chicago, 1980).

Grey, A., *Debates in the House of Commons 1667–1694*, 10 vols. (1763).

Hadfield, A., *Literature, Politics and National Identity: Reformation to Renaissance* (Cambridge, 1994).

Haley, D., 'John Dryden: Protestant in Masquerade?', *Cithara*, 30 (1991).

Haley, K., *The First Earl of Shaftesbury* (Oxford, 1968).

Ham, R., *Otway and Lee: Biography from a Baroque Age* (New Haven, 1931, repr. New York, 1969).

Hammond, A., 'The "Greatest Action": Lee's *Lucius Junius Brutus*', in A. Coleman and A. Hammond (eds.), *Poetry and Drama 1570–1700: Essays in Honour of Harold F. Brooks* (1981).

Hammond, P., *John Dryden: A Literary Life* (Basingstoke, 1991).

—— 'The King's Two Bodies: Representations of Charles II', in J. Black and J. Gregory (eds.), *Culture, Politics and Society in Britain, 1660–1800* (Manchester, 1991).

—— 'Anonymity in Restoration Poetry', *Seventeenth Century*, 8 (1993).

Harris, T., *London Crowds in the Reign of Charles II: Propaganda and Politics from the Restoration until the Exclusion Crisis* (Cambridge, 1987).

—— 'Was the Tory Reaction Popular? Attitudes of Londoners towards the Persecution of Dissent 1681–1686', *London Journal*, 13 (1987–8).

—— Seaward, P., and Goldie, M. (eds.), *The Politics of Religion in Restoration England* (Oxford, 1990).

Harth, P., *Contexts of Dryden's Thought* (Chicago, 1968).

—— 'Political Interpretations of *Venice Preserv'd*', *MP* 85 (1988).

—— 'Dryden in 1678–1681: The Literary and Historical Perspectives', in Wallace (ed.), *The Golden and the Brazen World*.

Henning, B., *The History of Parliament: The House of Commons 1660–1690*, 3 vols. (1983).

Hill, B., *The Growth of Parliamentary Parties 1689–1742* (1972).

Hill, C., *The Century of Revolution 1603–1714* (1961, repr. 1978).

—— *Reformation to Industrial Revolution* (1967, rev. Harmondsworth, 1969).

—— *The World Turned Upside Down* (Harmondsworth, 1975).

—— *Some Intellectual Consequences of the English Revolution* (1980).

Holland, P., *The Ornament of Action: Text and Performance in Restoration Comedy* (Cambridge, 1979).

Horwitz, H., *Parliament, Policy and Politics* (Manchester, 1979).

Howe, E., *The First English Actresses: Women and Drama 1660–1700* (Cambridge, 1992).

Hughes, D., 'A New Look at Venice Preserv'd', *SEL* 11 (1971).

—— *Dryden's Heroic Plays* (1981).

——'Otway's *The Orphan*: An Interpretation', *Durham University Journal*, 75 (1983).

Hughes, L., and Scouten, A., *Ten English Farces* (Austin, Tex., 1948).

Hume, R., *The Development of English Drama in the Late Seventeenth Century* (Oxford, 1976).

——'The Satiric Design of Nat. Lee's *The Princess of Cleve*', *JEGP* 75 (1976).

——'*The Maid's Tragedy* and Censorship in the Restoration Theatre', *PQ* 61 (1982).

——'The Unconventional Tragedies of Thomas Otway', in *Du verbe au geste: Mélanges en l'honneur de Pierre Danchin* (Nancy, 1987).

——'Texts within Contexts: Notes toward a Historical Method', *PQ* 71 (1992).

——'The Politics of Opera in Late Seventeenth-Century London, forthcoming.

——(ed.), *The London Theatre World 1660–1800* (Carbondale, Ill., 1980).

See also Milhous.

Hutner, H. (ed.), *Re-reading Aphra Behn: History, Theory and Criticism* (1993).

Hutson, L., *The Usurer's Daughter: Male Friendship and Fictions of Women in Sixteenth-Century England* (London, 1994).

Hutton, R., *The Restoration* (Oxford, 1985).

—— *Charles the Second: King of England, Scotland, and Ireland* (Oxford, 1989).

Jones, J., *The First Whigs: The Politics of the Exclusion Crisis 1678–1783* (1961).

—— *Country and Court* (1978, rev. 1986).

—— *The Revolution of 1688 in England* (1972, repr. 1984).

Jones, V., 'Methods of Satire in the Political Drama of the Restoration', *JEGP* 21 (1922).

Kastan, D. S., '*Nero* and the Politics of Nathaniel Lee', *Papers in Language and Literature*, 13 (1977).

Kaufman, A., 'Civil Politics–Sexual Politics in John Crowne's *City Politiques*', *Restoration*, 6 (1982).

Keeton, G., *Lord Chancellor Jeffreys and the Stuart Cause* (1985).

Kenyon, J. P., *Robert Spencer, Earl of Sunderland 1641–1702* (Cambridge, 1958).
—— *The Popish Plot* (Harmondsworth, 1974).
—— *Revolution Principles: The Politics of Party 1689–1720* (Cambridge, 1977).
Kinnaird, J., 'Mary Astell and the Conservative Contribution to English Feminism', *Journal of British Studies*, 19 (1979).
Klause, J., *The Unfortunate Fall: Theodicy and the Moral Imagination of Andrew Marvell* (1983).
Klein, B., ' "Between the Bums and the Bellies of the Multitude": Civic Pageantry and the Problem of the Audience in Late Stuart London', *London Journal*, 17 (1992).
Kubek, E., ' "Night Mares of the Commonwealth": Royalist Passion and Female Ambition in Aphra Behn's *The Roundheads*', *Restoration*, 17 (1993).
Landon, M., *The Triumph of the Lawyers* (University, Ala., 1970).
Langhans, E., *Five Restoration Theatrical Adaptations* (New York, 1980).
Legouis, P., *Andrew Marvell: Poet, Puritan, Patriot* (Oxford, 1965).
Lindley, D., *The Trials of Frances Howard: Fact and Fiction at the Court of King James* (London, 1993).
Loftis, J., *The Politics of Drama in Augustan England* (Oxford, 1963).
—— 'Political and Social Thought in the Drama', in Hume (ed.), *The London Theatre World 1660–1800*.
Love, H., 'State Affairs on the Restoration Stage', *RECTR* 14 (1975).
—— 'Who were the Restoration Audience?', *Yearbook of English Studies*, 10 (1980).
McFadden, G., *Dryden the Public Writer 1660–1685* (Princeton, 1978).
McFarlane, A., *Marriage and Love in England: Modes of Reproduction 1300–1840* (Oxford, 1986).
McKeon, M., 'Historicizing *Absalom and Achitophel*' in F. Nussbaum and L. Brown (eds.), *The New Eighteenth Century* (1987).
—— 'Historicizing Patriarchy: The Emergence of Gender Difference in England 1660–1760', *ECS* 28 (1995).
MacLean, G. (ed.), *Culture and Society in the Stuart Restoration* (Cambridge, 1995).
McMullin, B. J., 'Serjeant Maynard's Teeth', *NQ* NS 28/3 (1981).
McNally, D., 'Locke, Levellers and Liberty: Property and Democracy in the Thought of the First Whigs', History of Political Thought, 10 (1989).
Maguire, N., 'Nahum Tate's *King Lear*: "The king's blest restoration" ' in Marsden (ed.), *The Appropriation of Shakespeare*.

—— *Regicide and Restoration: English Tragicomedy 1660–1671* (Cambridge, 1992).

—— 'Factionary Politics: John Crowne's *Henry VI*', in MacLean (ed.), *Culture and Society in the Stuart Restoration*.

Markley, R., *Two Edg'd Weapons: Style and Ideology in the Comedies of Etherege, Wycherley and Congreve* (Oxford, 1988).

Marsden, J., 'Pathos and Passivity: D'Urfey's *The Injured Princess* and Shakespeare's *Cymbeline*', *Restoration*, 14 (1990).

—— (ed.), *The Appropriation of Shakespeare: Post-Renaissance Reconstructions of the Works and the Myth* (Hemel Hempstead, 1991).

Marx, K., *The Eighteenth Brumaire of Louis Bonaparte* (New York, 1963).

Melton, F., 'A Rake Refinanced: The Fortune of George Villiers, Second Duke of Buckingham, 1671–1685', *HLQ* 51 (1988).

Milhous, J., and Hume, R., 'Dating Play Premières from Publication Data 1660–1700', *HLB* 22 (1974).

—— 'The Prologue and Epilogue for *Fools Have Fortune; or, Luck's All* (1680)', *HLQ* 43 (1980).

—— 'Attribution Problems in English Drama 1660–1700', *HLB* 31 (1983).

—— *Producible Interpretations: Eight English Plays 1675–1707* (Carbondale, Ill., 1985).

Miller, J., *Popery and Politics in England 1660–1688* (Cambridge, 1973).

—— *James II: A Study in Kingship* (1978, rev. 1989).

Miller, R., 'Political Satire in the Malicorne–Melanax Scenes of *The Duke of Guise*', *English Language Notes*, 16 (1979).

Montano, J., 'The Quest for Consensus: The Lord Mayor's Day Shows in the 1670s', in MacLean (ed.), *Culture and Society in the Stuart Restoration*.

Mooers, C., *The Making of Bourgeois Europe* (1991).

Moore, J., 'Contemporary Satire in Otway's *Venice Preserv'd*', *PMLA* 43 (1928).

Moore, L., 'For King and Country: John Dryden's *Troilus and Cressida*', *College Language Association Journal* 26 (1982).

Morrill, J., *The Revolt of the Provinces* (1980).

Morrissey, L., 'English Street Theatre 1655–1708', *Costerus*, 4 (1972).

Munns, J., 'The Dark Disorders of a Divided State: Otway and Shakespeare's *Romeo and Juliet*', *Comparative Drama*, 19 (1985–6).

—— '"Plain as the light in the Cowcumber": A Note on the Conspiracy in Thomas Otway's *Venice Preserv'd*', *MP* 85 (1987).

Munns, J., 'A Note on Halifax and Otway', *RECTR* 5 (1990).
——*Restoration Politics and Drama: The Plays of Thomas Otway 1675–1683* (Cranbury, NJ, 1995).
Murray, B., 'The Butt of Otway's Political Moral in *The History and Fall of Caius Marius* (1680)', *NQ* NS 36 (1989).
Myers, W. (ed.), *Restoration and Revolution* (Beckenham, 1986).
Neman, B., 'Setting the Record Straight on John Crowne', *RECTR* 8 (1993).
Nenner, H., *By Color of Law: Legal Culture and Constitutional Politics in England 1660–1689* (Chicago, 1977).
Newman, R., 'Irony and the Problem of Tone in Dryden's *Aureng-Zebe*', *SEL* 10 (1970).
Ogg, D., *England in the Reign of Charles II*, 2 vols. (Oxford, 1934, rev. 1956).
—— *England in the Reigns of James II and William III* (Oxford, 1955, repr. 1984).
Owen, S., 'Drama and Politics in the Exclusion Crisis 1678–1683', Ph.D. thesis (Leeds, 1992).
——'"Partial Tyrants" and "Freeborn People" in *Lucius Junius Brutus*', *SEL* 31 (1991).
——'Interpreting the Politics of Restoration Drama', *Seventeenth Century*, 8 (1993).
——'"Suspect my loyalty when I lose my virtue": Sexual Politics and Party in Aphra Behn's Plays of the Exclusion Crisis', *Restoration*, 18 (1994).
——'"He that should guard my virtue has betrayed it": The Dramatization of Rape in the Exclusion Crisis', *RECTR* 9 (1994).
——'The Politics of John Dryden's *The Spanish Fryar; or, The Double Discovery*', *English* 43 (1994).
——'Sexual Politics and Party Politics in Behn's Drama 1678–1683', in J. Todd (ed.), *Aphra Behn Studies* (Cambridge, 1996).
Parker, G., 'The Image of Rebellion in Thomas Otway's *Venice Preserv'd* and Edward Young's *Busiris*', *SEL* 21 (1981).
Patterson, A., *Marvell and the Civic Crown* (Princeton: Princeton University Press, 1978).
Payne, D., '"And Poets Shall by Patron-Princes Live": Aphra Behn and Patronage', in M. Schofield and C. Machesk (eds.), *Curtain Calls: British and American Women and the Theatre 1660–1820* (Athens, Ohio, 1991).
Pearson, J., *The Prostituted Muse: Images of Women and Women Dramatists 1642–1737* (Hemel Hempstead, 1988).
Perry, M., *Elizabeth I, the Word of a Prince: A Life from Contemporary Documents* (1990).

Perry, R., 'Mary Astell and the Feminist Critique of Possessive Individualism', *ECS* 23 (1990).

Peters, J., *Congreve, the Drama and the Printed Word* (Stanford, Calif., 1990).

Pinto, V., *Sir Charles Sedley, 1639–1710: A Study in the Life and Literature of the Restoration* (1927).

Pittock, Murray, *Poetry and Jacobite Politics in Eighteenth-Century Britain and Ireland* (Cambridge, 1994).

Pocock, J., 'The Varieties of Whiggism from Exclusion to Reform', in *Virtue, Commerce and History: Essays on Political Thought and History, Chiefly in the Eighteenth Century* (Cambridge, 1975).

Pollard, H., 'Shakespeare's Influence on Otway's Caius Marius', *Révue de l'Université d'Ottawa*, 39 (1969).

Powell, J., *Restoration Theatre Production* (1984).

Price, C., *Cold Caleb: The Scandalous Life of Ford Grey, First Earl of Tankerville, 1655–1701* (1956).

Rahn, B., *Prose On Affairs of State: Popish Plot and Exclusion Crisis Pamphlets* (New York, 1985).

Richards, K., 'The Restoration Pageants of John Tatham', in K. Richards and D. Mayer (eds.), *Western Popular Theatre* (1977).

Roberts, D., *The Ladies: Female Patronage of Restoration Drama 1660–1700* (Oxford, 1989).

Roper, A., 'Drawing Parallels and Making Applications in Restoration Literature', in R. Ashcraft and A. Roper, *Politics as Reflected in Literature* (Los Angeles, 1989).

Rosenfeld, S., *The Theatre of the London Fairs in the Eighteenth Century* (Cambridge, 1960).

Rothstein, E., *Restoration Tragedy* (Madison, Wis., 1967).

—— and Kavenik, F., *The Designs of Carolean Comedy* (Carbondale, Ill., 1988).

Sampson, H., 'Some Bibliographical Evidence concerning Restoration Attitudes towards Drama', *Journal of Rutgers University Libraries*, 38 (1976).

Sawday, J., 'Re-writing a Revolution: History, Symbol, and Text in the Restoration', *Seventeenth Century* (1992).

Schille, C., 'Reappraising "Pathetic" Tragedies: *Venice Preserv'd* and *The Massacre of Paris*', *Restoration*, 12 (1988).

Schochet, G., *Patriarchalism in Political Thought* (New York, 1975).

Schwoerer, L., *The Declaration of Rights* (Baltimore, 1981).

Scott, J., *Algernon Sidney and the English Republic 1623–1677* (Cambridge, 1988).

—— *Algernon Sidney and the Restoration Crisis 1677–1683* (Cambridge, 1991).

Scott, J., 'England's Troubles: Exhuming the Popish Plot', in Harris et al. (eds.), The Politics of Religion in Restoration England.

Scouten, A., and Hume, R., ' "Restoration Comedy" and its Audiences 1660–1776', Yearbook of English Studies, 10 (1980).

Sengupta, S., 'Biographical Notes on John Crowne', Restoration, 6 (1982).

Sensabaugh, G., 'That Grand Whig Milton', Stanford University Publications in Language and Literature 10–11 (1952).

Shapiro, B., Probability and Certainty in Seventeenth Century England (Princeton, 1983).

Sharp, B., 'Popular Political Opinion in England 1660–1685', History of European Ideas, 10 (1989).

Shepherd, S., Amazons and Warrior Women: Varieties of Feminism in Seventeenth-Century Drama (Brighton, 1981).

Smith, N., Literature and Revolution (New Haven, 1994).

Solomon, H., 'The Rhetoric of Redressing Grievances: Court Propaganda as the Hermeneutical Key to Venice Preserv'd', ELH 53 (1986).

Speck, W., Reluctant Revolutionaries: Englishmen and the Revolution of 1688 (Oxford, 1988).

Spencer, C., Five Restoration Adaptations of Shakespeare (Urbana, Ill., 1965).

Staves, S., Players' Scepters: Fictions of Authority in the Restoration (Lincoln, Nebr., 1979).

—— Married Women's Separate Property in England 1660–1833 (1990).

Stocker, M., 'Political Allusion in The Rehearsal', PQ 67 (1988).

Stroup, T., 'Otway's Bitter Pessimism', in D. W. Patterson and A. B. Strauss (eds.), Essays Preseented to Dougald MacMillan, SP (Extra Series, 1967).

Styan, J., Restoration Comedy in Performance (Cambridge, 1986).

Szanto, G., Theater and Propaganda (1978).

Teeter, L., 'Political Themes in Restoration Tragedy', Ph.D. dissertation (Baltimore, 1932).

Todd, J., The Sign of Angellica: Women, Writing, and Fiction 1660–1800 (1989).

Trevelyan, G. M., England under the Stuarts (1965).

Tuck, R., 'A New Date for Filmer's Patriarcha', HJ 29 (1986).

Tumbleson, R., 'The Triumph of London: Lord Mayor's Day Pageants and the Rise of the City', in K. Keller and G. Schiffhorst (eds.), The Witness of Time: Manifestations of Ideology in Seventeenth-Century England (Pittsburgh, 1993).

Tumir, V., 'She-Tragedy and its Men: Conflict and Form in The Orphan and The Fair Penitent', SEL 30 (1990).

Turner, J., *The Politics of Landscape: Rural Scenery and Society in English Poetry 1630–1660* (Oxford, 1979).

—— (ed.), *Sexuality and Gender in Early Modern Europe* (Cambridge, 1993).

Van Lennep, W., Avery, E., and Scouten, A. (eds.), *The London Stage 1660–1800*, pt. 1: *1660–1700* (Carbondale, Ill., 1965).

Waith, E., *Ideas of Greatness: Heroic Drama in England* (1971).

Wallace, J., *Destiny his Choice: The Loyalism of Andrew Marvell* (Cambridge, 1968).

—— '"Examples are Best Precepts": Readers and Meanings in Seventeenth-Century Poetry', *Critical Inquiry*, 1 (1974–5).

—— 'Otway's *Caius Marius* and the Exclusion Crisis', *MP* 85 (1988).

—— (ed.), *The Golden and the Brazen World: Papers in Literature and History 1650–1800* (Berkeley, 1985).

Ward, C., *The Life of John Dryden* (Chapel Hill, NC, 1961).

Warner, K., *Thomas Otway* (Boston, 1982).

Weber, H., *The Restoration Rake-Hero: Transformations in Sexual Understanding in Seventeenth-Century England* (Madison, Wis., 1986).

West, M., 'Dryden and the Disintegration of Renaissance Heroic Ideals', *Costerus*, 7 (1973).

Western, J., *Monarchy and Revolution: The English State in the 1680s* (1972).

Wheatley, C., 'The Defense of the Status Quo and Otway's *The Atheist*', *RECTR* 4 (1989).

—— 'Romantic Love and Social Necessities: Reconsidering Justifications for Marriage in Restoration Comedy', *Restoration*, 14 (1990).

—— *Without God or Reason: The Plays of Thomas Shadwell and Secular Ethics in the Restoration* (1993).

White, A., *John Crowne: His Life and Dramatic Works* (Cleveland, Ohio, 1922).

Wikander, M., 'The Spitted Infant: Scenic Emblem and Exclusionist Politics in Restoration Adaptations of Shakespeare', *Shakespeare Quarterly*, 37 (1986).

Williams, R., *Marxism and Literature* (Oxford, 1977).

Williams, S., 'The Pope-Burning Processions of 1679, 1680 and 1681', *Journal of the Warburg and Courtauld Institutes*, 21 (1958).

—— 'The Lord Mayor's Show in Tudor and Stuart Times', *Guildhall Miscellany*, 1/10 (1959).

Willman, R., 'The Origins of "Whig" and "Tory" in English Political Language', *HJ* 17 (1974).

Wilson, J., *A Rake and his Times: George Villiers, Second Duke of Buckingham* (New York, 1954).

Wilson, J., 'Six Restoration Play Dates', *NQ* ns 9 (1962).
—— 'Theatre Notes from the *Newdigate Newsletters*', *TN* 15 (1961).
—— 'More Theatre Notes from the *Newdigate Newsletters*', *TN*, 16 (1961–2).
Wing, D., *Short-Title Catalogue of Books Printed in England, Scotland, Ireland, Wales and British America, and of English Books Printed in Other Countries 1641–1700*, 3 vols. (New York, 1945–51, rev. 1972–82).
Winn, J., *John Dryden and his World* (New Haven, 1987).
Withington, R., *English Civic Pageantry: An Historical Outline* (Cambridge, Mass., 1918).
Wood, E., *The Pristine Culture of Capitalism* (1991).
Zimansky, C., and Hume, R., 'Thomas Shipman's *Henry the Third of France*: Some Questions of Date, Performance, and Publication', *PQ* 55 (1976).
Zimbardo, R., *A Mirror to Nature: Transformations in Drama and Aesthetics 1660–1732* (Lexington, Ky., 1986).
—— 'Toward Zero/Toward Public Virtue: The Conceptual Design of Dramatic Satire before and after the Ascension of William and Mary', *Eighteenth-Century Life*, 12 (1988).
—— 'At Zero Point: Discourse, Politics and Satire in Restoration England', *ELH* 59 (1992).
Zwicker, S., *Politics and Language in Dryden's Poetry: The Arts of Disguise* (Princeton, 1984).

Index